LITERATURE, POLITICS AND CULTURE IN POSTWAR BRITAIN

Alan Sinfield

continuum
LONDON • NEW YORK

Continuum

The Tower Building
11 York Road
London SE1 7NX

15 East 26th Street
Suite 1703
New York
NY 10010

First published 1997 by
THE ATHLONE PRESS

This edition 2004

© Alan Sinfield 1997

British Library Cataloguing in Publication Data
A catalogue record for this book is available from the British Library

ISBN 0–8264 7702–X

Library of Congress Cataloging-in-Publication Data
Sinfield, Alan.
   Literature, politics, and culture in postwar Britain / Alan Sinfield.
     p. cm.
   Includes bibliographical references and index.
   ISBN 0–8264 7702–X (alk. paper)
   1. English Literature–20th century–History and criticism.   2. Politics and literature–
Great Britain–History–20th century.   3. Literature and society–Great Britain–History–
20th century.   4. Great Britain–Civilization–20th century.   5. World War,
1939–1945–Influence.   I. Title.
PB478.P64S5   1997
820.9'358—dc21
                                            97–26568
                                                CIP

Typeset by RefineCatch Limited, Bungay, Suffolk
Printed and bound in Great Britain by
Antony Rowe, Chippenham, Wiltshire

Contents

CONTENTS

Acknowledgements

I am grateful to acknowledge permission to reprint copyright material as follows. To Faber and Faber Ltd for lines from *Collected Poems* by W. H. Auden; for lines from *The Sense of Movement* and *My Sad Captains* by Thom Gunn; for lines from *Lupercal* by Ted Hughes; for lines from *The Whitsun Weddings* by Philip Larkin; and for lines from *Collected Poems* by Stephen Spender. To Martin Secker and Warburg Ltd for lines from *New and Collected Poems* 1934–84 by Roy Fuller; to Harper and Row Publishers Inc for lines from *Lupercal* by Ted Hughes (1960). Excerpts from 'The Unsettled Motorcyclist's Vision of His Death', 'On the Move', and 'To Yvor Winters, 1955' from *Selected Poems 1950–1975* by Thom Gunn, copyright © 1957, 1958, 1961, 1967, 1971, 1973, 1974, 1975, 1976, 1979 by Thom Gunn, reprinted by permission of Farrar, Straus and Giroux, Inc.; excerpt from 'Black Jackets' from *Moly and My Sad Captains* by Thom Gunn, copyright © 1961, 1971, 1973 by Thom Gunn, reprinted by permission of Farrar, Straus and Giroux, Inc. Lines from *Collected Poems* by Sylvia Plath (copyright Ted Hughes, 1965 and 1981, published by Faber and Faber) are quoted by permission of Olwyn Hughes and Harper and Row Publishers Inc.; passages from *The Journals of Sylvia Plath* (copyright Ted Hughes, 1982, published by the Dial Press) are quoted by permission of Olwyn Hughes.

Parts of this book have been published in other versions: 'The Migrations of Modernism: Remaking English Studies in the Cold War', *New Formations*, 2 (1987); 'Middle-class Radicalism', *Ideas and Production*, nos. 10–11 (1988–9).

Note on notes

At the end of the book there is a list of books and articles cited. Page references in the text are to titles in this list; when necessary, they are specified by the name of the author, with a brief title where the author has more than one entry. Where this cannot be done economically, references are in notes at the ends of chapters. Where appropriate, either in the main text or in the list of books, the date of the first publication as well as that of the edition cited is given.

References to 'The politics and cultures of discord (1997)' are at the end of that chapter.

A new introduction
Ideology and commitment: a personal account

For me the Second World War is not a conventional starting point: it is where my story starts. My mother, Lucy, and father, Ernie, married in 1937; he was an insurance clerk, she had been a typist in the West End. (For commentators on T. S. Eliot's *Waste Land*, the typist home at teatime, eating food from tins, receiving a house agent's clerk, and then putting a record on the gramophone is an instance of cultural dereliction; this, I always think, is how Lucy and Ernie might look like to a snobbish literary establishment.)[1] I suppose they were saving up before starting a family. I was born in December 1941, ten days after Pearl Harbor. For most of the war Ernie was away (in the air force); in November 1944 he was lost in action (harassing shipping off the coast of Norway). Lucy was carrying my brother Mark, who was born posthumously, in March 1945.

Lucy never got over Ernie's death. In our childhood he was an absent presence, often, but not always, forbidding (Daddy never did this, wouldn't have allowed that – never swore in the house, for instance). It occurs to me that to speak spontaneously and positively of him would have been too painful. Thirty years after his death, when she was in her sixties, she suddenly said: 'Perhaps your father and I wouldn't have got on!' After all that time, it crossed her mind that the fairy-tale marriage, of which she had been cruelly deprived, might not have been there anyway. Perhaps I wouldn't have got on with him.

At about the time of Ernie's death Lucy contracted Parkinson's disease. With the drugs that were then available, the apparent symptoms were loss of motor control, at times reducing walking to a shuffle, and passing at times into a trance-like state.

Parkinson's, together with the disability of not having a husband, moved Lucy, decisively, to the bottom of the pile – deprived of the meretricious blandishments of the consumer society and also, largely, of the benefits of citizenship. Her social life shrank almost to nothing. She didn't much like her father and stepmother; she loved her mother, who had died when Lucy was in her early teens, and Ernie's stepmother, Patience. The latter, and Ernie's father Jim, lived at the top of a five storey office building in the City (Patience was the caretaker, though her legs were swollen and she could hardly manage the stairs.) From Jim's roof garden we could gasp at the bomb craters all around and watch the pageantry of the Lord Mayor's Show; Mark and I would walk with Jim to the river to see the Tower of London and, if we were lucky, the opening of Tower Bridge. Lucy's brothers and Ernie's sister were also good to Mark and myself, and invited us at Christmas and Easter. Her pre-war friends got married and moved away. One or two neighbours and teachers were kind.

The 1950s were not a good time to be a lone parent. Going out was organised around couples; in a middle class neighbourhood it wasn't possible for a young woman to drop in on people, or to go into a pub. Lucy's impediments made it hard for casual acquaintances to appreciate her dry humour, her practical wisdom, her slightly quaint vocabulary, her belief in decorum and decency, and her capacity for love. Her life became focused on Mark and myself. At the time we took it for granted, but she made for us a secure, structured and remarkably full family life. Living on the war widow's pension and family allowance, we were poor and could never forget it. Clothes were often second hand; we walked to the next bus stop to save a penny; when carol singers came round at Christmas we turned off the light, so we wouldn't have to open the door and give them money. Nonetheless, Lucy thought of games to play, things to eat, places to go. We borrowed books from the Library; we collected (stamps, matchboxes, cigarette packets, cheese labels). We even went to West End shows – Whitehall farces and Agatha Christie mysteries (we saw *The Mousetrap* in 1954, when it was in its second year). For six or eight years we spent two idyllic summer weeks at Prestatyn Holiday Camp. Lucy encouraged our attempts to make music (Ernie had played several instruments and sung with the Royal Choral Society) and, above all perhaps, she encouraged us to do well at school, though she had had little joy there herself. Mark and I could read by the time we reached school: we learnt by watching the page as Lucy read Enid Blyton aloud.

To make ends meet and as a reason for getting out of the house, Lucy took a job washing dishes for a few shillings an hour in a local cafe. Being barely able to cope with the work, she was harried and hustled – we would now say bullied – on a daily basis. Yet she couldn't leave because it was doubtful what else she could do. With typical naivety and desperation, she conceived a loyalty to this employer that was in no way reciprocated.

My sense of anger at injustice in the world is undoubtedly rooted in the distresses of Lucy's life. Of course, I intend her also as a representative figure; innumerable people have been suffering in innumerable ways. Study of the war brought into focus, for me, the lives of ordinary people. Lucy spent the war in London, keeping a home for Ernie on his very occasional leaves and looking after me and Mark. Like many others, she could not shrug off the Blitz with a cup of tea, as the received version has it: she was petrified. I recall going to bed with her in a Morrison shelter (a steel box in the house). We must have been sheltering from the doodlebugs – flying bombs launched from France in 1944 – and I know she was petrified. Her trauma was evident again a little later, when I was older and for some reason the alarm siren was sounded while we were in the high street: she shivered and whimpered. Later she told me how, walking back from Jim and Patience's across the river Thames to Brixton one night, she looked back and saw the entire East End on fire. When she was expecting me she was relocated because the house where she was living was declared unsafe. When, prompted by a Sunday School teacher, I asked Lucy why she didn't go to church, she replied that the angels hadn't done anything for her in the war. Before, she and Ernie had belonged to church organisations for young people.

Lucy always sounded proud when she told me that Ernie didn't 'go' to the air force until he was 'called'. The ideological and even the physical authority of the war government did not go without saying. The myth is that everyone submitted heroically to a common purpose. However, class differences were indelible, and allowed a belief that the war was being fought, as always, for the benefit of better-off people. Many were sceptical, ironic and detached. They scrounged and skived, abandoned their jobs, went on strike, deceived their spouses, and made money on the black market. Such oppositional thinking helped me to think about the scope for dissident thought and action in modern societies. In the face of gross appeals to personal idealism and self-interest, unprecedented management of the media, and inducements to report disaffection, ordinary people were not taken in. (I write about this in Chapter 3, 'Literature and Cultural Production.)

As I show in Chapter 2, 'War Stories', the authorities were well aware that they needed to propagate stories that would maintain popular morale and inspire the necessary sacrifices. A principal theme was wide-ranging and insistent promises about what life would be like after the war. Looking back from the 1980s, when I was writing this book, it appeared that what we had got, for all the promises, was grudging, precarious, conditional. The ruling elite had demanded wartime sacrifices as necessary for the new society that was to follow. They owed us.

Lucy's largely thwarted life was and remains for me the perfect figure for the impoverishment and indignity which has continued to afflict disadvantaged people – those who are elderly, infirm, unemployed, black, queer, lone parents, and so on. It witnesses to the experience of many people, who are subject to the demands and indignities of landlords, employers and the care system, scarcely supported by friends and neighbours as each strives to meet the demands of work and conspicuous consumption. So much of this suffering could have been remedied if the ruling elite in business and politics had invested in it some of the money, imagination and determination that it has been ready to bestow upon a sequence of misguided wars. Some people question the idea that there is a ruling elite and a dominant social and ideological formation. I ask them, in whose interest has all this been?

The personal story of this book, then, is founded in a sense of disappointment, disillusionment and betrayal. The Labour movement appears the more culpable because more has been expected of it. That seemed clearer when I came to write a new chapter for the second edition of this book, 'The Politics and Cultures of Discord (1997)'. Since then, under the 'new' Labour administrations of Tony Blair, the sense of betrayal has become widespread.

To suppose that I might have derived from Lucy an articulated intellectual-political position would, of course, be sentimental. Political commitment, in my view, grows and thrives within a formation of like-minded people; in effect, a subculture. The stories that we, personally, find plausible tend to be those that are current within our milieu. By this I don't mean that intellectuals on the left have a tendency toward slavish compliance in some party line; indeed, the contrary is true – the tendency is toward competitive and disputatious individualism. Nonetheless, a shared agenda, subject to breaks as well as continuities, may be observed, and this affords a framework within which some responses, in any given situation, simply seem more plausible than others. I write in Chapter 12:

> political identity does not derive directly from class or gender or racial position, or sexual orientation; or simply from personal choice. It derives in large part, and this is not sufficiently remarked, from involvement in a milieu. So an individual discovers a certain kind of selfhood in relation to others, learns to inhabit certain preoccupations and forms. A subculture sets the framework of understanding – makes certain stories plausible. (p. 266)

Subcultural work, then, aimed at exploring outstanding issues, becomes a potentially productive political intervention.

Thus Tony Blair believed that there were Weapons of Mass Destruction in Iraq because the whole organisation of his political culture told him so. I, like all my friends, believed otherwise. The fact that we were right indicates not that we have superior access to intelligence information (evidently there was hardly any such information anyway), but that we have a superior framework of plausibility. I believe our view is better than Blair's also in relation to education and the health service: more would be gained by cooperation than competition.

The key moment of my own intellectual-political vocation lies in the early 1960s. This book moves towards that moment, placing or setting aside complicit versions of the literary apparatus, to arrive at Chapter 11, 'The Rise of Left Culturism', and Chapter 12, 'Intellectuals and Workers'. There I discuss the development of a youthful new-left subculture, organised typically around the Campaign for Nuclear Disarmament, drama associated with the Royal Court Theatre, some literary writing, and folk-music and jazz. This was the point at which I left my conservative school and discovered a new world of radical thought in the English Department at University College London. It is the moment of John F. Kennedy, Harold Macmillan and Harold Wilson; of the Sharpeville massacre and Martin Luther King; of the nuclear threat and the surrender of Empire; of *West Side Story* and *Oh What a Lovely War*; of the Beatles and the Rolling Stones; of guitar-strumming and hitch-hiking. *Literature, Politics and Culture in Postwar Britain* re-views that formation, making explicit some of its confusions and assessing their ongoing validity.

Part of the critical orthodoxy that prevails today is that literary studies in the 1960s were sunk in a Cold-War gloom until 'theory' rescued us all in the mid 1970s. Indeed at school, for A-level, we were advised to infer the author's intention, then to show how he had 'carried it out'. The teaching staff at UCL, however, included committed leftists, such as Charles Peake and John Chalker (they were also fine teachers). I recall the distinguished American new-critic, Cleanth Brooks, coming to speak, probably in 1963; he gave a close reading of poems by Yeats and Auden. In the pub afterwards we pondered what Yeats might have meant in 'A Prayer for My Daughter', and Chalker prompted the thought that the poem's stance was fascistic. (In the late 1970s, still, to speak thus about Yeats was sufficiently provocative to lead a senior colleague to question the suitability of a junior for his post.) In our course on European drama from 1880 to the present, Sean O'Casey, Bertolt Brecht and John Arden were taken as touchstones for the necessary political engagement of theatre, in a stand-off with 'Theatre of the Absurd' (Beckett and Ionesco).

Most significantly, our literary culture was not, in its larger part, something for the lecture, the assessed essay and exam revision. Most of the students I knew were writers, or were directly engaged in literary culture. We read Lawrence, Kafka, Scott Fitzgerald, Woolf and Orwell for guidance on writing and life. We disputed whether Hughes or Larkin had a serious engagement with the modern world, or whether this was attained by American poets (Berryman, Lowell, Plath).[2] Or was rhyming, stanzaic poetry exhausted, leading us to Allen Ginsberg and the Beat poets, whose bohemian lifestyle 'on the road' meshed persuasively with student mores? The college drama society found Brechtian potential in Georg Büchner's *Woyzeck* and Shaw's *St Joan*. This contemporary work, furthermore, seemed in an adequate continuity with the metaphysical poetry of John Donne, and with the drama of Webster, Tourneur, and Ben Jonson. Sympathetic teaching could rescue even the compulsory courses on Old and Middle English writing.

Such a specific and central engagement with the public realm of literary endeavour is far less common today, I believe. Student culture is located elsewhere, in music, video and the internet, offering realms of engagement that may outdistance the personal and political potential of traditional cultures. Undergraduates have little hostility to literature; it just doesn't fit very well with their other preoccupations. This is why many of my colleagues find their work with undergraduates unsatisfying. We try to close the gap though more directive and vivid teaching strategies; that risks sapping the students' independence. I notice with some dismay that the choice appears like that which faces the established churches in their relation with the old liturgy. We may either run to catch up with the contemporary world by tailoring our courses towards the presumed idiom of the students, or we may burrow back into the literary tradition, demanding that the students follow.

Literature presented itself to us in 1960 as a radical discourse, exploring the scope of human experience from an inevitably critical stance. This was within a general reliance upon existentialism, in which important issues of commitment had provoked authoritative treatment in philosophical and literary writing. The exciting and relevant new theatre (associated with the Royal Court) was not just, or even mainly, by the new British writers. The Nazi occupation of France had demanded individual heroism and shared responsibility. Political and ethical predicaments were analysed in plays by Jean-Paul Sartre (*Altona, Les Mouches* and *Les Mains Sales*), Jean Anouilh (*Antigone*), Eugène Ionesco (*Rhinoceros*), and Max Frisch (*Biedermann und die Brandstifter*), in some instances under the noses of the Gestapo. These plays were performed in London, and so was drama by Brecht. As I suggest in Chapter 6, 'Freedom and the Cold War', Sartre's exploration of *engagement* was much discussed – the commitment to freedom which the writer makes as a human being, and its relation to actual political formations (such as the Communist Party).[3] Sartre argued that in a class society the writer is alienated from his readers. Since a classless society is not in prospect, this amounts to a view of literature as perpetually avant-garde – which is how French culture appeared to be. Literature constitutes itself as a standing reproach to the bourgeoisie and its false claims for unity and wholeness.

In the wake of the international rebellions that we associate with 1968, and in the face of the tribulations of welfare-capitalism in the 1970s and the rise of Thatcherism in the 1980s, literary and artistic culture appeared out of its depth (see Chapter 13, 'The Ways We Live Now'). The utopias to which it had aspired seemed too remote, its grasp of them too halting. It had become dependent upon state subsidy and inured to the compromises required by that dependency. It seemed to find a confident voice only when complaining that support from the Arts Council and through higher education budgets was being reduced. Its assertion that art was a good in itself no longer appeared sufficient – and, indeed, was rivalled by arguments that the arts might encourage tourism, business relocation and urban regeneration. The Royal Shakespeare Company, for instance, had claimed a radical vision; now its efforts appeared piecemeal, gestural and complicit.[4] Many prized texts, inspected in the earnest light of multiculturism, feminism and gay liberation appeared racist, misogynist and homophobic. Furthermore, many texts were suddenly perceived as embedded in an essentialist, redemptionist vision, in which 'man' figured as a central but fixed entity, whose best move was to plumb the depths of his soul in order to discover how he might atone for his existence.[5] The heroic act was to acknowledge the wretchedness of man and the futility of his political aspirations. This stance was eased into a dominant position by the manufacture of Modernism (which is viewed in Chapter 9 as a conspiracy to seize the idea and authority of the modern).

Art and literature, in short, became subject to the mood of disappointment and suspicion that I have derived from broken wartime promises, and that others drew from diverse other sources. We had taken too much for granted, accepted literary culture too compliantly on its own evaluation. This was partly a matter of plot and character: simply, did the text promote demeaning images of women, gays, black people? These still seem to me viable questions. Indeed, the more compelling the writing, the more the need to read it with suspicion; this, after all, was Plato's point.

More fundamentally, many texts and commentaries appeared essentialist. This means that the world, from the global economic system to our personal loves and hates, is essentially as it is, of its nature. The counter argument is that this is false to human experience (which is manifestly various and malleable), and politically conservative (because it implies that people and the world are unalterable). Jonathan Dollimore took the epigraph for his book *Radical Tragedy* from Brecht's play *The Exception and the Rule*:

> We ask you expressly to discover
> That what happens all the time is not natural.
> For to say that something is natural
> In such times of bloody confusion
> Of ordained disorder, of systematic arbitrariness
> Of inhuman humanity is to
> Regard it as unchangeable.[6]

The political impetus in Brecht's proposition has become immensely stronger. If we cannot change the world, it is not going to last very much longer.

The leading project in most kinds of literary theory, therefore, became the deconstruction of essentialisms. This project embraced Colin McCabe in film studies, Catherine Belsey in literary criticism, Francis Barker on

Shakespeare, Terry Eagleton on literary theory, Homi Bhabha in post-colonial studies, Judith Butler in queer studies. Some feminists have held out for the essence of the female, but generally in the academy deconstruction rules. The characteristic critical task becomes the demonstration that, perhaps despite appearances, the text at issue actually displays an awareness of its own constructedness. The outcome is disconcertingly like a distorted mirror image of the discovery of the unity of the text in new criticism and Leavisism. In this book I have tried to conduct a materialist deconstruction; one that aims to evade formalist self-absorption by using deconstructive strategies to uncover the implication of the text in institutional, historical and ideological structures.

Suspicion of some of the claims made for some kinds of literary culture does not, of course, detach me from it. It is a resource that I share with friends and people I love; a repertoire of stories for thinking through. This is my culture. But, unlike many of my colleagues, I do not imagine that it is universal. Developments in literary and cultural studies did little for Lucy, however. She was very proud of the educational success of Mark and myself, but it set an unbridgeable gap between her and us.

Alan Sinfield, 2004

Notes

1 See for instance Helen Gardner, *The Art of T.S. Eliot* London: Faber, 1968), p. 95.
2 On these disputes, see A. Alvarez, ed., *The New Poetry*, 2nd edn (Harmondsworth: Penguin, 1956).
3 See John Mander, *The Writer and Commitment* (London: Secker and Warburg, 1961).
4 See Sinfield, 'Royal Shakespeare: Theatre and the Making of Ideology', in Jonathan Dollimore and Alan Sinfield, eds, *Political Shakespeare: New Essays in Cultural Materialism*, 2nd edn (Manchester University Press, 1994).
5 See chapter 7 below; Sinfield, 'Varieties of Religion', in Sinfield, ed., *Society and Literature 1945–1970* (London: Methuen, 1983); Leo Bersani, *The Culture of Redemption* (Cambridge, Mass: Harvard University Press, 1990).
6 Jonathan Dollimore, *Radical Tragedy* (Brighton: Harvester, 1984).

Foreword to the Second Edition

This book is an attempt to draw together a history of political change in the period since 1945, and a political approach to the literary and other cultural production that has been, in part, the agent and vehicle of that change. Such a project became feasible in the mid-1980s, when most of the book was written, as the collapse of the postwar consensus exposed the vulnerability of many customary left-liberal assumptions, while opening the way for a broader critique of the cultural apparatus. Time and again, even as I was writing, an event, movement or text which I had taken for granted as a component in my political and imaginative life took on a different shape, demanding a new awareness of the pressures and limits that had determined our history, politics and culture.

Because the book is a product of all that, I have not tried to splice into it subsequent knowledge and ideas. Yet, so revelatory was its moment, there is little that I would wish to change. This doesn't mean that I think it is all right, by any means; but the arguments and exemplifications have a purpose and a pertinence that I still wish to defend. There are things I want to add, of course, and they appear in a new opening chapter: 'The Politics and Cultures of Discord (1997)'. As well as an update, it offers a new frame through which to read the book, and therefore stands first. Apart from that, I haven't changed anything.

Alan Sinfield
Brighton, 1997

The politics and cultures of discord (1997)

When Margaret Thatcher lost the leadership of her party, in 1990, it was tempting to suppose that cultural workers would pick up where they had left off when she came into office in 1979. 'It was to many of us in the arts as if the curse had been lifted' Howard Brenton wrote. 'Perhaps now we can all get back to normal' said Roland Rees, director of the Foco Novo theatre company (whose Arts Council grant was discontinued in 1988).[1] But, of course, there is no going back. Anyway, where we were before wasn't good enough, I shall be arguing. Brenton writes of culture as 'a national café of the mind, in which we are all the clientele', deriving this notion, with only a slight qualm, from Malcolm Muggeridge. 'When the café's working, we all take part; the rows, the jokes, the outbursts of singing, the meals we eat together, give us our sense of identity.' But this genial, consensual model of culture is not adequate to our situation and it never was. I see, rather, the politics and cultures of discord.

Spotting Cultures

> Society invents a spurious convoluted logic tae [to] absorb and change people whae's [whose] behaviour is outside its mainstream.[2]

That is the thought of Renton, the main protagonist in Irvine Welsh's novel *Trainspotting*. The theme has haunted the period since 1945: for reformists and revolutionaries alike, the capacity of modern societies to contain dissidence has seemed to explain the persistence of unjust conditions. What, then, is the potential range of conformity and change, and how is it to be tilted in progressive directions? And how should we assess the idea that literature has been a site for the exploration of our individual freedoms? How do its universalist pretensions work in a multi-cultural and conflicted society? Such questions seemed central in the mid-1980s, when I was writing *Literature, Politics and Culture in Postwar Britain*; lately, they have taken new, or anyway more extreme forms. I am going to use *Trainspotting* as a way into some of them.

This novel was the scandalous literary success of 1993, such that for the cover of Welsh's fourth book, *Ecstasy* (1996), the publisher was able to invoke the major high-cultural gatekeepers. *Sunday Times*: 'Welsh writes with a skill, wit and compassion that amounts to genius. He is the best thing that has happened to British writing for decades'; *Guardian*: 'the most gifted of the younger writers working in Britain today'; *Times Literary Supplement*: 'Urgent, violent, bleakly funny prose. . . . He writes with style, imagination, wit and force'[3] *Trainspotting* was adapted for the theatre in 1994, had a West End run in 1996, and then toured again. It was produced as a film by Channel Four in 1995.

Yet this novel presents the argument about the capacity of modern societies to contain dissidence in terms that would have been excessive on the literary agenda of the mid-1980s:

> Suppose that ah ken aw the pros and cons, know that ah'm gaunnae huv a short life, am ay sound mind et cetera, et cetera, but still want tae use smack? They won't let ye dae it, because it's seen as a sign ay thir ain failure. The fact that ye jist simply choose tae reject whit they huv tae offer. Choose us. Choose life. Choose morgage payments; choose washing machines; choose cars. . . . Well, ah choose no tae choose life. If the cunts cannae handle that, it's thair fuckin problem. (pp. 187–8)

The thought that most of us are tied down by mortgages, cards and so on, and that non-conformists will resist all that, is not unfamiliar. Nor is the tendency to express such alienation through literary writing. 'The world is too much with us; late and soon,/Getting and spending, we lay waste our powers' – William Wordsworth. But Renton's claim for heroin addiction as an assertion of the free human spirit stretches the liberal imagination.

Trainspotting has other rebarbative aspects as well. The use of a Scots dialect places a severe impediment in the path of readers situated in what Renton calls society's mainstream. And the continual use of the word 'cunt', along with a great deal more emotional and physical brutality of language and action, offends both traditional decencies and progressive principles.

As I say, little of this is without precedent in literary writing; I think of James Joyce, Alex Trocchi, Hubert Selby, Jr, Edward Bond, James Kelman. Alan Sillitoe's *Saturday Night and Sunday Morning* is particularly relevant – it shocked and impressed the cultural establishment in 1958 (again, the film followed two years later). The cover to the third paperback printing of 1960 cites the *Daily Telegraph*: 'A novel of today with a freshness and raw fury that "makes *Room at the Top* look like a vicarage tea-party".'[4] Like *Trainspotting*, Sillitoe's novel draws together a bundle of stories around a central protagonist, illuminating the sex, violence and humanity of an unregarded (non-metropolitan) lower-class, youthful, urban scene (actually Nottingham; Welsh features Edinburgh and Leith). Like Renton, Sillitoe's Arthur Seaton has an anarchic contempt for the state, the ruling classes, empire and political parties; he too is pleased if his pleasures displease the system. 'Arthur was stirred by the sound of breaking glass: it synthesized all the anarchism within him' (p. 93). Seaton is having an affair with his friend's wife, Renton fucks his deceased brother's 'burd' at the funeral (the chapter is called 'Bang to Rites'); both Seaton and Sick Boy attack with air rifles people they dislike.

However, the level of explicit aggression, insensitivity and general disregard for the well-being and property of others is far more extreme in the later novel. Generally, Seaton likes to live and let live, but friends in *Trainspotting* abuse and threaten each other frequently, and street, pub and domestic violence, or the threat of it, seem unremitting; any passing stranger is likely to be attacked, especially if he supports the wrong football team. Begbie in particular is pathologically aggressive, and the others collude with him. Whereas Seaton only vomits over ordinary, decent folk, Welsh's characters cascade vomit, shit and piss over them. While Sillitoe's title highlights irresponsible hedonism, Welsh's indicates complete futility – collecting engine numbers at Leith Station where trains no longer run.

Welsh distinguishes his work from that of another contemporary Scots writer, James Kelman, on the ground that the latter 'seems ideologically to censor his characters. They are always non-sexist and non-racist'.[5] *Trainspotting* pulls no such punches. It 'seems designed to depress the liberal reader' writes Sean O'Brien in the *Times Literary Supplement*. 'While is charts Renton's halting progress towards abstinence, its reading of society is unsparing.'[6]

In fact, matters are not quite so bad because Renton affords something of a bridge to the liberal, middle-class reader. He was at university for a year, is thoughtful and likes books (he steals them because he wants to read them); he uses quite a few long words and can carry on a conversation about Brecht. He is uneasy at his friends' violent and exploitative behaviour. He is talked out of casual cruelty to animals, feels guilty about having supplied a friend's first shot of heroin, and gets to understand what it must be like for women when they are harassed. He is against 'Cunts that are intae baseball-batting every fucker that's different; pakis, poofs, n what huv ye' (p. 78). Like the standard hero(ine) of the bourgeois novel, he becomes wiser during the action of the book, reaches an accommodation with the world, and is ready, on the last page, to restart life from a new perspective (Seaton also follows that sequence).

If Renton's relative amiability may console the lover of literature, it may also make it more difficult for him or her to quarantine these characters as an extreme, no-good, drop-out group from another class. These days things like this could happen, almost, to people who read books that are recommended in the *Guardian* and the *Times Literary Supplement*. Further, the aggression occurs not only among lower-class young men and drug users. In a troubling incident, Begbie and Renton refuse to yield seats on a train to a couple who have reserved them, and browbeat the ticket inspector as well. The comfort, self-assertion and good fun of these boys require the intimidation, even in the face of reasonable authority, of decent, sensible people who book their seats in advance. Nicola Lezard in the *Independent on Sunday* declares: 'The real nastiness of the book, or the aspect that should make most people uncomfortable, is its depiction of the gulf that exists between the working class and most of the people reading this newspaper'.[7] Glossing 'real nastiness' as that which is unlike readers of the *Independent* puts it bluntly, but one can see what Lezard means.

What is even more uncompromising in *Trainspotting* is a resentful and dismissive attitude to high culture. This is indicated near the beginning when Renton, having shat in his pants in the street because he has inserted opium suppositories into his rectum in an attempt to tolerate withdrawal from heroin, finds a particularly noxious lavatory in a betting shop. He manages to catch a fly, and uses its juices to smear on the wall 'HIBS' (the football team): 'The vile bluebottle, which caused me a great deal of distress, has been transformed intae a work of art which gives me much pleasure tae look at' (pp. 25–6). This unpleasant, if cultivated, reverie is destroyed by Renton's realization that he has lost the suppositories – which he has to retrieve from the noisome lavatory bowl. And all this, he realizes in a concluding moment at the bus stop, on the first day of the Edinburgh Festival (p. 27). Reviews of *Trainspotting* often feature this episode.

The provocative bit here is not Renton's degradation – that is what is conventionally supposed to happen to drug addicts – but his claim to have produced art in some kind of relation with the Edinburgh Festival. Lovers of literature like to learn about other sorts of people; even nasty people when they can be placed as exemplifying a tragic predicament. Even so, they will find difficulty identifying with characters who are so determined to cancel the premises, as it were, of literary reading. If we are inclined to empathize with Renton's wish to evade two cunts who seem to be screaming at him and may give him a kicking, we may be discouraged to find Festival-goers being placed on a similar footing, when he notes how 'the noise fae the two arseholes has been replaced by the appreciative chattering ay groups ay middle-class cunts as they troop oot ay the opera' (p. 306).

As John Frow observes (discussing Andrew Ross's book *No Respect*), 'There are clear limits to the extent to which it is possible for intellectuals to associate themselves with anti-intellectualism; and there are limits to how far they can or should suspend their critique of, for example, racism, sexism, and militarism'.[8] Ross and Frow mean to reassess the wish, perhaps sentimental, of the middle-class intellectual to engage with popular culture: in practice, she or he will encounter there attitudes that are hard to take. Of course, one would not want to slide into an assumption that popular culture is fascist whereas high culture is enlightened. Rather, as John McGrath says, popular culture is 'the site of an ongoing struggle'. Describing the rewards and sorrows in running a committed theatre company in Scotland, McGrath regards himself as involved in 'the struggle for the "progressive" within popular culture'.[9]

The point I am pursuing here is that Ross and Frow envisage a relatively secure state of affairs: the literary-intellectual reader has his or her immediate culture and chooses to venture beyond, into other realms; it is there, in popular culture, that he or she may encounter illiberal attitudes. With *Trainspotting* the situation is different: disconcerting attitudes break into high culture.

This amounts to a break-down in the concept of literature, and in cultural authority generally. Many of the terms for this were evident already in the mid-1980s, when I was writing *Literature, Politics and Culture in Postwar Britain*. I described how, in the 1960s and 1970s, youthful, class-mobile impatience with the solemnity and triviality of leisure-class culture collaborated with commercial pressures to undermine the consensual cultural hierarchies that had masqueraded as 'universal', and to replace them, either with a more political dynamic (as in feminism, ethnic subcultures and lesbian and gay subcultures), or with an allegedly undifferentiated postmodernist collage (see chapter 13). Lately, these tendencies have accelerated.

Let's recap: the initial idea of literature and literary criticism was to discriminate between fine writing which generates a significant view of life, and crude or manipulative writing which exploits prurient emotions. It wasn't always specified in the theory that the latter was likely to be 'popular', but quite often it turned out that way. Writing about sex tested these boundaries: was it not pornographic? From the 1950s to the 1980s, the progressive move was to restrain pornography without interfering with art and literature. There were disagreements at the margins, as to whether certain texts were one or the other (over *Lady Chatterley's Lover*, for instance, in the defining court case of 1960), but few disputed that the distinction was viable. Literature was good, pornography was bad, and literary critics were trained to know which was which.

With *Trainspotting*, as for instance with the work of Robert Mapplethorpe, Dennis Cooper and Della Grace, it becomes far more difficult to posit a distinctive realism, let alone a superior realm, in which art and literature are created and appreciated. When, in their youth, Renton and Sick Boy photographed their penises in passport booths and put them behind the glass panels in bus shelters, they were rehearsing the confusion that has raged around Mapplethorpe's photographs. 'Wi used tae call thum oor public art exhibitions', Renton says (p. 200). The cover to Welsh's *Ecstasy* quotes the *Times Literary Supplement*: 'Irvine Welsh may become one of the most significant writers in Britain', Nick Hornby avers. So this *is* a kind of literature – it says so in the *TLS*. Moreover, Hornby warns, Welsh's voice is one which 'those alienated by much current fiction clearly want to hear': like it or not, this is the way the novel is going. The enemy has passed the gatekeepers.

'Fat, Rich Festival Cunts'

Welsh's purpose in registering and contributing to a collapse in authority and consensus in UK cultural life is not to celebrate the equality-of-access, level-playing-field, notion of cultural opportunity that is often imagined in postmodernist theory – as if roaming at will through the Internet and shopping without leaving our IKEA futons will comprise all the freedom that we could reasonably want. *Trainspotting* does not encourage the idea that cultural hierarchies are fading. On the contrary, it explores the intersection points of cultural and political power and resistance.

High culture comes under attack from Renton and Sick Boy because they regard it, in the main, as an alien class and national formation. Renton grumbles that you can't get a taxi for 'fat, rich festival cunts too fuckin lazy tae walk a hundred fuckin yards fae one poxy church hall tae another fir thir fuckin show' (p. 4). His girlfriend Kelly complains that the city is full of 'middle to upper-middle-English . . . white-settler types' and that the university has become 'a playground for failed Oxbridge home-counties types, with a few Edinburgh merchant-school punters representing Scotland' (p. 302).

The rebarbative style of the book registers this aggression and turns it on the literary reader. The writing in dialect and the violence of language and action are not just realism: they are designed as an impediment to the middle-class and non-Scottish reader. Actually, the language is not so difficult for the standard English speaker if she or he speaks it out loud; we might say that Welsh has achieved what writers since Robert Browning and Gerard Manley Hopkins have been trying to do, namely to slow the reader to a speaking pace. But what is accomplished specifically is that English people and other literary readers are prevented from supposing that they can readily assimilate Scotland, as if it were merely an extension of Englishness, or merely a tourist theme park.

There are two key points of comparison here with Sillitoe, writing in the early- to mid-1950s. First, for people in *Saturday Night and Sunday Morning* culture is simply and adequately expressive of people's feelings. They like Boris Karloff horror films and Laurence Olivier's *Henry V*. They have fun at the traditional Goose Fair and are entertained by television. They sing popular songs in the pub and listen to part of a Bach concerto on 'Family Favourites' on the wireless (pp. 170–1). Class difference is discernible here, but this is not where it is important; potentially, as Raymond Williams was claiming, everyone might share the same culture (see pp. 241–5 below). In *Trainspotting*, culture is political and dominated by money and class; it has become 'heritage'. Renton and Spud

> hate walkin along that hideous street [the celebrated Princes Street], deadened by tourists and shoppers, the twin curses ay modern capitalism. Ah looked up at the castle and thought, it's just another building tae us. It registers in oor heids just like the British Home Stores or Virgin Records (p. 228).

A poor woman from out of town is asked by the council where she would like to live: in Princes Street with a view of the castle, she says, naively. They laugh and give her a view of the gasworks (p. 115). Heritage is not for the likes of her.

For Seaton, Nottingham castle is a direct symbol of class rule, to be burnt down in a revolution (p. 159). For Renton, Edinburgh castle too is a repressive political edifice, but it signifies not as a seat of government but as an index of cultural inclusion and exclusion.

Second, while Sillitoe makes characters in *Saturday Night and Sunday Morning* aware of imperialism in Korea, Libya, Kenya and the Gold Coast, they give no thought to imperial relations within the UK. Irish people are remarked only as navvies, causing trouble in a local pub and then going to church; a visiting African soldier is treated respectfully; an Indian husband who speaks no English is said to be lonely. More conflicted attitudes were soon to appear. Colin MacInnes's novel *Absolute Beginners* (1959) alludes to the Notting Hill race riots and Brendan Behan's play *The Hostage* (1958) to the IRA. By the late 1970s, as is registered in such studies as *The Break-Up of Britain* by Tom Nairn (1977) and *Policing the Crisis* by Stuart Hall, Chas Critcher, Tony Jefferson, John Clarke and Brian Roberts (1978), relations among national, ethnic and religious communities, and between them and the state, seem to be at the crux of most social divisions in the UK, and indeed in many other Western countries.

When the Conservative Party formed the UK government after the general election of 1987, they took only ten of the Scottish seats, out of seventy-two, whereas the Labour Party took fifty. The government, spectacularly, had no mandate in Scotland.[10] Meanwhile, McGrath observes, 'the industrial, financial, land-owning and professional ruling groups of Scotland and Wales are tightly bonded with their partners in England, and increasingly their industries, banks, lands and practices are owned by English- or US-based companies'. Furthermore, 'almost every single important Arts administration post in Scotland, including the

Arts Council posts, was held by an English person' (McGrath, *Bone*, pp. 55–6).

The conflict in *Trainspotting* is linked explicitly with that in Northern Ireland; much of the street violence is between supporters of the local football teams, Hibernians and Hearts, who are attached to Catholic ('fenian') and protestant ('Orange') sectarian tendencies. IRA anthems are sung by some of the characters, while Renton's brother Billy is killed serving in the British army at Crossmaglen. There is racial oppression too, for Scots people, we are told, share the prejudices of the empire to which they significantly contributed. 'Ah sortay jist laugh whin some cats say that racism's an English thing', Spud says (p. 126); he describes a crude and malevolent taunting of his black friend Dode, leading to a vicious brawl. 'Do we have to rule the world to prove how much it hurts?' – the Scots band The Proclaimers link imperial ambition to forced emigration ('Letter from America').

These two points of comparison between Sillitoe and Welsh – the former's lack of interest in cultural hierarchy and in internal colonization – manifest the 1950s assumption that the central disruption was class, and that class was tangled up with socialism and hence with the Soviet Union, and hence with the Cold War. Arthur Seaton would sooner turn a gun on the English upper classes than fight the Soviets:

> They were angling for another war now, with the Russians this time. But they did go so far as to promise that it would be a short one, a few big flashes and it would be all over. What a lark! We'd be fighting side by side with the Germans that had been bombing us in the last war. What did they take us for? Bloody fools, but one of these days they'd be wrong. They think they've settled our hashes with their insurance cards and television sets. (p. 114)

In 1958 this was an extreme, but perhaps not uncommon, sentiment.

Welsh too is concerned with class, but in a changed context. '*Train-spotting* gives the lie to any notions of a classless society', Nicola Lezard says, picking up John Major's slogan.[11] Technically, though, Major may be right: the significant division today is less between classes, as they have been apprehended historically, than between those who have secure employment and those who don't. Will Hutton describes a 40–30–30 society: 40 per cent are relatively secure and hence privileged; 30 per cent are marginalized and insecure, without effective job-protection; and 30 per cent are disadvantaged – unemployed or economically inactive.[12] Yet it is alleged that history, and hence politics, came to an end with the collapse of the Russian empire and the end of the 'Cold War'.

Rectifying Our Anomaly

When I was finishing *Literature, Politics and Culture in Postwar Britain*, there were hopes that Eastern Bloc countries would discover an intermediate way, between capitalism and socialism; many people there must now wish that they had been able to do so. However, with regard to the Cold War, I stand by the analysis that I offered then.

The Russians were mainly concerned to establish buffer states against renewed invasion from the west; there was no serious likelihood that invasion or nuclear threat would result in Western Europe 'going communist'. Mostly, the Cold War was a way of defining and legitimising the ideologies of participant nation states. Western invocations of 'the Free World' not only justified ideological and physical surveillance, but also seemed to foreclose certain questions – whether 'your income' is your own or whether in any relevant sense it derives from your social situation; whether 'equality of opportunity' is, in practice, any kind of equality at all; whether the freedom to buy better education and healthcare than other people is, actually, cancelling some of their freedom; whether freedom of the press means exposing people systematically to lies and trivia; whether freedoms such as 'the right to work', which once were conventional trade-union parlance, are impossibly 'Red'; whether capitalism is worth dying for ('Better dead than Red', they said). As I try to show in Chapters 6, 9 and 11 particularly, these issues dominated ideas about art and literature – though this was hard to see, since one 'free world' dictum was that ideas about art and literature had nothing to do with anything else – even while being, by definition, anti-communist.

Now the 'Cold War' is 'over' and a new era of international peace is at hand, George Bush told us. The reason it is not working out like that is, of course, that most conflicts derive not from socialism but from capitalism. Yet the collapse of the Russian empire is being used to claim that socialism has 'lost', and the idea that it has lost is being used to claim that it is wrong. Neither inference is logically sound. First, we said repeatedly that international capital deploys immensely cunning and powerful ways of securing conformity, so insofar as socialism is currently being over-whelmed we should hardly be surprised. Second, the fact that capitalism is rampaging through the world does not make it right, and does not make us wrong to envision and work for a better system. My hunch is that socialism will be rediscovered, spontaneously by a new generation, in 2020 or so – because it remains, as it always was, the response which capitalism, through its own contradictions, provokes.

A question for the left at present, surely, is this: Since very few of us, in recent decades, have believed that a centralized, command economy and a Soviet-style political system are the way to socialism, why do we allow the idea that we have been thrown into disarray by the collapse of the Russian empire? What we call '1968' amounts, as much as anything else, to the decisive arrival of a generation of leftists who did not feel obliged even to entertain the proposition that the Soviet Union was a model for socialism. Something else, then, is troubling us. If we have lost, it is on another front.

There have been two broad patterns on the Western European left since the 1960s. Some of us have looked for radical new possibilities. These are envisaged, most often, as a kind of immediate local autonomy (not, by any means, Soviet-style centralized bureaucracy); we might think of this as the spirit of Greenham Common.[13] Others of us, the larger part, stayed with the pattern that had dominated since 1945: attempting to develop the progressive potential of the mixed economy as it emerged from the postwar settlement.

Let's locate that, briskly. In the 1930s, there seemed to be three kinds of future: fascism, communism and welfare-capitalism – a rejigging of capital-ism to make it fairer. These three fought it out between 1939 and 1946. Welfare-capitalism won in Western Europe; on the right as well as the left, it was agreed that a return to prewar conditions must be prevented. Welfare-capitalism would accord all the people a stake in society and adequate share of its resources – a job, a pension or social security, a roof over your head, healthcare, education. These promises were to be sustained by government management of the economy in the manner proposed by John Maynard Keynes (not by Soviet-style bureaucracy), which would even out the capitalist cycle of boom and slump. This is the consensus that broke down conclusively in the mid-1970s, when capitalism went into a slump after all, allowing a return to pre-Keynesian economic theories and authoritarian social attitudes. (It should be remembered, however, that in each of the elections that they won under

Margaret Thatcher's leadership, the Conservatives' share of the poll was around 42 per cent. The majority of voters preferred other parties.)

It is my contention that, whatever we were saying on the left, we hadn't really worked out a system to supersede welfare-capitalism. This is because, actually, so far from imagining a Soviet-style revolution, we envisaged capitalism continuing, though with vastly more of the 1945 promises realized. We often used a revolutionary rhetoric – and with justification, when we protested about nuclear weaponry, racism, unemployment and poverty, the Vietnam War; any number of imperial wars. But what did we really *intend* – when we cried 'America out', for instance, in Grosvenor Square in 1968? We pushed and shoved at the line of police, with the apparent goal of breaking through and reaching the US Embassy. But what were we going to do when we got there? Scratch at the walls with our fingernails, perhaps. Most of us hadn't thought about it.

I know this is not true of everyone; I mean to state the options provocatively. But for the most part, through diverse, more and less promising modes – trades unions, the Labour Party, the courts, the left-liberal press, canvassing, lobbying, demonstrating, infiltrating – we were looking for a delivery on the promises of 1945. The attraction of welfare-capitalism was that we might yet socialize – humanize – the system without having to go to the improbable length of overthrowing it.

Consider three significant movements. The Greater London Council in the mid-1980s aspired to combine the two main kinds of leftism that I have identified – an immediate, local autonomy and a more humane welfare-capitalism: the idea was to redistribute wealth and power through democratic municipal structures.[14] But how was this to be sustained, in the medium term, within the capitalist world order? If socialism in one country was unattainable, as Trotsky insisted against Stalin, what were the chances for socialism in one city? Perhaps it would be the lever for a greater change, but how would that develop, in the face of the capitalist state? I don't think we had thought very hard about it. But the Conservatives weren't risking it anyway: they abolished the GLC (is London the only capital in the world without a city government?).

Remember Bennism. Joint planning of the economy was the initial idea – the government was to call in the largest multinationals, to make planning agreements. The ambition was to shift the culture of business towards industrial democracy; here too, there was an idea of local autonomy within a more benign state.[15] But the project was both too weak and too strong: too weak to impact on the framework of capital, too strong to have been tolerated by big business.

Industrial disputes have constituted a third leftist mode of intervention. The pattern is epitomized by my own union, the Association of University Teachers. At one moment – one of many moments – our pay had fallen out of line with that of others with whom we thought it strategic to compare ourselves. The slogan we produced, with all the intellectual resources at our command, was: 'Rectify our anomaly'. A potent challenge to capital, if there ever was one. Even the coal-miners' struggle for a future set that future within an improved welfare-capitalism.

Leftist attempts to improve the system have not been in bad faith. We did believe, very many of us, that 1945 was a breakthrough, that we were forming effective campaigns, that there was potential for a slow and uneven, but steady movement towards equality and social justice. And it hasn't been all bad – especially if you disregard the fact that our relative wealth is premised on the poverty of most of the world. But, overall, it is dawning upon us now that this system is not going to deliver.

This is the flaw: welfare-capitalism raises expectations, with a view to governing through popular consent rather than through threats of deprivation and coercion. But only for a while can the system produce enough wealth to keep pace with those expectations. This is not a specially British problem; even in Sweden and New Zealand, where the chances looked best, welfare-capitalist aspirations have been hugely reined back. *That is the failure that has perplexed us*, not the failure of Soviet-style, centralized direction. Capitalism produces booms and slumps, just as it produces extremes of wealth and poverty; it can't be made compatible with a significant element of socialism. And this is so stunning that we cannot afford to recognize it. We prefer to allow the notion that it is Eastern Europe that has blown us off course; otherwise we will have to acknowledge the real poverty of our theories.

Looked at squarely, three-quarters of the world have been in continuous distress since 1945. A sleight of hand leads people to believe that being fully committed to the capitalist world order produces a 'successful' economy, such as that attributed until recently to West Germany. But what about, say, Zaire? That has been in the capitalist orbit throughout (for a moment there was a socialist leader, Patrice Lumumba, but he was assassinated by Western interests). We are invited to ascribe 'unsuccessful' economies to particular circumstances, or to an uninspected 'Third-World'-ness. But countries like Zaire are, in fact, more capitalist than the

UK – because the International Monetary Fund and the World Bank won't allow them even to attempt welfare programmes. They are in poverty because that is what happens to most people in capitalism, as it always did. The system is inherently cruel and inefficient. And socialists, whatever our confusions through the decades, are people who know this.

Materialism and Subculture

I regard the ideas and attitudes presented here as an application of a cultural materialist approach. One of the (several) ill-informed things that people say about cultural materialists is that, while they want to historicize everyone else, they don't do that to themselves. However, *Literature, Politics and Culture in Postwar Britain* is in intention, and I think in effect, a history of the political formation which fed the preoccupations of left-liberal intellectuals in the mid-1980s.

Cultural materialists investigate the historical conditions in which textual representations are produced, circulated and received. They engage with questions about the relations between dominant and subordinate cultures, the implications of racism, sexism and homophobia, the scope for subaltern resistance, and the modes through which the system tends to accommodate or repel diverse kinds of dissidence. In this approach, the terms 'art' and 'literature' (as I argue in chapter 3) are neither spontaneous nor innocent. They are bestowed by the gatekeepers of the cultural apparatus, and should be understood as strategies for conferring authority upon certain representations, and hence upon certain viewpoints.

A non-materialist approach alleges that high culture derives from the human spirit, and hence transcends historical conditions, constituting a reservoir of ultimate truth and wisdom and belonging thereby to all people indifferently. This approach has often been taken by leftists; it gained new validation in the postwar settlement, as art and literature were envisaged as good things which (like healthcare and social security) would be generally available within welfare-capitalism. It is largely through the failure of that vision that cultural materialists have been led to insist that art and literature contribute to the processes whereby cultural norms come to seem plausible, even necessary – the processes through which the prevailing power arrangements are legitimised and called into question.

This book shows, among other things, how cultural materialist theory has been fuelled by the disappointment of hopes that were generated initially by the postwar settlement of 1945, and then subsequently in the break-out that we call 'the 1960s'. The evocation of the war of 1939–45 in chapter 2 is designed to expose the patronising manipulations that were necessary to win the war; we were promised, and were owed, something better than we got. The account of the alienation of most of the literary establishment from popular needs and aspirations shows the extent to which high culture has been a class culture after all.

At the same time, up to a point, art and literature have been crucial vehicles for middle-class dissidence, which has been an important agent of social and political change through the New Left, the peace movement, the women's movement and other progressive formations. While my arguments derive, manifestly, from immersion in the left-liberal intelligentsia, from skiffle and the Campaign for Nuclear Disarmament in 1958 to Billy Bragg and Section 28 in 1988, I wanted nonetheless to treat that grouping as a historical phenomenon. The emergence of the New Left as a kind of subculture is traced in chapters 11 and 12, with a view to reassessing the anxieties and confusions that informed it.

It is noteworthy that the main discussions of the politics and cultures of race, gender and sexuality occur in other chapters, as topics in their own right rather than parts of the history and analysis of new-left attitudes. That, broadly, is how it seemed to be. While opposition to apartheid had been central, at least since the Sharpeville Massacre (1959), many leftist ideas about empire and race remained complacent – while literary discourse, I try to show, presented implicitly racist ideas as profound insights into the human condition. With regard to gender, it took most men on the left a good deal longer than we now like to remember to appreciate the justice and importance of the women's movement. Partly because it was becoming an orthodoxy that women had been excluded from literary writing, it seemed worthwhile exploring such a key figure as Plath in relations to her actual writing career. And sexuality had been recorded as a factor in the lives of many mid-century writers, but had hardly been articulated with a post-Stonewall gay politics.

Though part of my initial purpose in *Literature, Politics and Culture* was to explore queerness in the literary establishment, I didn't realize when I began writing that I would end with the argument that the best chance for literary and leftist intellectuals to make themselves useful lies in orienting their efforts, for the time being, towards a subcultural constituency – in my instance of lesbians and gay men. Instead of offering our efforts and talents to a disdainful or predatory mainstream, we may commit ourselves to subcultural fiction, history, art, political and cultural commentary. The same may be true for groups disadvantaged on ground of class, race, nation and gender; of course, that is for them to decide. I came to this conclusion by working through the pressures of the historical analysis as it unfolded; I have tried to develop it in subsequent writings.[16]

In 1997, my interest in *Trainspotting* is substantially to do with its repudiation of mainstream culture, in the interest of a national, class and generational specificity. A powerful comment by Renton indicates the subcultural orientation of the book. 'Ah don't hate the English. They're just wankers. We are colonised by wankers. We can't even pick a decent, vibrant, healthy culture to be colonised by. No. We're ruled by effete arseholes. What does that make us? The lowest of the fuckin low, the scum of the earth' (p. 78). That thought is not aimed at 'the mainstream' – effectively, the English, the Scottish establishment and international heritage tourists. It is for Scotspeople: Welsh is challenging them to ponder their own situation.

I am well aware that, in comparison with the global goals that socialists have envisioned, subcultural development may seem a limited project. However, since I am arguing that the failure of welfare-capitalism is a disaster that we can hardly bare, collectively, to contemplate, I cannot be expected to come up with a comprehensive new politics. Until someone does, there seem to be two options: (1) prepare for a future revolutionary conjuncture; (2) regard socialism, for the time being, as a relative condition – to be achieved in fits and starts where circumstances are propitious. Either way, a good strategy will be to sustain and politicize dissident groups.

The task, then, is to locate a subculture where one may claim belonging, and to work with and through that. The prospect of such subcultural commitment reorients the theme with which I began – Renton's thought about how 'Society invents a spurious convoluted logic tae absorb and change people whae's behaviour is outside its mainstream' (p. 187). In terms of literary production, this has seemed to be a question about how writing that is critical of the prevailing system is disarmed and accommodated. However, subcultural writing is not much concerned either to subvert or to reach an accommodation with mainstream attitudes; its primary goal is to intervene in the subculture, by (re)telling its myths in compelling and critical ways.

Making it Political

In practice it is not easy to kick free from the mainstream cultural apparatus. An interview with Irvine Welsh by Elizabeth Young in the *Guardian* in August 1993 concludes:

> In the meantime, *Trainspotting* stands as a crazed, splenetic rant against the sleek, self-congratulatory Edinburgh of the Festival. Welsh's is the voice from the pit, from a thousand freezing nights waiting to score drugs, a[nd] long days in front of dying televisions, a voice from the dark side . . .
> Irvine Welsh will be reading with Duncan McLean on August 30 at 12.30 pm – The Edinburgh Book Festival, Charlotte Square.[17]

The Festival has even more to congratulate itself on when it co-opts such a critical voice. But then, Welsh, like any writer, has to get his work into circulation.

Caryl Churchill's play *Serious Money* is read by Peter Holland as 'a harsh and exhilarating satire' on commercial institutions, and that is how a typical left-liberal audience heard it at the Royal Court in 1987.

> But in the later stages of its run at the Royal Court and even more explicitly when it transferred to the West End, *Serious Money* found itself confronting a new audience. Those the play attacked and ridiculed now watched it; the play became the excited preserve of the yuppie City world it savaged and the laughter of recognition replaced the laughter of astonished delight. The Royal Court stalls bar had never sold so many bottles of champagne.[18]

The financial viability of the Royal Court depends on transfers and runs that make its work accessible to mainstream audiences. As I argue at several points in this book, there is no innocent mode of cultural production, no way of jumping clear of the system. Even so, the point is not that nothing can be done, but that the struggle will have to be unremitting.

The extent to which ideas and attitudes may be provocative but constructive in subcultural contexts, and unacceptable in the mainstream, is illustrated by the film, *Trainspotting* (directed by Danny Boyle with screenplay by John Hodge, as a follow-up to their box-office success, *Shallow Grave*). Many of my (non-Scottish) friends liked it very much – though they had been put off reading the novel by either the experience or the report of it as hard-going. Unfortunately, the film diminishes or removes most of the challenging aspects of the book. This is not because film is a blunter medium – by no means – but because films as we plan and distribute them today cost a lot, and therefore tend to get made with international money for mainstream consumption. In the USA *Trainspotting* was the second most successful British film of all time, grossing over $20 million. (The play of *Trainspotting*, adapted by Harry Gibson, steers clear of sectarianism, but otherwise respects the spirit of the novel.)

Nothing remains in the film of sectarian conflict and almost nothing of class resentment; there is no attention to racial violence, domestic violence or gender harassment. The accents are toned down to the point where they are barely noticeable, and the Festival has only an inconsequential mention. There is nothing about Ireland and not much about Scotland. Generally, the film could be set anywhere.

Drugs are the problem most accessible to media consternation and liberal goodwill, and they are made into the entire theme – whereas in the novel they are one of the conditions of these people's lives. Even within this narrowed perspective, the film discourages several subversive ideas that are floated in the novel: that you can function sensibly while using heroin, that you can use it occasionally without becoming addicted, that you can finance it without too much difficulty, that you can protect against HIV infection by not sharing needles. In the film the boys all become more and more desperate, 'propelling ourselves with longing towards the day when it would all go wrong. . . . No matter how often you go out and rob and fuck people over, you always need to get up and do it all over again'. There is no equivalent to that kind of speech in the novel, and no such downward slide. In the film heroin is the source of all criminal behaviour, whereas in the novel Renton steals books because he wants to read them, Sick Boy becomes a pimp and a criminal *after* abjuring the drug, and Begbie is not a user.

Most disappointingly, the film suppresses the contrast between Renton and Sick Boy. In the novel the former is thoughtful and has a conscience, whereas the latter, he tells himself, is 'a dynamic young man, upwardly mobile and thrusting, thrusting, thrusting' (p. 30). So Sick Boy is the Thatcherite: 'The score is ah'm looking eftir numero uno', he declares when Renton expresses disgust that he is pimping (p. 174). However, the film shows Renton smartened up and enjoying himself as an estate agent in London during the late-1980s property boom, and credits him with Thatcherite sentiments: 'There was no such thing as society, and even if there was I most certainly had nothing to do with it. For the first time in my adult life, I was almost content' (there is no equivalent to any of this in the novel). The film also changes the ending, again bestowing Sick Boy's stance upon Renton (I won't spoil it by saying how). By destroying the distinction between them, the film cancels Renton's leftish rebellion, making Thatcherite selfishness the 'natural' way, on or off heroin, to live.

Cultural materialists are attacked as people who undermine cultural value by 'making it political'. We believe, of course, that culture is political anyway, and that the attempt to suppress that knowledge is itself a political manoeuvre. The translation of *Trainspotting* from subcultural novel to mainstream film highlights the politics of both texts.

In fact, it should be plain to see, capitalism is dissolving traditional hierarchies far more rapidly than leftist criticism. High culture used to be defined, in effect, as that which would not succeed in the market because its values were 'higher'. The New Right demand that high culture market itself, with anything earlier than 1970 packaged as 'heritage', is designed to rebuff the idea that there is any value beyond the market. When Conservative minister Michael Portillo was asked why a new royal yacht could not be financed commercially, he said it would be 'demeaning'; yet he is prepared to let the aura of Shakespeare, Constable and Elgar become tarnished with commerce. As I argue in chapters 11–13, high-cultural discourses have been colonized since the 1960s, in some measure, by a left-liberal ethos, and that is why right-wingers are prepared to forego such powerful ideological props.

During the 10 years since the writing of *Literature, Politics and Culture*, these de-mystifying tendencies have broadened and accelerated. Government, parliament, monarchy, the police, the judiciary, the churches and the press have fallen into new kinds of disrepute. Museums and cathedrals impose charges and anything that used to be dignified, from a stately home to an industrial process, is revamped as a theme park. Pubs near Nottingham are offering Shakespeare's *Macbeth* as a Karaoke option, with the main characters' speeches on a screen. 'CD Rom technology will then introduce other characters in the play in animated form and provide a soundtrack of ghostly wailings and other appropriate sound effects.'[19]

The marketing of books, art, theatre and classical music has come to depend more and more on advertising, launches, previews, prizes, cheap offers, package deals, discounts, celebrities, festivals, sponsorship, lottery handouts, personal scandals and every other kind of hype. It is taken for granted that a literary work, old or new, will achieve its full audience when it is adapted for film, shown on television and released on video.

Trainspotting reached the last ten on the Booker Prize list and was voted tenth in Waterstones' '100 Greatest Books of the 20th Century'; on the cover of *Ecstasy* Welsh is labelled 'the poet laureate of the chemical generation'; in the programme for the *Trainspotting* play he is 'the credible voice of rave culture'; in Dillons bookshop he is shelved in the 'Cult Fiction' section.

The potential disturbance in the present conjuncture resides not with the people who enjoy this circus, but with those who are hardly able to join in. Remember: welfare-capitalism was never wholly, or even primarily, altruistic. The idea was to head off the mass discontent that had given opportunities to fascism and communism. In *Saturday Night and Sunday Morning* the question was what would happen to the rebelliousness of Arthur Seaton now that he was earning good money in a bicycle factory. The prospect was that he would settle down, more or less, but his compliance should not be taken for granted.

In *Trainspotting* we have lower-class disaffection on comparable lines, but the factories have closed and the prospects appear to be living on your wits more or less outside the law, and suffering the illnesses that accompany drug dependency in a deprived environment. Secure employment is not on the agenda, and nor is purposive political action. What is, is persistent and omnipresent minor social disturbance, with the potential for something like fascist organization. The 'unsound looking cats' who attack Dode seem to be partly skinheads, partly Orangemen, partly Nazis (pp. 127–9). The entire culture is grossly sexist: Kelly is humiliated by what amounts to a 'lynch mob' (pp. 274–9). The return to economic and social policies of the 1930s has led where it led then: to a slump and a growth in fascism. Further, as Ellen Meiksins Wood points out, one consequence of globalization is that there is now nowhere for Western capitalism to displace its conflicts to; they will be experienced everywhere, including in the Western heartlands.[20]

A diluted form of welfare-capitalism – without the vision, lest we frighten international business – is still a significant response in the governing echelons of the European Union and in Tony Blair's 'new' Labour Party. It has been reasserted in principle in Hutton's bestseller, *The State We're In* (1995). Whether it will have another chance, and whether it will produce an improvement, are questions for another century. What it will no do is deliver on something like the promises and aspirations of 1945. There will not be full employment and social justice. Only by addressing the prevailing cultural arrangements as they are – implicated in an ideological structure that was mystified from the beginning – will cultural workers be able to gain a more secure political and creative ground.

Notes

1 Howard Brenton, 'The Art of Survival', *Guardian*, November 29, 1990; Brenton quotes Roland Rees.

2 Irvine Welsh, *Trainspotting* (1993; London: Minerva, 1994), p. 187.

3 Irvine Welsh, *Ecstasy* (London. Jonathan Cape, 1996), back cover.

4 Alan Sillitoe, *Saturday Night and Sunday Morning* (1958; London: Pan, 1960), front cover.

5 Quoted in Caspar Llewellyn Smith, 'The Credible Voice of Rave Culture', in the programme for the play *Trainspotting* at the Whitehall Theatre, 1996. I am grateful to Julie McGlynn for showing me this programme and for getting me to read *Trainspotting*. For a forceful essay by Welsh on themes discussed here, see the playtext: Irvine Welsh, *Trainspotting and Headstate* (London: Minerva, 1996).

6 Sean O'Brien, 'Schemies, Soapdodgers and Huns', *Times Literary Supplement*, October 1, 1993, p. 20.

7 Nicola Lezard, 'Junk and the Big Trigger: *Trainspotting*', Independent on Sunday, August 29, 1993, Sunday Review, p. 28.

8 John Frow, *Cultural Studies and Cultural Value* (Oxford: Clarendon, 1995), p. 158 and pp. 155–61; Andrew Ross, *No Respect* (New York: Routledge, 1989), p. 231.

9 John McGrath, *The Bone Won't Break* (London: Methuen, 1990), p. 64.

10 John Osmond, *The Divided Kingdom* (London: Constable, 1988), pp. 88–9.

11 Lezard, 'Junk and the Big Trigger'.

12 Will Hutton, *The State We're In*, revised edn (London: Vintage, 1996), pp. 105–10.

13 See Sasha Roseneil, *Disarming Patriarchy: Feminism and Political Action at Greenham* (Buckingham: Open University, 1995).

14 See Ken Livingstone, *If Voting Changed Anything, They'd Abolish It* (London: Collins, 1987).

15 See Tony Benn, *Arguments for Socialism*, ed. Chris Mullin (Harmondsworth: Penguin, 1980).

16 See Alan Sinfield, *Cultural Politics – Queer Reading* (London: Routledge, 1994).

17 Elizabeth Young, 'Blood on the Tracks', *Guardian*, August 13, 1993, p. 33.

18 Peter Holland, 'Communities: British Theatre in the 1980s', in *Heart of the Heartless World*, ed. David Margolies and Maroula Joannou (London: Pluto, 1995), p. 78.

19 *Long Eaton Herald and Post*, May 23, 1996, p. 3. I am grateful to Simon Shepherd for this cutting. See Alan Sinfield, 'Heritage and the Market, Regulation and Desublimation', in Jonathan Dollimore and Alan Sinfield, eds, *Political Shakespeare*, 2nd edn (Manchester University Press, 1994).

20 Ellen Meiksins Wood, 'Capitalism or Modernity?', *Review of International Political Economy*, Vol 4, No 3 (1997).

1
Introduction

> In acquiring one's conception of the world one always belongs to a particular grouping which is that of all the social elements which share the same mode of thinking and acting. ... The starting-point of critical elaboration is the consciousness of what one really is, and is 'knowing thyself' as a product of the historical process to date which has deposited in you an infinity of traces, without leaving an inventory. (Gramsci, p. 423)

Historically and currently, in most of the world, human societies have been and are generally controlled by force. If you don't do what powerful people tell you, they hit you, lock you up, throw you out of your house or burn it down, don't let you grow enough to eat or earn enough to subsist. Since what people of my generation call 'the war', meaning 1939–45, a distinctive attempt has been made in Britain and other parts of Europe to arrange things differently. The idea has been that we will all, or almost all, be persuaded to acquiesce in the prevailing order because we see that it is working generally to our benefit. This book reconsiders the hopes that were raised then, the way they were accommodated in the postwar settlement, how that was distorted by economic, political and cultural developments through into the late 1970s, and the implications of its abandonment now.

To win the war, people were encouraged to believe that there would not be a return to widespread injustice and poverty. The war exemplified (though not without contest) a pattern of state intervention and popular co-operation to organize production for a common purpose. And its successful conclusion afforded a rare opportunity to recast British society.

Full employment and the welfare state created, for a while, the sense of a society moving towards fairness, in which remaining 'pockets of poverty' would soon be eliminated. Now that this astonishing political experiment is under fundamental question, with social divisions deeper than for 50 years, it is important to investigate both the positive potential and the flaws in its conception, and how it went awry. So my intention is not just a work of scholarship, but an intervention in the way we see ourselves now, through a critical analysis of the period in which our present perspectives were constructed.

With that project in mind, this is a book principally about culture and especially literature – both as a range of influential writings that address current preoccupations, and as a complex apparatus that involves literary intellectuals and publishers, academic criticism and education. The hopes that have been placed in literature have been surprisingly close to the centre of the postwar settlement. The idea was that benefits that the upper-class had customarily arranged for itself would now be generally available – healthcare, education, housing, financial security. And 'good' culture, too, would be generally available. So what had hitherto been, in the main, the culture of the leisure class was proclaimed (to the discomfort of that class) as a universal culture. Literature and the arts were made to embody the spiritual and human values that consumer capitalism and 'mass' culture seemed to slight and, at the same time, were deployed as indicators for educational success and social mobility. The consequent confusions, hopes and frustrations were of a piece with others generated in postwar society, and 'good' culture is one place where the settlement has been disputed.

Through literary culture, in part, the left-liberal intelligentsia and the Women's Movement have established their identities and framed their critiques. And lately literary culture has been involved (like education, broadcasting, the Arts Council and local authorities) in the attempt of the New Right to wrest key cultural institutions from their association with a left-liberal ethos. My later chapters include assessments of the current scope for writing as intellectual resistance. The importance of literature, therefore, is not that it 'rises above' political circumstance (that idea is part of the formation under review), but that it has been a major contested category in the production of culture.

Societies have to reproduce themselves culturally as well as materially, and this is done in great part by putting into circulation stories of how the world goes. Diverse institutions are involved in this (the media, religions, political parties, education), and the texts designated 'literary', and the processes of that designation, contribute. They present the attempts of literary intellectuals, in the changing conditions of their medium and society generally, to make persuasive sense of the world. It is through such stories that ideologies are reinforced – and contested, for subordinate groups struggle to make space for themselves, and attempts to legitimate the prevailing order have to negotiate resistant experience and trad-itions. Literary texts raise complex questions of cultural affiliation and appropriation, while engaging with the most sensitive issues of our time. Chapters of this book discuss literary representations of class, race, gender and sexual orientation, relating them to institutional constraints and opportunities, other texts, and the wider ideological framework.

I am concerned particularly with points where literature intersects with other kinds of cultural production – after all, it has been defined as that which is not journalism, 'mass' culture and politics. A systematic account of other practices is not attempted; rather, discourses are juxtaposed with a view to unsettling customary assumptions. Placing 'good' culture alongside the discourses of imperialism and the Cold War, sexuality and the family, jazz and rock music, may help 'to disarticulate texts classified as literary from the system of ideological connections in which they are inscribed . . . to make them mean differently' (Bennett, p. 79). Inter-actions with the United States run through this work, manifesting a characteristic array of attitudes – deference, confrontation, strategic allegiance. Throughout, literature is shown as contested – between the class fractions and professions that would control it; within itself (for instance over formalism, Modernism and women's writing); and with other subcultures that negotiate its authority claims.

In summary, here, these ideas appear schematic and abstract; they are elaborated all through the book through numerous textual and historical instances. Because they are so intricately interwoven, I do not offer a simple progression – a historical sequence, or the demonstration of one or two main theses, or, certainly, any kind of 'coverage'. Each chapter explores a set of political and cultural developments (topics like the war, the Cold War, sexual orientation, imperialism, youth culture, the scope for women's writing), drawing upon appropriate historical, textual and theoretical resources (Chapter 3 is specially about theories of cultural production). Texts are selected for attention because they seem to focus key issues, and discussion of those texts is meant to be symptomatic rather than exhaustive. It is hoped that an uneven movement will prove stimulating.

However, there is an approximate chronological sequence together with a broad historical argument, and a distinct and persisting group of preoccupations should emerge, within an informing theoretical perspective and developing political debate. This debate is encouraging in so far as it moves through positive though often problematic interventions from the New Left, and towards significant new understanding in gender and sexual politics. But generally, the failure of the postwar settlement has allowed the initiative to pass to the New Right, and we experience a return to the conditions that the settlement was designed originally to avoid: unemployment, poverty, social rupture and authoritarian government. At the time of writing, the Postmodernist belief that all cultures are now on a level is disproved by new legislation discriminating against gay culture. However, I argue that there are still positive cultural strategies for dissident intellectuals and for subcultures.

One of my themes is that the pattern for current conditions was set by the late 1960s, after the passing up of an opportunity earlier in the decade to try once more for a fair society. I had once thought to work on through a further sequence of topics into the present, but the earlier material was so enlightening, in its aspirations and contradictions, that I present it confidently as a basis upon which to understand the ways we now live. I am not alone in this: Margaret Thatcher attributes our ills to 'Sixties culture' and says she wants to take us back to the 1950s, which she presents as 'an old-fashioned Britain, structured and courteous' (*Daily Mail*, 29 April 1988). My perception is different: in many ways the 1950s were an anxious, reactionary time, but from the middle of the decade fundamental economic difficulties and social dissatisfactions became apparent. A vivid phase of cultural and political challenge began, and 'old-fashioned Britain' generated its own supersession. An adequately complex understanding of this recent history is crucial in understanding how we got to be where we are today.

This is inevitably a personal book. I was born within ten days of the Japanese attack on Pearl Harbor, which brought the United States into the war and set the pattern of subsequent history – the defeat of fascism and checking of the ambitions of Germany and Japan, the placing of an east/west divide across Europe, the passing of the European empires to US domination; and, I suspect, the US fear of surprise attack that feeds its foreign policy (the Cold War, nuclear weaponry, the anxiety that some small Third World state might 'go communist'). I am re-viewing, in large part, my own intellectual history and configuration. In a characteristic phase of postwar social development, I have been drawn into the culture of intellectual dissidence: literary images and phrases jostle with a new-left subculture, and with other residues and alternatives – from *Hymns Ancient and Modern*, postage stamps of the British Empire, Lonnie Donegan and 'Round the Horne', through to 'EastEnders' and the Communards. Cultural contest enacts itself through our subjectivities. Some of the main formative interactions have been with people who have helped me with this book. Jonathan Dollimore and Mark Sinfield have read it all; Linda Fitzsimmons, Jacqueline Rose, Stuart Laing, Michael Butcher, Cedric Watts, Peter Nicholls, Alistair Davies, James Donald, Allon White, Pratap Rughani, Alison Light, Raphael Samuel and Rick Rylance have read parts; many students at the University of Sussex and colleagues at conferences have commented on its ideas; and teaching this period with Keith Middlemas and John Lowerson was very illuminating. One case that I argue is the importance of subcultural milieux in forming attitudes, and I gratefully acknowledge mine.

This book is likely to displease two groups of friends: those who will say that I place too much emphasis upon literary culture, and those who will say that literary texts are treated with insufficient sympathy and respect. To the former I repeat that it is a culture in which I have lived and a place where, in postwar Britain, all kinds of cultural affiliation have been formed and disputed. To the latter, I say that literature, as a discourse, is rendered uncritical and unserious by the notion that proper reading should entail acceptance; should preclude dispute with the text's assumptions. Male literary intellectuals have often identified themselves with Hamlet: that is where they discover a promising pole of sympathetic involvement – aristocratic, noble, troubled, profound. But Horatio is the character I mark: 'So I have heard, and do in part believe', he says. The hem-of-the-garment view of literature – assuming that sympathetic contact, of itself, imparts virtue – is likely to produce acquiescent people. And in a world as dangerous as ours we can't afford any more of them.

2
War stories

Bringing us victory

I just went down to the Post an' when I come back it was as flat as this 'ere wharfside – there was just my 'ouse like – well, part of my 'ouse. My missus was just making me a cup of tea for when I come 'ome. She were in the passage between the kitchen and the wash-'ouse where it blowed 'er. She were burnt right up to 'er waist. 'er legs were just two cinders. And 'er face . . . the only thing I could recognize 'er by was one of 'er boots . . . I'd 'ave lost fifteen homes if I could 'ave kept my missus. We used to read together. I can't read mesen. She used to read to me like. We'd 'ave our arm-chairs one either side of the fire, and she read me bits out o' the paper. We'ad a paper every evening. *Every* evening. (Harrisson, p. 266)

The words are those of an elderly man, an air-raid warden in Hull, from August 1941. One reason they are so distressing, to me, is the way they enact the man's loss. He speaks at first as though his house were there, and his wife, but he was standing among their remains. He cannot fully register the catastrophe that has befallen them. The comparison between his wife and 15 homes is manifestly inadequate (what would they have done with 15 homes?). But then, what else did he have, could he envisage, to lose? It would hardly be relevant to compare his wife, in the manner of traditional love poetry, to precious objects, since such things made no appearance in their lives. They had only their home and each other, and after the bomb they had neither.

What is not just distressing but, to me, enraging, is our glimpse of the life they had, in which the simplest activity – reading the paper – was a major pleasure, even a privilege. Probably they were hoping to learn what was really going on, in a society that was about to blow her and their home to pieces, and that had not bothered even to equip him with the second most important medium of human communication. And probably they had been sold a paper that systematically misled them, insulted their experience, their intelligence, her gender and their class.

If that man, who had most likely been in the trenches in the European war of 1914–18, and that woman were now living, they would be over 100 years old. By the time this book is published, no-one that fought in the war of 1939–45 and no war widows will be under 60 years old; most will be in their eighties. Yet the experience of those people, and the way the social order was adjusted in response, constitute a crucial turning point in the development of the modern world. In October 1940 Queen Elizabeth, wife of George VI, wrote to the king's mother: 'I feel quite exhausted after seeing and hearing so much sadness, sorrow, heroism and magnificent spirit. The destruction is so awful, & the people so *wonderful* – they *deserve* a better world' (Calder, p. 605). But they didn't really get it, and our current predicament is one consequence of that.

The blitz was on an entirely different scale from most natural disasters, or the routine fatal consequences of cost- and corner-cutting, lack of commitment and bad training in industry and communications. In the first three years of the war, more civilians were killed than soldiers (Minns, p. 187). Hull was attacked 70 times by night and 101 times by day over several months in 1940–1. The larger raids lasted from 9.15 p.m. to 4.00 a.m., there was 'incessant noise of aerial bombardment', whole streets of working-class housing were flattened. Poor people were reported as displaying a 'hopeless and indeed helpless incapacity to appreciate the significance of their plight, and the reasons for the disaster' – as well they might; for hours on end they were likely to be hit, and for months on end it was likely to happen again next night. Only 6,000 of the 93,000 homes in Hull escaped bomb damage (Harrisson, pp. 263–6).

How can younger European and North American people imagine the scale and intensity of the blitz? For instance, almost all my near relatives (grandparents, parents, aunts and uncles) were bombed out of their homes. By June 1941 more than two million houses in Britain had been damaged or destroyed; by the end of the war, two out of every seven houses were damaged, one-fifteenth of them beyond repair; in central London, only one house in ten escaped damage (Calder, p. 257).

10 May 1941 was the last and worst night of the London blitz. After that one night, 2,200 fires raged, and it was 11 days before the last water pumps were withdrawn; a third of the streets of Greater London were impassable; 155,000 families were without gas, water, or electricity; 1,792 people were seriously injured and 1,436 were killed (Calder, p. 247). Overall, two houses out of five in Stepney were rendered temporarily uninhabitable or worse. On the night of 14 November 1940, nearly one-third of all homes were rendered uninhabitable in Coventry. By April 1941, a quarter of the people of Plymouth had been made homeless (Harrisson, pp. 125, 133, 219). Thousands of people 'trekked' nightly from the towns where they worked to the countryside, often sleeping in the open. Up to 177,000 people slept, nightly, in filthy conditions in the stations of the London underground railway; when bombs exploded in those confined spaces, the deaths and maimings were counted in hundreds (Calder, p. 212).

In many ways, women bore the brunt. As Calder remarks, some men were said to have had 'a good war', but 'very few women can have come out of it with a better footing on the career ladder, or with enhanced personal prestige. The war trampled roughshod through women's sphere, the home'. The jobs into which they were conscripted were often frustrating and unpleasant, sometimes dangerous, and always lower in pay and status than those of men.[1] Harrisson prints an account of what a sailor's wife was supposed to do on the day after she was bombed out, one of her children killed and one injured, to re-establish her standing in the state. In her dazed and desolated condition, it entailed visiting 15 differently situated offices (pp. 224–5). That was a specific disaster. There was also the rest of the time. The myth has it that women had a good time with US servicemen (who were said to be 'over-paid, over-sexed and over here'; Minns, p. 164). There was a loosening of restraints on sexual behaviour; the illegitimacy rate had nearly doubled by 1945, to almost a third of all births. But considerable stigma attached to women who did not 'wait for' their forces 'sweetheart' (Minns, pp. 178, 182–4), and, anyway, most women were strongly socialized into fidelity to one man. Peggy Woods describes her experience like this:

> So to cut a very long and agonized war story short, he was away for five years. Now can you imagine that? I never loved anybody else. I had a few mild and meaningless flirtations and they always were just as meaningless as they had been at school. I wasn't interested. I was aware of needing sex, but I wasn't

prepared to have sex without love. Because I knew what sex was like with love . . . it's hard to explain to you what it was like emotionally that you kept faith for five years and it was perfectly normal. You waited for your bloke to come home. I find it hard to look at those wartime films, you know. I find it brings it all back. The deadly boredom of it. The War wasn't heroic, it was just a bloody bore. (McCrindle and Rowbotham, p. 173)

The blitz was designed to destroy civilian 'morale'. This is an interesting term: it signifies the people's willingness to go on accepting the government's claim to authority over them. The standard story is that Britons 'took it' all because of their intrinsic virtue and their commitment to king, country, empire and freedom. But research discovers 'a massive, largely unconscious cover-up of the more disagreeable facts of 1940–41' (Harrisson, p. 15). Very many instances of panic, despair and disaffection are recorded. Vera Brittain remarked that bombed-out people may appear calm on newsreels, but 'if people who have lost their homes, been blown up, injured, burned or buried were to be interviewed forty-eight hours later, the results would not always be so useful to the Sunshine Press' (Brittain, p. 145). Even this is naive: material for newsreels was carefully selected (Marwick, *Social Impact*). One government anxiety was that people would stop going to work. However, as Harrisson points out, people were so poor and unemployment was such a fear that they had to work to earn, whether they felt patriotic or not (pp. 140, 303).

The government evidently did believe in the possibility of civilian commitment failing, for it attempted to achieve just that in Germany. German cities were bombed at a cost of more than 8,000 British planes and well over 50,000 young, highly trained men (Harrisson, p. 304), including my father. In Tom Harrisson's view, 'Many Conservative and Liberal leaders never trusted the masses and in a way deeply, privately, despised them' (p. 21). The Ministry of Information's efforts included the notorious poster slogan: 'Your courage, your cheerfulness, your resolution will bring us victory'. People were not slow to notice the unintended admission that the war might be primarily in the interests of the ruling elite; that both fascism and the way it was being fought might be consequences of the international capitalist system. One magistrate acknowledged this perception by remarking, innocently: 'There is a war on and it is a people's war as well as ours' (Calder, pp. 70–1, 159).

Actually, the British governing elite had no conception of how most of the population lived, and therefore could neither anticipate nor understand their experience of the war. They installed a network of 'Home Intelligence' to find out. Prime Minister Chamberlain, learning of the malnutrition revealed in the evacuation of children, observed: 'I never knew that such conditions existed, and I feel ashamed of having been so ignorant of my neighbours. For the rest of my life I mean to try and make amends' (Addison, p. 22; was the hint of King Lear on the heath intended?). Prime Minister Churchill's wife remarked: 'He knows nothing of the life of ordinary people. He's never been in a bus and only once on the Underground' (Calder, p. 111). That is why the Labour landslide of 1945 was not expected. And it is why there was such a shocking lack of provision for civilian casualties and the homeless even when the blitz finally came, one year after war was declared. For instance, between 200 and 300 bombed-out people were sleeping on the floor of a school in Stepney, together with ten pails and coal scuttles being used as lavatories (Titmuss, *Problems*, pp. 260–1). These conditions were repeated everywhere, and were endured by some for weeks on end. 12,000 people were still sleeping in the underground and deep shelters on the day peace was signed with Germany.

After the war, Richard Titmuss was appointed to enquire into the 'problems of social policy' that had been revealed. By way of conclusion, he addressed the problem of morale—of how people coped so well:

> The proximity of death, the spread of physical hardship, and the ubiquity of destructive forces which were more intelligible to the ordinary man than the working of economic laws, gave existence a different meaning. . . . New aims for which to live, work that satisfied a larger number of needs, a more cohesive society, fewer lonely people; all these elements helped to offset the circumstances which often lead to neurotic illness. (*Problems*, p. 347)

In other words, most lower-class people survived wartime conditions because *materially* they were in many ways no worse off than under 'the working of economic laws'. Already, before war broke out, some two million families (17 per cent) were living from hand to mouth, in and out of debt, in cramped, cold, damp, insanitary conditions. Many more, over two-thirds, had 'next to nothing in hand from pay-day to pay-day' (Harrisson, p. 229). At least half of all working-class women were in very poor health, though they could not afford to take time off from work (Minns, p. 85). In Hull two-fifths of houses had no bath (Calder, p. 50). The point is epitomized in the fact that most people had a better diet under wartime rationing than before. In terms of *ideology*, or 'morale', Titmuss indicates that lower-class people already had precious little commitment to the social order anyway. The economic and political regime, of which they were victims rather than beneficiaries, did not afford them general goals to live for, only local engagements. Mass Observation surveys showed a steady, unsurprised cynicism about the powers that be. Through the 1944 volume, *The Journey Home*, runs this thought: 'It is widely believed that "they" have the power to put things right quite easily if "they" want to. But it is widely felt that "they" won't do so' (p. 122). So already, before the blitz, popular commitment to the British state was uneven – susceptible to stimulation by events like George V's jubilee, but generally acquiescent rather than enthusiastic.

For the total mobilization of modern warfare, general acquiescence was not enough. So when Churchill spoke from the steps of Bradford town hall in December 1942, he celebrated the unity that he knew he had to produce: 'All are united like one great family; all are standing together, helping each other, taking their share and doing their work, some at the front, some under the sea or on the sea in all weathers, some in the air, some in the coal mines, great numbers in the shops, some in the homes – all doing their bit' (Churchill, p. 245). Notice how the speech's extended geographical itemizing effaces a possible hierarchical one.

Some members of the governing elite feared revolution if the war did not result in social justice; the alliance with the Soviet Union, after all, was very popular, and there was the dreadful example of the 1917 Russian Revolution from behind the lines (Addison, pp. 134–41). The Archbishop of York believed that, if we were to 'slip back into our old ways', there might be 'such widespread and angry discontent that revolution would result' (Hopkins, p. 32). Sir John Anderson, Home Secretary, acknowledged in 1944 that full employment must be achieved to secure 'the fate of democratic institutions' (Beveridge, *Full*, p. 249). A much-quoted *Times* leader of 1 July 1940 declared that things would have to be different:

> If we speak of democracy, we do not mean a democracy which maintains the right to vote but forgets the right to work and the right to live. If we speak of freedom, we do not mean a rugged individualism which excludes social organization and economic planning. If we speak of equality we do not mean a political equality nullified by social and economic privilege. If we speak of economic reconstruction, we think less of maximum production (though this too will be required) than of equitable distribution. (Calder, pp. 158–9)

11

This mood was shared by middle-class intellectuals like Vera Brittain. In *England's Hour* she wondered 'what would have happened if all the energy, courage and resourcefulness which is now dedicated to the work of destruction, had been given to seeking a resolution for Europe's problems while time still remained' (p. 146). The most important literary expression was Richard Hillary's best-selling autobiographical book, *The Last Enemy* (1942). A pilot in the Battle of Britain, shot down and terribly burned, rehabilitated with immense surgical skill and then killed at the age of 23 back in pilot training, Hillary came nearest to satisfying the common call for a writer to parallel the war of poets of 1914–18.[2]

Hillary reminds us of what most upper-class young men at Oxford and Cambridge were like before the war: not committed Marxists like Cornford and Caudwell, or anxious liberals like Auden and Spender, or secret agents like Burgess, Maclean and Blunt, but 'held together by a common taste in friends, sport, literature, and idle amusement, by a deep-rooted distrust of all organized emotion and standardized patriotism, and by a somewhat self-conscious satisfaction in our ability to succeed without apparent effort'. In this, Hillary says, his college was 'a typical incubator of the English ruling classes before the war' (pp. 14–15). As a fighter pilot, his objectives were declaredly selfish: 'I am fighting this war because I believe that, in war, one can swiftly develop all one's faculties. . . . Back to individual combat, to self-reliance, total responsibility for one's own fate. One either kills or is killed; and it's damned exciting. And after the war, when I shall be writing, I'll again be developing faster than the rest of you' (pp. 119–20). This programme is not altered by Hillary's injuries, and hardly by the deaths of most of his friends.

At the end of the story, Hillary's outlook is transformed when he helps to dig out a dying mother and dead child from the ruins of a bombed building:

The woman who lay there looked middle-aged. She lay on her back and her eyes were closed. Her face, through the dirt and streaked blood, was the face of a thousand working women; her body under the cotton nightdress was heavy. The nightdress was drawn up to her knees and one leg was twisted under her. There was no dignity about that figure. . . . I was at the head of the bed, and looking down into that tired, blood-streaked, work-worn face I had a sense of complete unreality. . . . She opened her eyes and reached out her arms instinctively for the child. Then she started to weep. Quite soundlessly, and with no sobbing, the tears were running down her cheeks when she lifted her eyes to mine. 'Thank you, sir', she said, and took my hand in hers. And then, looking at me again, she said after a pause, 'I see they got you too'. (p. 244; my elisions)

This is a difficult passage to discuss. It is painful and humane, yet it is also shot through with apparently indelible class assumptions. The woman has 'the face of a thousand working women' because Hillary has never really looked at such people; the occasion produces an unaccustomed clarity of gaze. In his astonishment, Hillary registers both the suffering of her life and her moral superiority – her work-worn face and her capacity to notice sympathetically his disfigurement; and he allows us to conclude that they are connected. Before we have assimilated this insight there is a further implication: that in their suffering Hillary and the woman are one – 'I see they got you too'. Hillary comments: 'All humanity had been in those few words' (p. 246). This is the thought that is to transform Hillary's attitude at the end of the book. But what is left to pass unremarked is the woman's class deference: 'Thank you, sir'. Hillary's humanitarian, universalist conclusion includes, without apparent awareness, the class distinction that was at the root of the woman's life and his own initial selfishness.

So Hillary decides that it is 'impossible to look only to oneself, to take from life and not to give except by accident, deliberately to look at humanity and then pass by on the other side' (pp. 250–1). In the last sentence of the book, he welds together the sacrifice of the airmen and political commitment to a better future: if he can write for the common humanity he has scorned, he may claim fellowship with those who have died and with those 'who would go on fighting until the ideals for which their comrades had died were stamped for ever on the future of civilisation.'

To cash 'ideals' and 'civilisation', Hillary refers us back to earlier conversations with his friends, Peter Pease and David Rutter. Interestingly, this does not clarify matters as much as we might expect. Peter is a landowner and a Tory idealist. He would be as decent as he could to his dependents, would protect them and help them retain 'that ancient sturdy self-reliance of the true-born Englishman' (p. 122). On this programme, the war was fought to keep things structurally the same, with the future depending upon an (alleged) upper-class sense of responsibility. Peter does not see a problem of lower-class commitment to the war. Passing through the industrial Midlands he asserts: 'The people who live here love the grime and the stench and the living conditions. They've never known anything else and it's a part of them. That's why they'll fight this war to the end rather than surrender an inch of it' (p. 95). This is compatible with Hillary's sense of the dying working woman's common humanity, but it is troubled, in the book, by David Rutter's pacifist analysis.

David, before war is declared, asks: 'Whose war is it going to be? You can't tell me that it will be the same war for the unemployed labourer as for the Duke of Westminster. What are the people to gain from it? Nothing!' (p. 20). But the success of Hitler makes David decide that, this time, it is everyone's war (pp. 237–8). Unfortunately his struggle with his conscience about the special viciousness of Nazi Germany obscures his initial point about class in Britain. So, by default, the programme to be inferred from Hillary's new-found humanism is Peter's benevolent despotism – with class divisions subsumed into a vision of 'all humanity', which, by effacing them, maintains them. Hillary wonders whether there might be 'a new race of Englishmen arising out of this war, a harmonious synthesis of the governing class and the great rest of England' (pp. 174–5). 'Thank you, sir', she said. The first step, if such a commitment is seriously meant, should be for lower-class people to gain a reality and autonomy alongside Hillary and his friends.[3]

Consensus and its Enemies

I knew, because they told me, that a lot of people were fighting the war to keep Britain exactly as it had been', said J. B. Priestley (Lewis, P., *People's*, p. 230). Not everyone was enthusiastic about the 'levelling' tendency of the war, or contemplated with pleasure the prospect of a new programme for civilization. Evelyn Waugh rather gleefully points out in *Unconditional Surrender* (1961) that even under wartime restrictions he and his friends had ways of getting oysters, salmon, gulls' eggs, caviare and French cheeses (p. 23). But the great agony for Waugh and his kind was the disruption of class relations. In *Brideshead Revisited* (1945) the country house is evoked as a pastoral vision; like Keats's Urn, it is 'still unravaged' (p. 19). But the reprieve is temporary, for as the army arrives it brings with it what should have been a contradiction in terms: an officer who is not a gentleman, Hooper. He 'looks scarcely human', wears woollen gloves, says 'rightyo' and 'okeydoke' (pp. 13–17). 'The age of Hooper'

(p. 332) is hard on the heels of the pastoral dream. Waugh wrote in 1959 that, during the Labour Government of 1945–51, 'the kingdom seemed to be under enemy occupation' (*Spectator*, 2 October).

Angela Thirkell called her novel on the end of hostilities *Peace Breaks Out*: for her it is a further disaster, 'the Brave and Revolting New World' (p. 253). An eccentric and popular woman author (like Thirkell) declares, 'It is really good-bye to everything nice for ever' (p. 273). And the novel already has many indications of social decay – foolish government regulations, males in schools and colleges calling each other by first names, clumsy and impertinent social intruders. However, the novel ends hopefully. The upper classes are very decent with their menials, who are foolish and likely to vote Labour but nonetheless devoted to their superiors. So we may hope that tradition and good sense will win through eventually.[4]

Radical social change was generally anticipated. The typical wartime film included a reflective moment where someone asks 'What are we fighting for?' and the reply is something like, 'To create a world fit to live in.'[5] To improve and maintain war production, the government was obliged to do something about the employment, health, diet and housing of the people. Thus it was demonstrated, to all, that society and the economy could be made to work more effectively, that the world could be improved by political decisions. Sir William Beveridge drew the conclusions for the postwar world: 'All men have value when the State sets up unlimited demand for a compelling purpose. By the spectacular achievement of its planned economy war shows also how great is the waste of unemployment' (*Full*, p. 29). Beveridge was asked to produce a report on health insurance. To the embarrassment of many members of the war government, he proposed a comprehensive welfare scheme sprinkled with ringing declarations, such as 'A revolutionary moment in the world's history is a time for revolutions, not for patching', and admitting: 'Abolition of want just before this war was easily within the economic resources of the community: want was a needless scandal due to not taking trouble to prevent it' (*Social*, pp. 6, 166).

In major respects the Beveridge Report was regressive: it proposed a self-financing system with flat-rate contributions to be paid equally by all; and it insisted that married women (and only they) have 'vital work to do in ensuring the adequate continuance of the British race'. But the report and a summary sold at least 635,000 copies between them, and within two weeks a Gallup Poll found that 19 people out of 20 had heard of it and nine out of ten believed it should be implemented.[6] Kingsley Martin, having heard a 'charwoman' say, of flying bombs, 'We'll see the Government pays for this', wrote in the *New Statesman* that Beveridge was 'the last scheme which was likely to make possible a gradual change of our social order' (Martin, pp. 103, 109). Churchill and his Conservative colleagues, reluctant to talk of war aims and especially of any with an egalitarian tinge, were obliged to accept many of its proposals.

Younger Tories might recognize that the survival of capitalism required a more generous response. As Paul Addison has shown, a section of the governing class (including, for instance, Harold Macmillan) had been developing through the 1930s the idea that social reform was necessary (pp. 14, 35–44). Quintin Hogg spoke, in the Commons Beveridge debate, of the need to sustain community spirit to achieve a postwar reconstruction, and said this would require 'a complete measure of social justice to guarantee that we shall all suffer alike.'[7]

All suffer alike: we might have hoped for some pleasure and fulfilment as well; even so, the stakes are very high here. Who now proposes that we handle the current recession in that spirit? And there is evidence that many British people were ready for radical change. Public opinion during the war was found to favour the continuation of rationing, 'conscription of wealth', nationalization of land and essential industries, and a school leaving age of 16.[8] The Labour Party, it is well established, was unable and barely willing to respond to this mood.[9] Its leaders expected to lose the 1945 election, at which it gained 393 seats to the 213 held by the Conservatives and their allies. Even so, the Labour manifesto sustained the sense that something radical was going to be done, that a new deal was going to be struck between the people and capital. It spoke of 'hard-faced men', who with 'their political friends have only learned to act in the interest of their own bureaucratically-run private monopolies which may be likened to totalitarian oligarchies within our democratic State'. It concluded: 'The Labour Party is a Socialist Party, and proud of it. Its ultimate aim is the establishment of the Socialist Commonwealth of Great Britain' (Sissons and French, p. 310). Those were the days! – though on second reading the word 'ultimate' leaps into prominence.

Even so, the promise of full employment, a health service, universal full-time secondary education, nearly universal pension rights and public responsibility for housing were established. These were the good things of life that, traditionally, the upper classes had secured for themselves. Now the state was proposing to make them available to everyone. All the people were to have a stake in society, an adequate share of its resources as of right. It was an alternative conception of the social order.

The change was theorized by T. H. Marshall in two lectures at Cambridge in 1947. He saw an opposition, through the previous two centuries, between class and citizenship rights: class tends towards hierarchy, he said, whereas citizenship tends towards equalization. The latter is composed of civil, political and social rights. Civil rights – of property, speech and religion, justice before the law – developed in the eighteenth century; during the nineteenth and early twentieth century political rights were achieved; and now, in the postwar settlement, social rights were being added to citizenship: 'The components of a civilised and cultured life, formerly the monopoly of a few, were brought progressively within the reach of the many.'[10] 'Progressive' extensions of 'civilization' and 'culture' became the justification of postwar welfare-capitalism.

Historians dispute the idea that a historic shift towards a new kind of civilization occurred in 1945. Developments in welfare, health and education were the expected extensions of existing arrangements, and the effect on gender politics was conservative (Smith, H. L.). The reformers of the 1940s (Labour Party leaders and others) were timid, trapped in paternalistic Victorian assumptions, failed to think through what they were doing, and consequently became embroiled in disabling tactical compromises (Ashford, pp. 264–81, 300–6). 'Planning' was piecemeal, mainly in response to economic difficulties (Warren). And the need to bid for lower-class support was not new – Keith Middlemas locates at the end of the 1914–18 war a decisive point at which 'for the first time a British government was forced to bargain for national public support' in order to avoid political breakdown.[11]

Nevertheless, a distinctive *ideology* of welfare-capitalism was propagated, and it constituted an unprecedentedly ambitious project of state legitimation. Whereas most social orders have been sustained through religious authority claims and direct physical repression, welfare-capitalism aspires to legitimate itself by claiming that it is what people want. Many of the old symbols remained, but they were democratized (like the royal family) or seemed superficial (like evening dress). Like a great part of Western Europe, Britain was to pass through a phase unique in history and in the modern world, where the social order was secured – more or less – by consent, rather than by force.

The rights to be guaranteed by the state entered the rhetoric of politicians across the spectrum; they underwrote the consensual ideology within which party politics was conducted. Harold Macmillan wrote in 1948 of the Conservatives' proposed 'Workers' Charter': 'Security of employment and security of contract; extra reward for extra effort; every position, from the bench of the Board Room, open to every worker; full knowledge of all that concerns the business or industry; profit-sharing and co-partnership wherever possible'. It is hardly socialism, but it is more than is hoped for in the 1990s. And in the place of Germany Macmillan offers a new enemy – a new reason for pulling together and not making any trouble – Communism.[12]

The ideology of welfare-capitalism was sufficient to alarm those who believed the established system to be in their interest. This included many writers – I've mentioned Waugh and Thirkell – partly because they thought literature depended on a leisured elite (see chapter 4). When Harold Nicolson joined the Labour Party in 1947, in an attempt to get back into parliament, his mother said she never thought she'd 'see the day when one of my own sons betrayed his country' (Nicolson, 1945–1962, p. 94). Middle-class anxiety about social change is registered more interestingly in plays by Warren Chetham Strode, for they try to reach an accommodation with the new ethos. *The Guinea Pig* (February 1946) is about the Fleming Committee idea that private schools should be democratized, and rescued from economic difficulty, by a supply of lower-class pupils funded by local authorities (it wasn't found necessary; Calder, p. 627). The play is set in a school 'house', which has so little difficulty dominating the sole boy guinea pig and his deferential family that its values seem to prevail through their intrinsic virtues. At the end of the play the teacher in favour of the scheme takes over as housemaster; so a cautiously forward-looking attitude, we see, is the way to preserve tradition.

In *The Gleam* (December 1946) Chetham Strode takes on the health service and town planning. The play looks forward to 1949, and envisages much more decisive changes than actually happened. Doctors are directed around the country, medical decisions are taken by lay people, planning decisions are brisk, dictatorial and virtually without appeal or compensation. The question is whether true medicine can flourish in these conditions; the alternative is the lure of life in Kenya, where children 'are born with freedom in their blood, a heritage, believe me, that none of us who live there would ever give up' (p. 71; this refers only to the European settlers, of course; most of those 'who live there' aren't considered). However, medicine wins out – because it is a noble, caring profession, not because a health service is clearly needed. That issue hardly appears, because the play suggests that the lower classes are already well looked after by responsible doctors and employers (no doubt some were).

Ultimately medicine, in *The Gleam*, is a stalking horse for class. The play is set in the house of a wealthy employer, and all the challenges from the (supposed) new order are in effect class confrontations. In successive exchanges, traditional social authority stands on its dignity against crude and intrusive new power – whose source of authority is scarcely apparent. Like *The Guinea Pig*, *The Gleam* ends complacently; the ineradicable decency of the middle classes renders it inconceivable that they should not triumph.

One of the most disturbing books on these issues is Elizabeth Bowen's novel *The Heat of the Day*, begun in 1944 and published very successfully in 1949 (it sold 45,000 copies straight away; Lee, p. 187). Stella finds there are two men in her life: Robert, and the enigmatic Harrison; both work for the wartime security services. Robert is her lover (she is divorced); Harrison forces himself upon her with the claim – which proves correct – that Robert is a Nazi agent. We may not be surprised to find Harrison as the vulgar intruder, representing the obscure, impersonal power of the state; but Robert as the sensitive, personal, decent man of traditional middle-class values and a fascist – is a provocative move. Critics have found Robert improbable. But the precise project of the book is to entertain the thought that vulgarity dwells with the democratic victors of 1945, and civilization with fascism.[13] It is the postwar consensus, and its criteria of probability, that are in question.

Like most modern readers, Stella finds Robert's treachery very difficult to credit. Nevertheless, she is not unsympathetic to his anti-egalitarian position, which is argued in careful stages (unlike in Graham Greene's *The Ministry of Fear*, 1943, in which the case for fascism is no more than perfunctory). Stella does not dispute Robert's argument that the 'freedom' that is invoked in England is freedom to be muddled and mediocre: 'Look at your mass of "free" suckers, your democracy – kidded along from the cradle to the grave' (the Beveridge slogan). Robert says: 'I'd guarantee to every man the exact degree of freedom of which he's capable – I think you'd see that wouldn't carry us very far' (pp. 259–60). Stella puts the argument that Nazis are 'horrible – specious, unthinkable, grotesque' – an interesting case, founded in taste, decorum and class feeling rather than political principle. Robert replies, 'In birth, remember, anything is grotesque' – mature fascism may be better (pp. 264–5). Stella's remaining thought is for her brothers, killed in 1914–18, but here too she accepts Robert's point: they were heroes 'of a simplicity now gone'. In Robert's features she sees, finally, 'The face of a late-comer. He had been right: time makes the only fatal difference of birth. He was right: it was not for her brothers or their sister to judge him' (p. 268). So Robert's fascism is put down to English history: it is a necessary move for a basically decent man. And Stella's soldier son Roderick is tolerant of Robert's fascism too (p. 288).

There is much more of interest in this novel – Robert's location of Dunkirk as the last stage in a steady descent, the exposing of the dishonesty of British propaganda, the despising of popular wartime sentiment, Robert's stultifying, feminized middle-class family and its thwarting of masculinity (this theme was to occur throughout the 1950s, as I will show). But the difficult and crucial feature, for us, is the relatively evenhanded treatment of fascism. *The Heat of the Day* was not written from within consensual assumptions that welfare-capitalism is the best way to run the world. For Elizabeth Bowen, the celebrations of VE Day were as ominous as for Angela Thirkell's characters. She did not dance in the streets. She remarked: 'The intelligentsia, I learned later, remained in bed, drank and thought. I must say that I drank a good deal' (Glendinning, pp. 156–7). She wrote to William Plomer: 'I've always felt, "When Mr Churchill goes, I go". I can't stick all these little middle-class Labour wets with their Old London School of Economics ties and their women. Scratch any of these cuties and you find the governess' (Glendinning, p. 166; notice, as well as class, the accusation of feminization – wets, women and governesses).

In a postscript to the stories collected in *The Demon Lover* (1944), Bowen remarks that 'literature of the Resistance' is now coming in from France, and wonders 'whether in a sense all wartime writing is not resistance writing? Personal life here, too, put up its own resistance to the annihilation that was threatening it – war' (p. 199). French occupation by the Nazis is equated with the English experience of 'war': they constitute the same kind of affront to civilized life as Bowen has cultivated it; and 'personal life' is what Stella and Robert shared, together with a disaffection from the condition of England.

The lower-class subplot of *The Heat of the Day* concerns Louie, a rather simple war orphan with a soldier husband, who finds herself drawn into casual sexual contacts. She perhaps represents the life of the future: critics notice a resemblance between the concluding scene and that of Forster's *Howards End* (Lee, pp. 184, 188). Louie returns with her illegitimate child to the seaside village of her birth, sees the bombers passing overhead in support of the Allied landings in France and three swans flying to the west, and looks contentedly to the future. But there is a hint of disdain in the presentation of Louie throughout. For instance, she is extremely vulnerable to propaganda:

> Dark and rare were the days when she failed to find on the inside page of her paper an address to or else account of herself. Was she not a worker, a soldier's lonely wife, a war orphan, a pedestrian, a Londoner, a home and animal-lover, a thinking democrat, a movie-goer, a woman of Britain, a letter-writer, a fuel-saver and a housewife? . . . Louie now felt bad only about any part of herself which in any way did not fit into the papers' picture; she could not have survived their disapproval. (p. 146)

The way Louie fits into required roles sounds foolish; compare the way Roderick gains identity by inheriting an estate in Eire: 'He had been fitted into a destiny' (p. 168). Robert is summoned by destiny, Louie manipulated by propaganda. Better destiny, Stella reflects, 'than freedom in nothing'. Notice her anticipation of Robert's dislike of 'freedom': Louie's gullibility augurs ill for the new democracy.

The Heat of the Day requires us to see, in our confusion after the collapse of the postwar settlement, that there were ostensibly decent people who did not welcome the promise of welfare-capitalism, who would have resisted the (apparent) extension of citizenship to the lower classes. As Keynes remarked in 1926, many were 'incapable of distinguishing novel measures for safeguarding capitalism from what they call Bolshevism' (Addison, p. 29). Bowles and Gintis offer the illuminating thought that the 1939–45 war was in part a battle between two ways of dealing with 'the popular demand for democracy' (p. 38). Fascism and welfare-capitalism were *alternative attempts* to deal with the bargaining position that the development of capitalism was bestowing upon the lower classes. It is important, now, to review the initial hostility to the postwar settlement: as welfare-capitalism fails, Elizabeth Bowen helps us to see that not all subversives are on the left.

The Broken Promise

When the trades-union leader Ernest Bevin changed sides and became Minister of Labour in 1940, he declared: 'If our movement and our class now rise with all their energy and save the people of this country from disaster, the country will always turn with confidence to the people who saved them' (Lewis, P., *People's*, p. 112 and ch. 10). Welfare-capitalism implies a pact: capital produces most of the wealth, but the people are protected against and compensated for its disadvantages by a state-instituted welfare system, and by state intervention in the economy to secure full employment. At its simplest, capital sets up the factory, but the state makes it put guards round the machines so that people less often get mutilated or killed by them. So in education, health services, social security, environmental protection: the state supplies the human safety net that unfettered capitalism will not pay for.

Such state intervention is to the medium-term advantage of capital, provided that it does not use up too much surplus value. As I have argued, in the 1940s it was widely believed that capitalism needed some such bargain if it was to survive, and the war had shown that it should and could be done. Looking back on those years, we may see that the idea depended on a certain generosity of vision. The Mass Observation volume *The Journey Home* (1944) recalled the broken promises of the 1914–18 war, and declared that the need is

> not to find out what will make people acquiescent or co-operative *for a time*, but what will really resolve their deeper anxieties and help produce positive enthusiasm and some sort of stability over a long period. Plans based on what will 'keep people quiet' must lead to compromise, *ad hoc* patching and opportunist alteration in the future. For what will keep people quiet today will probably not keep them quiet tomorrow. . . . people can be *temporarily* palmed off with very little, and feel thankful to those who give it them. But if that happens, it does not mean that they will *permanently* forget the ideals and high hopes generated in years of war. (p. 71)

It worked for longer than Mass Observation anticipated, thanks to an economic boom; perhaps for long enough for people to forget the ideals generated to win the war. No one would deny that there have been considerable humanitarian advances but, as Bowles and Gintis point out, they have been more than matched by expansion in the power of capital (pp. 34–5). Joan Robinson has remarked: 'If the workers feel that genuine progress towards social justice is being made it will not be hard to solve the [inflation] problem' (Middlemas, p. 302). It is a question whether welfare-capitalism has really been tried (see chapter 13).

Already by the late 1950s, it was apparent that the postwar world was characterized not by a new fairness and dignity for most people, but by an economic system which J. K. Galbraith likened to a squirrel wheel, as people chased endlessly round a self-defeating circle of production and consumption (see below, pp. 106–9). In so far as there was a shared ethos, T. R. Fyvel pointed out in an analysis of the juvenile delinquency that seemed to indicate a faltering social system, it was that everyone must 'be drawn into the cycle of producing and consuming at the maximum level' (*Insecure*, p. 117). Bogdanor and Skidelsky observed: 'One of the para-doxical consequences of affluence and greater equality of opportunity was to narrow human life to the quest for goods, status, position. The more room at the top there was, the more energy was expended trying to get there' (p. 14).

Moreover, very many people were never included, even in this debasement of the dream of social harmony. As governments of all parties sought to spin the wheel faster and faster, in the hope that we would not notice the vacuity of the squirrel existence, those who could not pedal quickly enough, including war windows and the war disabled, were pushed to one side. At the end of the 1950s, when the affluent society was confidently invoked, journalist Gordon Thomas found in Brighton and Hove elderly people living mainly on toast and tea, giving up not just cigarettes and a drink in the pub but the radio because it was too expensive; Thomas estimated that there were 7,000 such in the district. Meanwhile, spending on advertising had grown from £114 million in 1947 to £454 million in 1960 (Montgomery, pp. 284–8). In 1987, Lanca-shire women who suffered terrible consequences from breathing in asbestos while making gas masks during the war were still unable to gain compensation; many of course, after ruined lives, were already dead. A wartime newsreel shows a government minister expressing pride in these workers as he opens their Blackburn factory. But they worked in a con-tinuous cloud of asbestos for up to 12 hours a day with no apparent precautions, although the dangers of asbestos were well known.[14]

The problems that the postwar settlement was devised to contain only return when it is abandoned. The most alarming story, for government, that went around in 1939–45 was that the king and queen had been booed by the people (Calder, p. 190; Harrisson, p. 326). At that point, the last symbol of authority would have failed, and direct force would be needed to control the population. That fear produced the postwar settlement. If welfare-capitalism doesn't work, we are back in the situation experienced through most of history and most of the world even since 1945, when the governing elite maintains itself and the forces and relations of production by direct repression.

Notes

1 Angus Calder, 'For Ever Walsall', *London Review of Books*, 21 March 1985, p. 7; Harold L. Smith, 'The Effect of the War on the Status of Women', in Smith, H. L., pp. 208–29. See also Minns. For many excellent pictures, see Lewis, P., *People's*.

2 Arthur Koestler witnesses to the myth in *The Yogi and the Commissar* (pp. 46–67), though he tries to disqualify Hillary's move in the book from existential motives to social idealism.

3 Among contemporary readers, V. S. Pritchett and John Middleton Murry thought the novel's conclusion phony (Gould).

4 On middle-class discomfiture, see David Pryce-Jones, 'Towards the Cocktail Party', in Sissons and French, pp. 216–39, and Hopkins, pp. 153–7.

5 Lewis, P., *People's*, p. 194; see Miliband, *State*, p. 106.

6 Beveridge, *Social*, p. 53. See Lucy Bland, Trisha McCabe and Frank Mort, 'Sexuality and Reproduction: Three "Official" Instances', in Barrett, Corrigan et al.; John Stevenson, 'Planners' Moon? The Second World War and the Planning Movement', in Smith, H. L., pp. 58–77; Calder, p. 609; Addison, pp. 217–22.

7 Calder, p. 49; see Titmuss, *Problems*, ch. 8; Bevan, *Why Not Trust the Tories?*, pp. 37–8. On the diversity of views among those committed to social reconstruction, see Jose Harris in Smith, H. L., pp. 238–57: Harris distinguishes Butlerite Tories, reformers like Beveridge, and Labour Party intellectuals.

8 Addison, pp. 161–3 and ch. 5; Calder, pp. 630–5; Mass Observation, pp. 103–4; Stanworth and Giddens, p. 57.

9 Miliband, *State*, pp. 106–13; *Parliamentary*, ch. 9. On the Labour Party's adoption of Keynesian assumptions, see Foote. On its confusion and lack of purpose, see Ashford, pp. 264–81.

10 Marshall, p. 47. Cf. Halsey, pp. 60–7; chapter 12; Laclau and Mouffe, pp. 171–5.

11 Middlemas, p. 114. See also Miliband, *State*, pp. 109–10; Bowles and Gintis, ch. 2. In 1917 Lord Russell declared that the masses should be enfranchised

'as a substitute for riot, revolution and the rifle. We grant the suffrage in order that we may learn in an orderly and civilised manner what the people who are governed want' (quoted by Paddy Scannell in McLennan et al., p. 150).

12 Macmillan, 'The Place of Government in a Free Society', in *Other People's Lives*, p. 83.

13 On upper-class fascists of the 1930s, see Branson and Heinemann, pp. 334–6. Glendinning (p. 152) and, even more, Lee (pp. 176–8) suggest that Robert's outlook may be related to that of Bowen's lover, Charles Ritchie. This seems altogether unfounded (see Ritchie, C., especially pp. 117–23 and 177). Ritchie meets a man he calls 'J.' whose 'line of talk, though a farrago of nonsense, is about the best a German agent in England could produce at the present time. I do not think it would be at all a bad thing to lock him up' (Ritchie, C., p. 144).

14 'Watchdog', BBC 1 Television, 3 April 1987.

3

Literature and cultural production

Telling stories

Paul Fussell, in *The Great War and Modern Memory*, has shown how the war of 1914–18, at the time, was not just presented but experienced through contemporary representations (rumour, myth and literature). The war of 1939–45 was understood at the time mainly through rumour, radio and writing: subsequently it too became myth, figuring, especially, the moment at which we shared the common purpose that consumer-capitalism can only imagine. Harold Wilson, faced with a run on the pound in 1964, told the Labour Party conference: 'They misjudged our temper after Dunkirk, but we so mobilised our talent and untapped strength that apparent defeat was turned into a great victory. I believe that the spirit of Dunkirk will once again carry us through to success' (Foot, p. 154). The wartime myth is invoked with the implication that we should forsake allegedly sectional concerns for the politician's version of the 'national interest'. However, though the Dunkirk spirit sounds plain, it uses only parts of the story of that British evacuation. It is not so convenient to remember 68, 111 killed, wounded and missing, and the chaos and misunderstanding, with small boats sometimes capsized by panicky men, and order sometimes maintained only at gunpoint (Gates, pp. 115–18). Miliband observes that notions like the Dunkirk spirit call the dead 'into service once again to help legitimate the regimes for which they have died' (*State*, p. 210).

It is through such stories, or representations, that we develop understandings of the world and how to live in it. The contest between rival stories produces our notions of reality, and hence our beliefs about what we can and cannot do. That is why governments seek to control what is written and said, especially when rendered insecure by war or some other difficulty. This chapter is about the processes through which we form and change beliefs, and the roles of literature within those processes.

The stories through which we make sense of ourselves are everywhere. In the media, they are not just in the articles and programmes labelled 'fiction' and 'drama', but in those on current affairs, sport, party politics, science, religion, the arts, and those specified as education and for children. They are in the advertisements. At work, the definitions of tasks to be undertaken depend upon them, and the relations between the people involved – some face to face, some very distant. And in our intimate relations there are stories telling us who we are as individuals, who other individuals are and how we relate to them. The conventional division, which I have followed in this paragraph, between the media, work and personal life, is itself one of the most powerful stories.

I am not quite sure that 'story' is the right term – it sounds rather informal, inconsequential; perhaps 'narrative' would be better, but I don't want its connotations of strategic organization. Carolyn Steedman distinguishes story and history: stories are not consciously ordered, whereas histories (like case studies) are interpretive devices, they suggest a coherence (pp. 138, 143). However, one person's anecdote is another's guiding light (as Steedman's book shows). I use 'story' (and 'representation') to accommodate the patterns of common sense alongside formal pronouncements, and to avoid prejudging adequacy. In oppositional work this has the advantage of throwing all systems, however authoritative, back to first base so that their claims may be re-evaluated. Stephen Greenblatt approaches the issue by comparing two other ways of regarding reality. On the one hand is a unitary, totalizing vision which claims an explanation for everything prior to experience (he instances psychoanalysis, or one version of it). On the other is the supposed uniqueness of each moment, leading to a stance of relativism, of neutrality (this is prominently represented in existentialism). Rejecting each of these, we are left with 'a network of lived and narrated stories, practices, strategies, representations, fantasies, negotiations, and exchanges that, along with the surviving aural, tactile, and visual traces, fashion our experiences of the past, of others, and of ourselves' (Greenblatt, p. 218).

This is not to deny individual agency (though it may make it less interesting); rather, the same structure informs individuals and the society. Present action is inconceivable (literally) without the past, but also it enters into multiple new interactions. Structural rules are drawn upon by actors, but through that very action those rules are reconstituted. Anthony Giddens, upon whom I am drawing here, compares the utterance of a grammatical sentence, which presupposes the lexicon and syntactical rules that constitute the language, but is individual and, through its utterance, confirms and modifies the language (pp. 69–71, 77–8).

The point to stress here is that stories are *lived*. They are not just outside ourselves, something we hear or read about. They make sense for us – of us – because we have been and are in them. They are already proceeding when we arrive in the world, and we come to consciousness in their terms. As the world shapes itself around and through us, certain inter-pretations of experience strike us as plausible because they fit with what we have experienced already. They become common sense, they 'go without saying'. Colin Sumner explains this as a 'circle of social reality': 'understanding produces its own social reality at the same time as social reality produces its own understanding.'[1]

For meaning, communication, language work only because they are shared. Even the question 'What is a chair?' makes sense only within a system of meanings; otherwise a chair might be a bundle of sticks for making a fire or beating an enemy about the head (Harris, *Beliefs*, pp. 36–7). If you make up your own language, no one else will under-stand you; if you persist, you will be thought mad. Meaning is interactive. This is apparent when we observe how people in other cultures than our own make good sense of their world in ways that seem strange to us: their outlook is supported by their social context (Sumner, p. 287). As much as oneself, others have frameworks of perception, maps of meaning, stories, that work in the real world and enable them to complete a circle of social reality. It is hard to challenge the prevailing stories – you will be thought implausible. Powerful stories – those useful to powerful groups – tend to drive out others.

The way stories work may be observed at the boundaries of plausibility – the point at which the dominant withholds even a willing suspension of disbelief. Nancy K. Miller remarks the way women writers are accused of falling prey to implausibilities in their fiction. They are said to manifest sensibility, sensitivity, extravagance – 'code words for feminine in our culture' – at the expense of verisimilitude.[2] Actually, the standards of plausibility are not universal but culturally specific – in this case specific to modern Western patriarchy. That is why some women's developments of the prevailing stories seem unsatisfactory. Miller argues, further, that the 'improbable' plots in novels like *La princesse de Clèves* (by Mme de Lafayette) and *The Mill on the Floss* (by George Eliot) may be regarded as comments on the current stories of women's lives – those inscribed in patriarchal reality. They manifest 'the extravagant wish for a *story* that would turn out differently' (p. 352). The wish of women for power over their lives cannot be expressed plausibly within dominant discourses, only as fantasy.

Stories, then, transmit power: they are structured into the social order and the criteria of plausibility define, or seem to define, the scope of feasible political change. Most societies retain their current shape not because subversives are infiltrated, penalized or neutralized, though they are, but because many people believe that things have to take more or less their present form – that they cannot, realistically, be improved upon, at least through the methods to hand. In other words, the prevailing stories are believed to be the most plausible ones; that is why it was effective for Margaret Thatcher to proclaim 'There is no alternative'. And it is why one recognizes a dominant ideology: were there not such a powerful discourse, people would not acquiesce in the injustice and humiliation that they experience. The power to make your story stick enables you to persuade people to buy your product, or vote for you, or put up with conscription, or unemployment, or stigma.

I have used the idea of 'telling stories' partly for its accessibility; a more substantial phrase is *cultural production*. Societies need to produce, materially, to continue – they need food, shelter, warmth; goods to exchange with other societies, a transport and information infrastructure to carry those processes and so on. Also, they have to produce culturally. They need knowledges to keep material production going – diverse technical skills and wisdoms in agriculture, industury, science, medicine, economics, law, geography, languages, politics and so on. And they need understanding, intuitive and explicit, of a system of social relationships within which the whole process can take place more or less evenly (see Althusser, pp. 123–8). Cultural production produces concepts, systems and apparently 'natural' understandings to explain who we are individually and collectively, who the others are, how the world works.

This is not to say that the dominant stories are uncontested; on the contrary, they need to be disseminated urgently lest they lose their grip. Social conflict manifests itself as competition between stories. Political change, Terry Eagleton observes, will be coupled with 'a fierce conflict over signs and meanings, as the newly emergent class strives to wrest the most cherished symbols from the grip of its rivals and redefine them in its own image' (*Rape*, p. 2). Before pursuing this thought I shall try to establish the role of literature in cultural production.

Literature as a Cultural Apparatus

Cultural production occurs all the time; but especially through what C. Wright Mills called the cultural apparatus – 'all the organisations and milieux in which artistic, intellectual, and scientific work goes on, and by which entertainment and information are produced and distributed' (p. 552). This includes an elaborate network of formal institutions in the law, education, religion, politics and communications; and also informal networks and conceptual structures ('the New Right' as well as the Conservative Party; 'progressive education' as well as the school system; 'the charismatic movement' as well as the Church of England; 'the arts' as well as the Arts Council).

It is important to insist on literature as a cultural apparatus because its institutional arrangements are often effaced, for instance in literary criticism, to the point where authors and texts seem to communicate with readers without such mediation (it is interesting that 'the media' normally means electronic media). Actually, books reach readers through publishers, reviewers, bookshops and libraries; and the reader's idea of what she or he is doing is influenced by instruction in schools, literary criticism, arts pages in journals, programmes on radio and television. Richard Ohmann finds, in respect of high-cultural fiction in the United States, that

> a small group of book buyers formed a screen through which novels passed on their way to commercial success; a handful of agents and editors picked the novels that would compete for the notice of these buyers; and a tight network of advertisers and reviewers, organised around the *New York Times Book Review*, selected from these a few to be recognised as compelling, important, 'talked about'.[3]

Notable changes in cultural direction usually involve both significant texts and institutional developments – the Shakespearean theatre and Hollywood cinema are obvious instances. Samuel Richardson was significant, Terry Eagleton observes, partly because he was a printer as well as a novelist. From this vantage point, he fashioned a whole social apparatus, 'placing himself at the heart of ethical controversies, education projects, religious and aesthetic contentions' (*Rape*, p. 7). In comparable manner, John Osborne's *Look Back in Anger* signalled a change in English theatre in 1956 in great part because it coincided with and helped to stimulate a new institutional arrangement: subsidized theatre. This not only gave opportunity to plays that might otherwise have been thought uneconomic, it designated certain kinds of theatre 'serious' – worth state subsidy, the responsibility of the Arts Council, appropriate for 'quality' newspapers, earnest conversation and examination syllabuses (see below, pp. 260–2).

'Literature' is another story. Even the concept has been culturally produced: it emerged in the eighteenth century and was not fully developed until the nineteenth century. Eventually it came to mean 'printed works of a certain quality' (Williams, R., *Marxism*, pp. 46–54), and suitable texts were assimilated, retrospectively, to it (as religious icons are put in art galleries). A profession of critical and scholarly experts grew up to support it, and its use in education followed. Michel Foucault points out that 'the author' is a function arranged by the culture – a way we have of speaking about texts, of controlling them by ascribing them (*Language*, pp. 113–38).

Usually, in our culture, literature is envisaged as 'rising above' its conditions of production and reception; as transcending social and political concerns and other such mundane matters. The argument most often presented for this is that great art has endured the test of time. That is an idealist position; the approach taken in this book is materialist. In my view the 'art' of other times and places that we 'appreciate' is, *ipso facto*, that upon which we can gain some kind of purchase from our own time and place, mediated through our particular institutions. We may not notice this because many texts have been so continuously worked upon that they are intertwined with our history, culture and institutions. Conversely, when we no longer admire the 'art' valued by earlier generations, we put that down to error, rather than remarking that the concept is inherently relative. We select and assemble 'art' to suit current needs, and its 'enduring relevance' (which we presumptuously imagine as universality) is thus a circular effect.

Literature is an institutional arrangement we have made to dignify some writing (at the expense of other). This is not surprising or sinister: any culture will value some texts more highly than others. But finally we are talking about *authority claims*. To have your work accepted as art or literature, or to be judged an expert, is to gain a voice in a discourse with certain claims to significance.

I have discussed elsewhere how the notion of art as transcending the utilitarian organization of society was fought out during the nineteenth century.[4] The romantic claim that artistic and political vision should combine was uncongenial to the developing bourgeois hegemony; it was too dangerous. Instead, poetry found itself with three choices: relegation as trivial; incorporation as a vehicle for the culture of utilitarianism and political economy; and a unique, autonomous role as the marvellous place where transcendent (non-political) experiences are represented. All three choices may be recognized today in the spectrum of poetic writing: verse in birthday cards is trivial; verse in advertising is incorporated; but with Modernism, at the turn of the century, the third choice – the repository of transcendent experience – came to define poetry as such. 'Art' and 'literature' followed the same trajectory: they are believed to be the product of mysterious forces working through the creative genius whose vision soars above material conditions, society, politics. But although this produces an honoured place for the arts, it is at the cost of limited influence, marginality, even irrelevance. Their protected status confines them to a reserve, like an endangered species insufficiently robust to cope in the modern world.

In idealist theory, art is envisaged, broadly, as one half of a binary formation. Poetry, literature, the arts, the spirit, nature, personal religion, intimate and family relations are constituted as 'the human', working counter to mechanical, urban, industrial and commercial organization in the modern world. But, actually, the whole framework belongs together and each part supposes the other. Art is constituted within the field of, in terms supplied by, the forces it opposes; it is their correlative. While we persist with this framework, therefore, we will never rescue the 'human', for it is set up as the necessary and weaker term in the binary – the other of political economy that enables it to know itself, the conscience of capitalism. The 'human' cannot triumph, because it affirms the binary through its very construction. And the further consequence is that other practices are released from the obligation to be spiritual, personal, human. We can build nasty suburbs, offices and shops if we list and preserve 'monuments to the human spirit'. One makes space for the other.

Idealist aesthetics often strives to discern an essential quality of literariness in admired texts, but actually a text may appear literary, or otherwise, depending on the contexts in which it is regarded. Not only does film become an art because people move it into that discourse; the kinds of film considered artistic are developed to include popular Hollywood genres. Tony Bennett and Janet Woollacott show how Ian Fleming's James Bond novels have been plausibly discussed as literature (Bennett and Woollacott, pp. 254–9). The literary, as it is deployed in our culture, is less a property of texts than a way of reading and placing texts (Fish, pp. 10–11). Conversely, respected texts may be read in non-literary ways. Entertain, for a moment, these temptations from an advertisement in the *Sunday Times* (8 June 1958) for a book club: 'Have you thought of what social standing it gives you and your family – having good books about the place? They put you a whole class up – in the eyes of your neighbours and business friends. You're "well-read" – the sort of family that's a cut above the rest . . . for less than the price of a TV licence' (Potter, *Glittering*, p. 120). This is a blatant version of the common assumption, that virtue must pass from the 'good book' to the person in its presence. But it all depends how the book is read; to suppose otherwise is the error of the censor and the aesthete.

However, although any reader may apply literary practices to a text not usually so read (pop songs, for instance), or read a canonical text in an unorthodox way, only well-placed people can give authoritative recognition to such readings (T. S. Eliot can bring Milton into disrepute; Christopher Ricks, a Cambridge professor, can promote Bob Dylan to literary attention, specially when broadcasting on the highbrow Radio 3). In literature, as with the other stories we inhabit, only certain tellers have the power, normally, to define the boundaries of plausibility. Literature is writing that is acknowledged as such within a powerful publishing, reviewing and educational apparatus. And therein lies the answer to the famous question about why monkeys and computers cannot write it (though it is interesting that they are thought suitable for comparison).

This is not to say that literature is trivial or false: on the contrary, it answers, albeit confusingly, to a real need. Marx noted of religion that, though illusory, it is 'a protest against real wretchedness' (Bürger, pp. 6–7). The need for 'art' is substantial, for it is the repository of all kinds of impulses that are produced and thwarted in our society. Moreover, despite the liberal-idealist attempt to quarantine literature from political import, it does disseminate, and with a distinctive authority, certain representations through the culture, inviting our assent that the world is thus or thus. It contributes, willy-nilly, to the making and legitimating of stories.

Saying this, I am not overlooking formal qualities or the distinctive character of literature. As with any mode of communication, literary texts make best immediate sense when read in ways that are appropriate to them (it would be a mistake to take an Absurdist play as 'slice of life' naturalism). But when we have done this the text is still, in the larger analysis, telling a story about the world, and therefore it has a politics. The fact that a text is regarded as literary does not destroy its political import. Stephen Spender acknowledges ruefully that authors he admires were influenced by facism: 'Their nostalgia led them into sympathising with whatever jack-booted corporal or demagogue set himself up in defense of order'. But, Spender says, 'they did put literature before politics' (*Thirties*, p. 165). Gerald Graff calls this a 'limited liability' theory of literary meaning, for it protects the author from the consequences of his or her utterances (*Professing*, pp. 151–2, 229–30). Now, we probably can read apparently right-wing texts in ways that will not add plausibility to their political stance. But that is how the case should be made; to assert that a book is 'literature' is not enough.

These arguments indicate, in themselves, that literature is a contested category. In 1942 C. S. Lewis remarked of F. R. Leavis, in their dispute about the literary merit of Milton's poetry: 'It is not that he and I see different things when we look at *Paradise Lost*. He sees and hates the very same thing that I see and love' (Lewis, C. S., p. 134). Rival stories about literature derive from alternative positions that are finally political, and the quarrel between them is about who is to define and dominate that cultural apparatus. I now discuss the conditions of cultural contest.

Contesting Stories

Despite the powerful institutions through which dominant stories are maintained, there are other stories – subordinated perhaps, but not extinguished. Marx and Engels, in *The German Ideology*, declared: 'The class which is the ruling material force is, at the same time, its ruling intellectual force. The class which has the means of material production at its disposal, has control at the same time over the means of mental production.'[5] The point is surely only sensible: those with material power will control the institutions that deal with ideas, and that is why people are persuaded to believe things that are neither just and humane, nor to their advantage. But it must not be taken too narrowly.

A principal insight of recent theory is that repression and resistance are involved in the same economy of power. Anthony Giddens observes: 'Power relations are always two-way; that is to say, however subordinate an actor may be in a social relationship, the very fact of involvement in that relationship gives him or her a certain amount of power over the other' (p. 6). Structure is enabling as much as constraining, therefore: it affords resources for both acquiescence and revolt. Another way to think this is to see that, for a subversive story to be handled and contained, it must be uttered, brought into visibility. To silence dissent one must first give it a voice; to misrepresent it one must first present it. And once that has happened, there can be no guarantee that it will stay safely in its prescribed place.[6]

Since cultural formations arise necessarily in relation to the social organization, one might expect the two always to be compatible. But the actual situation is more mobile and complex, due to the multitude of factors involved and with residual, dominant and emergent practices jostling together (Williams, R., *Marxism*, pp. 121–7). Any moment of stasis fades even before its shape can be fully appreciated. Dominant cultural formations are always under pressure, striving to substantiate their claim to superior explanatory power in situations where diverse features are resistant. Hence Raymond Williams's argument that culture has always to be *produced*: 'Social orders and cultural orders must be seen as being actively made: actively and continuously, or they may quite quickly break down' (*Culture*, p. 201).

For instance, when the first V2 rocket bombs fell in London in September 1944, with tremendous explosions, escalating in numbers by November to four and then six a day, the government told the press that they were to be treated as explosions of domestic gas; and the press co-operated. But Londoners guessed that this was a new weapon, and talked sardonically about 'flying gas mains'. So eventually Churchill admitted in the Commons that this was a new rocket attack (though not, he said, serious in its scale or results – in all 2,724 people were killed and more than 6,000 badly wounded; Calder, p. 649). Here, the government could not make its story stick – despite control of the press and the 'plausible' idea of gas explosions. People decided that the events better fitted another story from their experience – the flying bomb. The idea of 'flying gas mains' encapsulates both their awareness that they were being misinformed and their mockery of the government's supposition of their gullibility. They pretended to believe an implausibility – that gas mains might fly: since the government controls the official stories, alternatives are represented through self-conscious, deriding fantasy.

Again, the story of the Dunkirk spirit and British people coming through the war because they believed in the national purpose is not the only story. At least some trades unionists felt that they were fighting on two fronts:

> Just as working people were determined to defeat Nazism in the war with the Axis, they were equally determined to root it out wherever it appeared, albeit in diluted form, in the factories. ... As some contemporary commentators pointed out (generally in private), the engineers were fighting a war of their own which had begun long before September 1939.[7]

However, stories that powerful institutions don't want to hear are maintained at a cost. When Mass Observation evidence of the fear, helplessness and disaffection of blitzed people was produced in the early 1970s, not only did civic leaders, past and present, deny that such things had occurred: even those who had written the original reports were amazed at how little they tallied with their later recollections (Harrisson, pp. 323–7). We may glimpse here a cost in human anguish, as people interpreted their inability to match the official myth as shameful failure, and therefore suppressed it.

A principal reason for disturbance in cultural production is that institutions have specific conceptual organizations; it is necessary that they should do so, for the roles they perform. Thus, for instance, we would expect City financiers and Church of England bishops to express different views about the need to reduce unemployment. Financiers have to appear to be acting in the interests of their shareholders, whereas bishops have to be seen taking a moral and humanitarian stance. Also, institutions have their own histories and internal structures. The liberal outlook of many bishops at the time of writing derives from the fact that they took orders in the late 1950s and early 1960s, and were influenced by the progressive mood of that time. It has taken two or three decades for some of them to reach positions of seniority. In other institutions, progressive attitudes came to the top very quickly and then went into recession. Television is a good instance: there radicalism peaked by 1970 and has been on the retreat ever since. City financiers, again, were hardly affected by 1960s radicalism (except perhaps drug-taking), so their trajectory has remained in this respect even. Also, we have to allow for divergences between the short- and long-term interests of an institution. Capitalist publishers ought to be wary of publishing Marxist books, but the existence of an immediate opportunity for profit outweighs such considerations (Williams calls this kind of thing 'asymmetry'; *Culture*, pp. 98–107).

To allow thus much autonomy to institutions is not to embrace pluralism. A pluralist analysis sees society as a complex of competing groups and interests, none of them predominant all the time. It sees cultural institutions as bounded systems, enjoying an important degree of autonomy from the state, and controlled by managerial elites that allow considerable freedom to professional operators. The alternative analysis holds that modern societies are controlled by a power elite or ruling elite, perhaps divided into such distinct apparatuses as business, government and the military, but acting generally in harmony, in the interests of itself and the economically dominant class.[8]

The present study takes the latter view. There evidently are diverse power centres and there may be conflict between them; but some are much more powerful than others, the powerful ones tend to act broadly in concert, and few of us have much access to them anyway. The relative autonomy of institutions results not from democratic principle but from the specific and hardly avoidable conditions in which they operate, and generally the ruling elite contrives to constrain, negate or accommodate that autonomy. Such structural kinks are inevitable in an extensively elaborated system; John Rex calls it 'looseness of functional fit'.[9]

This case was made by Orwell in relation to the co-option of intellectuals into the wartime propaganda machine (interestingly, it undercuts the suppositions on which 1984 is based; see chapter 6 below). The government would have preferred to employ conservative people, he says, but the existing intelligentsia had to be utilized:

> No one acquainted with the Government pamphlets, ABCA lectures, documentary films and broadcasts to occupied countries which have been issued during the past two years imagines that our rulers would sponsor this kind of thing if they could help it. Only, the bigger the machine becomes, the more loose ends and forgotten corners there are in it. (*Essays*, II, p. 381)

The vast elaboration of modern society produces a looseness of structural fit between institutions and ideologies, and the very demands of maintaining the dominant order create conditions whereby contradictions in it may become apparent. In fact, commentators estimate that intellectuals in the propaganda apparatus contributed significantly to the mood that produced the election result of 1945 and the institution of welfare-capitalism. Alfred Duff-Cooper, for a time Minister of Information in the war government, lamented in 1944 that Conservatism 'had allowed itself to be deprived of the intellectual leadership of the nation' (Calder, p. 587).

The final evidence of the limits on the autonomy of cultural institutions is the way they are forcibly restrained when their relative freedom becomes embarrassing and 'goes too far'. Since much of the work I am drawing upon was done, economic recession, unemployment, racism and the Irish situation have undermined the consensual, 'arms-length' arrangements that were supposed to pertain in Britain (see chapter 13). The police, higher and secondary education, the BBC, the Arts Council, local government, trades unions – all have become subject to closer central control, as the linked crises of the economy and state legitimation have produced strains and stresses.

Even so, I have said, culture is necessarily under contest. Frank Parkin recognizes three major meaning-systems in Western societies: the dominant, the subordinate and the radical (*Class*, chapter 3). The dominant is the structure of understandings that successfully claims normative status; it is most fully and authoritatively represented in the cultural apparatus. Members of subordinated groups may subscribe to it through deference or aspiration. The subordinate system is accommodative: it adapts to, or negotiates, the dominant system, rather than endorsing or opposing it; this is characteristic of working-class culture and also, I would say, of the way many women handle the gender roles expected of them. The radical meaning-system promotes an oppositional interpretation of the social order; it is articulated, historically, through the politically aware sectors of both the working class and the middle class. The interaction of these systems in specific circumstances admits points at which change can be initiated.

Three further points may be made about the nature and scope of dominant and other stories. First, we should recognize the current range of subordinate and oppositional standpoints. These are constituted not only around class. As Summer puts it,

A developed capitalist economy creates social divisions according to non-property criteria. Age, sex and race are the most important criteria perhaps, but we must also recognise that social divisions also exist in terms of town versus countryside and intellectual versus manual labour. . . . They constitute real social relations, when put into practice, and generate contending ideologies founded upon them. These contending ideologies [generate] practices and organisations [which] are articulated in forms reflecting their class character, but which are not solely founded on class relations. . . . ideologies of sexism, feminism, racism, black consciousness, children's power, etc., have a solid structural basis in the economy and a basis which usually has developed political and cultural extensions.[10]

Cultural struggle, therefore, may derive from and draw upon diverse subordinated and oppressed groups, and may be articulated from complex and interlocking positions.

Second, the repertoire of oppositional strategies is complex and its effects hard to gauge. On the one hand, rejecting the dominant allows it to stigmatize or criminalize deviant practice, and leaves it unchallenged on its own ground. On the other, trying to work within the dominant, or to infiltrate and sabotage it, risks incorporation. The choices are difficult and so is analysis, for the dominant is adroit at recuperating dissent.[11]

Third, the subordinate and oppositional may not be continuously effective or fully apparent. Subordinate cultures which normally maintain an uneventful, negotiated relationship with the dominant, perhaps protecting their perceptions through distancing humour (Giddens, p. 72), may reveal inflammatory elements. Robin Blackburn invokes the instance of Vauxhall car workers at Luton, who were found in a social study to have a co-operative view of management and to be unlikely to experience 'discontent and resentment of a generalised kind'. About a month after the publication of the report, 2,000 workers tried to storm the management offices, singing 'The Red Flag' and calling 'string him up' whenever a director's name was mentioned (so it was reported in *The Times*). What the study did not allow, Blackburn concludes, was that the workers had two sets of attitudes. Generally they put up with a situation they could do little about and jogged along from day to day, deriving such happiness and fulfilment as they could from their immediate circumstances. But when roused by a particular incident, their dormant awareness that they were being systematically exploited was activated and found expression through traditional proletarian forms (Cockburn and Blackburn, p. 200). The point of principle here is that the subordinate or oppositional potential of a subcultural formation cannot be inferred from current practice.

Literature and Intervention

The foregoing considerations apply to cultural production generally and to the apparatus of literature. Literary culture has been produced and consumed mainly within the middle class, but it should not be assumed that individuals or groups in positions of (apparent) cultural power simply or necessarily promote the dominant viewpoint. Classes in modern societies, because of the specialization of occupational roles, throw off class fractions, which develop distinctive cultural formations. Raymond Williams instances the Godwin circle, the Pre-Raphaelites, and Bloomsbury.[12] I relate literature, in Chapter 4, to a dissident middle-class fraction, arguing that this generates a certain radical potential.

The literary text may be understood as an intervention: an attempt to render certain stories convincing. Orwell asked: 'How is it that books ever come to be written? Above quite a low level, literature is an attempt to influence the viewpoint of one's contemporaries by recording experience' (*Essays*, IV, p. 87). The word 'recording' is not right: writing inevitably arranges and interprets, and the impression of fidelity to experience is part of the reality-effect through which authors seek to be persuasive. However, by making representations of plausible reality, literary texts intervene in the world.

In my view, major academic theories to the contrary, writers' intentions may be inferred from their writing. We do this through the same kinds of understanding that we use to infer people's intentions all the time in diverse activities – previous experience, knowledge of registers, codes, forms and genres, internal coherence, the opinions of other people. Of course, we may get it wrong; that is always a condition of communication. This entirely normal process of understanding seems improper only when we're under the sway of the notion of the autonomous genius-author who transcends ordinary mortal conditions to create meaning as if out of nothing. Once that has faded, both the discursive positioning of the writer and the direction of his or her intervention in the self-understanding of that society may be appreciated. To be sure, writing is constructed socially but, also, writing is one of the constructing agencies: it influences discursive processes as well as being influenced by them. Otherwise how could the sequence ever begin, continue or change? In this process, we are made, and we make. Pierre Macherey says: 'The *act* of the writer is fundamental: he realises a particular crystallisation, a restructuration, and even a structuration of the data upon which he works.'[13]

Even so, the kind of intervention intended by the writer is not usefully considered as merely personal inspiration; it occurs within a framework of socially constructed possibilities (as speech and writing use the lexicon and grammar of the language). Nor need it dominate serious study, for once the text gets out into the world the conditions of reception are quite beyond the writer's control. Literary texts are certainly read, all the time, in ways the writer did not mean – that is the condition, no less, of continuing attention. The study of cultural meaning has to consider how texts are 'constituted as objects-to-be-read within the different reading formations which have modulated their existence as historically active, culturally received texts.'[14] So I shall be concerned with what Orwell's *1984* and Osborne's *Look Back in Anger*, and jazz and rock-'n'-roll, were taken to mean and by whom; more than with what we, today, think might have been intended, or take to be the most satisfactory readings. My quest is for the effects of the text in the world.

The contribution of literary texts to the contest over signs and meanings is not necessarily either conservative or radical. Those texts nominated 'literary' are chosen because they seem plausible, and therefore the main effect must be to reinforce prevailing understandings. Raymond Williams observes: 'The "persons" are "created" to show that people are "like this" and their relations "like this" ' (*Marxism*, p. 209): by appealing to a known model, the text tends to confirm the validity of that model. However, Williams goes on, literature, like other cultural practices, can break towards new understanding. There can be 'new articulations, new formations of "character" and "relationship" '. Whether this happens will depend on general circumstances, and particularly on the current state of literary institutions. In principle it's all open to contest, though in practice there are massive vested interests. The apparatus of literature has been made by people, and we can remake it. Texts may be read in different ways, different texts may be read (the Women's Movement has shown this), we may alter the boundaries between literature and other discourses, or cease to use the category.

So literary and other texts may be understood as powerful stories working in and beyond their initial historical moment, in our own lives and those of others. Notice how literary texts of any period return repeatedly to certain complex and demanding themes. This is because the stories that require most attention – most assiduous and continuous reworking – are the awkward, unresolved ones. They are what people want to write and read about. When a part of our world view threatens disruption by manifestly failing to cohere with the rest, then we must reorganize and retell its story again and again, trying to get it into shape – back into the old shape if we are conservative-minded, or into a new shape that we can develop and apply if we are more adventurous. The literary text, like all cultural production, is involved in these processes.

To repudiate liberal–idealist notions of literature is not, therefore, to diminish its consequence. On the contrary, it is to see just where its importance lies: not in the magical evocation of unreal worlds of merely formal significance, but as a discourse of authority in the dispute about how to extend our sense of the possibilities of human lives.

Notes

1 Sumner, p. 288. See Steedman, pp. 5–24; Stuart Hall, 'Encoding/Decoding', in Hall, Hobson et al.; Harris, *Beliefs*, ch. 2; Hall and Jefferson, pp. 10–11; Fish, introduction, chs. 13–16; Bennett and Woollacott, ch. 3; Jochen Schulte-Sasse, in Bürger, p. xxviii; Gagnon and Simon, ch. 1.

2 'Emphasis Added', in Showalter, p. 357.

3 Ohmann, pp. 203–4; see Naumann, p. 119; Stuart Laing, 'The Production of Literature', in Sinfield, *Society*; Wolff, pp. 40–8; Balibar; Macherey and Balibar; Bennett and Woollacott; pp. 108–9, 177, 291–3 below.

4 Sinfield, *Alfred*, pp. 11–21, 54–6. See also Bowlby, R., chs. 1, 6; Parrinder, pp. 85–119; Genette; Marcuse, *One*, ch. 3 and *Essay*, pp. 48–50; Brookeman, chs. 7, 8.

5 Marx and Engels, p. 61. Cf. Althusser, pp. 139–42, 170–2; Mills, C. W.; Macherey and Balibar; Bourdieu, 'Cultural'; Miliband, *State*, ch. 8.

6 Jonathan Dollimore and Alan Sinfield, 'History and Ideology: the Instance of *Henry V*', in Drakakis, p. 215. See Colin Gordon, 'Afterword', in Foucault, *Power/Knowledge*; Sumner, pp. 223, 288; Hall and Jefferson, pp. 10–13; Morley and Worpole, pp. 96–7; Williams, R., *Marxism*, pp. 108–27; Swingewood, ch. 3; Jameson, pp. 144–8.

7 Richard Croucher, *Engineers at War, 1939–1945* (London: Merlin, 1982), pp. iii–iv, quoted by Laurence Harris, 'State and Economy in the Second World War', in McLennan et al., p. 70; see also pp. 60–70.

8 See Stuart Hall, 'The Rediscovery of "Ideology" ', in Gurevitch et al., pp. 56–62; Christopher J. Hewitt, 'Elites and the Distribution of Power in British Society', in Stanworth and Giddens, pp. 46–9.

9 John Rex, 'Capitalism, Elites and the Ruling Class', in Stanworth and Giddens, p. 219. See also Westergaard, pp. 28–31; Bowles and Gintis, p. 119; Hindess, ch. 7.

10 Sumner, pp. 233–4. See Bowles and Gintis, ch. 4.
11 See Dollimore, 'Different' and 'Dominant'; chapter 8.
12 See Williams, R., *Culture*, pp. 74–83; Sinfield, 'Power'.
13 Macherey, p. 232; see Bennett and Woollacott, pp. 188–203, and Wolff.
14 Bennett, T., p. 74. E. Ann Kaplan specifies her reading formation and that of MTV (pp. 29–31).

4

Class/culture/welfare

Culture, Class and Dissidence

Sir Arthur Quiller-Couch in 1913 reviewed the poets of the previous century and concluded: 'A poor child in England has little more hope than had the son of an Athenian slave to be emancipated into that intellectual freedom of which great writings are born' (pp. 32–3; his exception is Keats). Virginia Woolf quoted and endorsed the point (*Room*, pp. 105–6). In the prevailing order of things before welfare-capitalism, 'good' culture was taken to be, in essence, the culture of the leisured upper-middle class; that is why it was 'high' culture. This doesn't mean that it was inaccessible to people of other classes. On the contrary, it was the most available aspect of the good life that poor people could see being lived by the wealthy: you had a far better chance of reading Shakespeare than of riding around in a carriage (horseless or otherwise), getting divorced, visiting Italy, or feeling secure from hunger and want.

Some lower-class people acquired aspects of 'high' culture out of deference, a belief that one should aspire to 'their' standards. This was to collaborate with upper-class attempts to 'civilize' the 'masses' – for instance, F. W. Robertson told a meeting at a mechanics' institute that poetry can 'enable the man of labour to rise sometimes out of his dull, dry, hard toil, and dreary routine of daily life, into forgetfulness of his state, to breathe a higher and serener, and purer atmosphere.'[1] In this scheme, poetry is the alternative to a change in material conditions. However, it would be quite wrong to regard all lower-class use of high culture as manipulation and delusion. Raphael Samuel has shown considerable overlap among artistic and socialist concerns between 1880 and 1935 (in Samuel, MacColl and Cosgrove, pp. 3–19): many working people were excited and enlightened by the breadth and sophistication of 'high' culture, and they found socialist inspiration in it. But two things were happening together there, producing a specific negotiation of high culture. Writers like Ruskin, Carpenter, Morris and Wilde were registering the ills of industrial capitalism partly as the destruction of beauty, elegance and sensitivity, and this is precisely characteristic of middle-class dissidence. And working-class socialists were making a distinctive selection from the high-cultural canon – favouring such writers as Bunyan, Shelley, Dickens, Shaw. Shakespeare's *Julius Caesar*, for instance, was raided for models of heroic achievement – 'I had as lief not be, as live to be/In awe of such a thing as I myself', roared out Tom Mann; however, it was also said that Shakespeare was biased against the workers (Samuel, MacColl and Cosgrove, pp. 36, 197). Once more, the point is not what you read but how you read it. Gramsci notes that there are songs composed by the people, for the people, and those which the people adopt because they conform to their way of thinking; it is the latter that count. Handel's *Messiah* took on 'quite a different social meaning' when performed by working people.[2] At the same time, there is always a danger of being appropriated by the tradition that you mean to appropriate.

With these points about working-class use of 'high' culture in mind, I reiterate that the formation – writers, institutions and readers – which mainly sponsored and consumed 'high' culture, which gave it coherence as a culture, which gave it the status 'high', was the leisured upper-middle class.

Certainly this is how it was regarded in the 1940s. In a compilation of essays called *Other People's Lives* (1948), Philip Toynbee explains that culture still depends on the middle classes:

> Brutal and philistine though the middle classes may in many ways be, there does lie within them a tenuous tradition of culture and civilisation. The middle class boy or girl can, if he or she be inclined to it, grasp and inherit this tradition. In their progress through school to university there is a certain ease and leisure. . . . (p. 40)

Cyril Connolly invoked in *Horizon* (April 1948) 'that highly cultivated well-to-do world bourgeoisie who provided the *avant-garde* artist – writer, painter, musician, architect – with the perfect audience' (*Ideas*, p. 193).

We should remember that Virginia Woolf required not just a room, but 'money' – £500 annually, unearned.[3]

Alan Pryce-Jones, editor of the *Times Literary Supplement*, found in 1956, still, that 'the writing of books remains an occupation of the middle and upper class' (in Lehmann, *Craft*, p. 39). There were writers of lower-class origin, it was acknowledged, but in the very act of becoming writers they were co-opted to middle-class forms. As Orwell put it, the educated working-class person 'writes in the bourgeois manner, in the middle-class dialect. . . . So long as the bourgeoisie are the dominant class, literature must be bourgeois' (*Essays*, II, p. 58). Even the best, such as D. H. Lawrence, Spender declared in *The New Realism*, 'have completely changed their environment, in order to write for a middle-class audience' (p. 15). Toynbee believed that Lawrence was 'broken by the superhuman task of escaping from his own class' (*Other People's Lives*, p. 38; see below pp. 258–9).

Identifying high culture as the culture of the leisure class is not to say that it is simply 'bourgeois' or 'capitalist'. Since the late eighteenth century, when enclosures, the factory system and urbanization helped to provoke the Romantic movement, the middle class has thrown up a dissident fraction partly hostile to the hegemony of that class. The stance is particularly attractive to intellectuals, who find their concerns slighted by aggressive commerce. From the end of the nineteenth century we may identify a line of critical intellectuals continuous with the present; it runs through the aesthetic movement, Fabianism, Modernism, Bloomsbury, 1930s public-school communists, Leavisism, and the New Left-CND nexus.[4] Dissident middle-class intellectuals may be right-wing, left-wing or liberal: they may imagine a 'return' to traditional structures, attempt an alliance with the working class or other oppressed groups, or try to find a compromise between radical intuitions and the prevailing system. The consistent feature is hostility to the hegemony of the principal part of the middle class – the businessmen, industrialists and empire-builders. Matthew Arnold was more hostile to middle-class 'philistines' than to aristocratic 'barbarians' or the lower-class 'populace'. The middle class is divided internally, and 'good' culture is proclaimed as the banner of dissidence.

The division was plain to see by 1900. In *Howards End*, by E. M. Forster (1910), the Wilcoxes represent imperial-industrial enterprise: they produce the wealth of the country, but are sadly vulgar, clumsy and dishonest. The Schlegels represent a finer culture: they are artistic, feminized, German in origin, gifted with human understanding, sincerity and even sexual spontaneity. Both, of course, are middle class: the Schlegels admit to living off money made by people like the Wilcoxes (pp. 58–9). The Schlegels' attempt to 'connect' succeeds only by way of the fantasy collapse of Wilcox resistance. George Bernard Shaw, in *Heartbreak House* (1919), opposed cultivated country-house society to the money-makers, represented by the pathetic Boss Mangan and a burglar. In his preface Shaw complains of the failure of 'cultured, leisured Europe' to make its dissidence effective: 'They took the only part of our society in which there was leisure for high culture, and made it an economic, political, and, as far as practicable, a moral vacuum' (p. 8).

Shaw's argument indicates that he had expected more of his cultivated ladies and gentlemen. In fact, a principal justification advanced for the existence of a leisured upper-middle class was that 'freedom and independence, based upon a secured income and a high standard of living, have produced a critical spirit and have given freedom to experiment in art, in science, and in politics.' So wrote Roy Lewis and Angus Maude in *The English Middle Class* (1949; p. 102). They defended 'the rentier, the man of independent means', arguing that 'the possession of some private wealth enables an individual to take a more long-sighted view of the public interest' (pp. 107–10). The argument derived from Karl Mannheim, who developed the notion of 'a relatively uncommitted intelligentsia'. He pointed out not just that the pursuit of intellectual occupations 'for their own sake is possible only to gentlemen of independent means', but also that 'the prestige does not come from the disinterested performance as such, but from the social position that makes it possible' (pp. 106, 112). Two uses of the word 'independent' are acknowledged here: independence of thought and independence of means; Mannheim is perhaps optimistic about their compatibility. In April 1948 Cyril Connolly acknowledged the Marxist charge that *Horizon* was bourgeois: yes, 'because we believe that the perfect medium for art and artists is an enlightened bourgeoisie with its guarantees of peace, privacy and a regular income and because intense hatred of the bourgeoisie is one of its most rewarding features' (*Ideas*, pp. 194–5).

How far we should credit this case is disputed. Thorstein Veblen suggested in *The Theory of the Leisure Class* (1899) that cultivation of the humanities is convenient for 'the leisure class' because it is a spectacular instance of 'conspicuous consumption' leading to the attainment of a certain status (p. 252). However, Jurgen Habermas, in the Frankfurt

School tradition, invokes 'bourgeois art' as a counter-culture 'hostile to the progressive-individualistic, achievement- and advantage-oriented lifestyle of the bourgeoisie' (Habermas, p. 85). This argument has been interrogated most complexly by Herbert Marcuse. He recognizes that 'only a privileged minority enjoyed [the] blessings and represented [the] ideals' of 'the higher culture', but believes that it may preserve 'images of a gratification that would dissolve the society which suppresses it' (*One*, pp. 56, 60). He suggests that the very lifestyle of those 'who have the time and the pleasure to think, contemplate, feel and narrate' haunts modern consciousness with the possibility of an unalienated existence (pp. 59–60). However, Marcuse also says that the notion of art as transcendent negates its radical potential: 'Separated from the sphere of labour where society reproduces itself and its misery, the world of art which they create remains, with all its truth, a privilege and an illusion' (p. 63). This is 'the contradiction, the self-defeat, built into art' (*Essay*, pp. 48–50; this is close to my argument in chapter 3).

Tom Nairn goes further, denouncing the politics of middle-class dissidence as nostalgic and gestural: it has been 'anti-machine, anti-money, and anti-city. It was not – of course – anti-bourgeois, or designed to impede the serious accumulation of capital. . . . It never intended to stop England becoming the world's workshop; but it did aim to inject into that fate as high a degree of conservative stability and rank as history would permit' ('English', p. 67). And Christopher Butler links experimental art with 'the phenomenon of the anti-bourgeois bourgeois, who accepts society more or less as it is, while at the same time entertaining a set of intellectual and artistic notions which are contradicted by his actual behaviour' (p. 122).

In my view there is truth in all these arguments. Middle-class dissidence has been subject to crucial limitations, but it has also been diverse. As I have said, it may be left, right or liberal: it is not a given, but an opportunity for contest. There is often scope for the push to the left that would produce a socialist, or feminist or gay or anti-racist, affiliation and activity. Perry Anderson allows that three main currents have fed the British left: working-class consciousness, classical English liberalism, and moral and aesthetic criticism (Anderson and Blackburn, p. 283). Identifying the structure, history and potential of middle-class dissidence is therefore an important project. In Chapters 11 and 12 I discuss CND and the New Left; in this chapter I consider the moment at which its prewar, rentier formation was displaced by a welfare-capitalist structure of assumptions.

'A Woolworth Life': Culture Under Threat

Elizabeth Bowen's wartime story 'Sunday Afternoon' is set at an Anglo–Irish country house in Eire – a particularly conservative venue, probably. Henry is visiting from London: his experience of the blitz separates him from 'the aesthetic of living' at the house, from its 'air of fastidious, stylised melancholy, an air of being secluded behind glass' (*Demon*, pp. 17–18). Their culture is so sensitive and personal that it cannot even address the blitz: 'One's feelings seem to have no language for anything so preposterous. . . . It will have no literature' (p. 19; my elision). Literature, here, is writing that engages refined feelings; and the story itself exemplifies the kind of delicately nuanced relations that Bowen and her friends valued and associated with literature.

Bowen's biographer Victoria Glendinning remarks: 'The big difference between then [the 1930s] and now was that the upper-middle-class world of society and the world of the arts very largely coincided' (p. 74). For Elizabeth Bowen and her circle, the war was destroying not only lives and homes, but the leisure-class refinement and sensibility fundamental to 'good' culture. In 'Sunday Afternoon' Maria, a young woman, is impatient with traditional decencies and excited by the idea of London. She seems to Henry framed 'for the new catastrophic *outward* order of life – of brutality, of being without spirit'. He thinks, 'with nothing left but our brute courage, we shall be nothing but brutes. . . . where shall we be when nobody has a view of life?' (pp. 23, 25; my elision). This is conservative dissidence, a disdainful recoil from the modern world. It almost parodies itself when Maria disturbs the tablecloth, shaking 'a petal from a Chinese peony in the centre bowl on to a plate of cucumber sandwiches. This little bit of destruction was watched by the older people with fascination, with a kind of appeasement, as though it were a guarantee against something worse' (p. 22). Such fastidiousness shows the leisured elite on the defensive in the 1940s, falling back on manners.

The threat to literature and the arts was often felt, by literary intellectuals, to reside in the whole trend of twentieth-century history, but the greatest danger was believed to be the strengthening of state power. The ultimate instances were the Nazi and Stalinist states, but anxiety was not limited to them, or even to the British state on a war footing. Many were impressed by James Burnham's argument in *The Managerial Revolution*. Orwell summarized:

What is now arising is a new kind of planned, centralised society which will be neither capitalist nor, in any accepted sense of the word, democratic. The rulers of this new society will be the people who effectively control the means of production: that is, business executives, technicians, bureaucrats and soldiers. . . . Private property rights will be abolished, but common ownership will not be established. (*Essays*, IV, p. 192)

The powers that the government had taken during the war seemed to promise such a development. Connolly in December 1944 was already transferring blame for the weariness of writers from Hitler to the British state 'Although it is Hitler who is responsible for this exhaustion, it is the State which appears as their enemy, for it is the State which continues to drain them by demanding new efforts' (*Ideas*, p. 7). He envisaged a time when 'it will no more tolerate private inspiration' (*Unquiet*, p. 55). John Lehmann thought, in 1946–7, that the need was 'to assert the rights and dignities of the individual human being against the pretensions of the state' (*Ample*, p. 37); he experienced 'the sense of a civilisation that had lost its way' (*I Am*, p. 271). This apprehension underlies Orwell's 1984 and Jocelyn Brooke's *The Image of a Drawn Sword* (1950).

The panic of literary intellectuals in the face of the postwar state is to be explained substantially by their assumption (deriving from the war experience in Britain and contrary to Burnham's thesis) that the working classes were about to take over. henry in 'Sunday Afternoon' registers 'the democratic smell of the Dublin bus' (*Demon*, p. 18). The bargain with the people proposed in welfare-capitalism, designed though it was, in great part to rescue the prevailing class structure, seemed to undermine both the idea and the economic basis of the arts. Welfare-capitalism implied that now all the people were to share in those good things that the upper classes had generally secured to themselves. But what, literary intellectuals asked, would happen to their cult of individual sensibility? The rest of us were not thought capable of attaining or appreciating that. In *The God that Failed* Spender explained his repudiation of communism largely in terms of his commitment to literature: he could not identify with the working class, he found, despite its oppression, because the sensibility of 'the creative artist. . . . which is decided for him in his childhood, is bourgeois' (p. 237). Therefore literary intellectuals defined themselves against an imaginary workers' state. In *The Unquiet Grave* Connolly asserted:

The English Masses are lovable: they are kind, decent, tolerant, practical and not stupid. The tragedy is that there are too many of them, and that they are aimless, having outgrown the servile functions for which they were encouraged to multiply. One day these huge crowds will have to seize power because there will be nothing else for them to do. (p. 48).

Then Connolly and his kind will not do well: 'The civilised are those who get more out of life than the uncivilised, and for this we are not likely to be forgiven' (p. 48). Observe the imprecision of 'get more out of life': it includes both cultural and material benefits, for Connolly does not care to distinguish between them.

Nigel Nicolson outlines the fears of his parents, Vita Sackville-West and Harold Nicolson:

they both believed that the world which they knew and loved would be irreparably broken by the war. They saw in it the end of *les douceurs de la vie*, represented by [their houses] Sissinghurst and King's Bench Walk. They thought that their past life of literature, Bloomsbury, 'the purchase of books and pictures and the unthinking enjoyment of food and wine', a large garden and sufficient servants, was now 'an obsolete tradition'. They feared the permanence of the new vulgarity which the war had introduced. 'I have always been on the side of the under-dog', wrote Harold Nicolson, 'but I have also believed in the principle of aristocracy. I have hated the rich, but I have loved learning, scholarship, intelligence and the humanities. Suddenly I am faced with the fact that all these lovely things are supposed to be "class privileges" '. 'We shall have to walk and live a Woolworth life hereafter. . . . I hate the destruction of elegance'. (Nicolson, 1939–1945, pp. 23–4).

However, Nigel Nicolson adds, 'their fears about the future were ill-founded. They continued to live after the war the same life as they had lived before it.'

Harold Nicolson was genuinely perplexed. A typical middle-class dissident of the period, he felt with the poor and hated the rich but loved learning, scholarship, intelligence and the humanities. He could not imagine a social order that would reconcile those principles, or a creativity that might draw upon other social, political, economic, human resources. This was the ethos of Bloomsbury, which remained the reference point for literary intellectuals. Bloomsbury 'appealed to the supreme value of the civilised *individual*, whose pluralisation, as more and more civilised individuals, was itself the only acceptable social direction' (Williams, R.,

Problems, p. 165). How far this pluralization could extend was rarely specified. In *Howards End* Leonard Bast is represented as the lowest class level at which cultural attainment might occur; but it fails because he is too poor ('I see one must have money'; pp. 44, 222). Forster's novel cannot get beyond this stage in the analysis. At one point the Schlegels and their friends discuss ingenious ways through which a millionaire at the point of death might 'do something' for Mr Bast, but although Margaret suggests giving him 'three hundred a year' (half her own unearned income), changing the social order is not seriously entertained (pp. 118–21).

In this context, we may understand T. S. Eliot's views on culture, education and society. In *Notes Towards the Definition of Culture* (1948) he distinguished elites and classes. Both, he thought, are necessary, and the upper class should provide and sustain the elite and high culture: 'I think that in the past the repository of this culture has been *the* élite, the major part of which was drawn from the dominant class of the time, constituting the primary consumers of the work of thought and art produced by the minority members, who will have originated from various classes, including that class itself.' He believed that the cultural elite must be attached to some class if they are to have 'their part to play', and therefore opposed, in Beveridge's phraseology, the extension of a national education system 'from the cradle to the grave'.[5]

Orwell traced the attitudes of Connolly and Eliot to the decline of the class fraction upon which their view of art and life depended. Poems like 'The Love Song of J. Alfred Prufrock', he said in 1942, were 'an end product, the last gasp of a cultural tradition, poems which spoke only for the cultivated third-generation *rentier*, for people able to feel and criticise but no longer able to act' (*Essays*, II, p. 275). In Connolly's *Unquiet Grave* Orwell discerned 'a cry of despair from the *rentier* who feels that he has no right to exist, but also feels that he is a finer animal than the proletarian' (*Essays*, III, pp. 364–5). Some privileged people thought that culture might protect them in the new political climate. *Other People's Lives* contains an unsigned article on the upper classes, which observes an 'attempt to strengthen the ties between the aristocracy and the arts'. The purpose of this is 'to bolster up the argument for survival based on the patronage of culture' (pp. 14–15). This move towards culture is accompanied, we are told, by a move to the right: 'Once indeed, it was fashionable to admit to a certain pinkishness, but now the great majority are becoming more and more outspoken in their hostility' (p. 16).

Even Orwell was not altogether unsympathetic to Eliot's elitism (*Essays*, IV, pp. 514–7). He had already been half persuaded by Sir Osbert Sitwell's 'A Letter to my Son' in 1944 that '*laissez-faire* capitalism is passing away, and the independent status of the artist must necessarily disappear with it. He must become either a spare-time amateur or an official' (*Essays*, III, p. 266). By 1954, Angus Wilson saw clearly that changing class composition had affected 'the novel' for a long time and now was making a critical difference:

> The English novel grew up with the emergence of a new social structure; the most serious novelists since James and Forster have reflected the decline of that structure in the very essence of their creation. Now that decline is complete, and the better novelists of today, who still belong to that vanished world, have been driven into the realms of childhood for their inspiration.[6]

However, the leisured upper-middle class retained control of high-cultural institutions well into the 1950s. In 1951 F. R. Leavis complained about 'an established tradition of coterie-power', specifying Bloomsbury, Spender, Keynes, unearned income, financial speculation, sartorial ostentation and society life ('Keynes', p. 50). And in 1955 Noel Annan demonstrated the network of upper-middle-class family connections within 'the intellectual aristocracy', remarking, cheerfully, how they enabled men of 'not outstanding ability' to reach 'the foremost positions'. Annan attributed to this formation 'the paradox of an intelligentsia which appears to conform rather than rebel against the rest of society.'[7]

Literature and Welfare-Capitalism

While some literary intellectuals lamented the wartime threat to the leisure-class life-style, many found an unprecedented opportunity to be useful. Not since the heyday of the Victorian sage, running through perhaps to Shaw and Wells, had literary intellectuals felt useful; indeed, they had constituted their activity as the principled alternative to usefulness, around ideas of aestheticism, feeling and sensibility.

The requirements of wartime 'morale' transformed the relationship between the state and cultural production. On the one hand there was censorship – it was an offence to circulate any report or statement 'likely to cause alarm or despondency'; news stories were suppressed and invented; the communist *Daily Worker* was closed down and the *Daily Mirror* was threatened (Calder, pp. 76, 155, 578–89, 331–3). On the other hand, new organizations were created to get people thinking along the right lines. It all gave employment to intellectuals. 'From 1938, with the establishment of the British Council to the formation during the war of the Ministry of Information film unit, CEMA [the Council for the Encouragement of Music and the Arts], the BBC third program, the Fire Brigade, ABCA lectures [Army Bureau of Current Affairs], and Artists for War, a new intellectual patronage system . . . came into existence.'[8] Opportunities for casual commissions increased greatly, and many intellectuals were actually salaried. T. R. Fyvel believes they had 'an unusual sense of fulfilment in jobs where one had not to worry about personal identity, nor pay' (*Intellectuals*, p. 50).

At the same time, the inequality apparent in the link between the leisure class and high culture threatened the project of drawing everyone into a shared national purpose. Some people tried to envisage a non-upper-class art. John Lehmann edited *Penguin New Writing* (quarterly from 1942). It had an egalitarian air about it, with limp covers and economy paper, previously unpublished young authors, attention to everyday experience, often in the relatively declassed context of the armed forces, and sales of up to 100,000 at 6d a copy. Lehmann believed these were 'revolutionary circumstances' for the development of literature and the arts, and encouraged articles that were 'based on personal experiences of people plunged into new circumstances by the upheavals of the war' (*I Am*, pp. 92, 95). However, the authentic personal note demanded by Lehmann kept *Penguin New Writing* within the orbit of Bloomsbury.

Others proposed more radical changes. Virginia Woolf, in 'The Leaning Tower', read to the Workers' Educational Association in Brighton in 1940, pointed out that privately educated men had produced virtually all English literature, and that the writer therefore 'sits upon a tower raised above the rest of us; a tower built first on his parents' station, then on his parents' gold' (*Collected*, p. 169). She anticipated a postwar world in which class distinctions would disappear – because of the promises being made to sustain the war effort and because income tax would stifle private education (p. 178). This would mean a loss: 'We shall regret our Jane Austens and our Trollopes; they gave us comedy, tragedy, and beauty. But much of that old-class literature was very petty; very false; very dull.' Woolf looks forward, instead, 'to a stronger, a more varied literature in the classless . . . society of the future' (p. 179). Boldly, she identifies herself, as a woman, with all those excluded from educational privilege – with 'the other class, the immense class to which almost all of us must belong' (p. 180).

Herbert Read welcomed the idea of proletarian art in a little book published in 1941 called *To Hell with Culture*. Read saw 'culture' and its specialized producers as consequences of industrialization, and as an aspect of the oppression of working people in the capitalist state; he thought Soviet-style state socialism equally at fault. Read says: 'The worker has as much latent sensibility as any human being, but that sensibility can only be awakened when meaning is restored to his daily work, and he is allowed to create his own culture' (pp. 43–7). He concludes: 'The whole of our capitalist culture is one immense veneer. . . . When Hitler has finished bombing our cities', let's build good new ones (p. 49). If such vivid egalitarian sentiments now seem crudely philistine, that is a measure of the extent to which the promise provoked by wartime needs has been forgotten. Read's book was in a series edited by Francis Williams called 'The Democratic Order'. Its aim was to take Churchill at his word and advance 'the forward march of the common people in all lands towards their just and true inheritance'. Williams wanted 'to make sure that this time there shall be no thwarting of just desires and rightful hopes' (Read, pp. v–vi).

An opposition between a workers' state and the bourgeois idea of art was recognized also on the Labour left. Aneurin Bevan, in *In Place of Fear* (1952; the title takes up the Beveridge promise of co-operation instead of domination), acknowledges 'the vicissitudes which afflict the individual' as an effect of current social change: 'Personal relations have given way to impersonal ones' (p. 36). Many believe this to be a decline, he says; but what is actually happening is 'a change from one type of society to another. Those whose habits and possessions are bound up with the vanishing social order are filled with pessimism' (p. 93). Nevertheless, Bevan thinks that art will do very well. The erstwhile commissioning of popes and monarchs should properly be regarded as a form of public expenditure on the arts, he says, and in the new society he expects the 'emancipation' of artists, 'restored to their proper relationship with civic life' (pp. 50–1). Connolly had already anticipated that Bevan might become the local equivalent of Zhdanov, Stalin's cultural policeman (*Ideas*, p. 126).

By the end of the war, state support for the arts was on the agenda. Lady Violet Bonham Carter defended the idea, but felt obliged to observe that historically 'the leisure and money of the "privileged" have guarded and preserved for the few much that was rare, precious and lovely. Whether or not the essential qualities of these values can survive intact, when they are shared by the many, still remains to be seen' (*Other People's Lives*, p. 89). In September 1946 *Horizon* asked writers what they thought they should live on while writing. Connolly agreed with nearly half the people asked, that the state must 'step in. It must give young writers scholarships and older writers Sabbatical years; it must, with its official blessing, thrust leisure as well as money on them' (*Ideas*, p. 124). In other words the state should preserve, for writers alone, the conditions of the threatened leisure class. But many still thought the state should be kept out. Edward Sackville-West (cousin of Vita) cried: 'Look at the way Shostakovitch has been ruined by the dogmatism of the Soviet regime' (*Ideas*, p. 113). Connolly proclaimed in October 1946: 'The artist who declares truly for individual freedom, aesthetic spirit or intellectual truth must be prepared to go once more into the breach against the Soviet view. . . . All we can do is see that it does not happen here' (*Ideas*, pp. 135–6). It was believed that it could happen here, such was the threat of the workers' state.

In the face of these anxieties, a key assumption of welfare-capitalism was instituted at this point in the 1940s: that the condition of culture is in substantial part a responsibility of the state, and that many intellectuals will be employed in state organizations. Wartime provision was continued with the forming of the Arts Council in 1945 and the BBC Third Programme in 1946; the extension of secondary education through the Butler act of 1944 was understood partly in the same terms. Culture, in welfare-capitalism, is one of the good things (like economic security and healthcare) that the upper-classes have traditionally enjoyed, and it is now to be available to everyone.

Culture Preserved

Of course, we now know, people's art did not take over in 1945, and literary intellectuals were not incorporated into a workers' state. Rather, the welfare-capitalist state turned out to be quite hospitable to them, and they flourished in institutions that Connolly's respondents despaired of or despised – the market, academia, and writing not normally thought of as literary. State intervention in culture took its tasks, its personnel and much of its tone from the current literary establishment, and the leisure-class idea of 'good' culture maintained its dominance, though the class did not. The 'high' culture to which everyone was now to have access was almost the same as that which had previously identified a class fraction.

Raymond Williams recalls:

> I thought that the Labour government [of 1945] had a choice: either for reconstruction of the cultural field in capitalist terms, or for funding institutions of popular education and popular culture that could have withstood the political campaigns in the bourgeois press that were already gathering momentum. In fact, there was a rapid option for conventional capitalist priorities – the refusal to finance the documentary film movement was an example. (*Politics*, p. 73)

In fact the Labour Party manifesto of 1945 hardly questioned the conventional idea of high culture: 'By the provision of concert halls, modern libraries, theatres and suitable civic centres, we desire to assure to our people full access to the great heritage of culture in this nation' (Borzello, p. 129).

Most of the Labour leadership were middle-class dissidents, brought up in the old middle-class manner. Clement Attlee 'suffered acutely if the port was circulated the wrong way at his dinner table' (Williams, F., p. 222). Their wish to extend 'good' culture was precisely of a piece with the paternalism that partly inspired the rest of the welfare state. According to his biographer Roy Harrod, Keynes, the leading strategist of welfare-capitalism, believed that 'the first claim upon the national dividend was to furnish those few, who are capable of "passionate perception", with the ingredients of what modern civilisation can provide by way of a "good life" ' (George and Wilding, p. 45). Keynes was opposed to communism because it 'exalts the boorish proletariat above the bourgeois and the intelligentsia who, with whatever faults, are the quality of life and surely carry the seeds of all advancement' (Lekachman, p. 40; Foote, p. 140). It is plain to see, now, that a genuinely unified cultural provision was not really attempted. It is a good instance of how ideology can set an agenda: the status of high culture, deriving from its class status, made a democratic cultural policy virtually inconceivable.

In *Hemlock and After* (1952) Angus Wilson sees that the state can be persuaded to co-operate with literature. Bernard sets up Vardon Hall to provide 'leisure and support for writers' – a substitute for the traditional unearned income; it is funded by a combination of private sources, institutions like universities and the Arts Council, and government grant (pp. 9–11). Instead of lamenting the state as the enemy of the leisure class, Bernard collaborates quite successfully with it – for, it turns out, the relevant civil servant is a literary man himself (p. 100). Opposition comes from local middle-class people, who dislike Bernard's democratic leanings (for instance, wanting Vardon Hall to be run co-operatively by the writers). They would have been happy if he 'had lived up to his position, had specialised in good food, a good cellar, and a "philosophy of life" that took you above everyday things.' Thus he could have confirmed 'their private conviction that the grievances and grudges they felt against a changing social order should be considered the reawakening of spiritual values' (p. 17). In other words, they want to hold literature to a traditional allegiance. However, Bernard's attempt to accommodate literary intellectuals in the postwar situation is destroyed by other difficulties (see below, chapter 5).

The way the wind was blowing became evident when the BBC opened the self-consciously highbrow Third Programme in September 1946. It was presented not as a reinforcement of privilege, but as potentially for everyone: that was the pact of postwar welfare-capitalism. The BBC's new Director General, William Haley, described his three programmes as 'a broadly based cultural pyramid, slowly aspiring upwards' (Hopkins, p. 227). He said 'his ambition, which he seemed to think readily achievable, was to lead listeners from the Light Programme to the Home and from the Home to the Third until eventually the Home and Light should wither away leaving the Third over all.'[9] The triumph of this moment in the BBC is Dylan Thomas's *Under Milk Wood* (1954): it developed out of Thomas's wartime broadcasting experience, and effects an excellent adjustment of 'poetic' language with the needs of a popular audience. These twin ambitions are apparent when Thomas says the idea was 'an impression for voices, an entertainment out of the darkness, of the town I live in' so that 'you came to know the town as an inhabitant of it' (Jones, T. H., p. 90). It won the Italia Prize for radio and was broadcast repeatedly through the mid- and late 1950s (Lewis, P., 'Radio').

But generally the Third Programme could not transcend the prevailing notion of the arts. Edward Sackville-West had opposed state funding, but he approved of the Third and persuaded himself that it was good for everyone: 'it may become the greatest educative and civilised force England has known since the secularisation of the theatre in the sixteenth century' (*Other People's Lives*, p. 90). Actually, its share of listeners fell to one per cent in 1949 and then dwindled to fewer than 36,000 (below the point that could be measured; Hopkins, p. 235). Connolly didn't see the Third as at all like Soviet promotion of approved culture. He welcomed 'a State which does not necessarily adopt social realism but encourages art for its own sake', and acknowledged the continuing closeness of the literary elite to the centre of power: 'Yet the State is ourselves, *l'état c'est toi*' (*Ideas*, p. 135).

The Arts Council, at its inception, was also supposed to have popular appeal. The terms of reference of its wartime predecessor, CEMA, included 'the encouragement of music-making and play-acting by the people themselves', but Keynes became chairman and was more concerned with high levels of professional accomplishment (Hutchison, pp. 44–50). The 1946 charter of the Arts Council included a responsibility 'in particular to increase the accessibility of the fine arts to the public throughout Our Realm', and to co-operate with other public bodies to develop 'a greater knowledge, understanding and practice of the fine arts' (Hutchison, p. 61). However, most of the money was committed immediately to turning Covent Garden, which had been a *palais de danse* run by Mecca with a two-month opera season, and of which Keynes was also chairman, into an international opera and ballet house. Even so, Keynes hoped that Covent Garden would justify its subsidy in popular terms by performing 'at least a month of Gilbert and Sullivan every year'. In June 1947 officers were still urging that 'the Council must not lose sight of its mandate to make the fine arts easily accessible to every section of the population' (Hutchison, p. 63). But by 1951 the Secretary-General was proposing: 'In reconsidering the exhortation of its Charter to "Raise and Spread" [appreciation of the arts,] the Council may decide for the time being to emphasise the first more than the second word' (Hutchison, p. 60). Generally, popular possibilities were cut back – promotions in Butlin's holiday camps, small exhibitions in schools, canteens, shops and factories, symphony concerts at one shilling a head, regional initiatives, local arts clubs.[10]

A residual Arts Council commitment to a democratic culture may still be invoked today, echoing thinly through decades of mystifying restatements. In 1977 Sir John Colville, former private secretary to three prime ministers, asserted: 'It is to opportunities for the many to learn, practise and enjoy, rather than to give the talented few the means to develop their genius, that this new patronage is directed.' However, he added, noticing how arts budgets had increased: 'It is tempting to conclude that the

Treasury Knights, being cultivated men, felt a sympathy for the arts' (Colville, pp. 268–9). When the Federation of Worker Writers and Community Publishers tried to get Arts Council support in 1980, they were refused because their work 'didn't really for the most part justify itself on literary grounds'. Everyone is welcome – so long as they abandon their culture and adopt that of the hegemonic elite. Questioned about the criteria of evaluation, Melvyn Bragg, chair of the Literature Panel, said: 'I think serious writing is represented by those people who think that they represent it at the time' – and they were on the panel.[11]

I am stressing here the role of the state. Of course, the market was the other crucial institution; welfare-capitalism is, precisely, a form of commodity capitalism. Book publishing, including literature, and sales of classical music records have flourished in the private sector, which has shared the growth and organizational developments of other capitalist enterprises in the period (see chapter 13). But theatre and live music have split, virtually, between the commercial (popular) and the subsidized (art), and the publishing of serious books has become dependent on education and public libraries.[12] State support was the new factor, and it was decisive in reorganizing the status and ideological role of literature and the arts. The sign of quality was no longer upper-class involvement, but the imprimature of the Arts Council and the examination syllabus.

So almost the traditional conception of 'high' culture persisted, but now with state validation, within the story that it was for all the people. The fraction that had nurtured literature collapsed, and a major part of its culture was proclaimed as universal. But the confusions and implausibilities that this involved meant that matters could hardly rest there. Deprived of their traditional class support, literary texts and aspects of the customary ways of reading them floated free. Three rapidly developing formations were ready to pick them up.

First, the salaried middle class expanded. Civil Service, managerial and professional jobs increased by 50 per cent between 1938 and 1951, and continued to grow (Hopkins, pp. 157–60). The new professionals were not leisure class, and at first it was doubted that they could sustain high culture. T. R. Fyvel noted in *Encounter* (June 1956) the decline of the old *haute bourgeoisie* and the rise of the new ideology: 'The keynote is that culture is no longer for a minority. Everyone must now participate. . . . The bureaucracy of the new ruling institutions has to some extent taken the place of the old bourgeoisie, but culturally it lacks the independence and confidence to become a new *élite*' (pp. 15–16). However, in the late

1950s a quite distinct dissident fraction was to develop, partly out of the new professionals, buoyed up by its own commitment to 'good' culture. By 1968 Fyvel was able to celebrate 'the flowering of a youthful British *avant-grade* in almost all the arts', associated with 'the new young administrators and technologists' (*Intellectuals*, pp. 54–5). The structure and dissident potential of this new fraction are discussed in Chapters 11 and 12.

Second, writing itself was increasingly professionalized. Among those who responded to Connolly's *Horizon* questionnaire about what writers should live on, a common figure was £1,000 a year (about three times the income of a bus-driver; *Other People's Lives*, p. 24); most thought it should derive, ideally, from a private income or a genteel, undemanding, semi-sinecure profession. Few thought that the writer could make a living in the market, or that he or she should be an academic (Connolly, *Ideas*, pp. 79–126). Since that time, the opportunities for writers have expanded vastly. They may have a private income; be financed by a spouse, lover, parents or friends; be employed in some other occupation (often university teaching); sell their work in the traditional 'free' market or in the multi-national corporate market; be retained in the market to produce a specified literary product; or in the state sector; work with others in a co-operative; or be unemployed and dependent on social security. Few of these options would have suited the leisure-class literary gentleman or lady. And there are numerous para-literary occupations. Fyvel observed in 1968: '90 per cent of writers are essentially literary technicians, turning out a precisely requisitioned product for advertising, for magazine, film or television editors' (*Intellectuals*, pp. 58–9). Not only writers, but publishers, editors and critics, have become salaried professionals. The literary apparatus has changed and thereby continued.

Third, literature became far more involved in education. The leisure-class person of letters knew about literature as part of his or her general ambience and scarcely needed teaching about it; and he or she didn't want a job, or would get one through family or school connections. But the new professionals needed qualifications and, especially at the pivotal moment when leisure-class authority was still substantial, literature seemed suitable. The new professional would not, of course, have the income or general outlook of a leisure-class person, but he or she might learn the culture – which, after all, was allegedly universal. This development was already under way by 1945; its rationale was Leavisism. The conflict in Cambridge and Oxford between the amateurism of the scholar-gentleman and the new 'rigour' of I. A. Richards, William Empson and F. R. Leavis has been thoroughly examined. Francis Mulhern credits Leavisism with influence in precisely the areas I have been discussing: 'the establishment of a new, professionally chartered discourse on literature', and 'the large-scale entry of a new social layer into the national intelligentsia'.[13] By insisting that literary appreciation was not a class accomplishment but an individual attainment, Leavis rendered it suitable for teaching and examining. So literature was presented as a universal culture, detached from the class fraction that had produced and sponsored it, and then used as a criterion for entry to a different fraction.

Discrimination

The position of the arts in welfare-capitalism has been like that of other services. They are presented as for everyone and the situation may well be better than before; but, nevertheless, structural privilege is preserved. One study shows that in 1976 the most affluent 20 per cent of households benefitted from over 40 per cent of public expenditure on theatres, sporting events and other entertainments, while the poorest 25 per cent received only 4 per cent. As with other state provision, despite the residual egalitarian ideology, the better-off get more (Le Grand, pp. 158, 126–8). For today's middle class, as for the readers of *Horizon*, 'the state, it's yours'. Notice also that the middle class benefits from subsidies to culture both as producers (cultural institutions employ many middle-class people) and as consumers. Middle-class culture is organized, by and large, from within the ethos of that class, whereas lower-class culture, in the market, is often organized by entrepreneurs with allegiances elsewhere.

As with other state services, the inegalitarian bias in cultural provision derives from two features: better resourcing for middle-class consumers, and cultural assumptions that freeze out and discriminate against the lower classes, ethnic groups, women. The final twist is that when lower-class people do not take to the arts, it is said to be their fault. Thus the idea of high culture tends towards not merely the self-justification of the upper classes, but the humiliation of the rest (if, that is, they defer to the hegemonic culture). This is a common consequence of the supposed incorporation of the lower classes into welfare-capitalism: now they can be held responsible for its failures, even though those failures may well derive from the fact that incorporation has been largely a pretence.

Aneurin Bevan warned already in 1945 that the working person, having been the drudge of history, had become now the scapegoat as well (*Why*, p. 82).

The same structure is apparent in the educational provision instituted in the 1940s. The 1944 (Butler) Education Act was peddled during the war under the slogan 'Free Secondary Education for All' and hailed, Harry Hopkins recalls, 'as a great advance towards a unified, modern society' (p. 143). But the retention of fee-paying schools and division of the rest into grammar and secondary modern, with an extension of 'intelligence' testing, continued prewar trends and 'ensured that privilege was perpetuated behind a facade of democratic advance.'[14] By the start of the 1960s it was found necessary to commission a report (Newsom) on 'average and below average pupils', which began by admitting the extent of talent not realized in the education system because of class privilege (*Half our Future*, p. 3). Another survey showed that upper-middle-class pupils were two and a half times more likely to stay at school beyond the leaving age of 15 than lower-manual working-class pupils; four times as likely to complete the following year (to GCE O level); and nearly six times as likely to start the year after. Frank Parkin observes: 'So far as the secondary modern school or its equivalent is concerned, one of its main socialising effects is to lower the ambitions of those who pass through it to accord with the opportunities in the labour market.'[15]

Literature teaching contributed.[16] It was already sometimes said by educationists that literature was not a class culture but a universal culture. Matthew Arnold had asserted that the aim and end of great literature is 'truth' and that its 'criticism of life . . . is permanently acceptable to mankind' (Arnold, p. 209). So the teaching of literature seemed a generous welcoming of an ever-widening range of people into full humanity. However, the incorporation of most of us was reckoned usually to be a very slow process and no great immediate change was anticipated. Leavisites disagreed on the extension of education: Boris Ford spoke up for experimentation and spontaneity in schools as against authority and tradition, but Denys Thompson and Geoffrey Bantock, following Eliot's line, anticipated a deterioration of culture.[17] For the latter, the 'universal' culture was that only in potential; for the time being it must be guarded jealously by the elite.

I have discussed elsewhere some of the mechanisms through which literature, despite the wish of many teachers, is used as a ground of discrimination (Dollimore and Sinfield, ch. 8). Of course many students whose home and neighbourhood culture was unsympathetic to literary culture found it strange, difficult, and perhaps unappealing. *Half our Future* reads this as weakness: teachers try not to 'think of the weaker boys and girls as living in a sort of nature reserve, debarred by lack of ability from the great things of our civilisation. That way lies apartheid. But in practice many of the weaker pupils never seem to reach the point at which real English begins' (p. 152). The stakes are admitted here to be very high – a nature reserve, apartheid – are all our children fully human? But the report only reinscribes the problem: namely that 'our civilisation' (whose?) seems not to include 'the weaker pupils'. In fact, it produces them and the criteria through which they are identified and excluded; for by what external criteria could they be judged 'weaker'? As with welfare-capitalism generally, the offer of full citizenship was apparently there, and it was our fault if we didn't do well on it. For those who did, it was at the cost of abandoning their native culture. The Bullock Report of 1975, entitled *A Language for Life*, says: 'In a very real sense the pupil is himself being judged each time he responds in class to a piece of literature. . . . Is he betraying himself, he may well ask, as one who lacks discrimination?' (*Language*, p. 131). He may well ask; but discrimination is what he is getting. The report thinks the answer is sensitive teaching: it doesn't notice that the student is being asked to internalize success or failure with particular cultural codes as a judgement on her or his potential as a human being.

Literature was presented as a universal culture, and this high claim ratified discriminations in teaching and examinations that, actually, were largely those of class and teachability. The alleged inclusiveness afforded mechanisms of exclusion.

How much damage is done by the welfare-capitalist recycling of high culture? Probably not as much as intellectuals might believe. The phenomena labelled 'art' are only a tiny part of anyone's cultural experience, compared with work and family relations and the media generally. The historic injustices, done to the lower classes, women, racial, national and sexual minorities through hegemonic representations, run through all cultural production. Conceiving 'art' as the ultimate insult and deprivation is to collude with the idealist notion of its import. Furthermore, as Rachel Sharp has observed, ideological reproduction cannot occur 'without simultaneously reproducing or reflecting the contradictions which latently are inherent in any capitalist society.'[18] I wrote in Chapter 3 of the scope for resistance in cultural production – for changing the stories through which we live. Cultural apparatuses are contradictorily situated, and may be used in part at least by dissident groups. The best argument for the reality of some kind of humanism is the resourcefulness with which subordinated groups manage to resist the recommended culture, or take what they want from it.

It may be, as Giddens suggests, that dominant groups are likely to believe their own ideology whereas others have a better idea of how the world actually works (p. 72). The boldest proposition, perhaps, is that the main losers from 'high' culture are those who cultivate it. Paul Willis writes:

> The dominant class is most victim to the illusions and false promises of its own ideology. What looks like the last gift of privilege – cultural attainment and a living sensual involvement with the world – turns out to be its opposite: stultification, reification and pretence. The conflation of art and culture with social elitism and exclusion leads to conformist hesitancy and the minimum strategy of knowing the accepted wisdom. (*Profane*, p. 5)

After Welfare

That the post-1945 understanding of culture, the arts and education was formed in the same ideological framework as the other main welfare institutions is confirmed when, in the 1980s, we see them all sharing the same process of disintegration. For although full employment, health, educational and cultural provision have in fact been of benefit to the middle classes, the notion that they were for everyone has required expensive provision, and this comes to seem extravagant and unnecessary. Moreover, it bears the ideological impress of a dissident intelligentsia. So cultural provision, like national utilities and health-care, is 'returned' to the private sector, where it can be shaped more precisely for those who can pay and who support the normative value system. This is plain in the policies of the National Theatre and Royal Shakespeare Company where, as sponsorship comes in alongside subsidy, allegedly universal ideas of art lose influence, and expensive up-market entertainments take over. And the targeted audience is no longer the traditional leisure class of the 1940s, nor the earnest left-liberal intelligentsia that succeeded it, but a secure and well-salaried 'yuppy' class fraction.

Notes

1 Quoted in Altick, p. 198, and Sinfield, *Alfred*, p. 161. See Baldick; Borzello.

2 Antonio Gramsci, *Selections from Cultural Writings*, ed. David Forgacs and Geoffrey Nowell-Smith, trans. William Boelhower (London: Lawrence and Wishart, 1985), p. 195; Morley and Worpole, p. 97. On self-education, see Levy.

3 *Room*, pp. 6, 39–40; on the relation of women to this formation, see chs. 5, 10 below. On relations between literature and the leisure class, see also Snow, *Variety*, p. 51; Ritchie, H., pp. 105–9; Kermode, *History*, chs. 2, 3.

4 See chs. 11, 12 below; Heyck; Levy. The term 'middle-class dissidence' is Williams's, referring to theatre from Ibsen to Arthur Miller and the Royal Court (*Long*, pp. 292–5). See also Inglis; Lovell, pp. 25–35; West, pp. 142–52. On class fractions, see p. 41 above and Williams, R., *Culture*, pp. 74–83. Martin J. Wiener has constructed a whole theory of the failure of British industrial and commercial strength out of the desire, which he attributes to the British middle class, to cultivate an aristocratic, rural life-style and imagery, in disaffection from industry, money-making and urbanization (Wiener).

5 *Notes*, pp. 42, 47. This was not new; already in 1939 Eliot had asserted that democracy was bad for art and culture because it was causing the social system to centre upon 'an illiterate and uncritical mob' (*Idea*, p. 66). On Eliot's involvement in wartime attempts to get Butler to propose a more congenial education system, see Jose Harris, 'Political Ideas and the Debate on State Welfare', in Smith, H. L. By 1948, according to David Pryce-Jones, Eliot had become an international focus for 'intelligent reaction against the new mass society' (Sissons and French, pp. 237–9).

6 *The Listener*, 29 April 1954; quoted by Hewison, *In Anger*, p. 80; see also pp. 74–84. The point about autobiography and childhood is made also in Lehmann, *Craft*, by Alan Pryce-Jones (pp. 26–43) and Francis Wyndham (p. 50–1).

7 Annan, pp. 284–5. See also Aron, pp. 215, 234–5; Stuart Hampshire, *New Statesman*, 28 April 1956, p. 457; Ritchie, C., pp. 111–12, 121, 177; Hewison, *Under Siege*, ch. 8. On the persistence of the prewar literary establishment, see Hewison, *In Anger*, chs. 1–3; Ritchie, H., pp. 174–83.

8 Stuart Samuels, 'English Intellectuals and Politics in the 1930s', in Rieff, p. 247; see also Calder, pp. 578–96 and Hewison, *Under Siege*, pp. 16–18, 84, 164–5, 175, 182–4.

9 Williams, F., pp. 271–2. In 1989 terms, think approximately of the Light, Home and Third as Radios 2, 4 and 3 respectively.

10 Hutchison, pp. 97–9, 90, 117–18, 48–9. See also Borzello, pp. 124–33; Appleyard.

11 Morley and Worpole, pp. 131–7; Borzello, pp. 134–9. On government arts policies from 1956 to the present, see chapters 11–13 below.

12 See Stuart Laing, 'The Production of Literature', in Sinfield, *Society*, pp. 122–35. The case of painting and sculpture was more complex, but the role of public institutions was great here too.

13 Mulhern, p. 318; see also pp. 22–34, 118–24; Eagleton, *Function*, ch. 4; pp. 232–5 below.

14 Calder, p. 627; see Deborah Thom, 'The 1944 Education Act: the "art of the possible"?', in Smith, H. L.

15 Parkin, *Class*, p. 63; for the survey, see Douglas, Ross and Simpson, p. 38. See also Willis, *Learning*.

16 For versions of this argument, see further Bourdieu, 'Cultural'; Macherey and Balibar; Balibar; Widdowson.

17 See Mulhern, pp. 220, 283–9; Baldick, pp. 31–6 and ch. 7.

18 Sharp, pp. 116–17. See Macherey and Balibar; Sinfield, 'Give an Account of Shakespeare and Education', in Dollimore and Sinfield.

5

Queers, treachery and the literary establishment

The Return of Ambrose Silk

'Outside the China of the mandarins, no great society has ever had a body of intellectuals so integrated with, and so congenial to, its ruling class, and so combining civility and refinement' – so wrote Edward Shils of Britain in 1955 (Shils, p. 152). This chapter is about the kind of civility and refinement cultivated by the literary establishment of the 1940s and early 1950s and how, despite the confident class position celebrated by Shils, its sexual politics rendered it strangely subversive and finally vulnerable.

Shils began his essay with an allusion to Evelyn Waugh's novel *Put Out More Flags* (1942):

> When Basil Seal joined the Commandos, Sir Joseph Mainwaring, an old Blimp, said, 'There is a new spirit abroad. I see it on every side'; and Evelyn Waugh, who was himself invaded by the new spirit, closed the book with the words: 'And poor booby, he was bang right'. He was bang right. It was the end of two decades of rebellion against society, against the middle classes, against capitalism, against British institutions and manners.

But for the upper-class Basil Seal and his friends to join the war effort, it seemed necessary that one person in his circle be excluded: that was the current stereotype of the literary intellectual. Waugh's novel banishes Ambrose Silk, quite brutally, to neutralist Eire. Silk is a writer and editor, an aesthete living after his time, and a homosexual: 'A pansy. An old queen' (*Put Out*, p. 41). He has no feeling for the war, although he is

Jewish and his Jewish lover, Hans, is in a Nazi concentration camp. So he founds a journal, reminiscent of *Horizon*, to sustain the arts: he values 'something personal and private in a world where only the mob and the hunting pack had the right to live' (p. 187). Thus he represents the stereotype of the effete literary intellectual, as it had come down from the 1890s, through Bloomsbury; this figure has to be exiled so that Waugh's other upper-class characters can reorient themselves towards the war.

Put Out More Flags misses no opportunity to stigmatize Ambrose Silk. He has 'pansy' mannerisms ('Why do I talk like this, nodding and fluttering my eyelids as though with a repressed giggle; why can I not speak like a man?' he asks himself; p. 61). He is made to accept expulsion from the community as his natural heritage as an artist, a homosexual who has always lived in fear of the police, and a Jew with 'the dark, nomadic strain in his blood' (p. 219). This stereotyping enacts, virtually, a fascistic centring of 'normal' Englishness by identifying and despising an outgroup. Silk, it seems, courts exile, it is his destiny, he deserves it. And, as if to mask this fascistic tendency in his treatment, Waugh makes Silk accept the Nazi view of such as himself and declare, indeed, that he is himself a frustrated Nazi: 'If I were not a cosmopolitan, Jewish pansy, if I were not all that the Nazis mean when they talk about "degenerates", if I were not a single sane individual, if I were part of a herd . . . I'd set about killing and stampeding the other herd as fast and as hard as I could' (p. 73). In this passage virtual admission of the Nazi case is followed by an assertion of liberal individualism, then by an endorsement of Nazi ideology which ratifies the idea of Silk's 'degeneracy' while removing the possibility of sympathy.

The overkill with which Silk is handled indicates the difficulty in cordoning him off from the leisure class that Waugh identified with, and which I presented in chapter 4 as the source, mainstay and general reference point of 'literature' as it was then understood. Looked at in this light, Ambrose Silk is close to the centre of the self-perception of the class fraction in which Waugh and his novels are involved (Waugh faced him again in *Brideshead Revisited*, 1945). His exile represents not the amputation of a minor limb, but a stroke near to the heart.

Nevertheless, other writers resorted to the queer stigma to signal their commitment to the war effort and their distance from the aesthetic. Orwell was annoyed by an attack on the involvement of writers in propaganda, and replied in verse with an indictment of pacifists as 'pansies': 'Yet where's the pink that would have thought it odd of me/To write a shelf of books in praise of sodomy?' (*Essays*, II, p. 343; also p. 216).

John Lehmann, the editor of *Penguin New Writing*, was disturbed by the persistence of a homosexual subculture in Soho:

> T. and the two boys came in, giggling and blowing kisses and chirruping away, discussing who they'd met at the Café Royal, what C.'s or B.'s latest *bon mot* was, where the new nightclub was and who'd be dancing there: I have to admit I was shocked at . . . this world existing now, so utterly out of touch with what's happening in the world all around us, so horribly unaesthetic to set beside the world of the Irish and Scottish soldiers I knew. (*I am*, pp. 76–7; see also p. 193)

Lehmann does not acknowledge in this volume of autobiography, published in 1960, that he was the lover of some of the soldiers he knew. His rejection of the 'pansy' world is related to his closeness to it – not just personally and sexually, but as a man of letters. Hence his statement that the 'pansy' boys were 'so horribly unaesthetic' in comparison with the soldiers: he seeks to shift 'aesthetic' away from an embarrassing identification. Lehmann tries to repudiate the 'sissy' image while actually giving it further currency. Ambrose Silk would not go away, so potent and intricate was his insertion in the social formation.

Although literary intellectuals believed co-option to the war propaganda machine to be necessary, they also believed it dangerous to their idea of civilization. Even as he wrote about recalcitrant 'pansies' Orwell was planning to resign from the BBC, complaining that it was 'a mixture of whoreshop and lunatic asylum' and that he felt like 'an orange that's been trodden on by a very dirty boot' (*Essays*, II, pp. 348–9). Lehmann felt he had to 'guard the free world of ideas from any military encroachment' (*I Am*, p. 165). Cyril Connolly's attitude, from the start, was not very different from Silk's: *Horizon* began in 1940 with an editorial distancing it from any commitment: 'Our standards are aesthetic and our politics are in abeyance'. Ambrose Silk represented literary values, and the war, by threatening those values, rendered him indispensable. He was not banished, but nurtured, cautiously and uneasily. The literary establishment, as the war ended and Labour came to power, was formed in the mould of Ambrose Silk.

Civilization and the 'Effeminate'

I showed in Chapter 4 how established literary intellectuals in the 1940s were implicated with and substantially belonged to a leisure-class fraction; they felt they were the bearers of 'civilization', which they believed to depend upon personal sensibility. Therefore they saw themselves as in opposition to the state and the working class. These oppositions proved unstable, principally because they were unnecessary and untrue.

There was a third opposition in play: masculine/feminine, and literary intellectuals were identified with what was perceived as the 'feminine'. This, again, was a Bloomsbury idea. Forster's Margaret Schlegel says theirs is a 'female house' – 'it was irrevocably feminine, even in father's time. ... it must be feminine, and all we can do is to see that it isn't effeminate.' The house of the Wilcoxes, the empire-builders who make things happen, is 'irrevocably masculine' (*Howards End*, p. 43). The 'feminine' correlates with the personal and individual, as against the masculine public world. Margaret muses: 'in public who shall express the unseen adequately? It is the private life that holds out the mirror to infinity' (p. 77). The feminine, as it was conceived, seemed more compatible with the sensitive and humane, with commitment to personal relationships, with the literary.

This may strike readers as strange, since diverse powerful studies have shown recently the extent to which women have been excluded from literature. I argue below (p. 211) that this case needs careful development, for there have been numerous women writers and they have been published. The problem has been their effacement or relegation, as is evident when committed presses rediscover them and reprint them. There were many prominent literary women in England in the 1940s – including Elizabeth Bowen, Rosamond Lehmann, Edith Sitwell, Rebecca West, Katherine Anne Porter, Elizabeth Taylor, Antonia White, Vita Sackville-West, Nancy Mitford, Pamela Hansford Johnson, Barbara Pym, Ivy Compton-Burnett, Storm Jameson, Angela Thirkell, Olivia Manning. Virginia Woolf died in 1941 and her influence remained strong.

Most of these women were so situated that they found it natural to maintain the identification of the individual, the personal and the literary with the lifestyle and outlook of the leisure class. Comments about 'what little luxury is left from this evened-out England' (Taylor), 'the levelling de-individualising new order' (Lehmann) and 'the last gleams of a murdered civilisation' (Thirkell) fall easily from the lips of characters in their novels, challenged only by the thought that things might, after all, be worse.[1] Elizabeth Wilson has observed the leisure-class pattern of response in such 'feminine' writing: 'It is not always clear at what point a minute and sensitive recreation in detail of the texture of daily life slips into snobbery and obsession with social nuances . . . and moral judgments become confused with the socially "correct".' The heroines, Wilson adds, become 'pure individual sensibility . . . a "woman's" sensibility taken to excess' (*Only*, p. 150). The presence of such women authors reinforced the prevailing notion of the literary, although men still dominated the main institutions.

The idea that literature is 'effeminate' goes back to the Romantics, it troubled the Victorians and broke through in the 1890s; Bloomsbury and the 1940s had only to keep it going. Its importance is evident from the attempts of men to change it. Sandra M. Gilbert and Susan Gubar have remarked how Modernism and New Criticism construct a literary history in which women play no part. At the start of this movement T. E. Hulme complained that 'imitative poetry springs up like weeds, and women whimper and whine of you and I alas, and roses, roses all the way. It becomes the expression of sentimentality rather than of virile thought.' A 'feminine' tradition had to be 'countered with critical ceremonies of male self-certification' (*No Man's*, p. 154). From another point of view, Richard Hoggart complained that the Arts Council is represented by journalists as 'a "fiddle" by a lot of "cissies" who despise the amusements of the plain Englishman' (*Uses*, p. 183). Writers and critics in the late 1950s and early 1960s strove to change this story, first through Leavisite, Movement and Angry work (see below), then by recentring Modernism (see Chapter 9). But first, as I show in this chapter, 'effeminacy' contributed to the insecurity of the leisure class in postwar England.

The masculine/feminine dichotomy in the construction of literary intellectuals overlaid another: masculine/homosexual. T. W. Adorno remarked that 'the stereotype of the artist remains the introvert, the egocentric idiot, frequently the homosexual.'[2] This second opposition could lurk almost unperceived in the shadow of the first because few people, initially at least, wanted to bring it into the open; and because homosexuals were generally perceived as displaced versions of the 'feminine' – 'effeminate'. Hence Leo Abse's analysis, in his speech introducing the second reading of the Sexual Offences Bill in December 1966:

Surely, what we should be preoccupied with is the question of how we can, if it is possible, reduce the number of faulty males in the community. How can we diminish the number of those who grow up to have men's bodies but feminine souls? It is clear from the number of homosexuals who are about that, unfortunately, little boys do not automatically grow up to be men. Manhood and fatherhood have to be taught. Manhood has to be learnt. (National Deviancy Conference, p. 163)

The last sentences here are revealing: they acknowledge that sex and gender roles are not natural but learnt. Yet this awareness does not stop Abse making the crudest assumptions about gender – that there are two precise and necessary categories, masculine and feminine, and that you are either one or the other or an unacceptable confusion of the two.

The ideological convenience of this way of thinking was that it effectively eliminated the concept of the homosexual male: such men were not really men (Marshall, J., pp. 135–6. Thus the demarcation masculine/feminine was secured, even as deviations from it were labelled. Newspapers in the 1950s and early 1960s pressed homosexual men into the 'effeminate' mould, and hailed the resolution of problematic cases (for instance, sex change operations, and the discovery that the disturbingly brave and patriotic homosexual was, after all, not really homosexual or not really brave and patriotic; see Pearce). Of course, all this was bad news for women as well.

Many homosexuals internalized the 'effeminate' stereotype.[3] Others knew it to be inadequate, but used it nevertheless, sometimes to signal their own relative 'normality'. Peter Wildeblood, speaking out with unprecedented boldness in his book *Against the Law* after his trial and conviction in 1954, asked for 'tolerance' for homosexuals – but *not* for 'the effeminate creatures who love to make an exhibition of themselves' (p. 7; also pp. 5, 106–7). This is thoroughly self-oppressed. Irving Goffman in *Stigma* explains how witnessing flamboyant instances of the negative attributes imputed to a stigmatized person may produce distaste, because he or she has internalized the norms of the wider society; 'but his social and psychological identification with these offenders holds him to what repels him, transforming repulsion into shame, and then transporting ashamedness into something of which he is ashamed' (pp. 131–2). This process informs John Lehmann's need to distinguish his soldiers from pansy boys. Lehmann tells also how, meeting a young travel writer, Alex Comfort (as it happens, the pacifist Orwell had attacked), he anticipated 'a tough young adventurer's contempt for all this intellectual theorising and sissy chatter about poetry'. But he found 'an enthusiastic follower of New Writing and of the left-wing writers' movement, an adoring fan of anyone with "glamour" in the world of theatre and ballet, gentle-voiced, sensitive and shy'; in fact, a 'young man whom a casual label-fixer might have written off as a "sissy".' But, better still, Comfort turned out to be 'cool and quite unshaken' as a doctor's assistant during air-raids, able to speak of it 'with a quiet objectivity' (*I Am*, pp. 124, 126). Again, Lehmann accepts the sissy identification even through the efforts he makes to repudiate it.

Homosexual and bisexual men and explicit sympathizers had dominated the literary establishment since the rise of Bloomsbury in the 1920s, when, according to Goronwy Rees, homosexuality at Oxford and Cambridge was 'among undergraduates and dons with pretensions to culture and a taste for the arts, at once a fashion, a doctrine and a way of life' (Hyde, p. 225). One view of this scene is given in *Brideshead Revisited*. Homosexuality was a further reason for commitment to the life-style of the leisure class, where its practice was most possible. There was more toleration than elsewhere, one might evade difficulties through the deployment of money or influence, and one was well-placed to gratify and impress lower-class young men – whole groups of whom, guardsmen for instance, learned how to play the scene. If you had enough money you could travel, for homosexual activity was not illegal in much of continental Europe; for many, abroad came to symbolize an open and fulfilling sexual and emotional life.[4]

Homosexuals, like the leisured elite, had grounds for anxiety about the modern state. J. R. Ackerley remarks, almost in passing, how he and his friends were 'outcasts and criminals in the sight of the impertinent English laws' (*My Father*, p. 120); Wildeblood said in 1955 that he 'would be the first homosexual to tell what it felt like to be an exile in one's own country' (Wildeblood, p. 55). None of the wartime leaders – politicians, journalists, wise men – who proposed a fairer society in compensation for the war said anything about equality for homosexuals (few of them say it now). Indeed, in so far as the anticipated workers' state was perceived as against the personal and the privileged, it seemed to threaten even those corners in which some homosexuals might feel secure. Prosecutions for homosexual 'offences' rose five times over in the 15 years from 1939, and the leisure class could not always escape. Sir Paul Latham, baronet, 36-year-old officer in the Royal Artillery, Conservative Member of

Parliament, old Etonian, millionaire, and husband of a daughter of the Earl of Drogheda, was tried by court martial in 1941 on charges of improper conduct with three gunners and a civilian, and also with attempting the suicide to which exposure had driven him. His wife divorced him while he was in prison and he died a broken man a few years after his release (Hyde, p. 237).

The Homosexual Disturbance

The paradigm within which literary culture was constructed may be represented thus:

dominant	the state	the working class	'masculinity'
literary	the personal	the leisure class	'femininity'

The characteristics in the lower part of the table were perceived as in opposition to the dominant characteristics above, and also in opposition diagonally across the columns (so that 'femininity' was regarded as opposed to the state and the working class, and the personal to the working class and to 'masculinity'). The paradigm was mutually reinforcing at each point – and might thus have constituted, in the lower part of the table, a defensible subordinate position.

However, it was vulnerable and unstable because of the concealed term, lurking behind the idea of the feminine: homosexuality. This problematized the class divide in the paradigm, because homosexuals often chose their partners across it (as Oscar Wilde had done), producing connections where the model envisages oppositions. The 'effeminate', leisured literary intellectual sought relationships – either personal or (equally provocatively) impersonal – with masculinity and the working class. So the paradigm falls into confusion. An impulse from inside the leisure class undermines the affiliations and barriers upon which it depends. Commentators sensed something amiss – for instance C. E. M. Joad complained, obscurely, that short stories in *Horizon* by Elizabeth Bowen, Denton Welch and T. C. Worsley manifest 'decadence' in their 'concentration on the abnormal' and their concern with 'the primitive and the perverted' (pp. 293–9).

Indirection was found necessary. Lionel Trilling apparently did not know that E. M. Forster was homosexual when he wrote admiringly of him in 1944; Terence Rattigan was obliged by the censor to remove from

Separate Tables mention of a man soliciting in a public lavatory; John Lehmann and Tom Driberg wrote, in effect, dual autobiographies – one about their public life and another, later and semifictional, about their sexual and emotional lives. Auden founded a theory of poetry on the indirection which he felt was required of homosexual men. 'The Truest Poetry is the most Feigning' (published in *The Shield of Achilles*, 1955) urges upon love poets the most elaborate style: 'Be subtle, various, ornamental, clever. . . . From such ingenious fibs are poems born.' Auden is worried not just about the instability of language and personality; the poet may be subjected to state violence:

> If half-way through such praises of your dear,
> Riot and shooting fill the streets with fear,
> And overnight as in some terror dream
> Poets are suspect with the New Regime,
> Stick at your desk and hold your panic in,
> What you are writing may still save your skin:
> Re-sex the pronouns, add a few details,
> And, lo, a panegyric ode which hails
> (How is the Censor, bless his heart, to know?)
> The new pot-bellied Generalissimo.
> Some epithets, of course, like *lily-breasted*
> Need modifying to, say, lion-chested . . .

The poem is written as if poets are all heterosexual men: they must 'Re-sex the pronouns' to adapt their love poems to a praise of the dictator. But the gender problem may be more complicated – after all, governments persecute homosexuals, not conventional love poets. Auden goes on to defend the poet against a charge of insincerity:

> Though honest Iagos, true to form, will write
> *Shame!* in your margins, *Today! Hypocrite!*
> True hearts, clear heads will hear the note of glory
> And put inverted commas round the story,
> Thinking – *Old Sly-boots! We shall never know*
> *Her name or nature. Well, it's better so.*

Auden picked up a phrase from here when he entitled his review of J. R. Ackerley's book *My Father and Myself* (1960), in which Ackerley describes how he discovered his father's possible homosexuality, 'Papa was a Wise Old Sly-boots' (Auden, *Forewords*, pp. 450–8).

The poem concludes with a theological justification:

> What but tall tales, the luck of verbal playing,
> Can trick his [i.e. man's] lying nature into saying
> That love, or truth in any serious sense,
> Like orthodoxy, is a reticence.

That Auden is covertly justifying the indirection of the homosexual writer is suggested by another phrasal similarity. 'Tall tales' very nearly appears in Auden's introduction to the poems of Cavafy (1961), where he says: 'Cavafy was a homosexual, and his erotic poems make no attempt to conceal the fact.' Auden defends this boldness on the ground that one duty of a poem is 'to bear witness to the truth'; but then seems to remember his own practice and theory and adds, parenthetically, 'In the arts, one must distinguish, of course, between the lie and the tall story that the audience is not expected to believe' (*Forewords*, p. 336). Homosexual desire was constituted as a submerged discourse – to be decoded by those in the know, but too dangerous to be spoken directly. Auden's poem presents itself as a quasi-philosophical meditation, requiring me to root around for verbal links to justify my analysis.

This subliminal status made homosexuals a convenient way to represent barely apprehensible threats of destruction and dissolution. They appear repeatedly in novels of the period as the *almost* unthinkable other. Their presence is permitted only on the condition that it is negated; yet as Jonathan Dollimore has shown, while the negated performs crucial functions for the dominant, it is liable to return to trouble that dominant (Dollimore, 'Homophobia').

The principal motif of the novels of Barbara Pym is an innocent Anglican lady finding that life is not quite as simple as she had thought. Homosexuality is used to suggest a vaguely threatening wider world. In *Excellent Women* (1952) it is just beyond mention. Mildred, the heroine-narrator, mentions the vicar to the unconventional Mrs Napier, who says: ' "He isn't married then? One of *those* . . . I mean", she added apologetically as if she had said something that might offend me, "one of the kind who don't marry?" ' (p. 25). Mildred, who has herself thought of marrying the vicar, seems not to understand this innuendo; or a later comment about the vicar and clergymen generally 'not knowing how to treat women and no wonder' (pp. 197–8). However, Mildred gets the point eventually, and when it is suggested that the vicar may 'throw himself into the boys' club' she found herself 'beginning to laugh, I cannot think why, and turned the conversation' (p. 217). As well as the stereotyping of the feared outsider (we don't get the vicar's point of view), we may observe here the process through which the unthinkable comes into consciousness. Even more interesting is the position offered to the reader, who is presumably expected to pick up rather more than Mildred does initially, though she is generally reliable as narrator and ethical touchstone. This makes homosexuality hover indeterminately between that which may be recognized – the novel asks the reader to recognize it – and that which the 'good' narrator hardly knows.[5]

The most profound threat constituted by homosexuality to the leisured world of literature derived from its tendency to disrupt class distinctions. Cross-class liaisons problematized the personal relationships upon which Bloomsbury prided itself, either by selecting the 'wrong' kind of partner or by validating non-personal relationships. In fact, the disruption of class distinctions was part of the attraction. In a television interview in 1974 Christopher Isherwood explained the excitement of 1930s Berlin as a release from conventional class relations: 'What I in fact started to encounter was the German working class: and there was an escape there from the upper-middle class to which I belonged – sort of landed-gentry background. And I wanted to be with these boys, not really just for sexual reasons, nearly so much as to escape into another sort of world.' Denton Welch in his autobiographical novel *Maiden Voyage* (1945) doesn't mask the erotic attraction. He presents his 16-year-old self, defiantly, as a 'sissy', fascinated by working-class men – 'When he bent forward with a lighted match cupped in his hands, I saw how horny and broad they were. They were nice, and strong, with dirty nails. I wished I had hands like them' (p. 110).

Any such liaison was interpreted as threatening the social order – like that between Lady Chatterley and her gamekeeper. In Forster's story 'Arthur Snatchfold' (substantially written in 1928, published in 1972), Sir Richard Conway has a brief but delightful sexual experience with a young man who delivers milk, but learns later from an acquaintance of his own class that they were observed by a policeman, and the youth, Arthur Snatchfold, is to be tried at the assizes. It is evident that the policeman avoided catching Sir Richard, and that Arthur refused to identify him even though it was made clear 'that he would be let off if he helped us to make the major arrest' (Forster, *Life*, p. 143). Forster undercuts his own Bloomsbury assumption that ethical superiority goes along with middle-class refinement by crediting the lower-class man with the superior personal morality. And he doesn't seek to rescue the liaison by making it a 'personal relationship'. On the contrary, in the concluding lines he makes Sir Richard both celebrate and lament the incident on the terms rendered necessary by the legal and social structure:

> It had all seemed so trivial. Taking a notebook from his pocket, he wrote down the name of his lover, yes, his lover who was going to prison to save him, in order that he might not forget it. Arthur Snatchfold. He had only heard the name once, and he would never hear it again. (p. 144)

Like that of Romeo and Juliet, the story of Arthur Snatchfold is ideal because it was not able to continue in the wordaday world (compare the ending of Forster's *Maurice*). However, Forster and others found eventually that cross-class relationships were possible, though often awkward. In *We Think the World of You*, an autobiographical novel published by Ackerley in 1960 but set in the immediate postwar period, Frank's association with ex-sailor Johnny leads him into complex jealousies and misunderstandings with Johnny's working-class family. We see how the relationship is tolerated yet excluded, despite Frank's money and authority as an upper-middle-class man (see p. 113). Johnny is imprisoned (for house-breaking) and Frank becomes devoted to his sheepdog, Evie. The dog is situated like Johnny: she is imprisoned and kept away from Frank, who wants to offer her a better life. But with the dog also, the legitimacy, let alone desirability, of Frank's relationship is not acknowledged. Frank is exasperated by his position and tries obsessively to manoeuvre within it; 'Incomprehensible people!', he thinks (p. 103). But gradually he sees that the behaviour of Johnny's family is 'ordinary' enough; from their point of view he must have seemed 'a tiresome and troublesome fellow' (pp. 131–2). He even comes to consider Johnny's eventual suggestion, 'What you've never 'ad you never miss' (p. 145); perhaps little is gained by trying to give a dog or a person a 'better' life-style. The solution is that Frank should have the dog, for she affords an almost legitimate relationship – only almost, for she snaps at and harasses other people. Evie jealously excludes others, as Frank has been excluded, and manifests all the devotion, excitement and intensity that he has failed to find among lower-class men – implicated, as they are, in the 'ordinary' lower-class family world.

How intricate and contradictory the web of class feelings could become is illustrated in Denton Welch's *Journals*. He meets a ' "superior"-voiced soldier' and is perplexed: 'I thought, I like you, yet I hate you being almost educated. I cannot admire you as I would if you were a clod. This is a terribly muddled state to be in. It shows that I can never be true friends with anyone except distant women – far away. I wish for communion with the inarticulate and can only fray and fritter with the quick' (p. 11; also pp. 40–2). Though Welch is 'muddled', he sees clearly how Bloomsbury notions of personal relationships fall into confusion when sexual desire crosses class boundaries.

The homosexual, leisure-class, literary intellectual was, therefore, in a strikingly contradictory position. He was *inviting in* the working class that was believed to be about to overwhelm civilized standards. He was a Trojan horse within the citadel of cultural power, smuggling in the class enemy.

The disruptiveness of the lower-class young man is explicit in Rosamond Lehmann's *The Echoing Grove* (1953). The main characters are two sisters. Madeleine has an unsatisfactory marriage; Dinah lives unconventionally and is on the political left, and consequently comes across Rob; he moves also among leisure-class homosexuals. Dinah says:

> They got their rotten rotting teeth in him. *They've* got the belts and ties and rings and bracelet watches. And all the words. *Avant garde* passwords. And the freedom of the hunting grounds. All the happy hunting grounds mapped out, combed over. Barracks, pubs, ports, tube stations, public lavatories. How could he possibly be missed! The classiest piece of goods on the market. Bought and paid for. (p. 179)

The novel does not notice that such exclusiveness as the homosexual subculture possesses has actually been created by its exclusion from ordinary society. As Wildeblood puts it, 'One of the charges often levelled against homosexuals is that they tend to form a compact and exclusive group. They can hardly be expected to do anything else, since they are legally excluded from the rest of the community' (p. 4).

Rob contaminates and threatens the leisure class with his lifestyle:

> He'd been kicked out of – someone's flat, for stealing; and then the police had got onto him and picked him up; and some wealthy nobleman or other he'd expected would rally to him and bail him out had refused to help him. . . . He

was going to blow the gaff on the lot of them, give 'em the works – blackmail – God knows what. (p. 182)

The horror of exposure and scandal enters with Rob. But the threat is also more specific. He is lower-class, masculine, criminal and not interested in or suitable for personal relationships. Dinah exclaims:

> An enemy of society. *Done time!* – actually done time – for housebreaking! *Actually actively* anti-bourgeois. A real moronic proletarian highbrow. . . . he looks romantic, but he isn't – not he! Would you believe it? – he's not interested in personal relationships! (p. 179)

'Housebreaking' captures the essence: Rob (the robber) enters and breaks up the world of the propertied class, trampling on the ethos of sensitive personal relationships. At least Leonard Bast respected their culture, and was weak. Rob is urgently desired, strong and determined, and opposed in principle to the fragile Bloomsbury ethos. He seems to represent the coming state of affairs: the whole fear about the workers' state is loaded onto him. Madeleine is upset even by his name: 'She hesitated over the semi-anonymous truncated name, feeling it stick in her throat, become a symbol for all she feared and hated – the levelling de-individualising new order' (p. 184). And Rob alone, in a novel committed to 'people, human relationships, personal feelings' (p. 272), is not presented at some point through his own thoughts and feelings. The anonymity and de-individualizing, we might say, are conferred by the novel, which cannot envisage or allow the subjectivity of Rob. He functions as vague, socio-political threat, not as a person.

Yet Rob does not take over, he is killed in the war. The man of the future is Jocelyn, Madeleine's lover: 'Humble background, scholarships all along . . . ruthless, sharp-witted orphan type . . . on the up and up.' Like Rob, Jocelyn is made to lack any sense of honour – it's the 'end of the code of the Decent Fellow' (p. 228). Behind this lies an awareness, by 1950, that the working class was not taking over, that other kinds of class disturbance are possible.

Towards the end, the novel takes a new turn. The rather ineffectual Ricky admits that he is strangely drawn to Rob: 'I'm not a pansy . . . never felt a touch of queerness since I left school – well, Oxford to be strictly truthful – but my sensations about him were very peculiar' (p. 246). Dinah believes 'a new gender may be evolving – psychically new – a sort of hybrid. Or else it's just beginning to be uncovered how much woman there is in man and vice versa.' If we can come to terms with this hybrid sexuality we may reduce the self-destructiveness that prevents people from sustaining 'a human relationship' (p. 292). This issue, Dinah adds, is 'much more fundamental than the obvious social economic one'. What this amounts to, in effect, is the Bloomsbury ethos with which we began, but proposed now in a framework that seems safer because it fantasizes the elimination of the differences that have disturbed that ethos – the social, the economic, the homosexual – including, no doubt, Corrigan, the stereotypically treacherous lesbian (pp. 122–4); and the dreadful Rob.

In his autobiographical *Orchid Trilogy* (1948–50) Jocelyn Brooke presents himself as a writer in the Bloomsbury tradition (p. 349) with some private means, and as 'effeminate': 'I was timid, a coward at games, terrified of the aggressively masculine, totemistic life of the boys at school; yet I secretly desired, above all things, to be like other people' (p. 21). Lowerclass men, and especially soldiers, are attractive, strange and – much more than for Denton Welch – threatening:

> In shorts and singlets, they plodded heavily across the rough fields, their naked limbs stained purple by the shrewd east wind, their red faces set in an expression of dull, stoic endurance. They seemed some curious variant of the human species. . . . Remote and alien, they passed me by without greeting, no flicker of human emotion betraying itself in their coarse, meaty faces. Watching them, I felt a stranger from another world: barred implacably from any friendly contact with these denizens of an alien country. (p. 249; see also pp. 181, 184, 258)

These members of the majority class are presented as a curious variant of humanity, 'Remote and alien'; yet Brooke feels himself to be 'a stranger from another world'. Each party in turn is the outsider, but despite the strangeness ascribed to the soldiers it must finally be Brooke: the literary intellectual cannot locate a coherent place in the dominant class and cultural paradigm because of his homosexuality. Perhaps once it was otherwise; Brooke associates soldiers, repeatedly, with a distant bugle call, representing a lost, mythic condition.

Other leisure-class homosexuals invited lower-class males into their houses or shared the neutral ground of homosexual haunts with them, but Brooke went to be with soldiers in the army.

I felt, in fact, about the Army, much as I had felt, in early adolescence, about sex: it was something difficult, rather disgusting and ultimately inevitable, which I dreaded yet longed to experience. Soldiers, too, were linked in some way with my childhood-heroes – the people I feared and secretly adored. (pp. 253–4)

After the war Brooke joined up again. He disparages writing and the literary world in comparison with army life. 'To spend hours, like Flaubert, polishing a phrase, was for me an impossibility; I would rather polish a pair of boots' (p. 422; also pp. 301–2, 315). The oppositions that define and protect the literary intellectual fall into confusion before the pressure of homosexual desire. Nevertheless, the contradiction remains. Brooke cannot change his identity, but he calls to account the coherence of the categories that customarily delimit it. Twice in the *Trilogy* he offers a typical lament of the leisured elite: 'We'll probably all be directed into coal-mines' (pp. 302, 315). But elsewhere coal-miners are among the workers he fears and desires (pp. 184–5), so perhaps he wouldn't have been unhappy in the mines after all.

The more familiar lower-class intrusion is invited by an Ambrose Silk-like friend of Brooke called Pussy; he is 'a perfect period-piece – a man of the nineties who had managed to preserve the authentic aroma of that (to me) still fascinating decade' (p. 371). Pussy takes up with a young Cockney soldier, Bert, buys him out of the army and engages him as 'a kind of chauffeur-valet-companion' (p. 375). Though likeable (to Brooke at least), Bert is also dangerous – a gigolo and blackmailer, liable to become obstreperous and violent. He uses his position to rise in society: to Pussy's chagrin, he accepts the protection of his sister, becomes a wireless mechanic, plays the Fitzrovian literary-homosexual pubs (p. 389), marries the sister and becomes an officer in the air force. The intruder takes over.

Tracing the sequence of Bert's coming to power, Brooke thinks of it as exemplifying the development of the state. He sees that it represents not lower-class rule, but new scope for social mobility:

It wasn't surprising I hadn't recognised him – even his accent had changed beyond belief; it was what might be called (for want of a better name) techno-cratic – the accent of the future: a hybrid affair in which the native intonation – Cockney, in this case – is overlaid with a quasi-'Oxford' blah-blah tempered by an American twang. . . . People like him, I thought, were the ones who mattered nowadays; Bert and his kind were almost a historical necessity. The fortunes of all of us lay in their hands: tough guys, clever with gadgets, with nice little places near Uxbridge – the technocracy of the future. (pp. 414–5)

It is to this kind of man that the leisure class has lost ground; the significant intruder was not the proletarian but the plausible technocrat. The trilogy concludes with Brooke's recognition that he has willed the destruction of his own class. Parting from Bert, he is overcome with laughter. 'The whole of my past, the whole, carefully built-up structure of my life and personality, had collapsed like a card-house', Brooke writes; yet 'I realised that, in my heart of hearts, I had always wanted the Moor [he means the barbarian] to triumph' (p. 437).

Treachery and After

The novels I have been discussing belong to the 1940s, to that point where the bourgeois world was in place alongside the social changes that were to destroy it. That was an old world dying; Angus Wilson's *Hemlock and After* (1952) launches us into the postwar world, struggling to be born.

Bernard's attempt to harmonize literature and the state (described above, p. 51) founders on his homosexuality. While he is discreet it's all right, but an 'unnecessary crossing and dotting of t's and i's' by the disreputable gatecrashers he has attracted (the Trojan horse again) almost destroys Vardon Hall (p. 149). *Hemlock and After* presents an accelerating alternation and eventual collision between the different worlds inhabited by Bernard, implying once more the difficulty of sustaining a coherent social identiy once the catalyst of homosexuality is admitted. Hence Freudian slips like 'One can pay too dearly for what one picks up in the Charing Cross Road' (p. 153): disparate cultures converge provocatively. Challenged by his daughter, Bernard offers an explanation in terms of social change: 'Any attempt to merge two quite different social patterns is bound to have some embarrassing moments' (p. 57). This is the optimistic interpretation, entertaining the possibility of greater social harmony in the postwar world.

However, a pessimistic interpretation is gaining upon Bernard: he has a 'growing apprehension of evil' (p. 13), and links aspects of the homo-sexual scene with it. At the party of Evelyn, an old-style hostess, are two groups: at one end of the room, survivors from the 1920s, sustaining an 'intricate web of personal values', and at the other end young homosexual men depending 'upon their wits and their social success to maintain themselves' (p. 102). The room is split between Bloomsbury and the intruders. Bernard moves between the two, finding special interest in this 'borderland between respectability and *loucherie* during his present pre-occupation with the nature of evil. He found in these young adventurers a state of moral anaemia' (p. 102). Here Wilson offers his own diagnosis of the current danger to civilization: it is not the working class, or the state, or a technocracy, but an amoral obsession with personal advancement. The shared social purpose that welfare-capitalism proposed to sustain beyond the war years is being undermined by petty corruption; the old leisure class is being displaced by 'spivs'. At Evelyn's party, 'with each year the "queer", more *louche*, more cosmopolitan elements drove out, like the tough tree rats whose grace disguises them as grey squirrels, the older, more effete, more established, more indigenous, fauna' (p. 103).

By now perhaps we should not be surprised, but the question offers itself: why should homosexuals represent this threat to the social order? Were there not heterosexual spivs? Looking again, the idea that Evelyn's party is divided between disreputable homosexuals and respectable heterosexuals doesn't hold up. It is lamented that the respectable group has long been disintegrating – 'Harry Norton a drunkard, Alice Lowndes always running after bruisers, poor old Janie shut up in her flat with her dark glasses, and Tim Rourke hanging around public lavatories' (p. 99). And there is Bernard himself. Wilson proposes the two groups as distinct because he is reaching for the customary pattern: lower-class homosexuals figure social disintegration, and specially among literary intellectuals. But the two ends of the room were already linked, and Bernard moving between them represents this. The 'older, more effete, more established' guests brought the 'young adventurers' with them, even as it is Bernard that draws the disturbance to Vardon Hall.

Paradoxically, Wilson works quite hard elsewhere in *Hemlock and After* to prevent the equation: homosexuality = 'evil'. The young men who figure in Bernard's life, Terence and Eric, and especially the latter, are treated sympthetically and shown to have gained morally during the action of the book and to have positive prospects at the end. They consti-tute a distinct revision of Leonard Bast. To represent complete corruption Wilson provides a group of Dickensian grotesques, centring upon the child-procuress Mrs Curry; eventually Bernard is prepared to invoke the law against them (p. 217). This brings us back to homosexuality, of course: ' "Sides of the law," Bernard said bitterly, "are hardly an issue on which *I* can take up a strong position" ' (p. 214).

Homosexuality is the ground upon which Bernard and Wilson focus the question of 'evil' and the law. Witnessing the arrest of a young man for 'importuning', Bernard is horrified by the 'sadistic excitement' he experiences when the young man is held pinioned before him by a policeman. Does the problem derive, though, from the law or from Bernard? – from the power structure that has set up this scene, or from an inner 'evil'? Wilson arranges the story so as to exonerate the law and incriminate Bernard: the young man has been complained of by a member of the public; he is not, as was witnessed by Wildeblood (p. 42) and experienced by Driberg (pp. 147–8), the victim of a police *agent provocateur*. And while Bernard experiences a 'hunter's thrill', the detective's attitude is one of 'somewhat officious but routine duty'. Literary intellectuals were accustomed to setting their moral sensitivity against the impersonal state but, the incident implies, in the last resort we must defer to the state's 'proper authority' (p. 109).

In a way, this is a courageous conclusion. But what puts the profoundest question to *Hemlock and After* is a sense that it is masochistic and, thereby, guiltily implicated in its own analysis. The sadism discovered by Bernard correlates with the beautifully witty but terribly spiteful observation of speech and behaviour throughout the book: this too is sadistic. It is also masochistic, for no opportunity is missed to reproduce virtually every homophobic remark made to that date. Similarly, the novel presents a series of conversations in which the homosexual is an embarrassment to a sympathetic character. The 'evil' of *Hemlock and After* is self-hatred. Despite the shrewdness with which Wilson is able to assess the forces producing the prevailing roles and oppression of homosexuals, the novel picks at a guilty spot. Stronger than its evocation of 'evil', or its implication that the law should be changed, is its illustration that oppression is bad for you.

Hemlock and After is a postwar book in the sense that it is little concerned with the communism of the 1930s (though Bernard's sister recalls that) and quite a lot with how communism was presented in the Cold War. As the t's are crossed and the i's are dotted in respect of Bernard's sexuality, he is taken to be a likely communist (pp. 149, 191). He thinks, of the local people, they 'were ready at the slightest crisis to label him, or any other person whom they associated, however vaguely, with their anxieties, as Communist' (p. 25).

Until the Cold War, homosexuality was a submerged discourse, only implicitly subversive of certain institutions. Once it could be linked, in a paranoid way, with communism, it could be invoked to reinforce the Cold War and stigmatized as treachery against the Western Alliance. The Labour Government in England initiated a purge of communists from the Civil Service (Hyde, p. 239). In the United States homosexuals and communists were hunted out of public life (Weeks, pp. 159–60). There particularly, homosexuality was attributed, by the political right, to artists and intellectuals because they were thought likely to be progressive. Gilbert Seldes, in his book *The Great Audience* (1951), described intellectuals, with their tendency towards radical commitment, as historically out of touch with US people; so cultural life, Seldes believed, became women's business and the artist became 'dandified'. In 1953 Adlai Stevenson's liberal presidential candidature was smeared as associated with 'egg-heads', who were said to be 'lacking in virility and resolution', 'fundamentally superficial, over-emotional and feminine in reactions to any problem', and prone to 'a watered-down Marxism' (Aron, p. 230). And, indeed, Stevenson did secretly represent for male homosexuals the first gay presidential candidate (Denneny et al., p. 291).

This nexus of fears was given perfect focus by the disappearance in 1951 of the British diplomats Guy Burgess and Donald Maclean. They belonged to the same cultivated-artistic-leisured world as the literary establishment. Burgess had known Rosamond Lehmann very well for many years; he had worked as a BBC producer in 1936–8 and during the war, and as part of the false trail he had laid before leaving England he asked Spender for Auden's address in Ischia.[6] Everyone was ready to tell their story – mainly to exonerate themselves. Stephen Spender told *The Observer* that he didn't believe the espionage thesis, and Cyril Connolly said the same in the *Sunday Times*. Connolly's views were printed in a pamphlet, *Missing Diplomats*: he revealed nothing about homosexuality, of course, but he hinted at the usual stereotypes, alleging that 'emotional maladjustment was the key to their personalities' (p. 43). Peter Quennell explained, in a preface to *Missing Diplomats*, that Connolly knew Burgess and Maclean – 'living as they did in that section of the London world where literature and politics converge, and where the appetite for ideas is qualified by the thirst for pleasure' (p. 9). He was careful to add that they and Connolly were not close associates.

However, John Lehmann was told by his sister Rosamond Lehmann that she had decided, thinking it over, that Burgess was a Russian agent;

and John Lehmann's friend Humphrey Slater said he had come to believe in recent months that Maclean was an agent. John Lehmann wrote of these suspicions in a letter to Spender, who was in Italy. And Spender gave the letter to attendant *Daily Express* reporters. The letter was reproduced on the front page (16 June 1951), Lehmann and his sisters were harried by journalists, the *Express* was sued and Lehmann's lawyers wrote to Spender. The literary establishment rallied indignantly to Lehmann (Lehmann, *Ample*, pp. 126–32).[7]

What was so upsetting, of course, was the link between communist treachery and homosexuality, and between them and the high-cultural establishment. After all, it was a Bloomsbury nostrum, printed just that year by Forster in *Two Cheers for Democracy*, that one would rather betray the state than one's friend.[8] The entire issue was much too close to home. Maudie Littlehampton and her husband, in Osbert Lancaster's cartoon in the *Daily Express* (19 July 1951), are looking across the room at a posh party, and one of them says: 'Now why on earth, darling, should you think it's either Burgess or Maclean? For all you know it's just as likely to be our host.' Now homosexuals were real subverters of the state and the elite.

A major consequence was a new persecution. For three weeks in summer 1952 the *Sunday Pictorial* ran a series entitled 'Evil Men' ('Most people know there are such things – "pansies" – mincing, effeminate, young men who call themselves queers. But simple, decent folk regard them as freaks and rarities'; Pearce, p. 308). And the authorities, probably at the instigation of the US government, stepped up their persecution.[9] Even the upper classes were not safe. On the contrary, it seems that the police, the Home Office and the Director of Public Prosecutions set out in 1952 to trap Lord Montagu of Beaulieu and his friends in order to prove to the United States that potential subversives in high places were being dealt with. Peter Wildeblood concludes this from the determination with which the case was prosecuted – including the brow-beating of two young airmen and the promise of immunity to them if they implicated others, the forging of evidence, searching without warrants, denying access to solicitors, manipulative extraction of a statement and manifest perjury (Wildeblood, p. 69).

The prosecution counsel made much of the crossing of class barriers: 'It is a feature, is it not, that inverts or perverts seek their love associates in a different walk of life than their own?' In his account of the case Wildeblood wrote proudly of his cross-class relationships:

The homosexual world knows no such boundaries – which is precisely why it is so much hated and feared by many of our political diehards. The real crime of Lord Montagu, for example, in the eyes of some 'Society' people, was that he became acquainted – on no matter what basis – with a man who (to quote the prosecuting counsel) was 'infinitely his social inferior'. (Wildeblood, pp. 77, 26)

The immediate outcome for the accused was periods in prison, but the police case was so unreasonable and so dishonestly conducted that a wave of sympathy was produced among the public, in parliament and in the press, even the popular press. The *Sunday Express* said: 'We have been encouraged to believe [the need for a search warrant] to be the vital difference between a Police State and a democracy. Have we been dcluding ourselves?' (Wildeblood, pp. 110–13, 127) Homosexuality was now subverting customary complacencies more directly than had been expected.

The other outcome was pressure for homosexual law reform, which produced the Wolfenden Report of 1957 and eventually the 1967 Act (which is still in force). Leisure-class homosexuals made relatively little contribution to this change in climate – they had less to gain from reform and, indeed, were probably unable to believe in it. This was both because they had internalized, to a degree, the estimate of themselves that they found in society, and because, relatedly, they were generally conservative and disinclined to welcome innovation. Gay Liberation, when it came, was a product of the 1960s and fiercely egalitarian. Although the cross-class relationships I have discussed were subversive, those involved did not want to change the class system. They shared the anxieties of others of their class; they were subversive despite themselves. The kind of changes thcy wanted, if any, would lead back towards prewar privilege, not forward into equality. As Jeffrey Weeks says in *Coming Out*, the existing law collapsed through its own contradictions rather than through the efforts of well-placed homosexuals (pp. 156–8, 163–4).

Sex and the Movement

The consequences of this inability, by and large, to be straightforward about homosexuality rendered established literary intellectuals vulnerable to attack as effete, hypocritical and snobbish. The sneer at the queer occurs again and again in the writings of the 1950s younger generation. Osborne reaches for the queer joke in *Look Back in Anger* (1956; pp. 35–6); the predatory homosexual is introduced to be rejected by the hero, purportedly in no doubt about his own virility, in John Wain's *Hurry on Down* (1953; p. 112) and John Braine's *Room at the Top* (1957; pp. 222–3). Doris Lessing makes the heroine of *The Golden Notebook* (1962) complain that there are no more 'real' men, just little boys and homosexuals (pp. 395, 470). These rising younger writers were probably in favour of Wolfenden-style reform of the law. But while homosexuals were manifestly oppressed and marginalized in general, in so far as they were associated with the literary establishment they seemed dominant and central. Younger writers, who by and large did not belong to the leisure class, felt justified in putting them down (see chapter 11).

Their mentors were F. R. Leavis and George Orwell. The latter had always been liable to tilt at homosexuals.[10] Leavis, as I have said, was striving to set up English as a university discipline and regarded the traditional person of letters as a cultural and class enemy. His literary preferences are expressed through male-sounding epithets such as healthy, mature, tough and robust. Chris Baldick remarks the stress on 'maturity' and how the Leavises elevated the 'fecund' Lawrence against the 'surprising radical adolescence' of Auden. We perhaps have a coded allusion when, in an article complaining of the 'coterie-power' of Spender's group and Keynes's 'sartorial ostentation and society life', Leavis writes of Keynes's 'recruitment' to Bloomsbury of 'young men of intellect and sensibility'.[11] Fred Inglis, still in the Leavisite line, is slightly too insistent when he describes earnest radicals as '*manly* in some very deep, pure sense' (Inglis, p. 25; his italics).

Anti-effeminacy appears everywhere in Movement writing. John Wain called for a revival of what Donne and Leavis called 'masculine persuasive force' (Morrison, p. 45). Donald Davie, in his poem 'Remembering the Thirties', remarked how that generation of poets had a 'craze/For showing Hector was a mother's boy'; when in retreat from the Movement, Davie admitted how easy it had been to make the 'conclusive sneer' against such as Cocteau and Gide.[12] Robert Conquest, in his introduction to *New Lines*, insisted that he and his colleagues had 'a new and healthy general standpoint', writing, as they did, for 'the whole man' (Conquest, p. xiv). J. D. Scott, in an article promoting the Movement, described the ethos as 'anti-wet; sceptical, robust, ironic'; Leslie Fiedler, with the freedom of a stranger, got to the point: the young British writer 'is able to define himself against the class he replaces: against a blend of homosexual sensibility, upper-class aloofness, liberal politics, and avant-garde literary devices'.[13]

The motif is prominent in Kingsley Amis's *Lucky Jim* (1954), where Dixon fights off provincial complacency in the persons of Professor and Mrs Welch, and effete metropolitan/cosmopolitan culture in the persons of Bertrand and his brother. Thus he wins his way to London and the upper-middle-class Christine. Bertrand, the artist, wants Christine, and is therefore to be presumed not predominantly homosexual. The thought lurks nevertheless: when it comes to a fight Dixon is confident of 'winning any such encounter with an artist' (p. 42), and on the last page of the book Bertrand and his father have 'a look of being Gide and Lytton Strachey'. There is also Welch's other son, referred to at least three times as 'the effeminate writing Michel' (pp. 13, 178, 250), as if this were a set colloca-tion in the manner of Anglo-Saxon verse. He is the absent other of the book in so far as it is about itself – about the possibility of Kingsley Amis writing a successful book, from outside traditional intellectual circles and mores, about his kind of hero and from his point of view. It is Michel and his effeminate writing that have to be displaced. He is made to appear in person only in the penultimate paragraph, at the moment of Dixon's triumph, 'on stage at last just as the curtain was about to ring down'.

It is interesting that Amis is not directly homophobic in *Lucky Jim*. It may be that he feared to be explicit at the date; I prefer to believe that he was genuinely progressive on the subject.[14] In an exciting story set in the army at the end of the war, 'I Spy Strangers' (published in 1962 in *My Enemy's Enemy*), Amis revises the whole received stereotyping of literary intellectuals and homosexuals. Social and political disturbance is envisaged – the phrase 'I Spy Strangers' is the parliamentary cry against intrusion on its dealings – but the mood and the analysis are unlike those of the leisure-class novelists. There is no Ambrose Silk figure and no crudely dangerous working-class young man. Intellectual concerns are evinced by an unpretentious, heterosexual, Amis-like young lieutenant, Archer, who has a university place to return to; and by a lower-class homosexual soldier-technician, Hargreaves, a courageous left-wing socialist with literary interests (p. 81). The latter is in an unselfconscious and apparently uncomplicated relationship with a soldier of his own class, and Archer tries to protect them from the bullying, reactionary major. Amis evidently saw potential for new kinds of relationship, between classes, sexualities and literature, here, at the high point of optimism about the just society that was to follow the war; a soldiers' mock parliament, facilitated by Archer and dominated by Hargreaves, is sitting during the story, passing socialist measures to the annoyance of the major. At that moment, in 1946, they are strong enough to fight off the major, and the fascistic Sergeant Doll plans to emigrate to Africa (p. 101). But the story is written with hindsight, and the major has the last thought: 'Despite everything that Hargreaves and Archer and the rest of them might do, England would muddle through somehow.' Prophetically, the major sees that the egalitarian vision will fail.

The repellent misogyny of much Movement and Angry writing (instances are too many and too obvious to need specifying) was part of the attempt to repudiate the perceived ethos of the literary establishment. Male hostility towards women often goes with hostility towards homosexuality. Geoffrey Gorer pointed out in 1957 that male authors and characters were jumping class in a virtually unprecedented way, and taking with them lower-class assumptions about accent and gender roles. In their culture, Gorer says, 'A light tenor voice, a la-di-da . . . accent, an extended vocabulary, restraint in the use of expletives, all carry the stigma of being cissy or pansy.' Feeling insecure, and marrying or seeking to marry upper-class women as a sign of their success, the upwardly mobile 'feel driven to emphasise their manliness' (Feldman and Gartenberg, pp. 315–9). In effect, the woman is taken as representing the hegemony of an effete upper class, and wooed and abused accordingly. This interpretation was taken further by D. E. Cooper, who saw the real target as 'the effeminate society' (Bogdanor and Skidelsky, pp. 256–67). Neither Gorer nor Cooper mention homosexuality explicitly, though they must have been aware of it; presumably it was unmentionable.

The tables were really turned, and in a way people still find difficult to cope with, in the poetry of Thom Gunn; for he, with new enthusiasm, reintroduces the rough young man. Gunn admired Leavis and was published in *New Lines*, though he was only marginally a Movement poet. His work was perceived as sufficiently masculine, indeed it is sometimes sexist, but more is going on. Stephen Spender had published in *Poems* (1933) an autobiographical piece that shows, quite boldly, the attraction and danger of the lower-class intruder:

> My parents kept me from children who were rough
> Who threw words like stones and who wore torn clothes.
> Their thighs showed through rags. They ran in the street
> And climbed cliffs and stripped by the country streams.

> I feared more than tigers their muscles like iron
> And their jerking hands and their knees tight on my arms.
> I feared the salt coarse pointing of those boys
> Who copied my lisp behind me on the road.

> (p. 23)

Gunn challenges this attitude in his poem 'Lines for a Book':

> I think continually of all the toughs through history
> And thank heaven they lived, continually.
> I praise the overdogs from Alexander
> To those who would not play with Stephen Spender.

> (*Sense*, p. 30)

Gunn's poem was admired for its tough male attitude, but to leave it there is an evasion. At the end Gunn celebrates

> The athletes lying under tons of dirt
> Or standing gelded so they cannot hurt
> The pale curators and the families
> By calling up disturbing images.

The poem welcomes images that disturb families; overall, it is rather *Greek*. It criticizes not homosexuality, but being wet and wimpish about it (though one should remark that Spender's poem is quite courageous).

From 1945 to 1950 and his arrival in Cambridge, Gunn has said, he 'couldn't yet acknowledge [his] homosexuality' (*Occasions*, p. 173). But by 1954 he was ready to go to the United States to be with his lover; there he experienced San Francisco gay bars and, in Los Angeles, 'the American myth of the motorcyclist' and 'the dirty glamour of a leather bar'. In San Antonio he heard Elvis Presley's songs and saw James Dean's films (*Occasions*, pp. 176–8). These experiences figure in poems in *The Sense of Movement* (1957) – in 'On the Move', 'The Unsettled Motorcyclist's Vision of his Death', 'Elvis Presley' and 'Market at Turk'. The last named presents a leather queen:

> prepared
> for some unique combat in
> boots, jeans, and a curious cap
> whose very peak, jammed forward,
> indicates resolution.

> (p. 32)

In *My Sad Captains* (1961), the gay identification is allowed to reach the 'I' of the poem. The other person in 'The Feel of Hands' is not specified as a woman or a man, but the poem makes more probable sense if it is a man – because of the anonymity, the impersonality, the initiative taken by the other. The first of the two poems printed together and both called 'Modes of Pleasure' (pp. 23–4) presents a gay cruiser, with the 'I' of the poem as onlooker:

> I jump with terror seeing him,
> Dredging the bar with that stiff glare.

But in the second poem the 'I' of the poem is himself seeking a casual liaison. The irony is in the unstated relation between the two: the essential difference between them is only age and degree of desperation.

Gunn's bike boys are typical objects of romantic homoerotic identification. The boy in 'Black Jackets' sees just leather, but the poet allows the syntax to slide, adding more exotic, romantic connotations:

> He saw it as no more than leather
> Which, taut across the shoulders grown to it,
>
> Sent through the dimness of a bar
> As sudden and anonymous hints of light
> As those that shipping give, that are
> Now flickers on the Bay, now lost in sight.
> (*My Sad Captains*, p. 29)

To be sure, it was a Movement strategy to show suspicion of high culture by going self-consciously down-market (see chapter 8). But Gunn is not reflecting ironically on conventional culture, he is trying to identify with bike boys.

Of course, Gunn's poems are about existentialism as well, and critics find it safer to concentrate on that, especially since he has been paired with Ted Hughes as a school author. The motorcyclists 'appear not as individuals but as the anonymous condition of man, embodied in their machinery' (King, p. 84); they 'are representatives of humanity, however flawed, and their collective action has therefore great interest and significance' (Bold, p. 26). The boys in 'On the Move' might, Alan Bold says, 'kick someone's face in', and the unsettled motorcyclist is 'simply a menace on the roads' (pp. 28, 30). The disapproval here is weirdly irrelevant; by taking the poems at the level of social comment, Bold keeps the discussion away from more disturbing topics.

What was wrong with Spender's rough boys, in Gunn's view, was the delicate and distant attitude towards them. The monster whom the fading literary establishment feared and yet admitted as if in a Trojan horse is now desired explicitly as a fantasy aspect of oneself; and Gunn has a number of poems, at this time, about split personality. In 'An Irish Airman Foresees His Death', Yeats glamorizes his hero, a wealthy scion of the Anglo–Irish ascendancy; Gunn replaces such traditional literary admiration for the family of an upper-class patron with 'The Unsettled Motorcyclist's Vision of his Death':

> Across the open countryside,
> Into the walls of rain I ride.
> It beats my cheek, drenches my knees,
> But I am being what I please.
>
> (*Sense*, p. 28)

That lower-class boys, and others, should be what they pleased had been the anxiety of the literary establishment. Gunn liberated them only in fantasy, but it was enough to provoke literary criticism into one of the services it has performed since the time when most of its texts were in Latin: that of rendering writing harmless to school students.

Notes

1 Taylor, E., *Wreath*, p. 87; Lehmann, *Echoing Grove*, p. 184; Thirkell, *Peace*, p. 95. However, I do not assume that these novels are straightforward, unfractured – they couldn't be; see Light.

2 Adorno, *Prisms*, p. 129. Adorno noted, as a prominent aspect of stereotyping in television scripts, 'the extremely popular idea that the artist is not only maladjusted, introverted, and *a priori* somewhat funny; but that he is really an "aesthete", a weakling, and a "sissy". In other words, modern synthetic folklore tends to identify the artist with the homosexual and to respect only the "man of action" as a real, strong man' (Rosenberg and White, p. 476). See also Ritchie, H., p. 231; Lovell, pp. 4, 144; Kermode, *History*, chs. 2, 4. Theatre management in London's West End was in fact dominated by homosexual

men who were prepared to exploit their position: see Darlow and Hodson, pp. 185–7.

3 Marshall, J., pp. 146–53; Worsley, pp. 26, 39–43; Sinfield, 'Why the Arts', 'Who's For Rattigan?'.

4 On guardsmen, see Ackerley, *My Father*, pp. 123–40; also Lehmann, *I Am*, pp. 191–4. On abroad, see Ackerley, *My Father*, p. 134; Worsley, pp. 127–31; Spender, *Thirties*, p. 80; Lehmann, *In a Pagan*; Davidson.

5 Later, in *A Glass of Blessings* (1958), Pym while deploying stereotypes represents prejudice against homosexuals as unloving and a failure of imaginative sympathy.

6 Penrose and Freeman, pp. 199, 214, 193–6, 259–60, 348. See also Green, *Children*, pp. 427–34. Elizabeth Bowen also moved in these circles, but her spy in *The Heat of the Day* was a fascist.

7 In 1956 Spender tried to persuade Goronwy Rees not to court further publicity by telling his story to *The People* newspaper, and in 1960 he helped to discourage Burgess from providing further embarrassment by visiting England to see his sick mother (Penrose and Freeman, pp. 362–7, 389, 393–5).

8 Forster, *Two Cheers*, p. 78; for a comparable sentiment expressed by Keynes and David Garnett, see Lekachman, p. 19.

9 Hyde, pp. 239 and 238–54; Wildeblood, p. 46; Green, *Children*, pp. 435–7.

10 E.g. Orwell, *Essays*, II, pp. 216, 343; III, pp. 18, 188, 192, 285; see Campbell, p. 99. On the influence of Orwell and Leavis, see Wain, *Sprightly*, pp. 174–8; Walter Allen, in Feldman and Gartenberg, p. 286; Hartley, pp. 50–3; Hewison, *In Anger*, pp. 32–48; Green, *Children*, pp. 406–27. And see below, pp. 181–4, 260–1.

11 Baldick, p. 217, and Leavis, *New*, p. 167; Leavis, 'Keynes', pp. 50, 53–5. See Morrison, pp. 31–3, 63–4, 73–4, 93–6, 113–16, 129–31, 206–7.

12 Conquest, p. 70; Davie, *Collected Poems*, p. 73.

13 Scott, *Spectator*, 1 October 1954, pp. 399–400; Fiedler, 'Un-Angry', p. 9. See Green, *Children*, pp. 457–65. David Storey felt that the northern part of his experience was masculine, the southern part feminine (Laing, p. 74).

14 Reactionary aspects of Amis's early writing and his subsequent career should not lead us now to read him as if he had always been right-wing in all respects. The Labour Party is endorsed consistently through into *Take a Girl Like You* (1960), and Amis voted Labour at the 1964 election (Hewison, *Too*, pp. 293–4). Davie refers to Amis in 1959 as wooing the readers of *Tribune* (Davie, *Poet*, p. 72). Morrison (p. 79) thinks the major in 'I Spy Strangers' is 'handled with considerable sympathy', but I think he is petty and spiteful.

6
Freedom and the Cold War

Existentialism and Politics

Anxious, as they were, about the role of literary culture in Britain after the war, Connolly and Spender travelled as soon as they could to Paris, to reassure themselves that their idea of the arts survived there. Connolly, in spring 1945, was exhilarated by what he found, and called his article about it 'Paradise Regained'. He wrote: 'London seemed utterly remote – a grey, sick wilderness on another planet, for in Paris the civilian virtues triumph – personal relations, adult-minded seriousness, aliveness, love of the arts. Literature is enormously important there . . .' (*Ideas*, p. 12).

Spender was deeply stirred by the desolation of much of Europe. But still he found Paris 'the market place of the human spirit, the central world exchange of civilised values' (*European*, p. 109). The mercantile imagery here proposes a link between 'free' literary culture and a 'free' market. Spender goes on, indeed, to acknowledge that the 'spiritual life' of culture 'is dependent on material things, even on a certain amount of corruption' – by which he means a black market. The thought that capitalist freedom is necessary to literature but yet might be corrupt was to worry the literary establishment through the 1950s.

In postwar Paris Spender found a particular challenge to 'the fusion of sensuous with spiritual experience' which he considered the distinctive French contribution to the modern world: it was the demand of Jean-Paul Sartre that literature should be 'engaged' (*European*, p. 111). Connolly, somwhat perplexedly, printed part of Sartre's introductory article from *Les temps modernes* in *Horizon* (*Ideas*, p. 20). Also in 1945, Raymond Mortimer introduced *engagement* to *New Statesman* readers. Through into the 1960s, Sartre's principle of commitment was a crucial intellectual influence in British culture: not because his ideas were followed, but because they were made to constitute the unthinkable other. Sartre could not be ignored – because he was the most significant intellectual currently writing; because he wrote from Paris; and because it could not be denied that he had one answer to the persisting anxiety about the status and roles of intellectuals. All the main texts and novels were rapidly translated.[1]

At the end of a war that had shown the terrible consequences of fascist ideology, that had ended with the use of a weapon of unprecedented power, and that had produced a popular impetus towards social reform, one might have expected political involvement. But, as I showed in chapters 4 and 5, the instinct of literary intellectuals was to defend traditional ground.

In relation to Sartre specifically, two factors made it easy for British intellectuals to misunderstand him. One was the Occupation, the other the French Communist Party. The Occupation, Sartre said, decisively discredited the traditional bourgeois order, through 'three betrayals': the compromise with Hitler at Munich, the capitulation to Germany in 1940, and the Vichy regime. He wrote in *What is Literature?*: 'Harassed, without a future, without guarantees, without justification, the bourgeoisie, which had objectively become the *sick man*, has subjectively entered the phase of the guilty conscience' (p. 185). This rendered the traditional middle-class allegiances of literature both shameful and ineffective – quite a different situation from that obtaining in Britain. Hence the French writer, Sartre held, was driven 'to join the proletariat' (p. 205), and that meant coming to terms with the Communist Party. The French Party, in Sartre's view, no longer represented the interests of the proletariat but sought instead to safeguard the interests of the Soviet Union (pp. 187–90). Nevertheless, it professed a version of Marxism, and about a quarter of the electorate voted Communist (in the elections of 1945 it emerged the largest party). This too was quite unlike the British situation.

Sartre's position is described fairly by Conor Cruise O'Brien:

> Sartre had condemned Stalinist crimes (and had in turn been hysterically denounced by the Stalinist press in France) but he had refused to treat those crimes as being a logical consequence of communist doctrine or of revolutionary experience, or to see either communism or the Soviet bloc as the sole or principal source of evil in the contemporary world. (p. 63)

However, Sartre's attempts to talk with French communists enabled British intellectuals to associate him with Stalinism, so evading the complex and subtle negotiation with Marxism that he was attempting.

Unfortunately Sartre's best essay on the topic, 'Materialism and Revolution', though written in 1946, was not translated into English until 1955. Here Sartre opposes 'materialism' – meaning the extreme theory of economic determinism which Stalin was imposing in the Soviet Union and on the world-wide communist movement. This repudiation of any concept of subjectivity, Sartre believed, left unexplained how a person might achieve political understanding: 'In short, it cannot account for revolutionary class consciousness.' Consciousness of any kind requires subjectivity, and 'in order for reality to be revealed it is necessary for a man to struggle against it.' Sartre argued that this was true for the worker, and also for the bourgeois like himself, whose commitment can be explained only if one admits 'the possibility of *rising above* a situation in order to get a perspective on it' (*Literary*, pp. 220, 231). So far from unthinking allegiance to a party line, with the goal of a state modelled on the Soviet Union, Sartre proposed commitment to the progressive building of socialism. 'It will be what men make it; it is the outcome of the soberness with which the revolutionary envisages his action. He feels responsible not only for the coming of a socialist republic in general, but for the particular character of this socialism as well' (p. 237).

What is exciting, and provocative, about Sartre's position is that he presents it in terms of *freedom*: 'Socialism is merely the means which will allow for the realisation of the reign of freedom' (*Literary*, p. 230). This emphasis reflects, of course, Sartre's wish to reconcile existentialism and socialism, and surely is too voluntaristic. The constraints on freedom, finally, are not metaphysical and they are only in part ideological; they are material. Nonetheless, the concept of 'freedom' afforded a provocative point of intersection with the ideas of Sartre's opponents – both the Stalinists and the western cold warriors.

This was the more so when Sartre asserted that literature too is bound up with freedom – it is 'the work of a total freedom addressing plenary freedoms', manifesting 'the totality of the human condition as a free product of a creative activity' (*What Is*, p. 206). The challenge, here, lies in Sartre's attempt to take seriously the proposition – shared by liberals and Marxist-humanists – that art and literature, potentially at least, are universal and speak to us in our ultimate human fullness and freedom. For the artist cannot address our humanity, Sartre says, while we are divided into oppressed and oppressors: the prevailing class structure deforms writing, causing it to be slanted towards a particular kind of reader. He refuses the middle-class basis of literature, dissident or otherwise (see chapter 4 above). In such conditions, the writer's freedom is only illusory: 'It is not enough to accord the writer freedom to say everything; he must write for a public which has the freedom of changing everything; which means, besides suppression of classes, abolition of all dictatorships, constant renewal of frameworks, and the continuous overthrowing of order once it tends to congeal' (*What Is*, p. 118). Only in such a society could the customary claims for the essential humanity of literature be realized: socialism is the precondition of the artist's free activity.

The present book takes a different line, arguing that literature as we know it is constructed in relation to specific organizations of class, race, sexual orientation and gender. If we were released from those organizations, a culture responsive to our universal humanity might be feasible, but that is hard to envisage. For the time being, Sartre's vision is important for the way it challenges the humanist idea by trying to take it at its word.

Alternative to Sartre's idea of artistic freedom was the belief that the intellectual preserves his or her freedom by avoiding political attachments. Ex-communists turned to autobiography (the confession of past error seemed to announce the integrity of the liberated self) to assert 'the individual' against Stalinist cultural theory. This left no apparent space for Sartre's careful distinctions. In his essay in *The God that Failed* (1949) Spender acknowledged, as he had before, a central contradiction in liberalism: that its economic theory proposes *laissez-faire* freedom of economic exploitation, whereas its social theory posits the equal freedom of all individuals; and that these two theories undermine each other. (Aneurin Bevan put it more sharply: 'Freedom for the worker means freedom from poverty, insecurity and unemployment. Freedom for the Tory means freedom of action to exploit the workers delivered into his hands by these'; *Why*, p. 86). Nevertheless, Spender reasserted the liberal notion of the artist's freedom: 'the artist is simply the most highly developed individual consciousness in a society', and the principal threat to art comes in political regimes that deny artists 'the freedom to express their intuitions' (*God*, p. 270). How this kind of freedom negotiates the contradictory economic and social theories of liberalism is not explained. Moreover, in this view artistic freedom is still limited, for the artist is restricted from dealing with political matters, except at the expense of art: 'the effect of centring art on politics would, in the long run, mean the destruction of art' (p. 269). This formulation exemplifies well the idealist framework I discussed in chapter 3, whereby the idea of art as the opposite of modern economic organization licenses and confirms that organization.

None of Sartre's opponents adequately answered his arguments. Instead they fixed upon Stalinism, or upon their idea of it, obscuring the possibility of intelligent socialist commitment. John Mander summed up in 1961: 'Whatever criticism Sartre might make of Communism in *What is Literature?* (and he ended up by rejecting any direct collaboration with the French Communist Party), Sartre's name acquired a fatal association with that of another would-be legislator of literature, Stalin's henchman Zhdanov.'[2] Mander found that, properly considered, 'commitment' was only what Coleridge, Arnold and Leavis had been urging all along (p. 23).

Literary intellectuals oriented towards the Western Alliance got their opportunity with the split between Sartre and Camus, which became explicit in 1952 over Camus' *L'Homme révolté* (*The Rebel*). In *The Myth of Sisyphus* (1942, trans. 1955), Camus had expounded *absurd freedom*: 'There is no future. Henceforth this is the reason for my inner freedom' (p. 57). Absurd freedom is quietist – it may best be experienced by the slave and the prisoner condemned to death: when 'all is collapse and nothingness' one can 'accept such a universe and draw from it his strength, his refusal to hope, and the unyielding evidence of a life without consolation' (pp. 58–9). In *The Rebel* Camus withdraws from that Stoic extreme and discovers a humanist concept of value: 'Man, by rebelling, imposes in his turn a limit to history and at this limit the promise of a value is born' (p. 216). Now Camus discusses 'freedom' mainly in terms of the individual in a tyrannical political system. He says oppression is endemic in all kinds of modern state, but his great preoccupation is with communism (see pp. 198–202). For instance, he condemns the determining role of 'the rhythm of production' in the modern world and declares that this condition is shared by Marxism and 'bourgeois ideology'; yet almost the entire development of the argument is in terms of the supposed communist state (pp. 185–6). This slippage pervades the book: destruction of freedom is said to be characteristic of the modern state but attention is fixed upon Stalinism – which is taken as the outcome of Marxism and of political activity generally.

Camus' quietism, anti-communism and general hostility to explicit political commitment were very acceptable in the Western Alliance. His work was promoted by intellectuals who supported the US Government, such as Nicola Chiaromonte who, in his article 'Sartre versus Camus, a Political Quarrel' (1952), represented Camus as the independent intellectual and Sartre as possessed by a Stalinist mentality and committed to spreading 'the intellectual confusion by which the Communist Party benefits'. Chiaromonte was director of *Tempo presente*, an Italian magazine covertly subsidized by the US Central Intelligence Agency (O'Brien, pp. 61–2). Time has not abated right-wing preparedness to misrepresent Sartre: Allan Bloom said in 1987, virtually as an aside, that Sartre supported the party line 'almost without fail' (p. 219). Lukacs's comment seems apposite:

> Today it is in the life interests of the imperialist bourgeoisie to annihilate the capability for social-historical orientation among the intelligentsia. Even if a considerable number of the intelligentsia cannot be made into absolute adherents of the imperialist reaction, they should at least be made to wander helplessly about in an incomprehensible world without the ability for orientation in it. (p. 275)

Like Sartre, but again also contrastingly, Camus carries his concept of freedom finally to the writer-artist. The latter is a rebel too: 'The artist's rebellion against reality, which is automatically suspect to the totalitarian revolution, contains the same affirmation as the spontaneous rebellion of the repressed' (*Rebel*, p. 223). Here again, there are two enemies: metaphysical 'reality' and the Stalinist state; other kinds of state disappear from view. Camus envisages two threats to freedom: communism and the 'human condition'. The first renders political action futile and throws the absurdist back upon the capitalist West. The second acknowledges that all is not well there either, but shifts the flaw from the economic and political order to humanity. When considering communism, we must make the political choice of capitalism; when considering capitalism, there is no choice. Amidst this confusion, socialism disappears altogether. Indeed, the rebellion of the artist makes political change unnecessary: 'Art realises, without apparent effort, the reconciliation of the unique with the universal of which Hegel dreamed' (*Rebel*, p. 223). Art achieves the totality which Marxism strives to realize in the world.

The English literary establishment took to Camus. In an introduction Connolly, celebrated *The Outsider* in 1946 as embodying the 'neopaganism' that he looked for in Parisian culture (pp. 5, 10). Introducing *The*

Rebel (trans. 1953), Herbert Read asserted, astonishingly: 'The nature of revolt has changed in our times. It is no longer the revolt of the poor against the rich' (whether this was because there were no more poor or because they had given up wasn't explained). Camus displays our 'metaphysical revolt, the revolt of man against the conditions of life, against creation itself' (pp. 7–8). This is the story many intellectuals of the Western Alliance wished to tell themselves.

A more balanced account was given by Iris Murdoch to BBC Third Programme listeners in March 1950. Her theme is why Sartre's compromise between existentialism and Marxism cannot work: existentialism focuses on the 'point at which our beliefs, our world pictures, our politics, religions, loves and hates are seen to be discontinuous with the selves that may or may not go on affirming them'; whereas Marxism claims to know the world ('Novelist'). Nevertheless, Murdoch is not unsympathetic to what Sartre is trying to do. Her concluding thought is that there is a predicament: the Marxist risks sacrificing critical intelligence, whereas the existentialist is likely to lose purpose and action.

Under the Net, Murdoch's first novel (1954), is set firmly within the French intellectual orbit. Jake is a translator from the French; the book begins with him returning from Paris, and it includes an evocation of left-bank and other notable places. Jake lives existentialism: his whole mode of feeling and action is dispersed and disconnected. Though, he says, he hates the contingent and requires the necessary (p. 24), many of his decisions seem arbitrary and are taken on the spur of the moment, and much of his narrative consists of the remarking of impressions as they strike him. He believes, 'The substance of my life is a private conversation with myself which to turn into a dialogue would be equivalent to self-destruction' (p. 31). Books mentioned as belonging to Jake are Beckett's *Murphy* and a clear model for *Under the Net*, Raymond Queneau's *Pierrot mon ami* (1942) (p. 15). It is all theorized by Jake's friend Hugo, who holds that each event is itself, that no general theories are possible and that describing states of mind falsifies them (pp. 58–61). We may have here the first use of the catch-phrase for absurdist theatre in England: 'So we never really communicate?' (p. 60).

With all this, Murdoch includes the character Lefty Todd, organizer of the New Independent Socialist Party. In discussion with Lefty, Jake admits to sympathy with socialist goals, membership of the Labour Party, and disappointment with 'English socialism' as merely 'welfare capitalism' (p. 99). Lefty has a political role for intellectuals which is precisely

Sartre's: he denies that 'society develops mechanically and ideologies just tag along'; rather, what is needed is 'consciousness' – 'not just to reflect social conditions but to reflect *on* them – within limits, mind you, within limits. That's why you intellectuals are important' (p. 100). Jake and Hugo are ready to act in Lefty's support when he organizes quite large demonstrations, which are broken up by fascists and large numbers of police with horses. Hugo says: 'I think Lefty's ideas are *decent'* (p. 223).

Murdoch was more inclined to the left at this time than most later commentators recognize; it stemmed, perhaps, from her fuller involvement with Parisian intellectual life. She said of herself and those linked with her as Movement writers: 'I don't think we have many tenets in common, except being all left-wing' (O'Connor, p. 54). That was perhaps true, as I have argued, of Kingsley Amis. Even so, Murdoch does not show Lefty to be effective. In fact, the whole dispersed movement of the book – the failure of characters to carry through plans, the tendency of events to work themselves out almost arbitrarily and yet generally in a genial manner – seems to render socialist purpose tangential to the way the world goes. The issues of the book are resolved within a broad human-ist framework. Finally Jake discovers a personal commitment: to work seriously at creative writing. Literature emerges as a value in itself, ratified by the quality of the personal commitment to it as a free activity. Camus' position seems to contain Sartre's.

The choice of a conservative interpretation of existential freedom was repeated in diverse writings of the decade. Auden went back to Kierke-gaard. Thom Gunn's existentialism derived from Sartre (Bold, pp. 26–8) and involved the constructedness of the self as well as immediate sensa-tion (pp. 168–9 below), but not political engagement. In Golding's *Free Fall* (1959) Sammy's membership of the Communist Party is shown to be insincere and pointless, and the good, rational socialism of Nick Shales as inadequate to reality. The moment when a free choice was made, for which Sammy seeks throughout the novel, is located, if anywhere, in the individual conscience, within an allegedly universal human predicament with guilt as the condition of transcendence. Similar attitudes informed the vogue for 'absurdist' theatre, starting with the London production of Beckett's *Waiting for Godot* in 1955. Eugène Ionesco explained his plays as the 'testimony of his anguish' in *The Observer* in 1958: 'No society has been able to abolish human sadness, no political system can deliver us from the pain of living, from our fear of death, our thirst for the absolute.'[3] This may be, but Ionesco's pronouncement tends to render invisible all those ills from which political change *might* deliver us.

In *The Outsider*, a sudden hit with reviewers in 1956, Colin Wilson called on numerous conservative writers and some others to establish a position very like that of *The Rebel*. Wilson and his friends actually thought of carrying forward their ideas of freedom by founding a neofascist political party, based on Wilson's belief that 'effective political power ought to be in the hands of the five per cent minority who were equipped to use it'; they had a meeting with Sir Oswald Mosley.[4] The prevailing trend in conventional party politics was sufficiently right-wing to render such unorthodox moves ineffectual.

The Cold War

In 1947 Sartre asserted: 'All is lost if we want to *choose* between the powers which are preparing for war' – namely the United States and the Soviet Union (*What Is*, p. 217). In *World Within World* (1951) Spender also resisted such a choice (p. 270), and in *The God that Failed* (1949) he declared that neither great power had the solution to the world's problems, and that 'the interests of the very few people in the world who care for the values of freedom must be identified with those of the many who need bread, or freedom will be lost' (p. 272). However, the Cold War made both these positions difficult to hold. Between 1952 and 1956 Sartre moved closer to the Communist Party than he had envisaged, and Spender became, as he later reported, 'largely taken up with anti-Communism' (*Thirties*, p. 122). These moves coincided with a massive further appropriation of the term 'freedom'.

In 1947 the British Government found that it could no longer afford its attempt to impose a military dictatorship upon Greece, so the United States took on the task. On 12 March 1947 the Truman Doctrine was enunciated, extending US imperialist pretensions, which the Monroe Doctrine had proclaimed in respect of Latin America, to the whole world. The leading motif was freedom:

> At the present moment in world history nearly every nation must choose between alternative ways of life. The choice is too often not a free one. . . . I believe that it must be the policy of the United States to support free peoples who are resisting attempted subjugation by armed minorities or by outside pressures.[5]

Truman said in conclusion: 'The free peoples of the world look to us for support in maintaining their freedoms.' So was inaugurated a whole sequence of US military, undercover and ideological interventions. 'Freedom', the term through which Sartre had invoked a classless society, and Spender an independent individual stance, was constituted as the watchword of one side in the cold war. Almost overnight, the rhetoric that had identified Nazism was recycled for a new enemy (and scientists who had worked for the Nazis were co-opted for the new crusade[6]).

To dispute who started the Cold War is to dance to its tune. As each side sought to consolidate its position in central Europe, US pressure enhanced the Soviet Union's sense of insecurity – which was in any case great because the capitalist powers had always been explicitly hostile, because it felt it had borne the brunt of Hitler's aggression, and because it perceived itself as encircled (see Higgins, ch. 1). From this point, the Cold War was built, stage by stage, out of that mutual paranoia that has proved its most enduring feature. Cold-War rhetoric, which formed the intellectual framework for many, seems to derive from the needs of US policy in the late 1940s. President Truman 'reduced a complicated international situation to the crude melodrama of a bad western film with himself in the role of a sharp-shooting sheriff', Hugh Higgins wrote in 1974 (p. 32) – when Ronald Reagan was hardly envisaged as a serious presidential candidate. To be sure, the United States suffered provocations: jostling in Iran and Turkey, the Soviet atomic explosion, Mao's victory in China, and the conviction (possibly rigged) of Alger Hiss for giving classified documents to Soviet agents. But these might have been handled with relative equanimity; after all, the power and prosperity of the United States was without parallel in modern history. How, Richard Freeland asks, 'did the idea take hold that any gain by communist forces, in whatever country, however remote and tiny, was a direct threat to American interests, to be opposed by the full force of American power?' (Freeland, p. 3).

The initial anxiety of the United States, in 1945–6, was not that the Soviets would sweep through Western Europe (which, after all, they were themselves occupying and could defend with the atomic bomb), but that Western Europe would be taken over more or less democratically by indigenous communist movements. In addition to the hopes for a juster society after the war, which produced the leftward swing in Britain, the continental left had resisted Nazism while others had collaborated. In January 1947 Harold Nicolson believed that within five years France, Spain, Italy, Germany and Greece would have 'gone communist', and that the Labour Party would '*probably*' split between its current leadership and the left wing, with the latter gaining ground among the working class because of poverty (1945–1962, p. 89). Marshall Aid was devised in 1947 to tie the European economy in with US capital, remedying what Secretary of State Marshall called 'economic, social and political deterioration' (Heffner, p. 286). It was administered by US businessmen who sought to encourage the buying of US goods and the development of docile trades unions. Even so, the idea of a threat from the Soviet Union was necessary to justify Marshall Aid to US Congress and public opinion. An interpretive framework calculated to command immediate public support was purposefully articulated: the necessary ideological confrontation between a fiendish Soviet scheme of world domination and the forces of 'freedom'. This proved so convincing that it was soon being used against the Truman Administration, which was alleged to be insufficiently vigilant against 'Communism'.[7]

Britain had its own reasons for contributing to Cold-War rhetoric. Its policy, said Lord Ismay (first secretary general of NATO) was to keep the Russians out, the United States in and Germany down. Churchill in 1946 spoke of an 'iron curtain' across Europe and called for 'bases all over the world' to combat the 'growing challenge and peril [of communism] to Christian civilisation' (Hopkins, p. 65). This outlook was shared by Ernest Bevin, Labour Foreign Secretary. The rhetoric took over when the US Government believed its own story and attributed the invasion of South Korea from the North to Soviet aggression.[8] The Labour Government accepted US pressure to increase 'defence' expenditure immediately by nearly 50 per cent, and from January 1951 by a further third over three years. Cold-War ideology was needed to justify this expense, which destroyed British economic reconstruction and threw the Labour Government into confusion. It was needed also to justify Western military practices – for instance, the invasion of North Korea, and the use of napalm: 'I saw a great sea of red, liquid fire beneath us', reported a US Air Force sergeant. 'No one could come out of it alive. Men, women, children, soldiers, and civilians, all were roasted alive' (Montgomery, p. 70). The Korean War caused a new crisis of conscience for Spender, who found that 'progressives who have been striving for years to improve the conditions of the masses, suddenly find themselves forced into opposition to these masses, in the name of democratic freedom' (de Huszar, p. 476). He could get no further than stating this seeming paradox.

The pattern was consolidated by the atomic bomb, since only the two world powers possessed, realistically, the resources to manufacture and deliver such weapons. Moreover, the doctrine of 'deterrence', to which the Western Alliance committed itself in 1950 because it seemed cheaper than conventional weaponry, demands the Cold-War perception of 'the other side' as permanently and constitutionally aggressive. That is why you are deterring them; and once you have thus labelled them, how can you afford to stop? Of course, by displaying this perception, you give the other side good reason to regard you as hostile – after all, you are pointing all those weapons at them. The pattern is self-sustaining, and international and even national politics, throughout the world, are suffused with it.[9] Overall, the world has been arranged to the advantage of a small proportion of the inhabitants of two power blocs, wasting vast amounts of human and natural resources in the midst of widespread hunger, poverty and oppression.

Cold-War ideology makes attempts at domestic political change appear at best misguided, probably complicit with alleged Soviet aggression; and it seems to justify all manner of interference around the world. Bertrand Russell observed:

> The elimination of dissent was achieved by identifying dissent in the popular mind with support of the 'enemy', the 'devil', the inconceivably wicked Russians. The nice thing about this was that it also became impossible to question the power-struggle itself. . . . the struggle for power with Soviet Russia has enabled American politicians to sanctify every oppressive act in the name of national security. . . . The sole criterion for support [of tyrannical regimes] has been subservience to American military needs and willingness to allow the resources and peoples of the respective countries to be exploited by American industry. (*America*, p. 359)

Russell published these words in 1963; Noam Chomsky said virtually the same in 1969 (Chomsky, pp. 178–235); as I write we have Nicaragua and 'Irangate'. At the height of the anti-communist witch-hunt, nothing was too ridiculous. The respected (ex-Trotskyite) political commentator James Burnham wrote, of Soviet infiltration of the United States:

> At the centre, checking and supervising every activity, are thousands of NKVD agents. There are then thousands of other agents, of the military intelligence, and of the various special commissions and bureaux of the Soviet state and the international party. . . . From the smallest sports clubs to the highest depart-

ments of government, from great trade unions to neighbourhood debating societies, from the established political parties to minute farm co-operatives . . . everywhere communist influence is actively penetrating.[10]

Through into the late 1950s dissident US artists, including Lillian Hellman, Paul Robeson, Charles Chaplin, Arthur Miller and Pete Seeger, were called before the House UnAmerican Activities Committee, and some were blacklisted, refused passports, sent to prison (Lewis, P., *Fifties*, pp. 83–5). In Britain the effect was much slighter, though it was still serious (p. 76 below; Hewison, *In Anger*, pp. 21–7). Left-wing thought and activity is still never safe from the accusation of Stalinism and treachery.

Cold War paranoia permeates and confuses C. P. Snow's novel about British scientists working to develop an atomic bomb, *The New Men* (1954). The novel and its narrator, Lewis Eliot, strive to maintain the liberal principle of fairness to all viewpoints, but the scientists experience three crises, and they lead in irreconcilable directions. The first crisis is the US use of the bomb on Hiroshima and Nagasaki, which appals most of those working to manufacture it. It is remarked that notifying the Japanese of the bomb might have been sufficient, that the Japanese were suing for surrender anyway, that it could have been dropped on unpopulated territory, that the second bomb can only have been for the purpose of comparing results (pp. 57, 149–50, 154). The danger of irresponsible power in the hands of Britain's main ally is plain, and it disrupts the careers and personal relationships of the principal characters. (The horrific triviality with which the decision to bomb Hiroshima and Nagasaki was taken has now been researched: Truman's main goal was to boost his confidence and defeat Japan 'before Russia comes in'.)[11]

The second crisis of the novel is the growing awareness that someone in the British team is passing information about the bomb to the Soviet Union. Despite the danger of US power revealed in the first crisis, the idea of balancing it up by helping the Soviets to defend themselves is hardly mentioned in relation to this crisis. Sawbridge, the spy, does not offer such a defence of his actions, though it would be his best argument (the main historical British atom spies, Alan Nunn May and Klaus Fuchs, said they wanted to help the Soviet Union gain parity with the United States). Sawbridge is denied this argument; instead he is presented as a maimed personality, and as evincing unreasonable class animus (p. 101). Although Snow indicates the dangers of US power, he cannot challenge the Cold-War thought that superiority over the Soviets must be maintained at any price.

Those two crises are informed and disturbed by third, a crisis of liberal humanism. Through the novel runs the anxiety that 'events may get too big for men'. This anxiety undermines the pleasant idea of some characters (forgetful of the record of the empire) that the British establishment might contribute a moral awareness that would retrieve the ethical legitimacy of the Western Alliance after Hiroshima (e.g. p. 157). But Lewis Eliot is reminded that he is 'living in a power equilibrium' with no place for 'the relics of liberal humanism' (p. 228), and his conscience fails to work for his colleagues and even for himself. In the final pages he is suddenly made to accept that even his concern for his brother has been selfish. Nevertheless, this acceptance is interpreted as validating a base-line concern with 'human relations', and so a relatively positive conclusion is managed.

Probably Snow means the whole texture of the novel to reinforce this final emphasis – the notion that a humanism endures in English middle-class culture at a fundamental level of personal interaction; and all the more for its persistence despite the failure of its explicit justification. But in its inability to achieve a coherent representation of its three crises, *The New Men* may be taken to reveal something more damaging, namely a servile adoption of the US interpretation of the Cold War and a consequent collapse of any serious political ethics. In this light, the civilized anxieties of the characters appear as the maunderings of a superseded power elite that has lost confidence in itself. Snow probably does not wish us to see his own role as writer in the character Hankins, a professional literary man who secures his career partly by getting in quickly with an article denouncing the passing of atomic secrets to the Soviets (p. 17). But Snow only arrives at the same situation by a more circuitous route.

By 1960 there was a relative 'thaw' between East and West, a peace movement, and a vivid new phase of left-wing thought and activity in Britain (see chapter 11). Also, the arms race was causing widespread anxiety – it is often overlooked that it was not Sartre, Russell or Marcuse who warned of the 'military-industrial complex', but President Eisenhower on the point of leaving office. However, right-wing stories are even more urgent when they are less plausible, and Constantine Fitzgibbon's novel *When the Kissing Had to Stop* (1960) responded to such a moment. It is set in the late 1960s, the peace movement has gained popular support, and the Labour Party is elected with many members committed to freeing

Britain from US bases. The US Government is represented as respecting the wishes of the British people in this (despite US intervention, to that date, in Greece, Iran, Lebanon, Dominica, and Guatemala). Members of the English establishment also behave very decently. But the Labour Party is led by men who are weak, self-interested and complicit with the Soviet Union; and the Soviet leadership is reimposing Stalinist rule after an interlude of liberalism, and plotting to occupy Britain. That is what happens if you drop your Cold-War guard.

One aspect of Fitzgibbon's scenario is at first surprising: he makes the police repressive and brutal *before* the Labour/Soviet takeover ('the police were very odd these days'; p. 11). As in Anthony Burgess's *A Clockwork Orange*, liberal democracy is shown as disintegrating out of its own weakness and inability to cope with the modern world. This breakdown precedes and facilitates the introduction of totalitarianism. So the answer is not just watchfulness against the Soviet Union and the left, but stronger political and social discipline. Both books seem to endorse the view of one character in *When the Kissing Had to Stop*, that the problem derives from national 'loss of will' (p. 200). So guarding against repression leads straight to the idea that a bit of repression would be a good idea anyway, since the Western Alliance cannot at the moment permit all the 'freedoms' for which it is renowned.

The Myth of *1984*

When the Kissing Had to Stop was admired by the *Daily Mail* because it 'relegates Orwell's *1984* and Huxley's *Brave New World* to the nursery' (an odd thing to be pleased about). *1984* anticipates well how dividing the world into superstates and maintaining reports of war or likely war between them helps to legitimate repressive regimes. Despite this, the novel was incorporated into Cold-War ideology. Kingsley Amis, in his pamphlet 'Socialism and the Intellectuals' (1957), placed a good part of the 'blame' for the 'present political apathy of the intelligentsia' upon Orwell, who had become 'a right-wing propagandist by negation, or at any rate a supremely powerful – though unconscious – advocate of political quietism'.[12] Whatever Orwell believed he was doing, he contributed to the Cold War one of its most potent myths.

A recurrent question about *1984* concerns the situation to which it alludes.[13] There are three possible frames of reference. First, it might refer to a development of socialism in England, with wartime restrictions on liberty continued by the Labour Government. This would amount to disillusionment with the possibility of humane, British socialism. Evidence for this view includes the manifestly English setting of the book, the allusion in the title to 1948 (backwards), and the description of Newspeak as 'devised to meet the ideological needs of Ingsoc, or English Socialism' (p. 241). As against such a reading, we should note Orwell's denial: 'My recent novel is NOT intended as an attack on Socialism or the British Labour Party (of which I am a supporter)' (*Essays*, IV, pp. 564, 566). A second frame of reference calls up the situation in the Soviet Union; in effect, this would constitute a warning against communist revolution and any relaxing of Cold-War suspicions. Evidence for this view includes the cult of personality around both Stalin and Big Brother, the intricate and vicious repression of dissent, and the similarity between the roles and ideas of Trotsky and Goldstein. A third frame of reference for the *1984* society is as a development of international corporatist capitalism. James Burnham in *The Managerial Revolution* (1942), upon which Orwell was drawing, had shown totalitarianism developing not from Soviet Communism, but from corporatist capitalism. Orwell's Britain has become Airstrip One in Oceania, a superpower based on the United States.

In my view it is not possible to resolve *1984* into one of these three readings, and so to attribute any precise political analysis to Orwell. That makes interesting reading now, but it facilitated the recruitment of the book to the Cold-War story. The danger of international corporatist capitalism disappeared from sight, leaving English or Soviet socialism as the obvious threats, and the simultaneous, undifferentiated presence of the latter two allowed it to seem that somehow England under a Labour government was already almost the same as Stalinism. Christopher Hollis declared in 1956: 'It was the deterioration of the English socialist party – in the name of resistance to totalitarianism taking upon itself an increasingly totalitarian nature – which he feared' (Hollis, p. 197). John Mander in 1961 was only repeating received wisdom when he spoke of 'the implicitly anti-Socialist *1984*', asserting, 'there is no escaping the fact that Ingsoc is a derivative of English Socialism' (*Writer*, pp. 72, 99).

Orwell's other writings allow no such easy collusion with Cold-War mythology. Though he is specially alert to Stalinism, he also observes repressive tendencies in the West. After all, his experience of cruelty, corruption and repression began in English private schools, and was enhanced in the British Empire ('You are not free to think for yourself. Your opinion on every subject of any conceivable importance is dictated for you by the pukka sahibs' code.')[14] Much of the impetus for *1984* came from the Teheran Conference, at which Stalin, Churchill and Roosevelt arranged to divide up the world (*Essays*, IV, p. 520). Orwell was even-handed in his condemnation of the initial consequences – he held that the Russian occupation of Poland was comparable with the British imposition of a right-wing government upon the Greek people, and with the continuing British occupation of India (*Essays*, III, pp. 349, 369; IV, p. 49). He specified the United States, along with Stalinist Russia, European imperialism and the Catholic Church, as likely to resist socialism in Europe (IV, pp. 426–8). And he criticized suppressions of thought in the West – 'When one looks at the all-prevailing schizophrenia of democratic societies, the lies that have to be told for vote catching purposes, the silence about major issues, the distortions of the press, it is tempting to believe that in totalitarian countries there is less humbug, more facing of the facts' (IV, p. 153).

Even more significantly, Orwell complained that the Labour Government was insufficiently socialist. He had looked forward to 'approximate equality of incomes . . . political democracy, and abolition of all hereditary privilege, especially in education' (II, p. 101); that was the price he thought would have to be paid for the co-operation of the people after the war (see chapter 2 above). He wrote of the Beveridge Report and welfare state as 'a capitalist bribe' (III, p. 29), and welcomed austerity in so far as it reduced class privilege and produced 'a democratising effect' (III, p. 111). He complained that the Labour Government had made no moves against the House of Lords, or towards disestablishing the Church or democratizing education; and saw danger in the failure to replace Tory ambassadors, service chiefs, senior officials, police chiefs, Special Branch and Military Intelligence officers (IV, pp. 58, 220–1; often such officials change with the administration in the United States, but in Britain the idea persists that they are 'above' politics).

In fact *1984* hardly derives from the Cold War at all, or even from Britain under the Labour Government. It was devised, Orwell said, in 1943 (IV, p. 507). Orwell had been obsessively anti-Stalinist since the Spanish Civil War, and he remained almost entirely impervious to the spirit of friendship towards the Soviet Union that prevailed during the war against Nazi Germany (*Animal Farm* was rejected by three publishers – Faber, Cape and Gollancz – because it was hostile to Stalin). Orwell had his anti-Stalinist story ready and virtually written by the time the Cold War began.

Orwell had a second preoccupation, with the supposed treachery of the English 'Russophile' intelligentsia. He offered as partial explanation of his purpose in *1984* his belief that 'totalitarian ideas have taken root in the minds of intellectuals' (IV, p. 564). So O'Brien in *1984*, like the pigs in *Animal Farm*, is an intellectual. Orwell believed that modern intellectuals 'look towards the USSR and see in it, or think they see, a system which eliminates the upper class, keeps the working class in its place, and hands unlimited power to people very similar to themselves' (IV, p. 212). This seems rather unkind to people like Spender and Orwell himself – who protested repeatedly that horror at poverty made them sympathetic to communism.[15] Of course, British intellectuals by the time when *1984* was published were by no means attached to Stalinism – though they tended to be anti-democratic (see Chapters 4 and 5). In this respect also, Orwell was replaying the scenario of the 1930s rather than attending to the social configuration around him.

Finally, because of its imprecision about the historical and political circumstances to which it alludes, *1984* may be read as a myth in the sense elaborated by Barthes:

> It abolishes the complexity of human acts, it gives them the simplicity of essences, it does away with all dialectics, with any going back beyond what is immediately visible, it organises a world which is without contradictions because it is without depth, a world open and wallowing in the evident, it establishes a blissful clarity: things appear to mean something by themselves. (p. 143)

The less specific (the weaker the political grounding), the more 'universal'. But the universal has political implications: it opposes political activity by making the present situation appear ineluctable; it produces a myth of 'the human condition'. Isaac Deutscher saw this in *1984*: 'The party is not a social body actuated by any interest or purpose. It is a phantom-like emanation of all that is foul in human nature. It is the metaphysical, mad and triumphant, Ghost of Evil' (Deutscher, p. 49). And, as Deutscher also observed, that suits Cold-War ideology (p. 194). US Secretary of State John Foster Dulles said he knew he was fighting 'absolute evil' (Williams, F., p. 344). Actually, it is improbable that Stalinist Russia ever was such a monolithic system; J. Arch Getty finds the decision-making at the time of the purges to have been mostly *ad hoc* and incoherent (pp. 1–3). There was no fiendish master-plan, no infallible organization. Saying this, my intent is not to understate the repression of the Soviet State under Stalin (on the purges of 1933–9, see Snow, *Variety*, p. 201), but to question the myth of a monolithic system beyond contradiction and hence change.

In the writing, Orwell has difficulty making the *1984* state mythically irresistible. Why should not the proles resist? Why should only Winston see through it all? How could such a degree of surveillance be maintained? In other contexts Orwell doubted that totalitarian systems could endure. He held that 'the crimes and follies of the Nazi regime *must* lead by one route or another to disaster', and that 'the Russian regime will either democratise itself, or it will perish' (*Essays*, IV, p. 214). He argued that systems of intellectual control must always be leaky (see p. 35 above). In fact, Orwell himself said the effectiveness of the Stalinist state was a 'myth' (IV, pp. 443, 457–8). But his counter-myth, in the process of exposing the repressiveness, helped to exaggerate the effectiveness. In the 1950s it was marvellous NATO Newspeak.

The Free World and Free Literature

As a concluding flourish to an account of literary criticism between 1945 and 1965, C. B. Cox and A. E. Dyson proclaim that books like *1984* 'remind us of societies, such as Russia, where great literature cannot be freely read and discussed' (Cox and Dyson, III, p. 462). The myths of free literary endeavour and the Free World help to generate each other. The writer is envisaged as a free mind, striking out beyond and above the material affairs, and hence unconstrained by history and the social order; and the reader is envisaged as similarly free. Literature is most itself in the Free World, both because of the shared attachment to freedom, and because the free activity of literature will eschew political commitment. The latter is not necessary in the Free World, because there is little to be political about; however, by its very being, literature manifests its opposition to communism. R. A. Butler, Chancellor of the Exchequer, 'reminded' the P.E.N. Congress in 1956, 'in a world where the word "peace" has now been replaced by that ugly circumlocution "competitive coexistence" ', that 'literature has no frontiers; that art should be held high above political passion; . . . and above all, that freedom of thought and expression is the most precious of pearls, which we barter only at our peril' (Butler, R. A., p. 15; note the market imagery again).

According to Christopher Lasch, the idea that 'good' culture is a distinctive characteristic of the Western Alliance was virtually established in the United States by 1948. A symposium on 'The State of American Writing' showed what was happening: the defence of "high culture" had come to be identified almost exclusively with anti-Stalinism' (Lasch, p. 56). In fact, critics were claiming exuberantly that Abstract Expressionism had shifted cultural power, in painting at least, from Europe to the United States. Clement Greenberg wrote in 1948: 'the main premises of Western art have at last migrated to the United States, along with the center of gravity of industrial production and political power' (Guilbaut, p. 172). Unsurprisingly, the 'main premises', in contrast with those that had prevailed in the 1930s, were formalist and abstract (and, as I show in chapter 9, Modernist). Any kind of social purpose was identified with Socialist Realism and the 'political' cultural theories of Stalin and Zhadanov. At the symposium on American Writing there was a rush to find 'alternatives to naturalism', amounting, as Leslie Fiedler said, to 'a search for alternatives to politics in general'.[16] The Abstract Expressionist's more or less random assault on the canvas seemed a graphic illustration of freedom. Guilbaut finds it ironic that

> in a society politically stuck in a position to the right of center, in which political repression weighed as heavily as it did in the United States, abstract expressionism was for many the expression of freedom: the freedom to create controversial works of art, the freedom symbolised by action painting, by the unbridled expression of artists completely without fetters. . . . Expressionism stood for the difference between a free society and a totalitarian one. (p. 201)

US art saw itself as 'the sole trustee of the avant-garde "spirit" ', even as the US Government saw itself as 'the lone guarantor of capitalist liberty' (Kozloff, p. 44).

Stephen Spender was already committed to this outlook in 1948. He wrote in the *New York Times Magazine* (25 April) under the title: 'We can win the battle for the mind of Europe', with the subtitle: 'The Europeans, even those behind the iron curtain, can still be swung to western culture'. He got the chance to help this process forward when he became one of the founding editors of *Encounter*, in 1953. The opening editorial celebrates the discrediting of Stalinism: now 'we shall be spared the tedious sophistry by which despotism could pose as a higher form of freedom.' Spender explains that they meant 'the defense of American and European democratic freedom against Russian Communism' (*Thirties*, p. 127). And the sign and guarantee of freedom was free literature: the editorial offered as its leading ideas 'a love of liberty and a respect for that part of human endeavour that goes by the name of culture.'

It was finally acknowledged in 1966 that the free financing of *Encounter* involved its backers, the Congress for Cultural Freedom, channelling funds from the US Central Intelligence Agency. To some degree the Congress influenced policy – 'simply', Spender admits, they 'had bright ideas about the kind of articles we should put in' (*Thirties*, p. 128; see Kristol, ch. 2). The secret role of the CIA here is not an unfortunate accident, but symptomatic of the fallacy in Free-World ideology: actually, cultural production is never free of ideological determinants. The editors had been misled about the financing; but they fell into the trap because they lived inside Cold-War ideology. As Lasch puts it, 'it was inconceivable to them that American officials were not somehow immune to the temptations of great power. The defense of "cultural freedom" was wholly entwined, in their minds, with the defense of the "free world" against communism' (Lasch, p. 72). They co-operated spontaneously: they were acting freely.

Encounter addressed generally cultured circles. Academic literary criticism had usually imagined itself as a disinterested study, and was already geared up to assert literature as a free activity, and especially its separation from social forces and political opinions. Even committed Christians at Oxford, such as C. S. Lewis and Helen Gardner, believed that they were only propagating attitudes that just happened to be in the literature; they didn't see that their selection and reading of texts was partizan. F. R. Leavis wanted literature to be culturally central in an English tradition, and concerned with positive moral values. Even so, he was opposed to relating literature to economic, social and political forces. He said: 'While you are in intimate touch with literature no amount of dialectic, or of materialistic interpretation, will obscure for long the truth that human life lives only in individuals: I might have said, the truth that it is only in individuals that society lives' (*Common*, p. 185).

North American New Critics aspired specifically to study the literary text free of all 'extrinsic' features. They proclaimed 'the heresy of paraphrase', 'the intentional fallacy' and that 'a poem should not mean but be'. Their origins were in the 1930s and the conservative South, but their maximum influence was in the 1950s. In 1945 a Harvard committee, which included an originator of New Criticism, I. A. Richards, reported on *General Education in a Free Society* and recommended exposure of students to the Great Texts of Literature, with as few 'ancillary studies' as possible, beginning with 'the greatest, most universal, most essential human preoccupations'. The president of Harvard College saw as the goal 'an appreciation of both the responsibilities and the benefits which come to them because they are Americans and are free'.[17] By 1962 such appreciation was widespread, and Wilbur Scott was writing in his collection of essays representing *Five Approaches of Literary Criticism*:

> Without question, the most influential critical method of our time is the formalistic. It . . . is, in fact, the method one almost automatically thinks of when speaking of contemporary criticism. . . . This leads them to shun all material such as the personal or social conditions behind the composition, the moral implications, and so on, so long as these are 'extrinsic' – that is, tangential to an understanding of the poem, and to concentrate on the structure of each poem, or on elements of that structure as they relate to the total poetic experience. (p. 181)

The adoption of this theory in England was, typically, even less theorized. John Wain explained in his introduction to *Interpretations*, a collection of essays on individual poems, that the poems were addressed entirely as discrete entities because 'analysis can only concern itself with one object at a time' (p. xv). The insidious effect of such an argument is that it appears to take no position: one just reads the poem. Even Englishness and historical sequence, which Leavis and T. S. Eliot had discovered in their tradition, disappear from view. It was a perfect aesthetic for the Western Alliance: intellectuals are confined to 'objects' falling narrowly within their expertise; those objects seem to dispose themselves naturally; no raising of the eyes from the page to the wider world is required; values, other than 'literary values', are not at issue. Christopher Lasch comments, 'the more intellectual purity identifies itself with "value-free" investigations, the more it empties itself of political content and the easier it is for public officials to tolerate it'; thus the state gains 'the cooperation of writers, teachers, and artists not as paid propagandists or state-censored time-servers but as "free" intellectuals capable of policing their own jurisdictions' (Lasch, pp. 94–5).

The Free Market

With the Free World goes what is called the 'free market' – the freedom to produce and purchase sufficient commodities to keep the market profitable. Actually most of it is not free, but controlled by the state and big business; and, moreover, it is confined by the ideological framework of welfare-capitalism. However, the free market was taken as a defining condition of the Free World; it distinguished the Western Alliance from 'communism'.

The slogan on which the Conservatives won the 1951 election (though with fewer votes than were cast for Labour) was 'Set the People Free'; this was understood to mean free from rationing and 'restrictions', so those who had money could buy more things. During the 1950s Britain followed the United States into a consumer boom, triggered by military expenditure on the Korean War, and at the end of the decade the Conservatives could suggest that we had 'never had it so good'. But in fact the British economy was lagging behind those of its competitors, as Michael Pinto-Duschinsky points out:

> While the increase in total British production had been about 40 per cent, that of France had doubled, West Germany's and Italy's went up two and a half times, and Japanese production quadrupled. The decline in Britain's comparative exporting position was in direct proportion to that of her total production. From 1951 to 1962 there was a 29 per cent increase in British exports; the increases of France, West Germany, Italy and Japan were 86 per cent, 247 per cent, 259 per cent and 378 per cent respectively. (Bogdanor and Skidelsky, p. 57)

At this point the decisive failure of investment in British industry occurred. However, the freedom of the Western Alliance seemed to be confirmed by the success of its free economic system.

By the late 1950s enthusiasm for the modern market had waned among many intellectuals. In the United States, J.K. Galbraith showed that, so far from production being organized to meet human needs, economic activity in modern capitalism serves production itself, which 'creates the wants it seeks to satisfy'. To keep the economy moving, new products must continually be devised, and then it is the role of the sales department and advertising to make people feel that they have to buy them (Galbraith, pp. 124, 134–7). A sequence of US studies raised profound questions about the life-style that was being produced – *The Lonely Crowd* (1950) and *Abundance for What?* (1964) by David Riesman, *The Hidden Persuaders* (1957) and *The Status Seekers* (1959) by Vance Packard, *The Organisation Man* (1956) by William H. White, *Growing Up Absurd* (1960) by Paul Goodman, *The Other America* (1962) by Michael Harrington, articles by Dwight Macdonald (see Brookeman). Aldous Huxley in *Brave New World Revisited* (1959) found that his prophecies of 1931 were coming true even more quickly than he had expected, especially through advertising, and 'even in those countries that have a tradition of democratic government' (p. 12); the West is no longer superior in its freedom, which will become an empty slogan (Huxley, pp. 118–19, 155–6). Dwight Macdonald, in 'A Theory of Mass Culture' (1953), almost reached the point of condemning capitalism (but note the proviso): 'If one had no other data to go on, the nature of Mass Culture would reveal capitalism to be an exploitative class society.' Politics and commerce occupy equivalent positions in the Soviet and Western systems: in one there is propaganda and pedagogy, in the other entertainment (Rosenberg and White, p. 60). The superiority of the Free World was, almost, in question.

Similar distaste, compounded of snobbery and sensitivity to exploitation, was felt by literary intellectuals in the British tradition of middle-class dissidence – Leavisites who had defined literature and themselves in opposition to 'mass' culture since the 1930s, some leisure-class affiliates, remaining left-wingers. Generally, until Raymond Williams's *Culture and Society* (1958; see chapter 11 below), an aspect of the free market was complained of but the whole system was taken as inevitable, natural. In 1954 J. B. Priestley, after visiting Texas, coined the term 'Admass':

> This is my name for the whole system of an increasing productivity, plus inflation, plus a rising standard of material living, plus high-pressure advertising and salesmanship, plus mass communications, plus cultural democracy and the creation of the mass mind, the mass man. (Behind the Iron Curtain they have *Propmass*, official propaganda taking the place of advertising, but all with the same aims and objects.) (Priestley and Hawkes, pp. 51–2).

The equivalence with the Soviet system both effects a critique and prevents Priestley sounding like a treacherous communist.

My point here is that the hostility of many intellectuals to the cultural effects of free enterprise constituted a scandal in Free-World ideology, for it discovers a disjunction between two cherished notions: the free choice of the people and the free market. The principle of people buying what they want seems less valid when we find the market turning them into 'masses' and manipulating their wants. Sartre's analysis comes into view: if people were free from manipulation, would they not be more likely to appreciate art?

That we are dealing with a weak point in Cold-War ideology may be inferred from the manoeuvres of its defenders. Anthony Hartley declared that 'much American "popular culture" caters at a high level of adequacy for perfectly respectable needs' – because he was enthusiastic about NATO and worried that 'American' was 'a term of abuse' among intellectuals and magistrates (pp. 82–3). Anthony Crosland, on the right of the Labour Party, recognized in *The Future of Socialism* that his advocacy of welfare-capitalism entailed approval of Free-World culture. So he denied that levels of design and general culture in the United States were generally low; or if they were, they weren't low in another instance, Sweden; and, anyway, US university professors were highly regarded (a strange criterion of culture!; pp. 245–6). More plausibly, Leslie Fiedler held that mass culture is democratic ('Middle'), and Edward Shils argued that the vast majority of people had always led degraded lives and that 'mass culture is now less damaging to the lower classes than the dismal and harsh existence of earlier centuries had ever been' (p. 606). Shils acknowledges right-wing hostility to 'mass' culture but declares: 'It is not accidental that most of the recent critics of mass culture are, or were, Marxian socialists, some even rather extreme' (p. 588). The free market is justified by the implication that its opponents are Stalinists. The dominant notion of culture in the United States in the 1950s became pluralistic, supposing a chorus of voices in general harmony and innocent of any power structure, with 'mass' culture teaching individuals how to adjust to and enjoy the fruits of consumer society (Ross, pp. 336–8).

As I showed in Chapter 4, many British authors of the 1940s feared bureaucracy and the state, believing that traditional capitalism suited them very well. It afforded, typically, a little private income or family support, cheap living in the country or abroad, undemanding employment for young men from the right schools, a network of independent gentleman publishers, and a fairly reliable middle-class readership. They were disconcerted to find that the problem was the Free-World development of capitalism, with large corporations looking, freely, for the largest markets. Already in 1947 Cyril Connolly saw how the US book market was going:

The crucial factor is the high cost of book-production which renders the printing of small editions (under 10,000) uneconomic; the tendency is therefore to go all out for the best seller and, with a constant eye on Hollywood, to spend immense sums on publicity so as to bring about one of these jack-pots. . . . The American public are cajoled into reading the book of the month, and only the book of the month, and for that month only. Last year's book is as unfashionable as last year's car. (*Ideas*, pp. 171–2)

In *The Craft of Letters* John Lehmann complained of 'the gap, long a feature of the American scene, between the best-seller and its less fortunate brethren among good books'; and of 'the exploitation of all that can appeal in literature to a mass, and mainly non-intellectual audience' (p. 4). Lehmann had reason to complain. After the close of *Penguin New Writing*, he built up a new publishing enterprise with finance from a printing company. But the company was interested only in profits and closed down Lehmann's subsidiary – to the general scandal of the literary intelligentsia. Lehmann's mother wrote to him: 'How splendid to have so great intellectual support: it does prove that true culture in this country is not commercial' (Lehmann, *Ample*, p. 187). Mrs Lehmann was both right and wrong: 'true' literary intellectuals felt themselves at odds with the capitalist organization of culture, but at the same time allowed their horizons to be bounded by it. C. Wright Mills observed that 'cultural work is not only guided: culture is produced and distributed – and even consumed – to order.' But the myth of the creative artist as 'the inherently and necessarily free man', deriving from the era of classic capitalism, 'is still clung to mightily, being identified with freedom itself' (p. 553).

Auden gave his version of the flaw in Free-World ideology in a guest editorial in *Encounter*:

Most poets in the West believe that some sort of democracy is preferable to any sort of totalitarian state . . . but I cannot think of a single poet of consequence whose work does not, either directly or by implication condemn modern civilisation as an irremediable mistake, a bad world which we have to endure because it is there and no one knows how it could be made into a better one, but in which we can only retain our humanity in the degree to which we resist its pressures. (April 1954)

The Free World is also a bad world, and poets have to 'endure', to 'resist its pressures'. But there is no thinkable political and economic alternative, so Auden attributes the problem to mechanization: the writer works 'by hand, by himself', unlike in the 'mass entertainment' of film, radio and television. However, at the end of the article he wonders whether printing (which, of course, dominated when the writer was supposed to be happy) should not also fall within his critique. He can't handle this, so he reiterates that 'no one knows' how the world might be improved.

Arthur Koestler's *Darkness at Noon* (trans. 1940) had made him a famous anti-Stalinist and best-selling author. In 1950 he was planning to live in the United States, but he felt there was 'something radically wrong with literary life' there, and especially with best-seller charts, as he explained in an interview for the *New York Times*. The issue, as Koestler saw it, was just the contradiction that we have been considering: 'Religion and art are the two completely noncompetitive spheres of human striving and they both derive from the same source. But the social climate in this country has made the creation of art into an essentially competitive business' (Koestler et al., *Strangers*, p. 101; also p. 140). Koestler adopts the definition of literature favoured in modern capitalism, then complains of the concomitant economic structures. This is not all. The interview was censored by the *New York Times*, and especially the references to bestseller lists. They asked: 'How can we run an attack on the very thing we do?' (p. 102). The incident is structural, and still informs dominant attitudes to the arts. It is because his book *The Age of Longing* was in the best-seller list that Koestler was interviewed: his chance to express himself depended, from the start, upon the market, and the market muzzled him when he tried to modify its conception of artistic activity.

Free – for What?

Until the 1950s, it was often said that intellectuals were characteristically dissident. Joseph Schumpeter suggested that capitalism, 'inevitably and by virtue of the very logic of its civilisation creates, educates and subsidises', in intellectuals, 'a vested interest in social unrest' (p. 146). But now their acquiescence was so marked that it became a topic of discussion. A *Partisan Review* symposium on 'Our Country and Our Culture' in 1952 found only Norman Mailer and Wright Mills unhappy with the assumption that US intellectuals were exhibiting a newly 'affirmative' attitude towards the United States (Ross, p. 334). Max Beloff remarked in *Encounter* 'the air of stability, this lack of any obvious wish to change the basic rules of British political life, this easy and far-reaching tolerance in our intellectual life' (June 1954, p. 51). At the end of the decade Daniel Bell pronounced the 'end of ideology'.[18] It seemed that we were free to think, in the Free-World, but there was nothing worth thinking about any more.

Functionalist sociology was developed to show that this was as it should be: it rendered conflict superficial and superfluous by holding that all parts of society must contribute to its ultimate stability. Shils defined the role of intellectuals as to reflect upon the world with a view to legitimating the existing arrangements (p. 4). This helping hand to authority is not offered subserviently, however: literature and philosophy are of course free, produced by 'the individual creator, working under his own self-imposed discipline' (pp. 10–11). Shils admits that intellectuals have tended to quarrel with the social order (p. 9), but he places this as part of a tradition of 'obstinate refusal to compromise' (p. 7) – not to be taken seriously. In fact, they sound pretty irrelevant – so 'remote' are they 'from the executive routines of daily life in family, firm, office, factory, church, and civil service, from the pleasure of the ordinary man and the obligations, compromises, and corruptions of those who exercise authority . . .' (pp. 15–16). It sounds as though Shils doesn't want these obstinate, quarrelsome folk getting in too close. When US intellectuals became dissident, during the Civil Rights movement and the Vietnam War, he found it unsettling, and frowned upon a lack of self-discipline, tradition and respect for authority (pp. 154–95, 265–97).

Ralf Dahrendorf made the implications plain enough by comparing intellectuals to court jesters. They question institutions so that they become more solid, and the toleration of criticism shows how little criticism is needed:

> to strengthen accepted positions – political, moral, pedagogical, religious, or whatever – by questioning them and therefore finding solid ground for them is the social task of the court jesters of modern society, the intellectuals. . . . Whether a society includes intellectual court jesters who critically question its institutions, and how it tolerates them, are a measure of its maturity and inner solidity. (Rieff, pp. 51–2)

The more active intellectuals are, the less they can or should make any difference. Their questioning occurs within a free system, and to question that system would be to undermine the very condition of intellectual activity.

However, the disabling of intellectuals, combined with the contradictions I have described, began to provoke its own critique. Despite the idea
of literature as the jewel in the crown of the Western Alliance, there were
courageously dissident literary texts. Arthur Miller's *The Crucible* (1953)
attacked the anti-communist witch-hunt ('a sheet of ice formed over the
first-night audience when it sensed the theme'); and in *Catch 22* (1961),
ostensibly about the 1939–45 war, Joseph Heller says he was 'trying
to deal with the climate of the Fifties during which there was great
disposition among Americans to trust their government' (Lewis, P., *Fifties*,
pp. 81–5). Lenny Bruce's nightclub act provoked US police harassment
and a ban on his entering Britain (Bruce, pp. 10–13). Political theorists
began to argue that the taming of intellectuals was a scandal – Marcuse
began the analysis of intellectual entrapment that was to be *One
Dimensional Man* (1964); Wright Mills has been mentioned. Interestingly,
left-wing thinkers tended to agree with functionalists that modern
capitalism has newly effective ways of incorporating dissent.[19]

Initially in Britain there was only an obscure discontent at the
impotence conferred by Free-World literary status. Contributors to
Lehmann's *Craft of Letters* lamented that English intellectuals are lonely
and without respect, that the writer is cut off from the main currents in
the modern world, that liberal culture cannot produce unifying belief
(pp. 30–5, 48, 75–6, 120–1). Yet political engagement was inconceivable.
Philip Toynbee believed that the only reason for serious writing now is
to say 'something about our present condition', but he had watched
Sartre's progress with 'disgust', and proposed 'concern' as the proper
attitude (though not such as to take any particular direction, or aspire to
make any difference to readers; pp. 64–8). E. P. Thompson argued in
'Outside the Whale' (1960) that intellectuals had capitulated in the face of
'Natopolitan' ideology: 'Few are silenced by force and few are bought
outright; but fewer still can resist the "natural" economic processes and
pressures to conform' (*Poverty*, p. 25). But this essay was itself part of
a substantial intellectual revolt in the late 1950s; I discuss it in chapters 11
and 12.

Even Spender was anxious about the affirmation of art as a value in
itself; he wanted it to be effective in the world. In an *Encounter* article
called 'Inside the Cage' he wrote that the thought of I. A. Richards breaks
'the connection of statements of the inner life of the imagination with any
kind of corresponding outward reality' (March 1955, p. 18). He proposed
as a principle: 'Art has a purpose which is to transform contemporary life'

(p. 22). But he couldn't say what direction the transformation should take; it was an attempt to devise a politics without politics. When Spender and Richards met and discussed the question, Richards's wife tried to move the conversation on to Colonel Nasser. But Richards said: 'Don't let's talk about things that don't matter' (Spender, *Thirties*, pp. 145–6). Spender doesn't suggest how they might have got literature, as he regarded it, to engage with the issue of Egyptian self-determination.

When dissent dwelt upon the situation of literature, it was often limited by an attempt to use Free-World ideology against itself. Literature and intellectual freedom stand against the tyrannical state in Ray Bradbury's popular US novel, *Fahrenheit 451* (1954). The title is the temperature at which books burn, for Montag is a fireman, in the unit that seeks out books, burns them and arrests their owners. Book-burning figures the intellectual control attempted by totalitarian regimes; also, it was a feature of the witch-hunt against 'communists' in the United States: librarians hastened to destroy books by suspect authors, including Sherwood Anderson, W. H. Auden, Theodore Dreiser and Edmund Wilson. Senator Joseph McCarthy denounced the US Information Service abroad for the 30 to 40 thousand allegedly communist books on its shelves (Lewis, P., *Fifties*, pp. 77–8). Bradbury's story is organized very like 1984. It credits the state with an entirely effective internal secret service and uncanny powers of psychological detection; yet some individuals and the central character particularly, despite his employment as part of the apparatus of control, experience an irrepressible 'human' impulse towards forbidden thoughts and activities. But in *Fahrenheit 451*, unlike 1984, the situation is recognizably the outcome of modern US capitalism; and the index of the inhumanity of that system is its inhospitality to literature and books. The stages that led to the present tyranny are specified as a levelling down of culture, the debasement of educational standards, compromises with mass culture, the production of digests of the classics (pp. 58–61). This makes Bradbury a liberal like Dwight Macdonald – accepting, basically, the Free-World notion of literature as an autonomous practice, crediting it with a mysterious suprapolitical virtue but without allowing it a politics, lamenting the effects of the market. Bradbury, like Macdonald, does not see that his informing definition of literature as a free practice depends on the ideology he is criticizing.[20]

Eventually it transpires that book-lovers are allowed to exist outside the cities and Montag escapes to join them. The authorities don't bother to chase them because they are peaceful, harmless folk, wrapped up in their reading (p. 148). At this point the novel falls into contradiction: literature, which has seemed so dangerous, is now defined as irrelevant because non-political – 'So long as the vast population doesn't wander about quoting Magna Carta and the Constitution, it's all right' (p. 148). This is the Cold-War confusion about literature: it is both a key institution in the maintenance of freedom, and something that stands beyond the modern world altogether. It is both immensely powerful and utterly harmless. The city and books are constituted as a binary, defining each other. Bradbury does not query this construction, but makes the books win, for the city is destroyed in an atomic war. Thus capitalism is made to auto-destruct, leaving the ideologically pure book-people to return and start again, perhaps producing an improved civilization from their wise reading.

One noted English poet went on publishing and trying to resist the Cold-War construction of art. Roy Fuller, who had begun writing in the 1930s, said in 1974 that he 'never lost, as other people did, the fundamental belief in socialism and the materialist conception of history' (Firchow, p. 128). While others cultivated the irrational modes of Dylan Thomas or T. S. Eliot, or the self-deprecation of Movement poetry, Fuller maintained an Audenesque manner through the 1940s and 1950s, bespeaking a belief in purpose, control and intelligibility – virtues that anticipate a responsible readership. In 'Poet and Reader', which concludes his 1954 volume *Counterparts*, he declares this in the face of contemporary gloom about 'mass' culture:

> The very act of warning
> Implies a faith in readers:
> It's not quite you I'm mourning,
> Rather the seedy leaders
> You are for ever spawning.[21]

The difficulties of this commitment and the dangers of abandoning it are addressed in 'Translation' (from the same volume):

> Now that the barbarians have got as far as Picra,
> And all the new music is written in the twelve-tone scale,
> And I am anyway approaching my fortieth birthday,
>   I will dissemble no longer.

> I will stop expressing my belief in the rosy
> Future of man, and accept the evidence
> Of a couple of wretched wars and innumerable
>   Abortive revolutions.
>
> I will cease to blame the stupidity of the slaves
> Upon their masters and nurture, and will say,
> Plainly, that they are enemies to culture,
>   Advancement and cleanliness.

(*Collected Poems*, p. 150)

The context sounds Roman, so the reader doesn't know initially how far we are to credit the dramatic speaker, though we may find the collection of reasons in the first stanza whimsical and the tone in the second somewhat off-hand. In the third stanza 'culture' at first seems straightforward, by itself at the end of line 11, but 'Advancement and cleanliness' are more doubtful criteria of virtue. We become suspicious of the speaker. Stanza four is particularly Audenesque: it reminds us of 'Spain 1937' and 1930s commitment ('the flat ephemeral pamphlet and the boring meeting'; Auden, *English*, p. 212); at the same time, by its tinge of irony ('daring verse', 'various protest'), it suggests that this stance is no longer credible; yet the last line sounds pompous, implying a limit to the speaker's wisdom:

> From progressive organisations, from quarterlies
> Devoted to daring verse, from membership of
> Committees, from letters of various protest
> I shall withdraw forthwith.

In stanza five we find that the speaker is Cinna, the poet killed in mistake for Cinna the conspirator when Brutus and Cassius overthrew Julius Caesar. In this light, his attempt to achieve security by abandoning political involvement is evidently futile:

> When they call me reactionary I shall smile,
> Secure in another dimension. When they say
> 'Cinna has ceased to matter' I shall know
> How well I reflect the times.

The ruling class will think I am on their side
And make friendly overtures, but I shall retire
To the side farther from Picra and write some poems
About the doom of the whole boiling.

Anyone happy in this age and place
Is daft or corrupt. Better to abdicate
From a material and spiritual terrain
Fit only for barbarians.

(p. 151)

Cinna the poet, historically, was a chief friend of Julius Caesar and hence of the reforming party, but he was killed when taken for one of the reactionary conspirators (Skeat, p. 122). So Fuller's speaker is deluded in his belief that he can escape by withdrawing from progressive politics. In fact, the barbarians were a long way off; the threat to liberty was from within, from corrupt leaders.

Criticism, generally, did not appreciate Fuller's concern with political commitment. Thomas Blackburn in 1961 complained that 'dogmatism mars the work of a good poet' and that Fuller has an inadequate sense of 'the wanderings and dangers of the human soul on its long journey' (Black-burn, pp. 137, 141). The volume in the Twayne English Authors Series offers no context through which Fuller's political situation might be understood; it concludes by admiring him for 'a worldliness, a flexibility, a balance, a totality of being' and likening his work to that of Philip Larkin (Austin, p. 135). That ignores Fuller's central preoccupation as a poet. He does sound sometimes like Larkin: he tried to negotiate with the prevailing mode, and often it makes him dull. But Fuller's 'flexibility' is grounded in the knowledge he attributes to Brutus in 'The Ides of March',

that what we built had no foundation
Other than luck and my false privileged role
In a society that I despised.

(p. 183)

This may sound like Larkin. But the difference, and in the 1950s it was all the difference in the world, is that Fuller strove to understand and express the political situation that made it so.

Notes

1 See Poster, *Existentialist*; Caute, *Communism*; de Mauny.

2 Mander, *Writer*, p. 8; see also Hartley, pp. 26, 170.

3 Ionesco, pp. 93, 95. See Sinfield, *Society*, pp. 104–5 (on *Free Fall*) and 181–4 (on the Absurd).

4 Holroyd, pp. 70–3, 76–9, 144–5; Ritchie, H., pp. 167–72. Holroyd dissociated himself from this 'extremism'.

5 Heffner, p. 283; see McCauley, p. 121.

6 'The Paperclip Conspiracy', BBC 1, 20 February 1987, discussed how Pentagon officers sanitized the records of Nazi scientists so that they could enter the United States and work on rockets; in 1948 the UK Government stopped identifying and prosecuting war criminals in Britain and the Commonwealth, because it saw that the Western Alliance would want to re-arm West Germany. See Marcuse, *One*, pp. 80–1.

7 See Carew; Higgins, pp. 46–9; Freeland, pp. 9–12; Grahame Thompson, 'Economic Intervention in the Post-war Economy', in McLennan et all., p. 102.

8 Calvocoressi, pp. 207–8; Higgins, pp. 77–82.

9 See Miliband, *State*, pp. 208, 222; Russell, *Has Man*, pp. 32, 44.

10 Burnham, p. 112; see Lewis, P., *Fifties*, ch. 3.

11 Rhodes, p. 688 and chs. 18–19. This attitude persisted: during nuclear testing on the Marshall Islands the people were not evacuated, and were returned, contaminated, to their atoll so that long-term effects of radiation could be studied. New York City Telenews presented the Marshall Islanders as 'savages' (cf. chapter 7 below): 'John, as we said, is a savage, but a happy, amenable savage' ('Half Life', Channel 4, 24 March 1988; Dibblin).

12 Feldman and Gartenberg, pp. 262–3; see also E. P. Thompson, 'Outside the Whale' (1960), in *Poverty*; Williams, R., *Politics*, pp. 384–92; Wain, 'Orwell'; and pp. 260–1 below.

13 See Hewison, *In Anger*, pp. 27–8; Calder, p. 578; Fyvel, *Intellectuals*, p. 50.

14 *Burmese Days*, p. 66; see below, pp. 118–19.

15 Spender, *Creative*, pp. 142–5; Orwell, *Essays*, III, p. 456.

16 Fiedler is quoted from Lasch, p. 56. See Kozloff; Ross.

17 *General Education in a Free Society*, pp. 205, 207, xv; see Graff, *Professing*, pp. 162–3; Bruss, pp. 10–13.

18 Bell, last ch. Seymour Martin Lipset declared, 'The political issue of the 1950s has become freedom versus Communism', and such critique as is maintained by intellectuals 'helps to maintain the conflict which is the lifeblood of the democratic system' (Lipset, pp. 369, 371). See Brookeman, ch. 2.

19 I discuss the scope for cultural resistance in chapters 3, 8 and 13. The point about the agreement of left- and right-wing thought is made by David Held,

'Power and Legitimacy in Contemporary Britain', in McLennan et al., pp. 303–6.

20 Even so, the novel makes some shrewd hits – for instance, Montag's anxious question: 'Is it because we're so rich and the rest of the world's so poor and we just don't care if they are? . . . Is that why we're hated so much?' (p. 74).

21 Fuller, *Collected Poems*, p. 159. See also 'Poem to Pay for a Pen' (pp. 143–4).

7
Cultural plunder and the savage within

In *England Your England* (1940) Orwell observed that the 'stagnation' of the British Empire in the years between the wars had specially affected

> two important sub-sections of the middle class. One was the military and imperialist middle class, generally nicknamed the Blimps, and the other the left-wing intelligentsia. These two seemingly hostile types . . . are mentally linked together and constantly interact upon one another; in any case they are born to a considerable extent into the same families. (*Essays*, II, p. 93).

This was my argument in Chapter 4: that the dissident middle-class intelligentsia was constituted in opposition to the empire-building middle class (the Schlegels versus the Wilcoxes); the two were in the same family, as Orwell suggests. Hence the complex feeling between Jimmy Porter and his father-in-law in *Look Back in Anger*. However, as I have shown, middle-class dissidence became predominantly conservative at the end of the war. So writers continuing the main literary tradition (that is, who did not identify themselves as a new generation; see Chapter 11) tended to associate decolonization with the threat to the leisure class and hence to 'civilization'. Anxiety about their own position as literary intellectuals merged with a wider confusion about British loss of imperial power.

Cultural Plunder

Literary intellectuals were concerned with decolonization also because they were self-conscious makers of culture. Orwell suggested that they took their cookery from Paris and their opinions from Moscow (*Essays*, II, p. 95); Osborne repeats this, adding morals from Port Said (*Look Back*, p. 17). What is recognized here is fundamental: as well as economic plunder, there is cultural plunder.

Mainly because of colonial enterprise, European identity has been constituted in contradistinction to that attributed to other races. The supposed inadequacies of colonial subjects position them as the inferiors that witness to European superiority. It is a massive act of cultural plunder. George Lamming develops the point through the figure of Caliban, in *The Tempest*, who has been given language by Prospero and is created by that language as an image through which Prospero delimits his own humanity. Caliban is 'an occasion, a state of existence which can be appropriated and exploited for the purposes of another's own development'. In Sartre's terms, 'the European has only been able to become a man through creating slaves and monsters.'[1]

At the most generous, the colonial subject is simplified, positioned as a simple creature of few, clear and inferior attributes. Lawrence Durrell went to Cyprus in 1953 to be a writer and schoolteacher in the sun and became press officer for the British administration, leaving as nationalist resistance and British repression approached their height in 1956. His book *Bitter Lemons* (1957) thus runs the gamut, from poetic evocation of the Mediterranean and transmission of metropolitan educational values, to reciprocal killing by the people and the colonial power. He writes: 'The British saw a one-dimensional figure in the Cypriot: they did not realise how richly the landscape was stocked with the very sort of characters who rejoice the English heart in a small country town – the rogue, the drunkard, the singer, the incorrigible' (p. 36). Durrell means to be positive, but for the usual single dimension he only substitutes four crude, external types (none female); he 'stocks' the landscape with delightful characters for the amusement of the English. Notice particularly the omission of subjectivity, self-consciousness, any kind of interior life. As Durrell says, this is similar to what is done to the lower classes in England.

The present chapter is meant not to be exploitative, but it also is written predominantly from a white English point of view. There are several possible justifications for this – that we have done enough of writing the histories of Blacks and Asians for them; that Europe needs to sort out its legacy of empire before it can address the experience of others; that we should concentrate on the things we might do something about. Finally it must be said that my history and institutional position enable me to do some things better than others. A comparable problem (evinced already in the quotation from *Bitter Lemons*) is the slippage, found all the time in uses of the 'English' language, between 'Britain' and 'England'; it represents confusion and manipulation in respect of the first and last colonies of the English – the more northern and western parts of the British Isles. For the domination of Celtic peoples and cultures has plainly been similar to overseas imperial enterprise (Hechter, pp. 8–10, 147–50, 342–4). Generally, Britishness is claimed for size and scope, Englishness for core distinctiveness. 'English Literature' works fairly straightforwardly as cultural plunder: it claims what it sees as the best Welsh, Irish and Scottish writers, regarding their acceptability to the English as guaranteeing 'universal significance', and abandons the rest as of quaint, local interest. In the present study it is often unclear whether 'England' or 'Britain' is the proper term, since many cultural phenomena might be said to derive from English hegemony, yet they do occur throughout the islands and to suggest otherwise would misrepresent experience as it is lived at the moment. It is in the structure of these issues that no clearly 'right' answer offers itself.

I pointed out in Chapter 3 that the stories requiring most attention – most assiduous and continuous reworking – are the awkward ones: it is the unresolved issues that people want to read and write about. Fiction and other evidence indicate that colonial Europeans spent a good part of their time producing anxious, self-justifying stories about the relationship between the natives and themselves. If colonial fiction 'can demonstrate that the barbarism of the native is irrevocable, or at least very deeply ingrained, then the European's attempt to civilise him can continue indefinitely, the exploitation of his resources can proceed without hindrance, and the European can persist in enjoying a position of moral superiority' (JanMohammed, p. 62). Flory, in Orwell's *Burmese Days* (1934), is exceptional in admitting this: 'I'm here to make money, like everyone else. All I object to is the slimy white man's burden humbug . . . the lie that we're here to uplift our poor black brothers instead of to rob them' (p. 37).

The mechanisms of colonial exploitation cannot be obscured completely or indefinitely; the attempt to make them seem just and reasonable is too fraught and contradictory. The stories therefore keep confessing their own construction. In Paul Scott's novel *The Birds of Paradise* (1962), the European boy is told, of his father's role: 'We had two jobs in India. The princes knew how to rule but we had to teach them democracy. The Indians of British India knew about democracy but had to be taught how to rule.' So both ways the British are necessary. The boy deduces: ' "We're like the Romans, aren't we sir? Like the Romans in Britain". It was a serious thought. I thought the Romans were fine fellows' (p. 36). However, the power relations which the flattering story is handling are plainer when the boy feels challenged by the rajah's son: ' "I can lick you any time", I said, "because I'm British and you are only a wog" ' (p. 88).

The attributes that are fastened upon the colonial subject are also fraught and contradictory, and therefore racial stereotyping is always uneasy. Homi Bhabha observes: 'The black is both savage (cannibal) and yet the most obedient and dignified of servants (the bearer of food); he is the embodiment of rampant sexuality and yet innocent as a child; he is mystical, primitive, simple-minded and yet the most worldly and accomplished liar, and manipulator of social forces.'[2] Such contradictions derive from the structure of the colonial situation: the natives have to be savage so that it is right to occupy their country and mistreat them; they have to be subservient so that they can be made to serve. They have to be innocent so that they can be dominated by the settler, and to be dishonest so that you never trust them very far. Therefore stereotypes of the native have continually to be reworked, rediscovered, reaffirmed.

Colonial stereotypes are insecure, finally, because they fit poorly with the evidence. The settler must seek confirmation continually, because every time he or she looks at a native (and the European's privilege is not to look, but always they must look), there is a risk of seeing not the stereotype but another human being. Further, the native might disconcert by returning a look not of acquiescence but of knowledge, and then authority falls under question. In *Burmese Days* the club servant says: 'I find it very difficult to keep ice cool now.' The reader unfamiliar with this kind of interaction should pause to consider what is unacceptable about the Asian's sentence. The colonist's objection is this:

> Don't talk like that, damn you – 'I find it very difficult!' Have you swallowed a dictionary? 'Please, master, can't keeping ice cool' – that's how you ought to talk. We shall have to sack this fellow if he gets to talk English too well. I can't stick servants who talk English. (p. 25)

Natives who undermine the distinction between themselves and Europeans are intolerable.

Almost all this analysis is presented in Doris Lessing's *The Grass Is Singing*, published in England in 1950 out of her experience in Southern Rhodesia (Zimbabwe). When settlers read of the killing of a white woman by her 'houseboy', in the opening paragraph, they 'felt a little spurt of anger mingled with what was almost satisfaction, as if some belief had been confirmed, as if something had happened which could only have been expected' (p. 9). The settlers are pleased to find evidence that suits their preconceived notions. Ambiguous instances trouble them – Charlie 'liked his natives either one way or the other: properly dressed according to their station, or in loincloths. He could not bear the half-civilised native' (p. 16). Lessing makes the contradictions apparent all the time. 'They are nothing but savages after all', says Dick, 'who had never stopped to reflect that these same savages had cooked for him better than his wife did, had run his house, had given him a comfortable existence, as far as his pinched life could be comfortable, for years' (p. 82). Anything which promises to draw attention to the artificiality of racial oppression causes anxiety – for instance 'the growing army of poor whites' who are thought shocking (unlike millions of poor Blacks) because of 'their betrayal of white standards' (p. 192).

Above all, it cannot be admitted 'that a white person, and most particularly, a white woman, can have a human relationship, whether for good or evil, with a black person' (p. 27). But that is what happens to Mary, Dick's wife – whom we know from the start to have been murdered (so, we may feel, it was inevitable). Her trouble begins when she takes her husband's place in the fields and is unable to understand an African man because she has not bothered to learn the language. ' "Don't talk that gibberish to me", she snapped.' So he speaks to her in English. 'But most white people think it is "cheek" if a native speaks English. She said, breathless with anger, "Don't speak English to me".' Her racism has led her into a typical contradiction, as the man perceives – 'shrugging and smiling and turning his eyes up to heaven as if protesting that she had forbidden him to speak his own language and then hers – so what was he to speak?' (p. 125). Mary sees a person, and that he doesn't respect her, and she strikes him with a whip. When he – his name is Moses – is appointed houseboy by her husband, she is unsettled. She sees him washing himself, he makes his resentment apparent, and it renders her hysterical:

What had happened was that the formal pattern of black-and-white, mistress-and-servant, had been broken by the personal relation; and when a white man in Africa by accident looks into the eyes of a native and sees the human being (which it is his chief preoccupation to avoid), his sense of guilt, which he denies, fumes up in resentment and he brings down the whip. (pp. 151–2)

From this point, Moses gains a strange ascendancy over Mary, she identifies him in dreams with her father and as obscene, he becomes insolent and domineering, a sexual relationship is probably established, and finally he kills her.

In *The Golden Notebook* (1962) Anna expresses dissatisfaction with her novel *The Frontiers of War*: 'I said nothing in it that wasn't true. But the emotion it came out of was something frightening, the unhealthy, feverish, illicit excitement of wartime, a lying nostalgia, a longing for licence, for freedom, for the jungle, for formlessness' (p. 82). The inter-racial sex-and-violence of *The Grass Is Singing* may well attract such a criticism. In this book Lessing is in danger of reproducing the racist system she repudiates; 'Even the works of some of the most enlightened and critical colonial writers eventually succumb to a narrative organisation based on racial/metaphysical oppositions' (JanMohammed, p. 61). The horror, as the settlers experience it, of black – white relations is hardly challenged in the novel. Moses is seen to have 'a malevolent glare' (p. 197), 'his face wickedly malevolent' (pp. 197, 199). We can't judge this, because there is no presentation of his thought. This is a crucial factor – whether the reader is invited to believe that the Black person has a consciousness, a subjectivity, comparable to the reader's own. Without this, he or she is easily regarded, by the reader as by the settlers, as the mysterious and violent other. Lessing's novellae and stories are sometimes quite different; in 'Hunger' (*Five*, 1953) a village boy falls in with 'bad' Africans, but also with politicians, and on the last page begins to achieve a commitment to work for the freedom of his people. All this is from the Black point of view. But in *The Grass Is Singing* we are told on the last pages: 'What thoughts of regret, or pity, or perhaps even wounded human affection were compounded with the satisfaction of [Moses'] completed revenge, it is impossible to say' (p. 218). Why should it be impossible? – any more than the thoughts of other characters, since Lessing has invented the whole thing. The 'unknowable' native is part of the stereotype. Kipling, in 'One Viceroy Reigns', says: 'You'll never plumb the Oriental mind/And if you did, it isn't worth the toil' (Williams, P., p. 95).

137

Moses is an instrument in a Lawrentian fable about sexual identity and domination – Mary sees him washing, like Mellors in *Lady Chatterley's Lover*. But whereas for Lawrence the challenge from class produces a personal and sexual relationship, for Lessing's novel the challenge from race is only frightening and violent. In *The Grass Is Singing* sexual intercourse can only be hinted at (pp. 196–8): for the novel, as for the settlers, it is unspeakable. Lessing said recently that she now finds Moses 'shadowy' as a person and would write it differently; but 'at that time you didn't *meet* any Black people except as servants. Or as politicos, which is just as much of a barrier, in fact.'[3]

Phobic and Structural Racism

Thus far I have tried to discuss racism as an ideological manipulation convenient to imperial rule, and I maintain that this is its most important role. *The Grass Is Singing* takes us into another realm, that of phobic hatred, and it is appropriate to consider the relationship between the ideology and phobia. For only some individuals is racism phobic; for the rest of us, it gets structured into the language, into the prevailing stories through which the society seeks to understand itself. It becomes 'common sense' (Lawrence, E.). Structural racism helps to legitimate the social order, but it may be relatively unimportant to the individuals who manifest it. Phobic racism, on the other hand, seeks to secure not just the economic, political and general psychic well-being of the European; the racial other is invoked, also, as a way of handling profound personal inadequacy. The phobic racist cannot leave the topic, he or she looks for people of other races in order to exercise again phobic feelings (the homophobe is similar). Structural racism is certainly not innocent; it affords a sympathetic milieu into which phobic racism may expand, and in extreme circumstances the two virtually merge. However, in other circumstances it is at least ameliorable: when pointed out it may be worked upon and changed.

Probably there is a more or less permanent phobic minority, the recruiting ground for the National Front and the Ku Klux Klan. Orwell presents all the characters in *Burmese Days*, including the narrator, as structurally racist. But Ellis is phobic. His abuse of Asians, which is shocking to read,

> went on for several minutes. It was curiously impressive, because it was so completely sincere. Ellis really did hate Orientals – hated them with a bitter,

restless loathing as of something evil or unclean. ... Any hint of friendly feeling towards an Oriental seemed to him a horrible perversity. He was an intelligent man and an able servant of his firm, but he was one of those Englishmen – common, unfortunately – who should never be allowed to set foot in the East. (p. 23)

Although *The Grass Is Singing* shows structural racism very well, it also folds it back into phobic racism. The distinction is important, because phobia seems ingrained and necessary, whereas structural racism is cultural, the product of historical conditions. Phobia may use many of the same themes and images as structural racism, but it affords neither a sufficient explanation for the racism of European societies nor an adequate theory of its implications. The two tend to support each other, but that is to the convenience of racists, and the more reason why they should be distinguished analytically; otherwise all racism may seem founded in deep phobia and therefore virtually natural. Phobia may even undermine structural racism, as it disturbs Flory in *Burmese Days*, through its manifest perversity.

A psychological analysis of 'Negrophobia' was in circulation in the 1950s:

There is a good deal of evidence to show that in modern Western civilisation erotic or sexual impulses are subject to a great deal of repression and renunciation. In so far as the Negro is popularly identified with the 'savage' and thought to live a life which is relatively free from the conventions and restrictions associated with 'civilisation', he is often believed to be free from sexual restraints. As a result it is suggested that the Negro comes to represent in the mind of the white man or woman that aspect of his own unconscious with which he is in a state of conflict. Hostility which the individual directs towards the part of himself that wants to break away from the sexual restraints is projected onto the Negro, who is accused of doing all the things that the white person himself would like to do, but dare not.[4]

This idea seems to underlie Mary's psychology in *The Grass Is Singing* – she is said to have been uneasy with her own sexuality from the start. But even the newcomer to southern Africa, Tony, is surprised to hear of white women having sexual relations with Black men: 'He felt it would be rather like having a relation with an animal, in spite of his "progressiveness" ' (p. 197).

Paul Scott's novel *The Alien Sky* (1953) allows race phobia to appear universal. Here it seems at first that the Indian servant will have a voice, but we follow his consciousness only briefly – just long enough to reveal the usual untrustworthiness and to set up subsequent development in the plot (pp. 15–16). And a militant Hindu nationalist puts his point of view, but is said to be fascistic and eventually revealed as merely ambitious (pp. 65, 256). The main action turns upon horror at the idea of mixed race in others or of it being known of oneself. The latter is Dorothy's fear; she says:

> 'Underneath all the so-called trust and understanding between white and black, there's mistrust and dislike. We fight them and they fight us.' She hesitated. 'Us? But then I'm not "us". A union between black and white is an act of treachery. Each side hates to be reminded of it. From time to time they can forgive each other and call the battle off, forget it for a while. But they never forgive themselves their own treachery. They never forgive my sort of people –.' (p. 204)

The Eurasian undermines racial stereotypes at the same time as affording unique opportunity for their reinforcement. In *The Alien Sky*, as in Lessing's novel, racial anxieties are shown to correlate with sexual anxieties (pp. 278–83). They are run together almost as the same issue, and race phobia is manifest by almost all the European characters. A Eurasian woman is introduced: 'Gower's eyes had the same look as Jimmy's. MacKendrick caught its meaning. Try as one would to ignore it, instinct said: This girl is a freak. Half-European, half-Asian, the only unity she has is a sexual one. Because of the colour of her skin one's mind immediately recalls an act of union' (p. 136). This opinion, which is not clearly that of any of the characters but lurks in the narration as a general truth, is not challenged in the novel. It is left as an adequate account of what 'instinct' says. Yet it displays not only racism but also sexual anxiety (why should one be so upset at recalling an act of union?).

Gower is the most sympathetic character. He and the novel have an astute moment when he fears for his servant as he, Gower, leaves India, but then corrects himself: 'No – that was the wrong outlook, the outlook of the Burra Sahib believing in his own omnipotence; this possessiveness, this feudalism, this benevolent despotism which passed for racial understanding' (pp. 109–10). Nevertheless, after the funeral of his European assistant, Steele, he is repelled by the sight of Steele's Indian lover and 'stunned' by realization that she is bearing a child: 'The child is obscene, sprung from an act of lust and the urgency of the flesh's need. The child was not Steele's, nor was it the girl's. Rather it seemed a growth, a canker, from which both would have turned in disgust, back to the inviolacy of their separate spirits' (pp. 253–4). Only one elderly woman speaks up briefly for Eurasians, but she is easily discounted, if we want, as optimistic and impractical (p. 36).

The Alien Sky makes objectionable reading because of the presumption that racism is inevitable, not just as a product of the colonial situation but as an 'instinct'. Yet even as this implication emerges, the novel cannot but belie it. For the thoughtful reader, the fact of personal and sexual attraction is established, however much the phobic may dislike it. The persistence of the forbidden relationship, despite such hostility, witnesses that only one race is involved, the human race.

Colonial Crisis

Imperialism began in a need for markets. Western European traders circled the globe, looking for enhanced opportunities to buy and sell goods and people. From the mid-eighteenth century, European governments consolidated the resulting trading posts and adopted them as extensions of their power and status. But African and Asian societies showed considerable capacity for adaptation and self-renewal, and proved good at assimilating European ideas and using them against the occupying powers.

Geoffrey Barraclough presents the consequences of European intervention in Asia and Africa in three stages:

> First, it acted as a solvent of the traditional social order; secondly, it brought about substantial economic changes; finally, it led to the rise of western educated *élites* which took the lead in transforming the existing resentment against the foreigner and foreign superiority into organised nationalist movements on a massive scale. (p. 171)

Imperialism produced, from within its own logic, 'both a new class of leaders and the material and moral conditions which ensured the success of the anti-western revolt which they led' (p. 174).

The colonial situation was so perverse that it generated quite specific reversals of effect at every turn. A stratum of educated natives was required to help run the place, but these were the people (some of them) who came to understand their oppression and developed the skills to resist it ('We lost the Indian Empire when we introduced Matriculation. . . . We've taught 'em to read and write a la bloody Whitehall so's they can write us our marching orders'; Scott, *Alien Sky*, p. 20). Again, nationalism in Africa was stimulated by the return of soldiers who had gained a wider perspective from being taken to fight in Britain's war in Asia. The first disturbances in the Gold Coast (Ghana) were caused when an English police officer fired on demonstrating war veterans, killing or wounding several. Nationalist leaders were even able to appeal to supposedly British values. In Cyprus Lawrence Durrell, initially at least, met people who declared their love for freedom *and* Britain: 'We do not have to teach you what freedom means – you brought it to Greece' (Durrell, p. 26). Durrell was pleased and embarrassed – the latter because he knew Britain had no intention of acceding to Cypriot demands.

Of course, exploitation did not end with decolonization – it can manage very well without colonies. George Lichtheim offers two current definitions of imperialism: 'the British and subsequently the American drive to throw foreign markets open to Western capital', and 'the transfer of surplus value from the poor countries to the rich through trade relationships which in practice discriminate against undeveloped economies' (Lichtheim, p. 126). On these definitions, imperialism certainly didn't end with 'independence'. On the contrary, it increased; one of the external stimulants towards decolonization was the impatience of US and multi-national corporations with the restrictive trade policies imposed by the colonial power. Now instead of moving labour-power to the centre, multinationals move capital and expertise to the periphery, exploiting cheap labour where it already lives and keeping the social and political consequences at arm's length (industrial and nuclear waste are dumped too). But still, when there is a critical moment in capitalism, such as the energy crisis, third-world countries are made to feel it first and most intensely, cushioning the effect in more powerful countries.

The Return and the Native

One way of thinking of imperialism is as the export of conflict and violence. Colonial emigration enabled Britain to remove to a safe distance diverse dangers – trades unionists, poachers and other lawbreakers; upper-class idealists and bullies; unemployment, hunger and disunity (see

Hechter, pp. 237–9). With the collapse of colonization, much of the violence comes back home. Sartre observed: 'Today violence, blocked everywhere, comes back on us through our soldiers, comes inside and takes possession of us. Involution starts; the native recreates himself, and we, settlers and Europeans, ultras and liberals, we break up.'[5] In France this worked explicitly, for the settlers brought their anger, resentment and humiliation back from Algeria to France and a putsch by them was averted only at the cost of one by de Gaulle. In the British case, many settlers moved on – from India to Kenya to Southern Rhodesia (Zimbabwe) to South Africa. But many came back, along with redundant administrators, soldiers and policemen, sometimes inured to racism and brutality. At the same time, some of the factors that produced decolonization helped to produce also the migration of some Blacks and Asians to what they had been led to regard as the mother country; a Sri Lankan remarks: 'We are over here because you were over there' (Moore, p. 16). Now colonial violence, physical and psychological, was reproduced in Britain, in housing, work and community relations, affording a consolation for the loss of empire and dividing working people against themselves.

Caribbean Blacks were recruited actively through the 1950s by the Health Service (with Enoch Powell as minister) and London Transport. Imported labour is free – you don't have to pay for its breeding and rearing; and during recessions it may conveniently be laid off, as *The Economist* pointed out in 1959 (Titmuss, *Essays*, p. 228). The people were pleased to come, even to menial work, though most of them were skilled, to escape unemployment and poor wages at home (drained of resources, colonies were left at independence with a large labour force and no capital to render it productive; in Jamaica unemployment was at 20 per cent and seven shillings a day was considered good pay for an unskilled labourer; Montgomery, p. 101). In another ironic reversal, Blacks were attracted in part by the image of the superior life in Britain that had been propagated in the colonies as a justification for imperial domination. Surveys showed that they believed Britain to be a Christian country of love and tolerance, ready to welcome strangers and care for them; that it was a generally prosperous country in which everyone lived in the manner of Europeans in the colonies (they were surprised to see white people doing manual work; Richmond, pp. 243, 246). And Commonwealth immigrants were in fact British citizens: the imperial relation, it seems, led Britain to use the settler concept of migrant labour rather than the *Gastarbeiter* model of continental Europe (Sivanandan, pp. 102–5, 143–6).

Nevertheless, racial discrimination was ubiquitous and continuous. Sam Selvon's novel *The Lonely Londoners* (1956) seeks to mediate generously between Caribbean and English attitudes. Blacks coming to London bring with them their customs of relating and their expectations about Britain. Generally, a genial air pervades the book, though some of the presentation of Blacks is defensively whimsical. However, there is also a persistent strain of perplexity and sadness (not resentment) at the unfairness, prejudice and hostility they encounter. 'In America you see a sign telling you to keep off, but over here you don't see any, but when you go in the hotel or the restaurant they will politely tell you to haul – or else give you the cold treatment' (Selvon, p. 24). It is only as you put the novel down that you may recall that no white English person has spoken with more than politeness (and sometimes less) to a Black all through.

Liberal optimism about the tolerance (let alone fairness) of English society was rudely undercut by outbreaks of violence against Blacks in Nottingham and then Notting Hill (London) in August and September 1958. Such incidents were not unprecedented and not the last. But they were fanned by the press and led to hysterical demands for immigration controls. Sivanandan remarks: 'Racism, though economically useful, was becoming socially counter-productive' (p. 105). Left-wing MP Tom Driberg asked: 'How can there be a colour problem here? Even after all the immigration of the past few years, there are only 190,000 coloured people in our population of over 50 million – that is, only four out of every 1,000, The real problem is not black skins, but white prejudice' (Fryer, p. 380). But there followed the 1962 Commonwealth Immigrants Act (Conservative), the 1968 Kenyan Asians Act (Labour), the 1971 Immigration Act (Conservative) and the 1981 British Nationality Act (Conservative).[6]

British prejudice was the continuation of the imperial assumption that it was right to exploit Africans and Asians because they were inferior. Sheila Patterson in her book *Dark Strangers* (1963) summarized her research:

A coloured skin, especially when combined with Negroid features, is associated with alienness, and with the lowest social status. Primitiveness, savagery, violence, sexuality, general lack of control, sloth, irresponsibility – all these are part of the image. On the more favourable side, Negroid peoples are often credited with athletic, artistic and musical gifts, and with an appealing and childlike simplicity which is no way incompatible with the remainder of the image. (pp. 212–13)

Despite all this – and she is not unaware that 'favourable' attributes like proficiency at boxing and jazz tend to reinforce ideas of violence, sensuality and lack of inhibition (p. 241) – Patterson says that the problem is not colour prejudice but a temporary misunderstanding such as afflicts any immigrant group and evaporates as the group becomes assimilated. But other immigrant groups, apart from the Jews, did not hold such a significant position in the British self-image, and the evidence Patterson quotes indicates widespread racism. In fact, it was part of imperialist ideology to believe that British people are rather good at race relations (as in the story about the generous granting of independence), and that Black people will put up with routine discrimination indefinitely.

Colin MacInnes's enthusiasm for (male) Black immigrants was partly sexual, partly humanistic, and partly a refreshing excitement at the new cultural opportunities offered by Blacks in a stodgy and boring English scene. In *City of Spades* (1957) Montgomery Pew becomes an Assistant Welfare Officer of the Colonial Department in London. Not accepting the view of his predecessor – 'that the Negro's still, deep down inside, a savage' (p. 14) – he spends his time investigating Black lifestyles in London, and specially that of Johnny Fortune, a Nigerian who shares the narration. Pew finds the Blacks 'bring an element of joy and fantasy and violence into our cautious, ordered lives' (p. 77). At points he falls into an enthusiastic myth-making that is the obverse of hostile stereotyping. He thinks, of Black US ballet dancers: 'As they danced, they were clothed in what seemed the antique innocence and wisdom of humanity before the Fall – the ancient, simple splendour of the millenially distant days before thought began, and civilisations . . .' (p. 206). The noble savage has always been the flip-side of the sub-human savage; here MacInnes is still using Blacks in a dispute about the quality of European civilization.

However, the presentation of Blacks is not generally sentimental in *City of Spades*, and Pew's attitude is challenged frequently, not least by Johnny Fortune, who accepts Pew as a friend calmly and straightforwardly, but generally without reciprocal enthusiasm. Pew complains that Blacks 'invade your soul: or rather, they did not, but your own idea of them did – for they were sublimely indifferent to anything outside themselves!' (p. 178). The distinction here between Blacks and Pew's idea of them shows awareness of the appropriation Pew makes. Equally valuable is his complaint about indifference, for it stresses that Blacks have their own preoccupations and aren't just figures in the lives of whites. The chapters in Johnny Fortune's narration reinforce this sense, centring upon the affairs of the Black community and attending to whites only when they become relevant. These may seem only minimal requirements for a good novel, morally, politically and technically – that diverse characters should have their own consciousnesses and concerns – but they are met only rarely in British writing where people of colour are among the characters. The culminating event is the framing of Johnny Fortune by the police – an audacious move by MacInnes, at that date, and owing something to his experience as a homosexual. Johnny admits that he is 'turning sour': 'Spades will stay sour, man, let me tell you, till they're treated right' (p. 275). In MacInnes's view, England spoils the utopian possibilities of Black culture. Finally Johnny returns to Nigeria.

The enthusiasm for the contribution of Black immigrants to British culture occurs again in MacInnes's novel *Absolute Beginners* (1959); the central character has all the left–liberal hopes of the day. However, as I argue in chapter 8, the optimism that pervades most of the book cannot cope with the Notting Hill riots. MacInnes and his characters are shocked, as Black immigrants were, by the attitudes of the police, the law and the press (Lamming, *Pleasures*, pp. 80, 82, 218). They had believed the official story about the basic fairness of British institutions.

> In the history books, they tell us the English race has spread itself all over the damn world: gone and settled everywhere, and that's one of the great, splendid English things. No one invited us, and we didn't ask anyone's permission, I suppose. Yet when a few hundred thousand come and settle among our fifty millions, we just can't take it. (*Absolute Beginners*, pp. 172–3)

However, families of immigrants have proved very resourceful at finding ways of surviving and flourishing in Britain. In the pattern we have seen earlier, the racism that conducts Black labour into the system is also the reversible circuit along which modes of resistance can move.[7]

Literature and the Metropolis

The institutions of literature developed in the nineteenth century in association, partly, with the idea of English imperial destiny (Baldick). The first public examinations in England were for the Indian Civil Service; in 1868 one of the examiners told the Taunton Commission:

I should take forty or fifty passages, taken from what I call fair authors – Shakespeare, Milton, Pope, and some of the later writers, Sir Walter Scott and Tennyson. I have set this question over and over again. 'Here is a passage. State where it comes from, explain any peculiarities of English in it, and state the context as far as you are able to do so'. (Althick, p. 184)

All too many readers of this book will be familiar with such exercises. No doubt they help sustain Margaret Thatcher's 'Victorian values'.

As I've said, the educating of colonial subjects was necessary but risky. In *The Grass Is Singing* Dick 'did not like mission boys, they "knew too much". And in any case they should not be taught to read and write: they should be taught the dignity of labour and general usefulness to the white man' (p. 164). It is not clear what effect the teaching of English literature had; generally it was promoted as part of the special genius with which England had been blessed, and as manifesting values that transcend commercial purposes. It symbolized the generosity that led Britain to share its culture with subject races, and helped to 'civilize' them – i.e. wean them away from other cultural and political allegiances. Tennyson's poems, for instance, were prefaced by professors of English Literature at Presidency College, Calcutta, with the view that 'the moral laws which he so strongly upholds are those primary sanctions upon which average English society is founded' (Rowe and Webb, p. xiv). George Lamming describes how it felt in the Caribbean:

The West Indian's education was imported in much the same way that flour and butter are imported from Canada. Since the cultural negotiation was strictly between England and the natives, and England had acquired, some-how, the divine right to organise the native's reading, it is to be expected that England's export of literature would be English. And the further back in time England went for these treasures, the safer was the English commodity. So the examinations, which would determine that Trinidadian's future in the Civil Service, imposed Shakespeare, and Wordsworth, and Jane Austen and George Eliot and the whole tabernacle of dead names, now come alive at the world's greatest summit of literary expression. How in the name of Heavens could a colonial native . . . ever get out from under this ancient mausoleum of historic achievement? (*Pleasures*, p. 27)

The native was proffered a cultural identity which in actuality she or he was not allowed, fully, to adopt – not being white; and in the process was removed from the culture of his or her (mainly his) family and locality.

I would add only this. Lamming assumes (as does James Baldwin in *Notes of a Native Son*) that Europeans generally are in secure possession of Shakespeare, Bath, Chartres, and such cultural monuments. However, the vast majority of Europeans have no particular stake there, in fact these monuments act as instruments of class domination in Europe rather as they do of racial and national domination across the world. For a lower-class English person to join the Civil Service, she or he also will have to forsake the culture of family and neighbourhood and acquire knowledge of Wordsworth and George Eliot, or some comparable area of middle-class culture. The same is true for the Welsh, Scots or Irish person. Dylan Thomas is often said to manifest Welsh *hywl*, but to do that in a way that would become widely known he had to negotiate English and literary culture. Raymond Williams observes that to become educated in Wales was to learn English modes (see p. 268).

A writer deeply implicated in these complexities is V. S. Naipaul, who was born in Trinidad of an Indian family and came to London in 1950. *A House for Mr Biswas* (1961) sets the life history of a man such as Naipaul's father in the context of changes in the Indian community of Trinidad. The house is the symbol of status and stability that Mr Biswas craves as he struggles from poor farm boy to journalist to government official, supported and confined by the extended family of his wife. But still he hasn't really made it: near the end of his life, hearing of a young relative's visit to Europe, he concludes: 'There, where Owad had been, was surely where life was to be found' (p. 540).

The presentation of Mr Biswas is a strange mixture of sympathy and satire, inwardness and distance. Consider these two passages, from the same page, about the materials with which, for want of money, the first house must be built:

> Mr Biswas hesitated. Of all wood cedar appealed to him least. The colour was pleasing but the smell was acrid and clinging. It was such a soft wood that a fingernail could mark it and splinters could be bitten off with the teeth. To be strong it had to be thick; then its thickness made it look ungainly.

> Mr Biswas examined the sheets as they were unloaded, looking for bumps and dents he could attribute to Sushila's maliciousness. Whenever he saw a crack in the rust he stopped the loaders. 'Look at this. Which of you was responsible for this? You know, I mad enough to get Mr Seth to dock your money'. That word 'dock', so official and ominous, he had got from Jagdat. (pp. 260–1)

The first passage is in there with Mr Biswas, sharing not just his opinion but his perception; we can almost feel, with him, the wood yielding under his fingernail. The second passage is external and mocking. The narrative voice is split, between identification with Mr Biswas and near-contempt for him. In effect, though it is not said and cannot be literally true since he is not present or even born for most of the action, the narrator's is the voice of the son Anand, who is successful in the school system and escapes to England. The uncomfortable treatment of Mr Biswas is that of the native boy who is drawn into the culture of the Europeans.

The grounds for assessing the complex partiality of the narrator are there in the presentation of Anand. Just before the passages quoted above, he sees that his father is going to use second-hand sheeting for the roof, and displays his disappointment and shame at its impoverished appearance (p. 259); it is from those feelings that both the identification with and mockery of Mr Biswas come. Anand is said to have a 'satirical sense', and 'contempt, quick, deep, inclusive. . . . It led to inadequacies, to self-awareness and a lasting loneliness. But it made him unassailable' (p. 413). However, this account of a self-protective stance is not applied, explicitly, to the narrative voice. Further down the same page we read of relations arriving: 'nondescript people'; but the dismissive phrase is not attributed to the aspirations and self-protection of one such as Anand. It is offered as sufficient. It seems to come from the wise, omniscient narrator of the English novel – the voice Anand and Naipaul heard in their education.[8]

A House for Mr Biswas has been accepted into the tradition of the English novel, probably because sniggering at the social aspirations of lower-class people sometimes passes for wisdom there. On the back of the Penguin edition Francis Wyndham is quoted as saying the book is 'conceived and executed within the great tradition of the humanist novel'. And Professor Arthur Pollard, chief 'A' level examiner for the conservative University of London Board, declared in 1982: 'The fact remains that, with the possible exception of Naipaul, there really is nothing in African and Caribbean literature to match in quality those works which are normally found within the substantive body of texts set at Advanced Level.'[9] But the interest of *A House for Mr Biswas* lies not in its secure humanist conception and execution, but in its inability to assess and confess the specificity of its narrative voice.

In the Castle of my Skin (1953) by George Lamming, another migrant from the Caribbean to London, criticizes the education in European culture provided in Barbados (which is perhaps why the novel doesn't achieve the 'quality' required by the University of London examinations board). Pupils are taught about Barbados being 'Little England', the goodness of Queen Victoria, the Battle of Hastings and the Wars of the Roses, but not that their forebears had been taken from Africa as slaves. When they hear of that they find it incredible (pp. 56–8, 98–104, 221). The central character is the boy who gets to high-school and experiences alienation from the village community, but without fully assimilating school values ('He said they were trying to make gentlemen of us, but it seemed I didn't belong'; p. 225). He is caught between two worlds, and at the end of the book leaves for Trinidad, still in search of an identity.

The consequence of such an alienated position – and it was invitable if you were to get from a Bajan village to the point of writing a novel that could be published in the general world-market for fiction in English – is, again, a disturbed narrative stance. But rather than obscuring this, *In the Castle of my Skin* admits and uses it, moving between several points of view – the boy's, the villagers', and the informed narrator's. This movement manifests the difficulty of gaining a coherent perspective from within a colonial situation. The villagers have been persuaded to believe that the local education system is excellent, that it is unfortunate if your skin is too black, that Big England and Little England go hand in hand in the world. How would they know better? Even the wise old man and woman and the politically aware shoemaker mistake the intentions of the white land-lord and his Black successor. The informed narration can explain what is happening (for instance, the current of envy and suspicion that runs through the village is attributed not, as in *Mr Biswas*, to merely personal malignancy, but to the imposition of a Black overseer between the white landlord and the people, so that the people's resentment is turned upon themselves and anyone who seems to be joining the enemy; pp. 26–7). But the narrator's knowledge is separated, by definition, from the people's experience.

This gap is closed at the end of the book, when the boy is about to leave. His friend Trumper returns from the United States, bringing an outside analysis of the injustice that is taking place in the village (these people are not getting houses, as was Mr Biswas, but being evicted). Trumper has learnt that Blacks are his people – he plays Paul Robeson's recording of the spiritual 'Let My People Go' (pp. 293–8). In the United States, Trumper says, 'They suffer in a way we don't know here. We can't understan' it here an' we never will. But their sufferin' teach them what we here won't ever know. The Race, our people' (p. 296). This is almost beyond the boy's comprehension, but it may be the answer to his insecurity about his identity. In the last pages of the novel Trumper says: 'A man who know his people won't ever feel like that.' The boy goes, with the blessing of the old man, to find out for himself.

Naipaul pursued the theme of cultural identity in *An Area of Darkness*, which tells how in 1962 he spent a year in India, trying to come to terms with a culture which was in a sense 'his'. He is stirred, nostalgically, by remnants of the English occupation, and declares: 'Indians could walk among these relics with ease; the romance had always been partly theirs and now they had inherited it fully. I was not English or Indian; I was denied the victories of both' (p. 104). Despite this sense of being neither one thing nor the other, Naipaul identifies consistently in this book with a European point of view. He criticizes again and again the dirt, corruption, inefficiency and cultural insecurity of India, without expressing any sense that such things might occur in other forms in Europe (for instance, that class might, compared with caste, have its own disadvantages; p. 79). He is specially sensitive to people he perceives as mimicking English manners, though not, apparently, because they make him think of his own indirect acquisition of English culture.

Mimicry is a dubious concept. Naipaul describes '*the* Indian army officer' (my italics: are they all the same?):

> He even manages to look English; his gait and bearing are English; his mannerisms, his tastes in drink are English; his slang is English. In the Indian setting this Indian English mimicry is like fantasy. It is an undiminishing absurdity; and it is only slowly that one formulates what was sensed from the first day: this is a mimicry not of England, a real country, but of the fairytale land of Anglo–India, of clubs and sahibs and syces and bearers. (p. 61)

Now, all this may be roughly true. But if we were describing natives of Britain dressing up nowadays in the clothes of the prewar leisure class to attend the opera, or in the manner of 1950s teddy boys, or in 'hunting pink', would we say they were mimicking? Possibly we would, but it wouldn't be the obvious or necessary way to put it. It would be more suitable to speak of the adoption of a distinctive style in order to display allegiance to a certain set of social attitudes. Even if we disliked those attitudes, we would recognize the legitimate choice of a feasible stance from the repertoire of cultural resources. But 'mimicry' suggests something intrinsically foolish and unrewarding.

What is at work, at least in some uses of the notion of mimicry, may be seen from this passage in Scott's *Birds of Paradise*. A rajah, after independence, speaks of himself: 'Look at me, old man. I speak the same language as you. We laugh at the same kind of things. I don't *ape* English manners, they were drilled into me by old Nannie and the Princes' College. But underneath my princely Indian flesh I have the bones of the serf I always was' (p. 231). Notice, first, the give-away excess, 'old man', suggesting at once a synthetic quality in the rajah's speech. He denies that he 'apes' – that he is less than human – but admits he was 'drilled into' 'English manners', implying that they were not his by nature. Yet how, we might ask, is the rajah's acquisition of culture different in principle from the way people in England pick up their habits and speech, dress and appearance? And suppose his mimicry was perfect, what then? How would we distinguish him from 'the real thing'?

The answer to these questions, within the idea of mimicry, is that nothing the rajah could do would be the real thing – because he is Indian and therefore by definition not allowed to join the dominant race. Therefore his acquisition of English culture cannot be like that of English people; only the white is genuine. In fact, in relation to the dominant race he is no more than a serf, as he tells us himself. One of the things the rajah learnt as part of his 'English' education was that Indians are inferior, and it is this notion that undermines his confidence in the coherence of his personality. Homi Bhabha has argued that mimicry is 'at once resemblance and menace', that it menaces through 'its *double* vision which in disclosing the ambivalence of Colonial discourse, also disrupts its authority' (Bhabha, 'Of Mimicry', pp. 199, 201). I think, rather, that colonial discourse coped very well with the imperfect representation of itself which it received back from educated Indians, reading those imperfections, as Naipaul and Scott do, as evidence of the natural and necessary superiority of Europeans. For Naipaul, however, the 'mimicry' of Indian army officers may constitute a threat, because he needs to reassure himself that his own English identification is not mimicry. He is imprisoned by the construct that he adopted with the purpose of gaining his freedom.

In 1967 Naipaul audaciously extended the idea of mimicry in his novel *The Mimic Men*. Here it appears that everyone with secondary education in the formerly British Caribbean is merely mimicking:

We, here on our island, handling books printed in this world [i.e. Canada and Belgium], and using its goods, had been abandoned and forgotten. We pretended to be real, to be learning, to be preparing ourselves for life, we mimic men of the New World, one unknown corner of it, with all its reminders of the corruption that came so quickly to the new. (p. 175)

Consequently, it seems, the narrator, an exiled political leader, lacks a personal centre and sees himself only as role-playing, and this condition is said to pervade Third-World politics. So, in effect, Naipaul supplies the notorious absence in Conrad's *Nostromo* – the explanation of why Decoud, the brilliant young political leader committed to his country's freedom, is so hollow at the centre that when left on his own for a few days he kills himself. In Naipaul's novel this is integral to the post-colonial situation. Now mimicry is not the folly of particular groups, but the general condition of three-quarters of the world. So determined is Naipaul's Englishness that he can't envisage any serious life outside it.

A Crisis of Self Esteem

European intellectuals were vulnerable to a particular inference about decolonization, namely that it called into question the value of European culture. The point was taken explicitly by Sartre, though intellectuals in England tried not to hear him: 'We must face that unexpected revelation, the striptease of our humanism. There you can see it, quite naked, and it's not a pretty sight. It was nothing but an ideology of lies, a perfect justification for pillage; its honeyed words, its affectation of sensibility were only alibis for our aggressions.'[10] A cornerstone of imperial ideology was that European culture represented the apogee of human achievement, and the others were the savages – that is why they had to be rendered servile in their own countries. And this alleged savagery included both incompetence and violence. The Duchess of Manchester said, during the Kenya Mau Mau resistance: 'The niggers – that is what *we* call them – have a list of Europeans they want to get rid of. But they can't manage without us, and they will have to see reason eventually. It is difficult to explain this to them because they have no brains, you know – only animal cunning' (Montgomery, p. 100). But what if Africans, Asians and Caribbean peoples were competent, did not need Europeans, did not respect their humanism, wanted them to leave? And what if the Europeans were violent, unjust and, further, hypocritical about it? European self-esteem and the superior status of European culture were at stake.

In Anthony Burgess's *Malayan Trilogy* the central character is Victor Crabbe, a schoolteacher. Through him, Burgess attempts to handle two divergent thoughts: that the British have valuable knowledge and culture to contribute to Malaya, and that they have become irrelevant. The three component novels represent successive adjustments through the early and mid-1950s – they are *Time for a Tiger* (1956), *The Enemy in the Blanket* (1958) and *Beds in the East* (1959). The most pronounced attributes of the British seem to be drunkenness, lechery and pettiness; nevertheless, the main impetus of the trilogy is to find meaning in the British enterprise, and when that fails everything is represented as disintegrating.

At first, in *Time for a Tiger*, Crabbe feels that the cultural influence is two-way. Through interaction with his students he sees that 'a white skin was an abnormality, and that the white man's ways were fundamentally eccentric'; he draws 'great breaths of refreshment from the East, even out of the winds of garlic and dried fish and turmeric' (pp. 56–7). It is not a very equal exchange, but this novel nevertheless proposes a strong resolution of cultural disjunction: absorption. Crabbe is told: 'You will lose function and identity. You will be swallowed up and become another kind of eccentric. You may become a Muslim. You may forget your English, or at least lose your English accent' (p. 193). And something like this is anticipated in the cheerful final episode, where people speak to each other in diverse languages and 'it became Whitsun more than Christmas, for the Tower of Babel lay with the empty bottles' (p. 202).

In *The Enemy in the Blanket* such a harmonious resolution comes to seem implausible. Crabbe's wife argues: 'Are you so blind? Don't you see the beginning of the end already? They don't want us here. They're talking about Malaya for the Malayans. There's no room for Europeans any more' (p. 273). His fall-back position is that it is 'his duty to show Malaya those aspects of the West which were not wholly evil, to prepare Malaya for the taking over of the dangerous Western engine' (p. 301). Though Malayans manifestly don't want British rule, they may still be grateful for some culture and wisdom. But this idea is criticized as typifying the third episode, so to speak, of Wagner's *Ring* cycle, when actually the twilight of the gods is at hand (pp. 312–3). 'Malaya did not want him. The romantic dream he had entertained, the dream that had driven Raffles to early death, was no longer appropriate.' Even so, it is implied that Crabbe and English culture have something of value that is being displaced. Burgess is unable to say quite what this is; instead, its disregard is linked to a supposed general decline of human possibilities. If the British Empire is not wanted in Malaya, there must be 'no longer any room for the individual . . . nothing now that any one man could build' (p. 361). The huge expansion of opportunity for people in Malaya doesn't count.

In *Beds in the East* the bruised English sensibility imagines that everything must disintegrate together with its own role. The presence together of Malays, Chinese, Tamils and Sikhs is now seen as threatening an independent Malaya: 'There was, it's true, a sort of illusion of getting on when the British were in full control. But self-determination's a ridiculous idea in a mixed-up place like this. There's no nation. There's no common culture, language, literature, religion' (p. 447; the same might be said of several European countries). So the British are once more part of the solution, not of the problem; and now Crabbe's mission is not to impose English culture, but somehow to referee the others. He holds a party for the purpose but it turns into a brawl (pp. 485–8). And he encourages the musical talent of Robert Loo, and tries to get the State Information Officer to take up his symphony as 'the first bit of national culture you've ever had' (p. 455). But Robert Loo is confused and distracted by too many and diverse musical influences, and especially by the interference of US culture.

The ambivalent effect of US power – helping to stave off communism but tending to corrupt (producing, for instance, juvenile delinquency: *Malayan*, pp. 442–3) – is a recurring theme in British literature of decolonization. In Scott's *Alien Sky* the US person, MacKendrick, is told: 'The British are going and now it's your turn. Whether you like it or not, all they're doing here is exchanging the Union Jack for the dollar sign' (pp. 31–2; notice the implication that US imperialism is more directly to do with money). I discuss elsewhere (in Chapters 8 and 9 particularly) the attractions of US cultural power and the resentment it caused; part of the damage to British self-esteem was that the beneficiary of the break up of the empire was the United States. The halting of the 1956 Suez adventure – an attempt to invade Egypt and teach a lesson to any nationalist leader who thought he could defy British (or French) wishes – by pressure from the Eisenhower–Dulles Administration, showed that the United States saw no reason to encourage European powers to maintain their imperial pretensions. In *Beds in the East* the United States moves in as Britain moves out ('nature abhors a vacuum'; p. 544 – the natives are empty space). It seems that US ideological techniques are to be more sophisticated. There's the linguistic angle. Then there's the angle of inter-racial relations. And there's method of teacher training, time-and-motion study in industry, behaviour patterns, statistics, sociological surveys and, of course, demographic studies. A great deal to do. It'll cost a lot of money, of course, but it's the best possible investment. We can't afford to let the Communists get away with it. (*Malayan*, p. 548)

In Burgess's tone, admiration and envy struggle with a residual claim for superior British good sense.

Crabbe is killed, finally, by the jungle (a scorpion), and is absorbed into Malaya not culturally but physically. Wounded European self-esteem falls back upon appropriated, vague mysticism ('The jungle called "OM", like the Malay showman of the shadow-play, one and indivisible, ultimate numen'; p. 580). If Britons aren't wanted to rule and give culture to the world then they might as well die, there is nowhere to go.

Where there were few white settlers and little strategic military significance, the withdrawal from empire occurred without too much physical violence. In 1948 there were riots in the Gold Coast/Ghana, by 1950 there was a Black government under a British governor, and in 1957 independence. In other places – Kenya, Cyprus, Aden (People's Democratic Republic of Yemen), Southern Rhodesia (Zimbabwe) – there was a period of bloody repression and resistance. Fanon remarked: 'So they say that the natives want to go too quickly. Now, let us never forget that only a very short time ago they complained of their slowness, their laziness and their fatalism' (*Wretched* p. 59).

Often the perceived need to prevent local self-determination led to shameful European methods. Sartre observed: 'Rage and fear are already blatant; they show themselves openly in the nigger-hunts in Algiers. Now, which side are the savages on?' (Fanon, *Wretched*, p. 24). The Kenyan struggle was precipitated by settler agitation against political progress, the detention of Jomo Kenyatta and other African leaders, and the forced removal of 100,000 people from Nairobi. It was conducted viciously on both sides. Sections of British public opinion were shocked by reports of British actions – arbitrary killings, torture and beatings of prisoners, collective punishments, concentration camps for suspects detained without trial, wholesale removal of peoples from their lands, executions, a shoot-to-kill policy, the bombing of tribespeople thought to be harbouring guerrillas, and the holding of people without trial. On 5 June 1954, the Colonial Secretary announced, 6,741 people were being held on detention orders, 6,937 in work camps on restrictive movement orders, and 22,553 for 'screening' on short-term detention orders (Richmond, pp. 188–202).

There were ways of trying to disavow the implications of such reports. The psychologist William Sargant quoted from *The Times* (1 September 1955) court evidence on the treatment of a Kikuyu prisoner, Kamau Kichina:

> Throughout Kamau's captivity no effort was spared to force him to admit his guilt. He was flogged, kicked, handcuffed with his arms between his legs and fastened behind his neck, denied food for a period, and was left out at least two nights tied to a pole in a shed, not surrounded by walls, with only a roof overhead, and wearing merely a blanket to keep out the cold.

Although a day or two before his death he was no longer able to stand properly, no medical attention was sought; he was never brought before a magistrate. This episode is used by Sargant as evidence of the subtle viciousness of the Kikuyu! – on the ground that their powerful indoctrination techniques were proof against 'crude beating-up methods' (Sargant, pp. 150–1; of course, this overlooks the possibility that Kamau Kichina was 'innocent').

But to many people it was apparent that there were problems with the ideology of European superiority. Lamming developed the analogy of Prospero and Caliban: 'Now it is Prospero's turn to submit to the remorseless logic of his own past. . . . He cannot deny that past; nor can he abandon it without creating a total suicide of all those values which once sanctified his acts as coloniser' (*Pleasures*, p. 85). The colonial enterprise cannot be forgotten, because it has been the locus of all kinds of cherished beliefs about Europe; yet it must be acknowledged as a history of violence and oppression.

Writers tried to register the shock and shame of such contradictions. David Caute's novel *At Fever Pitch* (1959) shows British soldiers continuously drunk and riven by sexual disturbance in an African country moving into independence. The most sympathetic officer panics when confronting a rioting crowd without adequate support and shoots 25 people, but he is saved from prosecution by the threat that British troops, supporting the government, will be withdrawn. In Alan Sillitoe's novel *Key to the Door* (1961), Brian Seaton is in Malaya on National Service, and finds that sympathy with the communist insurgents is the obvious continuation of his instinctive leftishness and anti-racism. So he has easy relations with his Chinese woman, who says most people support the communists (p. 337), and when he overcomes a guerrilla who attacks him in the jungle he lets him go. In a survey, *The Novel Now*, Anthony Burgess attacks Sillitoe's book for wilful ignorance and political innocence (p. 150). Burgess has a point: the case against the communists – that they were promoting the minority Chinese as against the Malays and other peoples – is put but not answered in *Key to the Door* (pp. 330–4). The final impression is that Seaton is using Malaya, in the way we keep seeing, as an item in an argument about Europe. It is unclear how far Sillitoe means us to reach that conclusion.

Plays at the Royal Court associated with the New Left (see chapter 12) took up the topic. Osborne's *The Entertainer* (1957) invokes the Suez invasion as part of the shambles that British imperial power had become. *The Long and the Short and the Tall* by Willis Hall (1958) is set in Malaya in 1942, but its theme of British military incompetence and loss of morale, leading to the killing of an unarmed prisoner and general defeat, was topical. *Serjeant Musgrave's Dance*, by John Arden (1959), is based on an actual event in Cyprus, where the killing of a British person was followed by the killing of five Cypriot people during a 'search' operation. It gradually becomes apparent that Musgrave intends to multiply by five again and kill 25 of those in power (mayor, parson, policeman) in the town from which the dead soldier came. The play is optimistic in its treatment of the British situation, for striking miners are alert both to local oppression and to the danger of irrational violence by such as Musgrave. As they reflect on the fable they have witnessed, they, and the audience, may learn to transform their society. In Edward Bond's play *Saved* (1965), the young men who murder a baby in its pram seem to think they are still in Malaya, 'shootin' up the yeller niggers' – 'Looks like a yeller-nigger', one of them says (pp. 28, 66). If you teach such young men how to kill and little else, Bond is saying, you shouldn't be surprised if you get violent behaviour.

The Savage Within

A principal ideological adjustment attempted by British literary intel-lectuals was to focus upon the concept of *the savage within*. This is, of course, an idea with a long history. Conrad gave it classic formulation in

Heart of Darkness – 'They howled and leaped, and spun, and made horrid faces; but what thrilled you was just the thought of their humanity – like yours – the thought of your remote kinship with this wild and passionate uproar.'[11] Aldous Huxley put it pithily in his appendix to *The Devils of Loudun* (1952):

> No man, however civilised, can listen for very long to African drumming, or Indian chanting, or Welsh hymn singing, and retain intact his critical and self-conscious personality ... if exposed long enough to the tom-toms and the singing, every one of our philosophers would end by capering and howling with the savages. (Quoted by Sargant, p. 149)

I am happy to witness that this is not true.

Since the eighteenth century, the notion of innate human depravity, as received through some Christianities, has been persistently challenged by ideas that people are either innately good, or neither one nor the other and therefore improvable. In the eighteenth and nineteenth centuries, in the period of imperial enterprise, progress seemed easy to demonstrate, in science and technology, economic and political institutions, in the arts and humanitarian concerns. An ideology of progress appeals to a rising class – it seems to bespeak its coming dominance.[12] The Darwinian theory of evolution seemed to threaten this optimism, but it could be accommodated. Tennyson exhorted:

> Arise and fly
> The reeling Faun, the sensual feast;
> Move upward, working out the beast,
> And let the ape and tiger die.
> (*In Memoriam*, 118)

The savage was that which European Man had left, or was leaving, behind, and imperial enterprise could be taken as the sign of that achievement. Even in *Heart of Darkness*, where Kurtz succumbs to temptations to join the savages, Marlow manages to maintain his equilibrium.

The debate was intensified in the 1950s by awareness of Nazi cruelty, Stalinist oppression, the atomic bomb and the general success of science. In 1955 Bertrand Russell said: 'There is no end to what science can do by way of destruction, and also no end to what it can do in the opposite way' (Thompson, *Poverty*, p. 2). Doris Lessing took up the thought in *The Golden*

Notebook (1962): 'the dream of the golden age is a million times more powerful because it's possible, just as total destruction is possible' (p. 459). The European intelligentsia's crisis of self-esteem at the expulsion from empire – the repudiation of its claim to superior rationality and general culture – contributed a specific inflection. Imperialist ideology was readjusted, to produce a myth of 'human nature': it is savage. Other motifs contributed to this formation, but imagery of the savage returns again and again. Consider William Golding's comment that atrocities committed during the war of 1939–45 'were not done by the headhunters of New Guinea, or by some primitive tribe in the Amazon. They were done, skilfully, coldly, by educated men, doctors, lawyers, by men with a tradition of civilisation behind them, to beings of their own kind.'[13] European atrocities are understood through comparison with Third-World people, who are taken as the benchmark of savagery. In this further tactic of cultural plunder it is not our superiority to the natives that is demonstrated, but our likeness: they are positioned as the image of the worst truth about us. Even so, the implication of Golding's last phrase is that people in Brazil and New Guinea are not of our 'kind'.

The myth of universal savagery is the final, desperate throw of a humiliated and exhausted European humanism. It is informed by both an anxiety about and a continuing embroilment in imperialist ideology. It works like this: when it was just the natives who were brutal, the British were enlightened and necessary rulers. But if the British are (have been) brutal, that's human nature.

There are three advantages in this move. First, the development of the idea of universal savagery may, of itself, be presented as an index of European moral and philosophical profundity. Second, no analysis of colonialism or the continuing effects of Western imperialism need be conducted, since it is all human nature anyway. Third, Europeans may imagine themselves even now to possess at least 'a veneer of civilization', and hence retain the superior position. Moreover, as the final insult, the traditional imperial myths of race, savagery, primitivism and the jungle are now redeployed as the language for misrepresenting European aggression as determined by a universal savagery – of which Third-World peoples are the alleged ultimate instance. These themes appear again and again during the period of decolonization and through into the present, and especially in a potent compound of popular science and what has seemed to be England's profoundest literature. It is a modern myth comparable in potency only with that of the Cold War.

Graham Greene believed that in the colonial situation 'Man' is revealed at his most elemental. In *The Heart of the Matter* (1948) Scobie wonders why he loves 'this place so much? Is it because here human nature hasn't had time to disguise itself? Nobody here could ever talk about a heaven on earth. . . . Here you could love human beings nearly as God loved them, knowing the worst.' When Wilson enters an African brothel the situation is even more extreme: 'Here a man's colour had no value: he couldn't bluster as a white man could elsewhere: by entering this narrow plaster passage, he had shed every racial, social and individual trait, he had reduced himself to human nature' (pp. 30, 186). The shedding of white status is the ultimate reduction: not to have authority over Blacks is to get down to their level, namely that of basic human nature.

In Greene the savage-in-everyone idea ties in conveniently with the Christian notion of 'original sin', and so it does in Golding's novels. The whole idea of *Lord of the Flies* (1954) is that English boys are reduced to the complete stereotype of the savage – with nakedness, warpaint, ululating, superstition, sadism and pointless cruelty. The book is Golding's corrective to *The Coral Island* by R. M. Ballantyne (1857; see Whitley), where Fijian people are represented as fiends, demons and cannibals, delighting in fearsome cruelty. Ballantyne's British boys declare: 'We've got an island all to ourselves [the locals don't count!]. We'll take possession in the name of the king; we'll go and enter the service of its black inhabitants. Of course we'll rise, naturally, to the top of affairs. White men always do in savage countries' (Ballantyne, p. 21). It all proves rather more difficult, but that only shows to better advantage the qualities of the British boys. In fact, there are 'white savages' as well in *The Coral Island* – pirates, 'more blameworthy even than the savages, inasmuch as they knew better' (pp. 146, 180). This is the classic nineteenth-century formulation: anyone *may* be savage (because of 'the strange mixture of good and evil . . . in our own natures'; p. 142), but there is little sign of it in the three decent British boys who represent imperial domination. Golding's distinct post-colonial inflection is to attribute savagery, in principle, to the British ruling elite.

It is possible, if you try, to find cultural-materialist implications in *Lord of the Flies*. We might think of the novel as displaying the effects of the brutal culture of English private schools, for the violence into which the boys degenerate is theirs already when they arrive on the island, in forms which they have learnt at school (see Tiger, pp. 162–4). Jack cries excitedly, 'We'll have rules! . . . Then when any one breaks 'em –', and the other children supply: 'Whee-oh!' 'Wacco!' 'Bong!' 'Doink!' (pp. 32–3). Violence, we might conclude, is acquired culturally from the adult system which is training the boys for imperial and class rule. And the pig's head speaks to Simon 'in the voice of a schoolmaster' and says schoolmasterly things like 'This has gone quite far enough' and 'I'm going to get waxy' (p. 137). Also, the imperialist stereotype of the savage may actually be discerned in the making within the novel, for it is Piggy who introduces and develops it. 'After all, we're not savages. We're English'; 'What are we? Humans? or animals? or savages?'; 'Which is better – to be a pack of painted niggers like you are, or to be sensible as Ralph is?' (pp. 42, 87, 171). In these comments, savagery can be seen as a part of Piggy's political strategy, and it would be amusing to argue that the novel shows the boys' degeneration as consequent upon their acceptance of this imperialist construction of human possibilities. But most readers see the book as demonstrating innate savagery, not cultural construction; and Golding says his theme is 'the fallen nature of man' (*Hot Gates*, p. 90). Piggy's stereotype is adopted by the narration: we are told: 'They understood only too well the liberation into savagery that the concealing paint brought' (p. 164); and towards the end of the book the boys opposing Ralph are referred to consistently as 'the savages'.

Despite its distrust of modern rationalism, *Lord of the Flies* draws some of its strength from an allusion to the way some anthropologists describe 'primitive' peoples. Golding found another pseudo-scientific myth of the savage for *The Inheritors* (1955). The peaceable, co-operative Neanderthalers are displaced by Cro-Magnon people, the direct ancestors of *Homo Sapiens*; the Cro-Magnons have, again, the 'savage' configuration, and the book asks us to recognize in them ourselves. Thus Golding reverses H. G. Wells's version in his story 'The Grisly Folk', where it is Cro-Magnon people that are threatened by Neanderthalers, and the victory of the former is taken as offering hope for future human progress: 'What leapings of the heart were there not throughout that long warfare! What moments of terror and triumph! What acts of devotion and desperate wonders of courage! And the strain of the victors was our strain . . .' (Wells, pp. 691–2). This is precisely the vision of positive human potential that Golding wishes to disqualify.

The idea that the ancestors of modern humans had established their ascendancy through their particular disposition towards violent aggression was topical and controversial in the early 1950s (Golding says he read everything there was to read on the subject; Biles, p. 105). Raymond Dart argued in 1953 that the damage to the bones he had discovered demonstrates that 'man's predecessors differed from living apes in being confirmed killers', and hence that 'the loathesome cruelty of mankind to men forms one of his inescapable, characteristic and differentiative features.' Dart proposes a link between the innate savagery attributed to early humans and that supposed of Third-World peoples when he cites Bantu and other African tribespeople and Pacific and American peoples as instances (pp. 206–9). This was made fully explicit by the right-wing popularizer Robert Ardrey. In his book *African Genesis* (1961) he concludes that only the European has learnt to control his thoughts of 'the pleasure of massacre, the desirability of human slavery, the practicality of castrating one's captured enemy, and the ritual satisfaction of consuming a stranger, preferably alive' (p. 365). Everyone is savage, but the Africans are still the real savages. This was published in South Africa in the year following the Sharpeville Massacre!

Another source for notions of innate human savagery is ethology – trying to understand people through the study of animals. It combines well with popular anthropology and palaeontology, and was given wide currency by Konrad Lorenz's *King Solomon's Ring* (1952). We read there, for instance, of male fighting-fish, that 'the war-dance of the male . . . has exactly the same meaning as the duel of words of the Homeric heroes, or of our Alpine farmers which, even today, often precedes the traditional Sunday brawl in the village inn.' The primitive and remote human is the link between 'us' and the animals. Again, of female fish: their 'wonderful love-play . . . resembles, in delicate grace, a minuet, but in general style, the trance dance of a Balinese temple dancer' (pp. 25, 30).

A key ethological concept is territory – animals deploy elaborate rituals to establish and defend it against others of the same species. Territory is often invoked as a key to Harold Pinter's early plays, where characters fence aggressively for the possession of the room, the security of their boundaries. In *A Slight Ache* (1959) Edward invites in the Matchseller, who stands mysteriously outside his house, threatening his boundary, and shouts in exasperation: 'God damn it, I'm entitled to know something about you! You're in my blasted house, on my territory, drinking my wine, eating my duck!' (pp. 34–5). In *The Dwarfs* (1960) Pete and Mark are described as predatory animals, while Len lurks in his room like an animal in its lair: 'This is the deep grass I keep to. This is the thicket in the centre of the night and morning. . . . Here is my arrangement, and my kingdom' (*Slight*, pp. 96–7). But whereas animals are said to have rituals for deciding domination and subordination, Pinter's characters fight with a blind and bitter determination that transcends any immediate provocation; and the interloper is not just physically repelled, he is attacked at the core of his being and pursued to destruction. It seems second nature. All this is often said; my purpose is to observe its continuity with other writing about the savage within, and the political implications of the appeal to an alleged savage human nature. Mick tells Aston at the end of *The Caretaker*: 'You're nothing else but a wild animal, when you come down to it. You're a barbarian' (pp. 73–4). It's all there: the barbarian caps the wild animal, and there's nothing else when you come down to it.

The other great literary proponent of the animal analogy is Ted Hughes. His 'Hawk Roosting' (*Lupercal*, 1960) seems to invite comparison with humankind, while appealing also to evolutionary origins:

> My feet are locked on the rough bark.
> It took the whole of Creation
> To produce my foot, my each feather:
> Now I hold Creation in my foot.

Hughes denies that he believes violence to be necessarily destructive; he says, rather, that it is the error of 'our rationalist, humanist style of outlook' to try to refuse 'the elemental power circuit of the Universe'; we need 'rituals, the machinery of religion' (Faas, pp. 200–1). But in the poems the special human attribute of self-consciousness seems often, as with Golding's New People and Pinter's human animals, to cut us off irretrievably from the straightforward relationship with violence apparently enjoyed by other creatures. Hughes's thrushes experience

> No indolent procrastinations and no yawning stares,
> No sighs or head-scratchings. Nothing but bounce and stab
> And a ravening second. . . .
> With a man it is otherwise.

('Thrushes', Lupercal)

What complicates 'Hawk Roosting' is that the hawk says 'There is no sophistry in my body' and 'No arguments assert my right', and this sounds like a proclamation of freedom from self-consciousness. But the fact that the hawk says this sounds, contradictorily, like a self-justification – an act of self-consciousness. So the reader is caught between the image of the animal and the interference of 'human' consciousness – producing, perhaps, an enhanced sense of the incompatibility of the two.

The other principal discourses supporting this outlook have been psychoanalysis and psychiatry. Freud thought 'Jung had excellent grounds for his assertion that the mythopoeic forces of mankind are not extinct', and that in dreams and neuroses 'we come upon the *savage* . . . upon the *primitive* man, as he stands revealed to us in the light of the researches of archaeology and of ethnology.'[14] It all hangs together, the savage is within. The association of Third-World peoples with mythopoeic forces, drives, instincts, the id, and other such terms for the savage within, facilitates once more the imperial ideology and obscures political determinants, even while giving the impression that the human situation in the modern world is being confronted at its most profound and demanding.

Psychoanalysis and psychiatry interact with and support the ideas and texts I have already considered; their contribution is to claim knowledge of the present organization of ancient savagery in the depths of our minds. In Hughes's 'The Bull Moses' (*Lupercal*), the boy peers into the darkness of the bull's byre and it is 'a sudden shut-eyed look/Backward into the head'. Hughes's poem 'To Paint a Water Lily' (*Lupercal*) describes the surface of the pond, which is violent enough in this account. But

> Think what worse
> Is the pond-bed's matter of course;
>
> Prehistoric bedraggoned times
> Crawl that darkness with Latin names,
>
> Have evolved no improvements there,
> Jaws for heads, the set stare . . .

'Prehistoric' savagery is currently beneath. Golding writes: 'We stand where any upright food-gatherer has stood, on the edge of our own unconscious' (*Hot Gates*, p. 105). In Golding's *Free Fall* (1959) the central revelation of human inadequacy is reached through interrogation by a Gestapo officer who is called one of the 'psychologists of suffering' (pp. 131–2). Forced to confront the horror inside himself, Sammy cries for help: it is 'the cry of the rat when the terrier shakes it, a hopeless sound, the raw signature of one savage act' (p. 140).

Psychoanalysis and psychiatry seemed to license theories such as that of J. A. Carothers, in his book *The African Mind in Health and Disease* (1953), to the effect that 'the value of preliterate cultures lies' in their representation of 'a certain stage of human social evolution', namely that corresponding to the underlying 'selfish drives' postulated by 'the psychoanalysts' (Carothers, p. 168). From this point of view, imperialism appears as the imposition of reason and control upon the primitive drives that are within all of us but, as usual, more pronounced in colonial subjects. And these drives 'must be stamped on from an early age' – like the natives, no doubt. O. Mannoni proposed that the European attitude to Blacks derived from a 'Prospero complex': 'The savage, as I have said, is identified in the unconscious with a certain image of the instincts – of the *id*, in analytical terminology. And civilised man is painfully divided between the desire to "correct" the "errors" of the savages and the desire to identify himself with them in his search for some lost paradise' (Mannoni, p. 21). Both Europeans and natives are subject to this complex: the former want to dominate, the latter to be dependent. And it is the withdrawal of settler authority which leads (as with parents and children) to native resentment and rebellion (as if there were no other reason). Mannoni has the effrontery to apply this theory to the uprising in Madagascar in 1947, when 80,000 Malagasy people were massacred (see Fanon, *Black*, ch. 4).

Sylvia Plath's poem 'Daddy' seeks to identify a fundamental source of psychic violence and oppression in the male authority figure and the Nazi killer of Jews. But there runs through the poem, also, an unemphatic but insistent association with black: black shoe, black swastika, blackboard, black telephone, black heart, 'A man in black with a Meinkampf look', and

> In the picture I have of you,
> A cleft in your chin instead of your foot
> But no less a devil for that, no not
> Any less the black man who
>
> Bit my pretty red heart in two.
> 			(*Collected Poems*, pp. 223–4)

And in 'The Arrival of the Bee Box' – another image, for Plath, to do with Jews, Nazis, her father and deep-seated violence –

> I put my eye to the grid.
> It is dark, dark,
> With the swarmy feeling of African hands
> Minute and shrunk for export,
> Black on black, angrily clambering.
>
> (p. 213)

In his introduction to the Penguin *New Poetry* (1962) A. Alvarez recommended the poetry of Plath and Hughes and castigated Movement poets for turning away from 'primitivism' and 'the forces of disintegration which destroy the old standards of civilisation'. He declared: 'It is hard to live in an age of psychoanalysis and feel oneself wholly detached from the dominant public savagery.' And he made explicit the link between this perception and the expulsion from empire: 'Once upon a time, the English could safely believe that Evil was something that happened on the Continent, or farther off, in the Empire where soldiers were paid to take care of it' (pp. 26–7; see pp. 194, 227 below).

Nature and Culture

A principal irony of the persistence of imperial ideology in the concept of innate human savagery is that the most pronounced human qualities actually displayed in former colonies are a generous capacity to forgive and forget. Throughout the world, peoples who suffered colonial occupation have striven for friendly relations with their former masters, both internationally and in personal kindness to European visitors (despite continuing insults to their citizens when they visit Britain). Unfortunately Europeans have difficulty recognizing this optimistic evidence of human possibilities, since it is presented by people they have learnt to look down upon.

The story of the savage within aspires to the nature of myth – namely the representation of a permanent truth about 'Man'. But there is no such thing, no essential 'Man'. The claim to be presenting a myth is only a way of trying to add status to a reactionary story. I am trying, steadily, to promote an alternative framework of human possibilities, arguing that the network of stories in which we live and which constructs our world has been made by us in history and society, and may be remade. The idea of a fixed human nature, especially a savage one, means that there is no point in trying to change society: the underlying condition will remain the same and you will probably make things worse. So it seems better to submit to the world as it is, to acquiesce in existing power relations. I discussed the Cold War as a myth of this kind in chapter 6, especially in relation to 1984. E. P. Thompson observed its workings there and in 1950s politicians; in 1983 Conservative cabinet minister Nigel Lawson said: 'I am not a great believer in progress. . . . Man doesn't change. Or man's nature doesn't change. The same problems are there in different forms.'[15] Such an approach underwrites the Cold War: negotiation would be pointless with an 'evil empire'. In Chapter 9, when I discuss the reinvention of Modernism as the artistic mode that sounds the depths of the supposed 'modern condition', a similar anti-progressive pattern will appear.

The key strategy of the myth of the savage within is the surface/depths model. In our culture, this model is a powerful means through which one side of an opposition can be credited with the authority of profundity, and the other dismissed as superficial. It helps proponents of the myth to discount evidence of human behaviours that do not make for their case. This model is bolstered by a present/past model and an us/them model. So, for instance, in *The Naked Ape* (1967), Desmond Morris asserts that our social life comprises 'in reality' – that's the claim for depth – 'an incredibly complicated series of interlocking and overlapping tribal groups' – that's us/them: the concept derived from Africans is applied provocatively to 'us'. 'How very little', Morris continues, 'the naked ape has changed since his early primitive days' – that's present/past (p. 163). We see the same structure when Morris evokes 'the dramatic progression that led [Man], in a mere half-million years, from making a fire to making a space-craft. It is an exciting story, but the naked ape is in danger of being dazzled by it all and forgetting that beneath the surface gloss he is still very much a primate' (p. 21).

The surface/depths model helps to produce a belief that the truth about 'Man' is to be discovered in extreme situations. This facilitates the dismissal of instances of constructive human interaction as superficial. But people act in diverse ways in diverse circumstances within diverse cultures. None of these behaviours is more quintessentially human than another. They are all what people do. The person who betrays her or his comrades under torture, who eats them to survive an aeroplane disaster, who kills them under intolerable stress, is no more 'real' than the caring and co-operative person we see in more congenial circumstances. They are all parts of the picture of human behaviours. It is merely tautologous to show that people behave in extreme ways in extreme conditions. The task of political action, educational and social policy, and even cultural analysis, is to avoid placing people in such conditions. None of us can be sure what she or he would do if ordered to become a concentration camp guard; the point is to avoid the establishment of concentration camps. Revelling in the most appalling events of our century, as literature of the savage depths does, obscures the political determinants and distracts from positive tasks of analysis and action.

A savage human nature means, moreover, that all kinds of restrictions and controls are necessary: it helps to legitimate authoritarian attitudes. It takes sides in the uneasy stand-off between co-operation and competition that underlies welfare-capitalism. Beveridge addressed the argument that human nature requires the fear of suffering to produce social discipline. He quoted from *The Times* (23 January 1943): 'The first function of unemployment (which has always existed in open or disguised forms) is that it maintains the authority of master over man.' Beveridge believed that 'a civilised community' should find better modes of social cohesion (*Full*, p. 195). The myth of the savage within says the quest would be pointless.

Many scientists repudiate the uses of their disciplines that we have been discussing. Bronislaw Malinowski attacked 'the search for origins', for 'primaeval man, the missing link' in anthropology, and the simplification of 'modern savages' into 'stage properties' for 'myth-making':

> It cannot be said too emphatically: first of all, we shall never be able to reconstruct man's original nature in one single term, or even in two or three terms; man has always been more or less what he is: a very complex mixture . . . in short, the savage, the primitive, the man-ape, was probably very much as you and I are. In the second place, whatever primitive man might have been means nothing, absolutely nothing, to what he is going to become. (pp. 111–3)

Of course, if 'savagery' were really the main characteristic of human beings, we would have destroyed ourselves long ago. If we are to use these terms at all, it is only common sense that aggression or competitiveness must work alongside amity or co-operation. The use of violence depends upon the social and economic circumstances in which people find themselves; establishing territory is a tactic in the repertoire of political manoeuvres, not our essential nature.[16] Richard Leakey believes, on the evidence of palaeontology, that 'reciprocal altruism', not violence, is the source of the ascendancy of the human species: 'We are human because our ancestors learned to share their food and their skills in an honoured network of obligation.'[17]

The idea of territoriality has been taken up by the New Right. Modern racism often does not confess itself, but asserts the need for nations to defend their territory against intrusion. Enoch Powell writes: 'I do not believe it is in human nature that a country, and a country such as ours, should passively watch the transformation of whole areas which lie at the heart of it into alien territory' (Barker, *New*, p. 39). National Front pamphlets proclaim:

> Sociobiology has shown us that evolutionary processes have genetically and therefore immutably programmed human nature with instincts of competitiveness, territorial defence, racial prejudice, identification within one's group (nation), instincts which the Marxist fantasy said were socially determined and which could and should be eradicated.[18]

Martin Barker's reply to this is that the primary characteristic of human beings is to plan, and to co-operate. No particular kind of social system may be presumed to follow from this – 'even with an exploitative social relation there is cooperation' (pp. 172–3). We are born into the history that has been produced by the plans developed so far, and what we do with the future will depend on decisions that are being made now.

The issue is not just territory and racism, Barker argues; there is a whole package, a project of innateness, that reaches into sexual and interpersonal relations, education, industrial relations, class relations (pp. 134–55). Difference is both suppressed and insisted upon. We are all said to be genetically programmed and fundamentally the same, and thereby positive change is disallowed; meanwhile, variations in power and access to resources are said to reflect essential qualities and to be inevitable. Certainly the implications for gender politics are reactionary. Anthony Storr's *Human Aggression* (1968) is relatively reasonable, but it begins with our 'savage impulses' (p. ix) and proceeds inexorably to statements such as: 'However emancipated a woman may be, she will still, at one level, want the man to be the dominant partner' (p. 65). 'At one level' is the recurring strategy: if things appear otherwise, you appeal to depth.

Edward Bond, in his plays and prefaces, holds that people – and animals – respond aggressively only when deprived and threatened (*Lear*, pp. v–vi). In the preface to *The Fool* he derives current aggression from the culture required by the capitalist system: 'Our economy depends on exploitation and aggression. We expect business to be *ruthlessly* aggressive' (p. vi). In the attempt to control the aggression it stimulates, capitalism uses the myth of innate violence 'to justify force and preserve social relationships. As the toys of affluence become brighter and faster and noisier, so it becomes necessary for capitalism to take an increasingly pessimistic view of human nature' (p. x). That was in 1976. Since then, the aggressive drive of capital is undiminished, but it now appears that only some people are to be consoled with the toys of affluence. A substantial underclass is denied even such incorporation into the prevailing ethos, and must be disciplined more directly. The myth of savagery-that-must-be-controlled is even more convenient.

Notes

1 Lamming, *Pleasures*, p. 107; Sartre, in Fanon, *Wretched*, p. 22.

2 Bhabha, 'Other Question', p. 34; Williams, P., p. 95; Fanon, *Black*, p. 53; Nandy, pp. 11–18.

3 Lessing speaking on 'Bookshelf', BBC Radio 4, January 1987. On sexuality in the colonial situation, see Nandy, pp. 4–11, 42–6.

4 Anthony H. Richmond in his Pelican book *The Colour Problem* (1955), drawing upon I. D. MacCrone's study published by Oxford University Press in 1937, *Race Attitudes in South Africa*, p. 296–309 (Richmond, p. 245).

5 Fanon, *Wretched*, p. 24. See Peter Worsley, 'Imperial Retreat', in Thompson, *Out*, pp. 115–20.

6 Fryer, pp. 381–6; Moore, chs. 2, 3; Sivanandan, pp. 101–26.

7 Hall, Critcher et al., pp. 348–62, 389–90.

8 See Foucault, *Language*, pp. 124–30; JanMohammed, p. 63.

9 Quoted by Kenneth Parker, 'The Revelation of Caliban: the "black presence" in the Classroom', in Dabydeen, p. 197. Parker proposes a multi-racial literature syllabus. Many Indians and West Indians felt that Naipaul was betraying them (Lamming, *Pleasures*, pp. 30, 224–5); but compare the perhaps less than confident defence by Gāmini Salgādo in 'V. S. Naipaul and the Politics of Fiction', in Ford, *Present*, p. 326.

10 Fanon, *Wretched*, p. 21; see also Hartley, pp. 67–74; and Peter Marris, 'Accessory After the Fact', in MacKenzie.

11 Conrad, p. 104; see Miller, C. L., ch. 4; Watts. Paul Johnson, disliking Fanon's anti-imperialism, calls him 'the black French intellectual who turned into a savage' and compares him to Kurtz (p. 249).

12 See Passmore; Barthes, pp. 141–2.

13 Golding, *Hot Gates*, p. 87. The association of Nazis and Blacks became customary. The Mau Mau were compared to Nazis (Russell, Lord, p. 59; Richmond, p. 192). Sir Robert Boothby said Nasser's was 'the language of Hitler and the rule of the jungle' (Lawrence, E., p. 68). Fanon reports that people associated words like 'Negro' with 'Nazi' and 'SS' (*Black*, p. 166).

14 Freud, *Case*, pp. 222–3; see also Freud, *Totem*, on 'primitive men and neurotics', pp. 89 and *passim*. In Pinter's *The Room* (1960), psychic disturbance is apparently associated with a blind Negro who's been 'Just lying there. In the black dark. Hour after hour' (*Plays: One*, p. 121).

15 Thompson, *Poverty*, pp. 26–9; Lawson is quoted by Margot Heinemann, 'How Brecht Read Shakespeare', in Dollimore and Sinfield, p. 203.

16 See Tiger, pp. 162–4; Sack, p. 217. Bertrand Russell argued against the necessity of the arms race, on the ground that human nature is almost entirely custom, tradition and education, and after a few generations without war it would seem as absurd as duelling (*Has Man*, pp. 46–7).

17 Leakey and Lewin, p. 125; also p. 213, and Leakey, pp. 223–37.

18 Richard Verrall, quoted from *New Nation*, no. 1 (1980), by Barker, *New*, p. 100.

8
Making a scene

Putting on the Style

Several of the preoccupations of this book so far are focused by rock-'n'-roll: contradictions and discontent within the postwar settlement; attitudes to US culture and to the commercial organization of 'mass' culture; the anxieties of literary intellectuals and the attempt of younger writers to make space for themselves (they preferred jazz); the processes of cultural appropriation; the scope of subordinate cultures for resistance.

Rock-'n'-roll, basically, was a combination of Black blues, known as 'race' music, and white country music. This was not unprecedented – white popular music has experienced a sequence of infusions from Black culture. I discuss jazz later on; Jimmie Rodgers in the 1920s had drawn on Black music, but since then country music has been specialized as white-only (Hatch and Millward, pp. 33–4). In the early 1950s white performers started playing Black music ('Shake, Rattle and Roll', for instance, was taken from Joe Turner by Bill Haley). Elvis Presley was called 'the King of Western Bop' and 'the Hillbilly Cat', schizophrenic combinations of Black and white terms; both Black and white radio stations refused to play his 1954 pairing 'That's Alright, Mama' (blues) and 'Old Blue Moon of Kentucky (country). Buddy Holly and the Crickets were thought to be a Black band when, after the record of 'That'll Be the Day' (1957), they were first booked outside their native Texas. The excitement of Black music and the circumstances in which it was generated were co-opted by white people to address a range of feeling that lay beyond their own culture. The irony, as with jazz, was that the music appropriated as unfettered self-expression derived from some of the least free people in the world.[1]

In Britain the Black dimension of rock-'n'-roll was relatively unappreciated; on the contrary, rock was appropriated especially by teddy boys, and they were notably aggressive towards Caribbean and African immigrants. For the teds and other young British people, rock-'n'-roll meant the exotic excitement of the United States in a generalized version of gangsters, 'automobiles' and Hollywood (James Dean and Marlon Brando in particular); it was fantasized in the decor of coffee bars and juke-boxes.

Rock-'n'-roll didn't create teds; they took it over in September 1955, when the film *Blackboard Jungle* (notice the savages again) gave them the chance to dance in cinemas to Bill Haley's 'Rock Around the Clock' and rip out the seats that impeded them. Bill Haley was an unlikely teenage hero – paunchy, baby-faced, almost 30, the father of five. But he made sense to teds because they perceived him in the light of the story they were telling themselves; that is how subcultures are formed. They rioted when *Rock Around the Clock* was shown in August and September 1956, despite the film's theme that rock-'n'-roll is unjustly maligned, just good fun really, decent and wholesome.

Teds were named from their 'Edwardian' style of dress – another instance of cultural appropriation. This style had been designed by smart Savile Row tailors for upper-class young men to remind them of a happier time for the upper classes, the supposed Edwardian summer. But it was adopted by lower-class boys, initially from south London, a group with some money but not much status, now trying arrogantly to assert itself.[2] However, if the teds' idea, initially, was to acquire status, it didn't last long, because the upper-class wearers quickly abandoned the style when it became associated with the teds. 'The whole of one's wardrobe IMMEDIATELY becomes UNWEARABLE', 'explained a disconsolate young ex-Guardee over a champagne cocktail', for the benefit of readers of the *Daily Mirror*.[3] Headmasters and army officers forbade ted garments, and Savile Row sought to produce new, less imitable styles for its clientele.

My perspective here elaborates that of Chapter 3, where I wrote of cultural production as contest between the stories that we tell ourselves about ourselves and the world. A subculture is a group collaboration to build a common story and establish it against rivals. This process is always in the making, and its strategy is characteristically appropriative. The mechanisms of imperialist plunder, and defence against it, described in Chapter 7, are in principle similar. Subcultures are not founded always, or even particularly, in opposition and resistance; more mundanely, they are *ways of coping*.[4] They afford to those who live them stories of their own identities and significance. They help groups who are ill at ease in the dominant culture to manage the diverse, often contradictory, histories and demands that they experience. We notice subcultures most when they disconcert the system, but even then the element of resistance is often incoherent or implicit. For resistance is first of all a way of retaining a degree of collective identity and individual self-esteem in the face of the humiliation and frustration suffered by people within the prevailing relations of production.

The rock-'n'-roll subculture was consolidated by hostility to it. The banning of the film *Rock Around the Clock* from many towns, and the denunciations of clergymen, magistrates and headmasters, told the fans that their allegiance was significant. Habitual notions of the popular, the lower classes, the United States, anything disorderly, coalesced around rock-'n'-roll. It became the focus of a 'moral panic' – an opportunity for right-thinking people to restate the boundaries of the permissible by denouncing deviants. Sociology, criminology and the media became preoccupied with 'juvenile delinquents'. Steve Race spoke for jazz and the music business when he declared in *Melody Maker*: 'For sheer repulsive-ness coupled with the monotony of incoherence, "Hound Dog" hit a new low in my experience' (Chambers, p. 30). The BBC allowed only tiny space to rock, but this forced listeners over to Radio Luxembourg, which added the sensation of a forbidden pleasure or guilty secret, the signal tantalizingly fading and coming again. In 1964 Paul Johnson, editor of the *New Statesman* wrote, of television audiences for 'Juke Box Jury' and 'Oh Boy!': they have 'faces bloated with cheap confectionery and smeared with chainstore make-up, the open, sagging mouths and glazed eyes, the hands mindlessly drumming in time to the music, the broken stiletto heels, the shoddy, stereotyped, "with-it" clothes' (Frith, *Sound*, p. 252). Something was bothering him.

Of course, there had long been popular music, its fans had sometimes behaved excessively, and highbrow anxiety about it was not new. Already in 1951 it was alleged that 'modern ballroom dancing may easily degener-ate into a sensuous form of entertainment' leading to 'unruly behaviour and not infrequently to sexual immorality' (Frith, *Sound*, p. 203). I showed in Chapter 6 how 'mass' culture embarrassed intellectuals in their

Free-World enthusiasm for the free market. Some Frankfurt School commentators held that 'mass' culture was implicitly fascist. Adorno believed that 'the aim of jazz', which he failed to distinguish from other popular music, was 'the mechanical reproduction of a regressive moment, a castration symbolism. "Give up your masculinity, let yourself be castrated", the eunuchlike sound of the jazz band both mocks and proclaims.'[5] However, the debate about 'mass' culture paid far less attention to music than to the printed word (where intellectuals felt drawn to distinguish their own aspirations). Bernard Rosenberg and David Manning White's collection of 49 essays, *Mass Culture*, includes only a couple devoted primarily to popular music (by S. I. Hayakawa and David Riesman). Richard Hoggart, in *The Uses of Literacy*, remarks: 'Popular songs do not so plainly show the effect of modern commercial organisation as does popular reading' (p. 222). These volumes, both published in 1957, were written before the impact of rock-'n'-roll – though Hoggart does have a bitter passage on 'juke-box boys' in 'harshly lighted milk-bars' (subcultures need meeting places): the decor is vulgar, the music synthetic and too loud, the boys apathetic and of low intelligence. They 'waggle one shoulder or stare, as desperately as Humphrey Bogart, across the tubular chairs . . . living to a large extent in a myth-world compounded of a few simple elements which they take to be those of American life' (p. 248).

The main accusation levelled at popular music before rock was that it is trivial: it presents unrealistic notions of the world and makes us passive and dependent – 'the directionless and tamed helots of a machine-minding class' (Hoggart, p. 250). This view persists in hostility to rock-'n'-roll but alongside it, much more strongly, comes the belief that rock is dangerous – violent, aggressive, like the teds. Several singers recorded 'Rip It Up' in 1956:

> Well it's Saturday night
> And I just got paid:
> A fool about my money
> Don't try to save.
> Gonna rock it up,
> Gonna rip it up,
> Gonna shake it up,
> Gonna ball it up,
> Gonna rock it up
> And ball tonight.

From a parental point of view the song is worrying. The context ('just got paid') is specific and alludes to the common anxiety about the spending power of teenagers; 'fool about my money' confesses that sensible injunctions to save have been heard but disregarded. The variations in the refrain seem calculated to alarm. 'Rock it up' probably just means 'have a party', though that could damage prized objects and upset the neighbours. But 'rip it up' sounds like the notorious teds and the cinema seats; 'shake it up' perhaps implies a general threat to the social order. But worst of all, you don't need much hip lingo to know that 'ball' may mean to have sexual intercourse, threatening the ordered continuance of family life. Those able to hear the precise pitching and controlled wildness of Little Richard's singing of the song (and many claimed to hear only cater-wauling) would be even more disquieted, for it implies that this is no casual disturbance, but deliberate, mocking and determined.

The danger was that a section of the population might be getting out of hand. Youth clubs were often reckoned to be the answer. One youth worker admitted in July 1957: 'So scared are we that boys and girls will become "teddified", promiscuous or Communist, that we try, often unconsciously, to impose upon them our own sets of values, so that they may "fit into" our society and thus not wish to change it' (Gillis, pp. 198–9). Teds were the first significant dent in the postwar settlement, the first sign that not everyone was feeling consensual. This is not to romanticize them as a challenge to capitalism and the state – on the contrary, their futile posturing and violence towards people no better off than themselves typifies the difficulty of perceiving, in welfare-capitalism, a constructive outlet for dissidence. Nevertheless, the spectre of young working-class males not imbued with customary social values was disturbing, and the consensus, by definition, had no way of handling it. That was the danger in rock-'n'-roll.

The 'Americanization' in British rock culture was part of the issue. The ascendancy of US culture became a major topic, as Harry Hopkins recalled in 1964 – notice how these innovations now seem 'natural' parts of the British scene:

> From hula-hoops to Zen Buddhism, from do-it-yourself to launderettes or the latest sociological catch-phrase or typographical trick, from Rock'n'Roll to Action Painting, barbecued chickens rotating on their spits in shop windows to parking meters, clearways, bowling alleys, glass-skyscrapers, flying saucers, pay-roll raids, armoured trucks and beatniks, American habits and vogues now

crossed the Atlantic with a speed and certainty that suggested that Britain was now merely one more offshore island. Striptease clubs completed the 'Fordisation' of sex, supermarkets of shopping and Wimpy bars of eating. (p. 454)

Colin MacInnes, in an article 'Young England, Half English', noted that British performers such as Tommy Steele sang in US accents but spoke in between with UK accents, and wondered whether the English are 'ceasing to be a people in any real sense at all' (MacInnes, *England*, p. 15). But if 'Americanization' was indeed cultural imperialism it was also, for the teds and other young people, a mode of resistance. They were deploying a fantasy image of US cultural power against a home situation that offered them little.[6] The use of US culture to unsettle traditional elements in the local culture is common all round the world.

Even more than lower-class disorder, there was a fear of 'bad' teenagers leading the rest astray (Frith, *Sound*, p. 186). I argued in chapter 4 that cultural attainment was used in schools as a criterion of success, facilitating upward social mobility and seeming to justify the failure of the majority. From this point of view, it was convenient for lower-class young people to adopt a cultural form that could be demonized, since that reasserted the boundaries of proper behaviour and ratified the 'good' choice of those who proceeded into middle-class occupations and lifestyles. The fear was that the disaffection of rock subculture would spread, creating a new, supposedly classless category called 'youth', infiltrating decent middle-class and aspiring young people, and undermining the literary-educational ethos with which they were being inculcated. Ray Gosling recalls how he had teddy-boy clothes and hairstyle despite being in the sixth form: 'One moment I was a choirboy singing "Jesu, Joy of Man's Desiring", and the next moment it seemed I was running in my luminous socks from an affray at the Cow Meadow Fair, bawling through the streets up to the bus station: "Hail, hail rock'n'roll, deliver me from days of old" ' (*Personal*, p. 33). There was much comment about Paul McCartney's GCE successes and Mick Jagger's time at the London School of Economics. For the fact was that rock culture ran purposefully counter to school culture.

What established commentators were reluctant to see is that rock subculture was partly produced by school, youth clubs, the BBC and the churches; and especially by school. For the extension of schooling trapped all young people there while allowing only a proportion of them to feel more than occasional pleasure, pride or dignity in the experience. The whole idea of selection, streaming and examining was that some people should do well but most should fail – that is what the economy needed them to do. It was said that they would feel all right because they were 'good with their hands' (the implication that heads aren't required for hand-skills is absurd – as you'll know if you've ever tried even to plumb in a washing machine). But every time that was said, it was contradicted by someone else saying that if you didn't work hard and succeed in the examinations then you wouldn't get a good job and be a full person. Therefore rock culture was not something that had unfortunately escaped the control of the school, the product of malign outside agencies such as coffee bars, television and record promoters, to be countered by more effective schooling. Rock culture (like trades unions in relation to the factory system) was developed in specific opposition to school, as a defence against it.

The educationists' approach is exemplified in Donald Hughes's thoughtful essay in the Leavisite volume *Discrimination and Popular Culture*, edited by Denys Thompson in 1964 in response to a National Union of Teachers' conference of October 1960 (see Laing, ch. 7). Jazz and folk music, even skiffle, are good, though popularity and commercial recording tend to spoil them, because they are spontaneous and composed by the people rather than for them. But pop has to be standardized for a mass market, 'typed to a degree where most of its original creativeness has been driven out'. Actually, a characteristic of youth culture is earnest differentiation between groups of fans.[7] Hughes insists on the sameness of pop music, but never gets close enough truly to inspect it. He says, 'It is never the frustration of everyday human circumstance; always the singer and the object of his or her song inhabit a dream world' (p. 164), and quotes a current example:

> Come outside, there's a lovely moon out there,
> Come outside while we've got time to spare.

Hughes's instance is very unlucky, for there surely were and are recordings such as he describes, but the one he quotes, which presumably he hadn't heard, is not one of them. 'Come Outside' topped the hit parade in July 1962. Sung by Mike Sarne in an exaggeratedly 'common' London accent, it is a humorous song, with the 'romantic' sentiment undercut both by the evidently sexual intent of the boy, and by the knowing but resistant replies of the girl. The song offers precisely what Hughes says we don't get: frustration, everyday human circumstance, and an alternative to romantic attitudes.[8] Probably Hughes is evincing a submerged anxiety – that when she finally agrees to come outside, sexual intercourse will occur. He makes the 'trivial' attack, leaving the 'dangerous' one unstated. The point is not that 'Come Outside' is a 'great' song, but that it could be a number-one hit, used so inappropriately in the argument, and not be noticed by any of the people producing the book.

Music and Movement

Most literary intellectuals were hostile to rock-'n'-roll, and so, from the late 1950s, was the New Left (see Chapter 11). However, as I showed in Chapter 5, younger writers, and especially those linked with the Movement, were also opposed, in part, to traditional cultural attitudes. Where teds appropriated rock-'n'-roll, writers adopted another initially Black music: jazz. The relation between the two musics made it specially urgent to distinguish them. John Wain wrote that the decline of jazz after 1948 had left the ground to become 'choked with a particularly noxious weed they called rock-and-roll' (*Strike*, p. 254). In *Blackboard Jungle* the kids, in a symbolic moment, smash up the jazz 78s belonging to a friendly teacher.

When Larkin met Amis at Oxford in 1941, their friendship was founded on their passion for jazz, and Wain's brief connection with Larkin at Oxford also featured jazz (Larkin, *Jill*, pp. 16–18). Movement fiction gives symbolic status to the jazz enthusiast. He (usually he) is significantly absent in Larkin's *Jill* (1946). The novel presents two main kinds of wartime Oxford student: snobbish, selfish and brutal upper-class types, and anxious, innocent and intense scholarship-boys from the north of England. The jazz fan is elusive; only at one point is heard 'from somewhere in the College itself, the hysterical crying of a jazz record' (p. 40). The young man playing the record doesn't appear, presumably because he doesn't associate with either of the class stereotypes; he has a distinctive culture. It is pleasant to deduce that it is he, like Larkin, who possesses the knowledge, detachment and sensitivity to narrate the novel of which he is the absent moral and technical centre.

The typical Amis protagonist is a jazz fan; in 'I Spy Strangers' Archer hopes the victory of the Labour Party in 1945 will produce 'my England, full of girls and drink and jazz and books and decent houses and decent jobs and being your own boss'.[9] Jazz affords a social and cultural allegiance, a bench-mark against which other life-styles are examined and found wanting. In *Lucky Jim*, when Jim Dixon returns from the pub he sings 'The Wreck of the Old Ninety-seven' – the kind of thing Lonnie Donegan was performing with the skiffle group of the Chris Barber jazz band.[10] The reader is not told what this is; if we recognize the reference, we are in the know. Dixon objects to this strategy when used by Professor Welch. But then, despite his hostility to high culture, Dixon does recognize the composer when he complains of a 'skein of untiring facetiousness by filthy Mozart' (p. 63). And he is able to specify 'the "rondo" of some boring piano concerto' which he hums as his Welch tune (p. 87). He is good at these games – it augurs well for class mobility.

As Larkin explains, jazz had in the 1930s some of the forbidden danger that rock'n'roll acquired in the 1950s. It was 'something we had found for ourselves, that wasn't taught at school' (*All What*, pp. 1–3). The BBC and other cultural institutions were hostile; when the Duke Ellington Band visited England in 1933 *The Times* wrote: 'The expert who could disregard their emotional effect might conceivably derive aesthetic enjoyment from his rhythms, but the ordinary listener probably does not, and is probably not intended to do so. It is enough the effect be immediate and violent' (Godbolt, pp. 101, 196–7). Jazz, like rock, was disreputable and exciting because it came from the United States. Eric Newton recalls 'the prestige and horrible fascination of the USA in the heyday of Henry Ford, Wall Street, Lindbergh and Prohibition' (p. 63).

Most of this carried through to the 1950s. Jazz seemed to side-step the class system. It attracted lower-class young people belonging to 'the world of the grammar school and public library'. For them 'it was part of achieving intellectualism the independent way (and often the hard way) by self-education' (Newton, pp. 247, 258). Also, jazz attracted adherents in public schools and universities, for whom it was a way of refusing upper-class norms:

> Polish was unimportant, even suspect. . . . When the Magnolias played jazz they felt themselves soul brothers to Bunk Johnson and Louis Armstrong. The blacker they sounded the better. It was a mistake of history and of nature that Bob [Dawbarn] and [Mick] Mulligan had attended a British public school, but they were doing their best to atone.[11]

With jazz, intellectuals who were uneasy about 'mass' culture and the free market could respond with clear conscience to the excitement of US culture. They could think of jazz as despised and rejected by the US mainstream (though this was not actually so after 1947, when the US Government took it up as 'propaganda for the "American way of life" in the Cold War, and use[d] it to penetrate the East–West barrier, flooding the air with daily jazz broadcasts and sending prominent musicians abroad as "cultural ambassadors" ' (Newton, p. 72).

Indeed, jazz could be appreciated as an 'art'. This seemed to establish its status – Roger Taylor says the middle class 'could not allow itself to be interested in anything less than art, so what it is interested in must be art' (p. 56). Art was linked to exclusiveness. Jazz fans were continually defining jazz, identifying purer forms of it, providing it with a canon, a tradition and elite interpreters (Newton, pp. 232,255). Amis in his *Observer* column preferred New Orleans and revivalist bands (Allsop, p. 55). Larkin really wanted to listen only to the records the already possessed and others that were similar (*All What*, p. 4). Subcultures thrive on exclusiveness. So Leavisism with its 'line of wit' and 'great tradition', and late-1960s bike-boys who would listen only to the original rock records (Willis, *Profane*, pp. 63–4, 70–1).

Better still, jazz was not a conventional art. It was 'music of the people', quite unlike the elite culture of the leisure class. Reviewing John Lehmann's autobiography, Amis noted the privileged cultural background of the typical pre-1939 writer, and contrasted 'the intellectual of the Fifties' who went to grammar or minor public school. The latter's extra-literary interests, Amis says, involve not Dürer and Monteverdi, but Louis Armstrong. But this doesn't mean that he holds 'defiant, dour, scholarship-boy views of culture': his commitment to jazz is more vital than the philistinism of the dilettante (Amis, 'Editor's Notes'). This is a Leavisite move: exclusive, earnest commitment is preferred to the unthinking 'good taste' of a leisure class that takes its culture for granted. The intellectual jazz fan disdained the prevailing notion of the artistic while demanding its redeployment on new terms.

In the 1950s jazz became, in effect, the rock-'n'-roll of the younger intelligentsia. It appealed to those who were cut off from the teds by class and educational aspirations, but were drawn nonetheless towards youth culture and were uneasy with the roles officially available (I discuss class mobility in chapter 11). In a way jazz was compatible with school – you could study and 'appreciate' it; but this made it potentially more insidiously rebellious, displacing the required studies. Brian Jackson recalls the appeal of the jazz club at Huddersfield grammar school to working-class boys at odds with the school ethos: 'If the life of New Orleans was an exaggerated image of working-class life, the stimulating generalised emotions of jazz were a hazy image of what the world of art could offer. The school avoided the first and didn't particularly lead to the second' (Jackson, p. 129). Jazz improved on both neighbourhood and school.

An offshoot, skiffle, deriving from the harsh experience of such as Lead-belly and Woody Guthrie, was even closer to rock music. George Melly suggests that Lonnie Donegan appealed to lower-middle-class youngsters, projecting a violent world but in a safely distanced rendering. Skiffle was even less like an art – Larkin disdained 'the high nasal Glasgow – American version of some incident from transatlantic railway history'.[12] It tilted the careful balance jazz fans had constructed; anyone could do it. In fact, the Beatles were doing it.

Blacks, Existentialists and Beats

I argued in Chapter 3 that meaning and value are not intrinsic to cultural artefacts, but dependent upon the context of interpretation; and that social change occurs through contest among cultural formations. This is true of jazz also: there have been numerous articles and books aiming to define jazz, but although these appear to be analysing a phenomenon, they are actually claiming a concept. Jazz is a cultural token of some power, susceptible to diverse political appropriations, worth getting on your side. 1950s British jazzmen Chris Barber and Kenny Ball ended up in the late 1970s playing to raise funds for Margaret Thatcher; she said she liked 'New Orleans Jazz, especially Duke Ellington' (Godbolt, p. 1). In the postwar period diverse subcultural groups struggled for control of the concept 'jazz'.

Most importantly, Blacks were trying to get their music back. One musician said, in a book published in 1953: 'When we had it – the old type of jazz – the whites came, and they liked it and imitated it. Pretty soon it was no longer our music. No negro can play New Orleans jazz today with a clear conscience. A few old ones still do, but no coloured man listens to them.'[13] The young ones, starting in effect with Charlie Parker in the 1940s, took advantage of a new phase of Modernism in the United States to develop 'modern jazz'. British traditional fans contested this reappropriation. Larkin was well aware of the issue – 'a desire to wrest back the initiative in jazz from the white musician, to invent "something they can't steal because they can't play it" ' (*All What*, pp. 7–8). He was the more annoyed because this was a version of Modernism: 'Parker was a modern jazz player just as Picasso was a modern painter and Pound a modern poet. . . . There could hardly have been a conciser summary of what I don't believe about art' (p. 11; see p. 183 below). Larkin had cultivated jazz because it didn't have conventional high-cultural pretensions, and now it was being reorganized in just those terms. He had looked to it for innocence and simplicity, and it was producing John Coltrane – whom Larkin attacked on the occasion of his death in August 1967 for his 'squeals, squeaks, Bronx cheers and throttled slate-pencil noises' (*All What*, p. 213; for those who consider Larkin lacking in passion, it is instructive to see where he could feel strongly; the *Telegraph* declined to publish the piece).

Larkin said: 'The tension between artist and audience in jazz slackened when the Negro stopped wanting to entertain the white man' (p. 12). The trouble was that white jazz enthusiasts wanted to take over the black person along with the music. As Fanon put it, 'In their eyes jazz should only be the despairing, broken-down nostalgia of an old Negro who is trapped between five glasses of whisky, the curse of his race, and the racial hatred of the white man' (Fanon, *Wretched*, p. 195). John Wain addresses the topic in a radio play, 'Good Morning Blues', broadcast on May Day 1986, on Radio 4. Well-spoken British schoolboys become jazz enthusiasts and performers, and meet up with the aged New Orleans trumpeter Ulysses Baker. He is happy to play with them in the traditional manner, but his daughter Roxane, who has graduated from business school, refuses to be friendly to whites, pointing out their exploitation of Blacks and of jazz in particular. However, the action is slanted against Roxane, who is ruthless and vengeful: 'Every black person . . . hates every white person that walks the earth.' Wain hears the Black case, but cannot accept its implications for his own cultural allegiance.

Other literary groups were also making use of jazz. New Orleans had been a French colony, and some musicians lived in Paris. It was all tied in with the literary scene. Sidney Bechet was resident at the Vieux Colombier club, beneath the theatre where Sartre's *Huis clos* was produced. The writer and trumpet-player Boris Vian ran the Jazz Club de Saint-Germain, which presented modern jazz and became a principal stopover for US performers. So jazz became associated with existentialism, intellectuals and bohemians. Sartre wrote about in in *Les Temps modernes*; already in *La Nausée* (1938) it is a jazz record of a black woman singing 'Some of These Days' that presents, uniquely, the possibility of pure being; the song *is*, as Roquentin has wanted to be (p. 248). In 1947 *Life* magazine did a feature with photographs of young people 'discussing philosophy' to a background of jazz and poetry readings; *France-Soir* attacked noisy jazz club patrons as 'delinquents, drug traffickers and tarts who should go and philosophise elsewhere'; and Sartre defended jazz dancing as 'an innocent, gay and healthy exercise'.[14]

Then there were the US Beat writers. 'Holy the groaning saxophone! Holy the bop apocalypse! Holy the jazz bands marijuana hipsters peace & junk & drums!', Allen Ginsberg wrote in 'Footnote to Howl'. Norman Mailer, in his essay 'The White Negro' (1957), grossly appropriated the Black jazzman as necessarily an existentialist, an affront to the American way of life:

> One is Hip or one is Square . . . one is a rebel or one conforms, one is a frontiersman in the Wild West of American night life, or else a Square cell, trapped in the totalitarian tissues of American society, doomed willy-nilly to conform if one is to succeed. . . . The Negro has the simplest of alternatives: live a life of constant humility or ever-threatening danger. . . . and in his music he gave voice to the character and quality of his existence, to his rage and infinite variations of joy, lust, languor, growl, cramp, pinch, scream and despair of his orgasm. For jazz is orgasm, it is the music of orgasm. (Feldman and Gartenberg, pp. 290–1).

The link between Beat writing and modern jazz was taken up by British 'Underground' performance writers such as Michael Horovitz and Jeff Nuttall. Horovitz declared: 'The boppers' recognition that the artistically impoverished conditions which moulded Traditional and standard styles had been rendered obsolete is echoed by the release of poetry from the dusty iambic grooves of book (society) culture' (p. 329). Jazz had become a major cultural token in a struggle for meaning and power.

Black, Parisian-existentialist and Beat ideas of jazz arrived together in Britain from the early 1950s. They were misunderstood, diluted, combined and appropriated; they were mingled with images of Marlon Brando in *The Wild Ones* (1955 – 'What're you rebelling against?' 'Whatta ya got?' – banned in Britain) and James Dean in *Rebel Without a Cause*

(1956); of Holden Caulfield in J. D. Salinger's *Catcher in the Rye* (1951) and Colin Wilson sleeping out on Hampstead Heath to write *The Outsider* (1956); of Elvis Presley, Jimmy Porter and Lonnie Donegan. There were even hit singles.[15] It was all quite confused, but it was different, optimistic, and open. The stodginess, as it was perceived, the stuffiness and hypocrisy of insular cultural modes was being challenged. The young hero of David Stuart Leslie's novel *In my Solitude* (1960) felt that in jazz jiving 'you're spitting in the eye of the dreary grey city of Tubes and traffic-jams, the middle class in bowlers, the upper class in Daimlers, the Daily Telegraph, the BBC, and Morning Service from St Paul's' (p. 98). This, like rock music, was hardly coherent as a rebellion; but, as I show in chapter 12, it became a reference point in a new-left subculture.

Briefly, jazz became trendy. Upper-middle-class young men who were to be the self-publicists of the 1960s picked up on its cosmopolitan, 'classless' excitement. Alexander Plunket Greene, who with Mary Quant opened their first 'Bazaar' boutique in the King's Road, Chelsea, in 1955, was an amateur jazz trumpeter from a public school (Booker, p. 38; see chapter 13 below). Former-Etonian Andrew Sinclair wrote about Cambridge students in his novel *My Friend Judas* (1959). The hero-narrator is made for the 1960s and *Private Eye* – irreverent and abrasive, crossing ostentatiously cultural barriers that were crumbling anyway, dropping names from a self-consciously surprising range of reference, making a boast of lack of principles, yet with a final hint that there may be a soul inside (p. 195). Jazz – more or less any jazz – is part of the style:

> Judy fixed me a whisky, and I began to hit the keys. I tell you, I hadn't tapped black-and-white for near on a month. I started on a sort of Shearing, Lullaby in Birdland stuff. Then I got really sent down the Street. I took it on my own, and it *was* my own, and I was sending it away and me along with it. It's when I'm solo on the improvisation that I really send it away. It's all in there, left hand, right hand, pulling it in together, the drive and the beat of the old Kansas City, with Bartok and Stravinsky humming in the harmonies, and Bach on the set-square seeing I don't finger over the line. (p. 73)

The Modernist, Parisian and Beat appropriations of jazz combine to exacerbate each other's pretentiousness.

By 1960, the year the film of *Saturday Night and Sunday Morning* (directed by Karel Reisz) was released, there was a repertoire of sub-cultural music. In an early scene in the pub, working people sing a traditional pub song, 'Lily of Laguna' – one of those attributed by Hoggart to 'the finest period in English urban popular song' (pp. 156–7):

> She's my lady love,
> She is my own, my lady love.
> She's no girl for sitting down to dream,
> She's the only girl Laguna knows.
> I know she likes me,
> I know she likes me, because she says so!
> She is my Lily of Laguna,
> She is my lily, and my rose.

(I quote from memory; it is romantic, but everyone singing grins at line 6.) Against this, earlier in the evening, we have current pop – a singer with ineffectual electric organ and drums, singing 'What Do you Want if you Don't Want Money?' (recently recorded by Adam Faith). None of the people in the pub is taking any notice: the performance appears trivial and unimpressive, set against a lively community culture; and the title is of course significant. However, there is more rock music – at the fairground when Arthur is threatened with physical violence in retribution for his adultery with his friend's wife. Now rock is vigorous and aggressive, representing a real threat. So the film uses the two preoccupations: rock is trivial and dangerous. However, the score for the film as a whole has a discreet jazz ambience – it's by Johnny Dankworth, the modern jazz bandleader. This is the choice of the director, made for those he hopes will really appreciate his film.

Reasons for Attendance

Willy-nilly, Movement writers became caught up with the changing imagery of jazz. They were promoted alongside the Beats as comparable discoveries in Britain and the United States.[16] But they didn't like any of it. They had wanted the amoral, cross-cultural excitement of jazz, but not quite like that. Furthermore, the new popularity of jazz was edging it towards pop culture and rock-'n'-roll and the renewed ferment of youth subculture of the 1960s. Larkin looked at modern jazz on the one hand and rock on the other, and suggested that jazz had 'split into two, intelligence without beat and beat without intelligence' (All What, pp. 13–14).

Movement writers began to feel beleaguered, and tried to sort out the pattern through their writing, defining subcultural alternatives and their own affiliations.

Larkin distinguishes the thoughtful and the casual jazz fan in 'Reasons for Attendance' (in *The Less Deceived*, 1955):

> The trumpet's voice, loud and authoritative,
> Draws me a moment to the lighted glass
> To watch the dancers – all under twenty-five –
> Shifting intently, face to flushed face,
> Solemnly on the beat of happiness.
>
> – Or so I fancy, sensing the smoke and sweat,
> The wonderful feel of girls. Why be out here?
> But then, why be in there? Sex, yes, but what
> Is sex? Surely, to think the lion's share
> Of happiness is found by couples – sheer
>
> Inaccuracy, as far as I'm concerned.
> What calls me is that lifted, rough-tongued bell
> (Art, if you like) whose individual sound
> Insists I too am individual.
> It speaks; I hear; others may hear as well,
>
> But not for me, nor I for them; and so
> With happiness. Therefore I stay outside,
> Believing this; and they maul to and fro,
> Believing that; and both are satisfied,
> If no one has misjudged himself. Or lied.

The poet is drawn to the club by the trumpet's authority, but he dislikes the ambience created by the young dancers. As Newton observes, true enthusiasts avoid dancing – 'They stand or sit by the bandstand, soaking in the music, nodding and smiling at one another in a conspiracy of appreciation, and tapping their feet' (p. 232). For the poet, the trumpet takes the (religious) form of a 'rough-tongued bell', and this 'individual sound/Insists I too am individual'. His preference (I suppose the speaker to be male) is dignified, off-handedly but the more personally for that, as 'art, if you like'. The poem sets serious aspirations in the jazz scene against its more popular aspects.

It would be a mistake to believe that because the poet is outside the window, he therefore 'remains apart as a result of his commitment to an art which is to record and preserve life' (King, pp. 4–5). The poet is right in there, not recording the dancers but giving a thoroughly slanted version of them, mainly as 'sex'. Thus he reduces their experience, not admitting other kinds of excitement, happiness, involvement that might be there. And the consequence – it is serious, and a characteristic consequence of stereotyping the other – is that the poet's own possibilities are reduced. In the last stanza he insists on the polarity between these two kinds of jazz subculture and wonders, finally, whether anyone has misjudged himself or lied. The immediate reading is that the speaker has overstated his position: perhaps he too might like a sexy feel of a girl after all. The slanted restriction of the possibilities is left for the reader to challenge.

In 'For Sidney Bechet' (in *The Whitsun Weddings*, 1964), Larkin begins with the thought that the music permits the listener to develop his or her own fantasy – 'appropriate falsehood';

> That note you hold, narrowing and rising, shakes
> Like New Orleans reflected on the water,
> And in all ears appropriate falsehood wakes.

The poet goes on to dissociate himself from several of these falsehoods – the idea of community, with 'Everyone making love and going shares'; the imagery of the brothel; the studiousness of 'scholars *manqués*'. The implication is that the poet's idea is purer, so we seem to have another instance of everyone else appropriating while oneself has the true insight. However, the poet has already himself, in the second line quoted, said that Bechet's playing invokes 'New Orleans reflected on the water', and the 'imaginative' quality of that image bespeaks the poet's particular mode of attention. In the final lines he moves, boldly, to affirm that appropriation:

> On me your voice falls as they say love should,
> Like an enormous yes. My Crescent City
> Is where your speech alone is understood,
>
> And greeted as the natural noise of good,
> Scattering long-haired grief and scored pity.

The New Orleans (Crescent City) of the poet's imagination is even more ideal than the image produced by other listeners: it is the place where

Bechet's music is most fully itself, in its original culture. The poet claims to leap beyond the current formations of the British fan, to achieve in imagination the ideal moment of New Orleans, the moment before appropriation. My contention is that this is impossible, for culture is always in the making and you cannot step into the same river twice. The poem itself is a recontextualizing of jazz – and in characteristic Movement manner. Notice, for instance, the placing of the enthusiasm of jazz lingo when the spontaneous injunction: 'Oh, play that thing!' is incorporated into these careful verses. The manner of the poem signals, in itself, an appropriation of New Orleans and jazz, contradicting the poet's claim to transcend subculture.

In *Strike the Father Dead* (1962), John Wain seeks to represent the culture of the authentic British jazzman and to fight off rivals. Jeremy takes up jazz piano as an alternative to school and, particularly, his father, who has the ultimate stuffy occupation of classics don: 'He'd given me the idea, without actually saying it in words, that playing or listening to jazz was a disreputable act, something like masturbating' (p. 42). Jeremy's fantasy idea of the United States is 'a big shape on the map, full of film stars, skyscrapers, hot dogs and people playing jazz' (p. 142). He plays with a Black US musician, Percy, who is made to say: 'To a coloured man [jazz] comes easy. He knows they can't take his music away from him. They can take everything else, but that only makes him put more into his music' (p. 315).

However, we might say that Jeremy takes Percy's music, and even the moral qualities associated with it, and reads them into his own story. He comes to realize that his father's emotional constriction derives from his experiences in the war of 1914–18, and that he, Jeremy, is not dissimilar to his father. He has his father's courage (he stands by Percy when he is attacked in the London race riots of 1958), and his father's commitment to his talent: 'I saw, now, that my way was really the same as the old man's. You played music, as you studied the classics, because you had chosen it as your own particular skill, the contribution you were going to make, the thing you were good at' (p. 315). So Jeremy's devotion to jazz was compatible with his father's values all along. It was not the opposite of parents, high culture, educational attainment, tradition and respectability, but an additional way of expressing them. This discovery epitomizes the Movement generally: even in its most distinctive, unorthodox feature, it was striving to find a way to occupy the ground that it appeared to repudiate.

As do Larkin and Amis, *Strike the Father Dead* suggests that jazz should have stopped at 1948, and Jeremy's playing is said to take little from Parker, Gillespie and bebop. The novel celebrates traditional jazz as the music of Blacks, pretending not to know that the repudiation of it by radical Blacks was not just musical, but economic and political. Jeremy resents other 1950s developments of jazz. Playing in Paris, he finds that jazz fits the mood of existentialism and players are taken for philosophers. But neither 'Percy or I, or any of the chaps who came along to play with us and stayed varying lengths of time, were the type to bother with any such pretensions' (pp. 202–3). Again, at a concert Jeremy sits next to 'one of those people who've taken up jazz since it became part of official vogueishness' – evidently from Cambridge and talking 'half-digested bunk' to an 'adoring female' (p. 263). Typically in the process of subcultural formation, false versions have to be disqualified.

Above all, Jeremy objects to rock-'n'-roll.

> The kids were shouting the refrain with him – at least some were, and the rest were just screaming aimlessly, like animals trapped in a burning arena. I just stood there with Percy and we looked. First at the band, with this big phony slob in his white suit gyrating up and down, then at the kids in their jeans, check shirts and jerseys, hopping up and down with excitement and bawling. (p. 307)

The drift of this account is partly that the behaviour is arbitrary ('aimless'), partly that it is contrived ('phony'). However, Jeremy has a better understanding than this of how subcultural formation works, for the observes that by 'cool' the kids mean 'anything that conformed to the values of their world, the one they had created out of their own needs and preferences' (p. 307). The kids have taken from jazz talk ('cool') what they can use. Jeremy doesn't apply this analysis to himself, though: his needs and preferences, he believes, are authentically his own – and his father's. The musical allegiance of the kids is either 'aimless', 'phony' or appropriative, whereas his own is set in a framework of individual attainment and traditional values. Jeremy cannot tolerate rock-'n'-roll because of what it implies for his own appropriation of US music.

Other writers were more adventurous. I showed in Chapter 5 how Thom Gunn undermined the 'blokeish' ethos cultivated by other Movement writers with intimations of unorthodox sexuality. He did this, furthermore, through the complex of jazz-inflected, rebellious affiliations that other Movement writers resisted: existentialism, Beats, and lower-class youth subculture. So far from placing bike-boys, Presley, leather jackets and juke-boxes with thoughtful detachment in terms of art, individualism, seriousness, and 'good' culture, Gunn presents and justifies the social construction of subcultures. In the poems in *The Sense of Movement* (1957) he acknowledges that meaning is produced through group identification, and that new possibilities occur through improvisations on current formations:

> Men manufacture both machine and soul,
> And use what they imperfectly control
> To dare a future from the taken routes.
>   ('On the Move')

In 'Elvis Presley' Gunn writes: 'Whether he poses or is real, no cat/Bothers to say': it doesn't matter about authenticity, the point is what the cats make it mean.

Culture constructs the literary person also, Gunn suggests in 'To Yvor Winters, 1955':

> And in the house there rest, piled shelf on shelf,
> The accumulations that compose the self –
> Poem and history: for if we use
> Words to maintain the actions that we choose,
> Our words, with slow defining influence,
> Stay to mark out our chosen lineaments.

The books are of poetry and history, and the self also is both a poem (an apparently autonomous artefact, always read in the present) and a history (composed of its successive states). The books, to which Winters has committed himself, now define him.

I discussed Colin MacInnes's *City of Spades* in Chapter 7. He was virtually the only established writer to celebrate youth culture and try to develop its subversive potential. He was affiliated neither to the Movement nor to the traditional literary establishment. He had connections with the leisure class, for his mother Angela Thirkell had both belonged to it and written for it (see pp. 71–72 above). But MacInnes had no delusion that its ethos could or should survive, though he was gay or bisexual. So he struck out in his own direction. He harked back to the radical social concerns of Wells, Shaw and Orwell, and anticipated the new journalism of the 1960s – fast-moving, welcoming the new, launching into superficially unpromising topics.

Absolute Beginners (1959) is a journalist's book (and none the worse for that – see pp. 199–201). MacInnes falls over himself trying to include as much as possible of the vitality of parts of the London scene at that date, as well as his idea of where that vitality should go. The (unnamed) young hero starts by enthusing about youth and pop: teenagers, 'absolute beginners', could, if they knew their power, 'rise up overnight and enslave the old tax-payers, the whole dam lot of them – toupets and falsies and rejuvenators and all' (p. 14). However, the boy is mainly into jazz – the Modern Jazz Quartet, Billie Holiday, Ella Fitzgerald. He has both trad and modern friends, and describes them neatly in terms of their subcultural styles and outlooks (pp. 62–3). But he doesn't need to choose between them, or to repudiate rock-'n'-roll. For him, jazz is a commitment to humanity: it goes along with lack of interest in party politics and the royal family, with opposition to war, the Cold War and commercial and media exploitation (especially of youth culture), and with passionate commitment to Blacks, who represent everything that is needed in a country that is dreary, lifeless, blind and busy over trifles (p. 44). In this utopian fusion of subcultural forms, MacInnes produced a vision rather than a record: he intuited, in 1958, that pop and youth culture might stand for and create a new mood of tolerance and geniality. As a general prescription for national happiness it was absurd, but as a utopian inflection it has some resonance. However, as MacInnes also foresaw, it was all too easily captured for media hype.

There are of course disruptions, at least three, in the vision of *Absolute Beginners*. One is suppressed by the book: it is that the experiences of the boy were open to only the tiniest minority of young people. The main structure is an odyssey in which he meets the most diverse and extraordinary people MacInnes could think of – or in fact knew, since most of them are based on acquaintances and friends. The boy moves through it all without a hint of surprise or anxiety. The only place where he has a problem is the bank – not because he hasn't any money, but because the cashier won't take him seriously (pp. 27–9, 48). No doubt there were lower-class young men who lived like that – making him a photographer is another touch of prescience. But along with so much else about the 1960s, MacInnes is anticipating the fallacy of the classlessness of youth. The boy is more like a mod than anything else (the Italian style may be dated to 1957–8) – hence the smart dressing, the affinity with Blacks, the hostility of teds, the general cool. But most mods exercized their cult 'in the pockets of free time which alone made work meaningful' (Hebdige, p. 53). The boy's time is his own, money problems miraculously disappear, and he has no difficulty meeting interesting and influential people. The impression is that subculture can cut you free from other allegiances: that if you listen to jazz, dress snappily and stay cool, then the rest of it needn't bother you. But subculture is a response to class, gender and racial pressures, not an alternative to them.

Two other disruptions are allowed by MacInnes to tear the book apart. Evidently they were lived by him as he wrote it, and their appearance in the book is organized with none of the tidy structural anticipation that is supposed to characterize the literary. They burst upon the reader as they do upon the boy, as do events in the real world, cutting through the utopian vision. One is the teds. For most of the book we have the impression that the potentially violent teds are a throwback and the boy's outlook is unstoppable. But the teds attack the Blacks, as they did in Notting Hill in 1958 (see pp. 126–8 above), and the vision of a society transformed by fun and cool collapses in incoherence and impotence. The point is not merely that the book has been over-optimistic; but that one should expect change to be resisted, since it threatens identities that are only precariously constituted. Partly because they were out of date, marginal (the Notting Hill riots marked the end of their significance), the teds were dangerous.[17]

The other disruption is the boy's assumption, unspoken until the riots break out, that the social order is fundamentally benign and held in place by adults who, however dreary, are competent and well-intentioned. 'They'd never allow it!', he exclaims – 'The adults! The men! The women! All the authorities! Law and order is the one great English thing!' (p. 136). But the police do nothing or arrest the wrong people, and the press and government statements are implicitly racist. The vision of cool and fun has ignored the general framework of power, assuming that it will honour its own ideology.

However, the boy maintains his belief in cultural action. Like MacInnes in real life, he wants to organize 'public figures' to declare that Blacks are welcome in Britain, to retrieve the possibility of racial harmony. So humane values are not tied back, as in Wain's novel, into the humanism of the classics, but depend upon the absoluteness of the beginners. The boy is tempted to leave for Norway, but the novel ends with him running to welcome Africans arriving from a plane: 'They came down grinning and chattering, and they all looked so damn pleased to be in England, at the end of their long journey, that I was heartbroken at all the disappointments that were there in store for them'. Finally 'they all burst out laughing in the storm' (p. 203), but it is a desperately sad and optimistic moment. As when Bond's Lear ends the play by starting to demolish the wall by himself, the boy's commitment gives us hope but the odds against encourage despair.

Lipstick on Your Collar

Much of the anxiety about the rock subculture was aroused by what was intended and perceived as sexual aggression. Even when it was forbidden to show Presley below the waist on television, the *New York Times* objected: 'He injected movements of the tongue and indulged in wordless singing that was singularly distasteful' (Lewis, P., *Fifties*, p. 132). In Britain, aggressive male sexuality was used to signal rejection of the 'feminine' authority of home and marriage and, as with Movement and Angry writers, rejection of class privilege that was regarded as effete (the secondary-modern boy dismissed the grammar-school boy as 'sissy'). Such attitudes were held not only by men. Sheila Rowbotham, who was reading Sartre, Camus, 'Howl' and *On the Road*, found that rock music fuelled 'a dislike of upper-class arty people': 'Every rock record simply was. The words were subordinate to the rhythm and the music went straight to your cunt and hit the bottom of your spine. They were like a great release' (Rowbotham, *Woman's*, p. 14). In so far as Rowbotham shared the same oppression as young men, she shared their liberation. In so far as she was a woman, she had to wait for the next episode (see Chapter 10 below).

Early Presley tracks such as 'Lawdy Miss Clawdy' and 'Milk Cow Blues' (1955) assume the earthy, adult sexual imagery of southern Blacks and poor whites. Only after Presley was successful did it appear that the main audience consisted of fairly inexperienced teenagers, preoccupied with dating and petting rather than women who 'ball every morning, don't come/Home till late at night' ('Lawdy Miss Clawdy'). Their problem was with parents when they got home late ('Wake up Little Susie', by the Everly Brothers, 1957; 'It's Late', by Ricky Nelson, 1959). Music companies adjusted accordingly (hence perhaps the redirection of

Presley's talent and its relative failure). This dilution of rock-'n'-roll restored much of the previous pattern of the popular-music business, where fans had 'swooned' over 'crooners'. When Pat Boone covered Little Richard's 'Long Tall Sally', *Melody Maker* found that it acquired 'clarity and an engaging relaxation' (Chambers, p. 9). The consequent division into what has been called teeny-bop and cock-rock runs through to the present (Frith, *Sound*, pp. 225–8).

Songs of both kinds invited the listener to share the story that chief fulfilment in life is to be found in consenting relations between two heterosexuals (even in cock-rock the woman is usually expected to flatter the male by submitting voluntarily). Very many were sung by male singers for female ears. Some were sung for third parties, apealing to male and female listeners on behalf of the disconsolate male.[18] Generally, women were objectified as the necessary complement to male desire – 'There's only one cure for this body of mine,/And that's to have that girl that I love so fine' (Presley, 'All Shook Up'). As Teresa de Lauretis says of film viewers, the female fan is doubly implicated: she is represented as 'the negative term of sexual differentiation . . . the looking-glass held up to man'; and she is also a spectator-subject, called upon directly, rendered 'complicit in the production of (her) woman-ness' (p. 15; the role of feminist criticism is to develop awareness of such processes). We should not imagine that these songs were merely false; it is likely that they addressed real needs, though in such a way as to help keep women in their place.[19]

Most postwar youth cultures, including hippies but with the partial exception of mods, have been heterosexist.[20] Connie Francis was a 'strong' female singer, and was successful with songs telling boys infidelity would not be tolerated:

> You had your way,
> Now you must pay,
> I'm glad that you're sorry now.

And 'Lipstick on your collar/Told a tale on you' (1958–9). But these are still variations on the usual story. Between the initial phase of rock and the appearance of the Liverpool groups (1958–65), 'girl groups' were the most lively part of the scene, but the songs are mostly celebrations of The Boy ('I met him on a Sunday and my heart stood still' – the Crystals). However, contradictions in the positioning of women in the dominant stories were certainly discernible in the 1950s (see chapter 10). Greil Marcus hears in girl groups the struggle 'of the singer – a young girl, black as likely as not – against the domination of her white, male producer' (Miller, J., p. 154). And girls had diverse kinds of experience, at home and at school, from which to construct a complex reading formation. 'All the cats want to dance with/Sweet little sixteen', Chuck Berry tells us (1958),

> Oh but tomorrow morning
> She'll have to change her trend,
> And be sweet sixteen
> And back in class again.

Perhaps adulation of boy-stars prepares women for subordination to the boy next door and men generally; but perhaps it provokes dissatisfaction with the boys they are actually meeting. For Ellen Willis it was Janis Joplin who 'never made me feel as if I were crashing an orgy that consisted of her and the men in the audience' (in Miller, J., p. 260).

An intriguing feature of youth culture is a strain of male narcissism. John Berger has said: 'Men look at women. Women watch themselves being looked at' (*Ways*, p. 47). This is not altogether true – a good deal of male youth display has been for the gaze of the same sex. Lately there have been gay and gender-bending artists, and they may be traced back, through Gary Glitter, David Bowie, Lou Reed, Mick Jagger and Little Richard. Mods were distinguished by a gentleness that was perceived as 'effeminate' (so, perhaps, *Absolute Beginners*). But it goes back before that, to the teddy boys and their concern with dress. 'Blue Suede Shoes' didn't carry a conventional gender message: it said that your clothes and the way you wear them are the main thing. An informant told T. R. Fyvel: 'Even if they all weren't effeminate [he meant homosexual], though I know some of them were, the main thing with these Teds was that they had to out-shine the way the girls were dressed.' 'Many parents viewed with alarm what they took to be an undertone of effeminacy: the interest which young men took in patterns, clothes, fashions and materials seemed to them degenerate', John Montgomery reports.[21]

Male narcissism in youth culture doesn't mean that lots of boys were 'really' homosexual, though in some instances such feelings were at work (more explicit expression being illegal and taboo).[22] Rather, I think, received wisdom underestimates the extent to which, generally in our culture, men check themselves out against men – and women against women. Male narcissism did little for girls, who were expected to wait around until noticed. But some may have found it a relief that the boys were looking at each other and leaving them in peace for a while to develop other interests.

Jazz has sometimes been preferred to popular music on the grounds of its gender politics.[23] But the British jazz scene in the 1950s was very heterosexist. Dick Hebdige notes 'a beery "blokeish" ambience' (p. 51; in Movement and Angry fiction alcohol allows the male protagonist to manifest the emotional intensity that would otherwise embarrass him but shows him to be a real human being). Larkin, in 'Reasons for Attendance', says a young man might enjoy, along with the beat, 'The wonderful feel of girls'; *Strike the Father Dead* is notably misogynist. Francis Newton remarks: 'Of all the arts in mid-twentieth-century Britain, this is so far the one with the overwhelmingly strongest heterosexual tradition and ethos' (pp. 237–8). It allowed 'commitment to the art concept' without being 'open to the interpretation of effeminacy and obedience to the values of the social system'.[24]

The gender politics of the jazz scene are well captured in Amis's *Take a Girl Like You* (1960). The issue is whether Jenny will be seduced by Patrick. It is expressed as traditional morality versus modern sophistication, and the latter is associated with jazz. Patrick is educated in classics and literature, belongs to the Labour Party (from liberal conviction), and moves fairly effortlessly in quite wealthy, smart circles where, it turns out, people are quite decent (there's a lot of alcohol). And the index of his sophistication, his proto-1960s 'classlessness', is his readiness to attend jazz sessions although 'persons of inferior education and breeding were to be found there, many of them engaged in contemporary-style dancing and calling out to one another in unpolished accents' (p. 133). Jenny is initially mystified by Patrick's records:

> In between the singing there were long bits where the sax or the vibes made it up as he went along and played as many notes as he could in the time . . . Jenny found that nearly all of what she had thought of as jazz was really called pop, and was not as good as what was called jazz by the people who knew. When she said she liked Dave Brubeck, though, she was obviously starting to do better, and spent a few happy minutes being told about him. There was always something they liked telling you about. (p. 57)

This is by no means unsympathetic to Jenny, though full appreciation of the humour depends on knowing more about jazz than she does. The narrative is divided in its sympathies. However, Jenny gradually comes round to jazz and Patrick's way of thinking.

Amis is ready to give points to Jenny because she represents a more conservative morality which he now wants partly to validate (she is preferable to the new teenager who likes rock stars and gets pregnant). Jenny's argument is persuasive when she notes that being 'frank, free, and open' seems restricted to situations where women give in to men, whereas 'to tell them all to drop dead, however frankly, freely, and openly, did not count as that' (p. 185). And although Patrick is sometimes afflicted by conscience about his seduction programme, he is mainly selfish and shallow. This is figured by a liking for modern jazz. He buys some 'East Coast stuff':

> After a frugal tune had twice been announced in unison, an alto saxophone offered a sixty four bar contribution to the permanent overthrow of melody. Just when it seemed that the musician must break out into verbal abuse, a trumpet began to rave. Several kinds of drum and cymbal continued a self-renewing frenzy in what had at one time been called the background, while underneath it all the string bass plodded metrically on as if undismayed. (p. 169)

The humour is not all Patrick's – he has bought the record; some of it is Amis's mocking disapproval, and it encompasses Patrick.

Frustrated in his persuasions, Patrick rapes Jenny while she is drunk. He is guilt-stricken and a 'good' friend tells him off, so Amis is not cavalier in the matter; we might read the rape as the outcome of a shallow and amoral outlook. However, although Jenny tries once more to reject Patrick, she decides on the final page that she should take the rough with the smooth and give in. So masculine 'needs' win out after all. Interestingly, there is the shadow of an alternative in view. Jenny has been approached also by the lesbian Anna, and while initially this is allowed to take the colouring of Jenny's fear, Anna turns out to be a valued friend. Ten years ahead, Anna might have been starting a Rape Crisis Centre, but here marrying the man seems the only way forward for Jenny.

Commerce and Authenticity

An anxiety about authenticity runs through attitudes to culture in our society. It is related to the process of cultural appropriation: when people lived inside the culture they were brought up in and hadn't the opportunity to piece together bits from diverse cultures from all over history and the world, authenticity didn't arise. Donald Hughes, for one, implies that we can get back to that innocence:

> The discriminating music-lover should look beyond the pops back to their origins – to the truly popular or people's music which grew as a direct response to the need of everyman for expression of his feelings, loves, sorrows and cares. He may then see jazz, particularly the traditional variety, as a music coming straight from the hearts and minds of the Negro people. (p. 171)

Supposing jazz was such a music, it is no longer that when taken up by British whites. Because jazz is so blatantly appropriative, it specially activates the anxiety of authenticity; we see it in Hughes's reservation 'particularly the traditional variety'. One answer, Simon Frith points out, was to make sincerity, 'playing from the heart', the criterion of true jazz ('Playing', pp. 19–20).

Rock-'n'-roll also puts sincerity under stress. Gradually it changed the organization of popular music, away from the sequence: composer →sheet-music-publication→performer, whereby diverse artists would adopt a song, towards the sequence: composer-performer→live-performance→recording (Hatch and Millward, pp. 71–3). In the former, the conjunction of song and performance is almost casual. The latter combines three kinds of authenticity claim: the specific commitment of the folk artist to his or her material, the 'live' occasion, and the idea of the disc as permanent record of a unique event. At the same time, contradictorily, rock music is manifestly subject to extreme pressures from the market and (in Europe) state-run media.[25] It cannot be chance that when Jimmy Savile plays on BBC Radio 1 the Kinks' record 'Lola', which is about a boy's self-discovery through meeting a man in a transvestite bar, he says it is for girls named Lola. Or that when he plays Marvin Gaye's record 'Abraham, Martin and John', about how people favourable to Blacks in the United States (Abraham Lincoln, Martin Luther King, John Kennedy) get assassinated, Savile comments: 'Abraham, Martin and John, good biblical names'. Or that when he plays 'Happy Birthday', by Stevie Wonder, which promotes the idea of a holiday to mark the birthday of Martin Luther King, Savile says it is for everyone whose birthday is this week. The political impact of the songs, which Savile has to play because they were in the charts, is being interfered with; and the aspiring record producer can see what kind of thing is preferred. However, those records were made, released, promoted and successful, so the effect is not all one-way.

Discourses of art and literature also invoke authenticity. In fact, they depend on the 'commercialization' of 'mass' culture to set up, by contrast, their own superiority. If 'mass' culture did not exist, high culture would have invented it (arguably, it *has* invented it). They are 'dialectically interdependent phenomena'.[26] The alleged degradation of commercial culture is invaluable in handling the embarrassing effects on culture of the free market. Celebrating literature as rising above the rest, criticism often neglects to notice that advertising, pornography and gutter-journalism are not unfortunate excrescences upon the consumer economy, but principal discourses through which it reproduces itself.

The persistent illusion is of a 'higher' culture that is not commercially organized. But jazz was business in the New Orleans brothels, and it was still business when Dave Brubeck and Thelonious Monk gained prestige and publicity by recording on the CBS label, taking on some of its 'aura of power, mystery and devastating sophistication' (Morse, p. 107). And literature is business. Movement writing, notoriously, was promoted by London journalists – the editor of *The Spectator* told his staff to be 'more influential, more sensational, and so more circulation-building, more money-making', so they decided to run articles on the Movement (!).[27] Richard Ohmann finds in US publishing 'a nearly closed circle of marketing and consumption, the simultaneous exploitation and creation of taste, familiar to anyone who has examined marketplace culture under monopoly capitalism' (Ohmann, p. 202; and p. 208). In a familiar manoeuvre, corporate capitalism seizes and adapts to its own purposes anything that aspires to evade it, from punk rock to health foods. One of Donald Hughes's arguments for classical music is that people actually buy it: 'There are numerous listed recordings of Beethoven's Fifth Symphony; and a popularly priced disc of one version only of such a major classic may sell between 20,000 and 50,000 copies' (p. 173). Hughes seems not to notice that, on his earlier argument, such market success should involve a lowering of 'standards'. In fact, commercial promotion is a feature not specially of rock music, but of the capitalist mode of production. Culture of all kinds, increasingly, is designed and packaged for a market slot.

This said, commercial and media involvement in youth subcultures is certainly blatant. More, it is integral. The band being toned down by its record company and ripped off by its manager, the release of records at strategic intervals, the tee-shirts and fanzines, the stereotyped 'personal' interviews, the romantic attachments leaked by publicity agents, the inferior B sides, the use of session men and women not 'in the band'; lately, the hint of sexual deviancy and political purpose implied and repudiated – all this is not incidental to rock-'n'-roll, any more than the guardsman fainting is to the trooping of the colour, or the professional foul to football. It's part of the structure.

In fact, the anxiety that surrounds popular culture is connected to the way it overstates key motifs in the organization of consumption. Walter Benjamin noted how in the film industry mechanical reproduction preserves 'not the unique aura of the person but the "spell of the personality", the phony spell of a commodity' (Benjamin, p. 233). So the aura of traditional culture – as natural, expressing fundamental truths, proceeding from the individual genius author – is set aside. The pop record seems the ultimate instance of the useless, synthetic product, contrived and promoted to fit a market slot. While it is nice to be affluent and enjoy leisure and buy things you didn't know you wanted, the pop industry seems altogether too much – trivial and wasteful. One way for 'deviants' to disturb the dominant is by developing its recommended values (conspicuous consumption, material aspirations, masculine aggression) with an unacceptable excess.[28] Rock music is consumer capitalism writ too large, and some performers, especially since punk, cultivate artificiality rather than authenticity.[29] However, it would be optimistic to construct a subversive role for rock music from the refusal, or failure, of much youth culture to conceal its own contrivedness as an object of consumption. Plainly people are using the music in different ways; if some are finding subversion, the dominant seems able to cope with it. The strength of authenticity as a value in our culture is so great that the refusal of it permits a critique by which the artificial may be abused and hence contained.

As there is no essential meaning or value to the artwork, so with popular music: it is not essentially either subversive or conformist. Rather, there is a contest between diverse and shifting strategies of subversion and containment. On the one hand, there is no single-minded conspiracy to dilute rock music; on the other there is no pure moment of subcultural formation – not the local band or the small record label before they are taken up by large companies.[30] The people in that initial situation are already implicated in the prevailing order, and their rebellion is structured in relation to it. There is nowhere else to be, no miraculously free space.

Hence the failure of successive youth cultures to build an enduring resistance, despite a persistent strain of disaffection, and hence their violence, racism, sexism and heterosexism. Subcultural meaning, like all meaning, works through a strategic reordering of what is to hand. Its stories make sense because they key into existing stories, adapting some aspects and repudiating others. Subordinate cultures are tangled up with the oppression that they are trying to handle; these are the conditions in which people try to negotiate cultural space.

The same conditions afford opportunities for resistance: as I argued in chapter 3, they are enabling as well as constraining. They supply language, images, institutions, strategies, points of entry – and the enemy's campaign plan. Resistance derives from the same source as conformity: from contradictions in the economic, social and political order and in the system of signification. 'The language of denial has, in its "material", always been the same as the language of affirmation' (Marcuse, *Essay*, p. 41). Which effect predominates depends upon the balance of relations at that conjuncture. There was a moment, in 1971–2, when reggae was prominent and Blacks and skinheads shared a multi-racial youth culture (Mungham and Pearson, p. 108). It could have developed differently if some people had tried harder. Every ideological effect can be deconstructed, no subcultural alignment is permanent, all forms can be appropriated. 'Smarten yourselves up', they were told, so they bought some new winkle-picker shoes.

Notes

1 Frith, *Sound*, pp. 15–23, 263–4. See also Palmer, pp. 206–7; Marcus, p. 177; Peter Guralnick, 'Elvis Presley', in Miller, J., pp. 33–5.

2 Melly, *Revolt*, pp. 33–9; Hopkins, pp. 422–9; Fyvel, *Insecure*; Montgomery, ch. 12; Nuttall, pp. 26–9; Blishen, pp. 177–80; Tony Jefferson, 'Cultural Responses of the Teds', in Hall and Jefferson, pp. 81–6; Phil Cohen, 'Subcultural Conflict and Working-class Community', in Hall, Hobson et al.; John Clarke and Tony Jefferson, 'Working Class Youth Cultures', in Mungham and Pearson.

3 Paul Rock and Stanley Cohen, 'The Teddy Boy', in Bogdanor and Skidelsky, p. 290. This article is excellent on how teddy boys were 'created' by the media as a 'moral panic'; Fyvel, *Insecure*, ch. 4; Cohen.

4 Work deriving from the Birmingham Centre for Contemporary Cultural Studies (prominently, Hall and Jefferson; Hebdige) overstates the resistance

in postwar youth movements (see Cohen, pp. i–xxxiv; Geoff Mungham, 'Youth in Pursuit of Itself', in Mungham and Pearson; Born; Nowell-Smith). But it also provides the basis of the theory presented here. See Sinfield, 'Making Space', in Holderness.

5 Adorno, p. 129; however, Marcuse lauded the political potential of 'the subversive, dissonant, crying and shouting rhythm' (*Essay*, pp. 52–3); see Brookeman, chs. 5, 8; Swingewood, pp. 10–18. On pop before rock, see also Melly, *Revolt*, pp. 31–2.

6 See Robert Christgau, 'The Rolling Stones', in Miller, J., p. 185 – referring specifically to the mythology of the United States cultivated by the Stones in Songs like 'Route 66' and 'Down Home Girl'.

7 Hughes, D., pp. 155–63, 169, 170; the same opinion is voiced by Denys Thompson in the same volume, pp. 12–13. On specificity in pop allegiances, see Morse, p. 43; Frith, *Sound*, p. 217. On how the students negotiate the culture of the school, see David Reynolds, 'When Pupils and Teachers Refuse a Truce', in Mungham and Pearson.

8 For further instances of interesting songs from this period, see Cohn, pp. 26, 38–41; on Mike Sarne, see Melly, *Revolt*, pp. 66–7. On the earlier campaign against 'horror' comics, see Barker, *Haunt*.

9 *My Enemy's Enemy*, p. 101; see pp. 80–1 above. The hero is a jazz fan in *Lucky Jim* (1954), *That Uncertain Feeling* (1955) and *Take a Girl Like You* (1960; discussed below). In *One Fat Englishman* (1963) dislike for jazz indicates a superficial and unpleasant protagonist. Amis wrote jazz criticism for *The Observer*, Larkin for the *Daily Telegraph*.

10 *Lucky Jim*, p. 54. The song appears on the Donegan LP *Showcase* (1956), with a sleevenote displaying a typical anxiety about art and commercial success: 'Many a case-hardened critic automatically wrote off any artistic merit in performances which netted such huge disc sales and so high a rating on the best-sellers lists.'

11 Oakes, p. 152. See also Newton, pp. 249–50. 264–8; Melly, *Owning Up*, pp. 10–11, 21, 141, 246; Frith, 'Playing', pp. 20–3.

12 Melly, *Revolt*, p. 30; Larkin, *All What*, p. 5; and see Chambers, pp. 29, 44–8; Nuttall, p. 40. Jazz faded during the 1960s because its role as sixth-form music was captured (from about *Sergeant Pepper*) by an up-market form of popular music (see chapter 13).

13 Quoted by Newton, p. 213; see also pp. 88–90, 213–22; Wilmer, pp. 21–4. On US Modernism, see chapter 9.

14 Webster and Powell, ch. 4; Wilmer, p. 251; Newton, p. 244.

15 See Nuttall, pp. 37–8; Gosling, *Personal*, p. 37; Booker, pp. 33–40. Colin Wilson wrote in his diary, published in the *Daily Mail*: 'How extraordinary that my fame should have corresponded with that of James Dean, Elvis Presley, Bill Haley, Lonnie Donegan' (Allsop, pp. 168–70). The hit singles were: in

April 1959, Monty Sunshine and the Barber Band playing 'Petite fleur' (a Bechet composition); in November 1961, Dave Brubeck's 'Take Five'; and thereafter the commercially targeted singles of Acker Bilk and Kenny Ball (Melly, *Revolt*, pp. 58–62).

16 In 1955 several Movement-connected writers were presented by G. S. Fraser in *New World Writing* as a British 'new movement'; the opening piece in this volume was 'Jazz of the Beat Generation', in fact part of Jack Kerouac's *On the Road* ('Dean was in a trance. The tenorman's eyes were fixed straight on him; he had found a madman who not only understood but cared and wanted to understand more and much more than there was . . .'; *New World Writing*, p. 9). Wain and Amis both appeared in *Protest* (1958, ed. Feldman and Gartenberg) alongside writers of 'The Beat Generation'.

Amis and Larkin expressed their reservations about being 'on the road' in poems called 'On Staying Still' and 'Poetry of Departures'; Wain described 'Howl' as 'a "poem" remarkable chiefly for its badness' (*Sprightly*, p. 195); to Donald Davie, Beat poets were 'illiterate apostles' ('Pentecost', *Collected Poems*, p. 206).

17 See Rock and Cohen, 'The Teddy Boy', in Bogdanor and Skidelsky, pp. 309, 314. David Puttnam's film of *Absolute Beginners* is perhaps hectic rather than cool, reflecting the 1980s, but worth seeing.

18 E.g. 'Heartbreak Hotel' (Presley) and 'Bye Bye Love' (the Everly Brothers); see Kaplan, E. A., pp. 98–101 – discussing Paul Young's 'Every Time You Go Away'.

19 See Modleski, pp. 37, 108; also Angela McRobbie, 'Dance and Social Fantasy' and Erica Carter, 'Alice in the Consumer Wonderland', both in McRobbie and Nava; Frith and McRobbie.

20 See Willis, *Profane*, pp. 27–31; McRobbie, 'Settling'; Angela McRobbie and Jenny Garber, 'Girls and Subcultures' in Hall and Jefferson; Frith and McRobbie; Taylor, J. and Laing; Frith, *Sound*, pp. 225–43.

21 Fyvel, *Insecure*, p. 50; Montgomery, p. 157; the point about 'Blue Suede Shoes' is made by Cohn, p. 26. See also Taylor, J. and Laing; Lewis, P., *Fifties*, p. 120.

22 See Gosling, *Personal*, p. 37; Gosling, *Sum Total*, p. 99; Leslie, p. 89.

23 S. I. Hayakawa, 'Popular Songs vs. the Facts of Life', in Rosenberg and White, pp. 396–403; Hayaka wa's best case is from recordings by Bessie Smith.

24 Taylor, R., p. 148. See Wain, *Strike*, pp. 72, 98–100, 207, 254.

25 Simon Frith observes three principal mechanisms in 'the capitalist control of rock practice': confining it to leisure, freezing its audience into a series of market tastes, and presenting it always as an individual matter (*Sound*, pp. 270–1). Dick Hebdige specifies two processes that recuperate the challenge of subcultures: the conversion of their style into mass-produced objects,

and the labelling and redefining of their behaviour by the media, police and judiciary (p. 94).

26 Fredric Jameson, 'Reification', pp. 133–4; cf. p. 302 below. Galbraith remarks how disapproval of advertising is not allowed to reach into the structure of the system (pp. 134–5). Peter Fuller points out that the art/advertising distinction slants our sense of the scope of visual material produced in capitalist society (pp. 78–9).

27 Morrison, pp. 47–54; Oakes, pp. 219–23; Davie, *Poet*, pp. 73–4. See also Sutherland, *Action*, ch. 2; Debray.

28 See Bennett, Muncie and Middleton, p. 39; Matza and Sykes; Dollimore, 'Different' and 'Dominant'.

29 See Chambers, pp. 1–7; Dave Laing, *The Sound of our Time* (London, Sheed and Ward, 1969), pp. 150–1; Cohen, pp. 188, 192; Frith, 'Art'; Kaplan, E. A., ch. 3.

30 Frith, 'Making'. This is Volosinov's point about the multi-accentual property of the sign (pp. 23–4). See also Stuart Hall, 'Notes on Deconstructing the Popular', in Samuel, *People's*; Kaplan, E. A., chs. 2, 4, 5. See further pp. 265–6, 300–4 below.

9

Reinventing Modernism

The fashion now is to proclaim that Modernism has given, or is giving, way to Postmodernism. Before settling on this agenda, it is worth recalling that Modernism has not maintained an even or unbroken domination over twentieth-century theory and practice of literature, art and criticism. We have important accounts of how English 'rose' in Britain as a certain kind of study – in complex implication with ideologies that were imperialist, nationalist, empiricist, sexist, elitist.[1] But how did we get from the peak of that tendency – in the 1950s – to the point where the question is how Postmodernism superseded Modernism? Socialist accounts of English studies have overlooked the effective political impetus of the reinvention of Modernism in the United States, dwelling instead upon an Englishness and Leavisism that is in fact only residual.

Anglo-Saxon Attitudes

We associate *Scrutiny* with the championing of Eliot, Yeats, James, Conrad and Lawrence, but that did not constitute an endorsement of Modernism. Four defining characteristics of Modernism, as generally understood, did not match Leavis's views: cosmopolitanism and internationalism; self-conscious experimentation with language and forms; the idea of the artwork as autonomous; and the concept of the artist as alienated by the special intensity of his (usually his) vision of the 'modern condition'. Leavis wanted literature to be central in an English tradition, and therefore it should be English, relatively comprehensible, concerned with positive moral values, not avant-gardist. Leavis and his associates read Eliot, Yeats, James, Conrad and Lawrence so as to emphasize the qualities they could use and marginalize the others. As Harold Rosenberg has demonstrated, *Scrutiny* published articles opposing many Modernists – Marianne Moore, Faulkner, Bergson, Apollinaire, Laforgue, Mallarmé, Valéry, Gertrude Stein, Pound, Wyndham Lewis and Joyce (*Finnegans Wake*). Rosenberg observes: 'No writer after Lawrence was ever permitted to affect the magazine's perspective. For Leavis, such men as Kafka, Kierkegaard, and Sartre might as well never have existed. . . . Leavis embraced the modernist revolution in order to bring it to an end' (*Case*, pp. 35–8, 40).

Leavisism informed the rapid expansion of higher education and teacher-training in the 1950s. In its liberal aspect, it claimed to define the 'good' culture that most pupils were to enjoy under welfare-capitalism; in its conservative aspect, it insisted that only 'the best' would do and promoted a call for 'standards' (see p. 56). Although *Scrutiny* closed in 1953, *The Use of English* (1949) and *Critical Quarterly* (1959) were founded on Leavisite principles, and *Universities Quarterly* was edited by Boris Ford from 1955. Well after 'the moment of *Scrutiny*' (the title of Francis Mulhern's book), after 1953, significant work was published by Leavis, L. C. Knights, D. A. Traversi, D. J. Enright, H. A. Mason, D. W. Harding, Denys Thompson, David Holbrook, John Speirs, Wilfrid Mellers, A. E. Dyson and C. B. Cox. The Pelican Guide to English Literature appeared between 1954 and 1961: edited by Boris Ford, it placed a fundamentally Leavisite canon and set of interpretations within every student's reach at five shillings per volume.

Movement writers came, at about the same time, to seem the major new force in literature, and they often acknowledged an allegiance to the *Scrutiny* school (Morrison, pp. 31–5, 63–4, 113–16, 206–7); D. J. Enright had published often in *Scrutiny* from 1941 to the end, and he edited a key volume, *Poets of the 1950s* (1955), in which Movement writers introduced their work with brisk statements of their aims and beliefs. This overlap of literary and academic fashions was, in itself, contrary to the spirit and practice of Modernism, which had sought to release literature from established institutions. In fact, anti-Modernism was a key feature of Movement writing. I've remarked that Larkin didn't like modern jazz partly because it was Modernist – which according to Larkin meant indulging in 'irresponsible exploitation of technique in contradiction of human life as we know it', wading 'deeper and deeper into violence and obscenity', and 'tending towards the silly, the disagreeable and the frigid'; and all because the artist is 'piqued at being neglected'. John Wain declared that the idea 'that all ardent, youthful spirits would naturally write in a "modern" manner . . . was manifestly absurd by 1950.' 'What poets like Larkin, Davie, Elizabeth Jennings, and I had in common at that time', recalls Thom Gunn, 'was that we were deliberately eschewing Modernism, and turning back, though not very thoroughgoingly, to traditional resources in structure and method.'[2]

I have proposed already (in Chapter 6) a relationship between cultural theories and Free-World ideology. Within that overarching determination, the political impetus of British anti-Modernism in the 1950s may be sketched, quite rapidly, in terms of three frames of reference: literary institutions, class and nation. Within the institutions of literature, Movement and Leavisite anti-Modernism contributed to the attack on the 1940s establishment (see chapter 5): among their other shortcomings (as it seemed), leading figures such as Connolly, John Lehmann, Spender, C. M. Bowra, Edith Sitwell and Dylan Thomas were associated with a left-over Modernism that was, its opponents felt, both watered down and desperately extreme. Younger writers saw little scope for development there, and cultivated self-consciously unpretentious styles; their books are funny.[3]

At the level of social class, anti-Modernists regarded Modernism, perhaps correctly, as a rebellion effectively within the leisure class that had traditionally hosted literature. As John Holloway explained in the *Hudson Review*, even the prominent left-wing writing of the prewar period had come from the upper classes: 'behind it, at varying degrees of half-discredited remoteness, stood literary Bohemia or Bloomsbury or the literary country-house weekend.' Not only did the Movement writer come from a lower-middle-class and suburban background, 'he is on the whole staying there. If he is teaching it is not in an upper-class preparatory school, but in a "red-brick" university. The automatic decanting process into upper-class England has been interrupted. Perhaps it is no longer wanted' (Holloway, pp. 592–3). Exactly the same analysis may be applied to the Leavisite academic (of course, several Movement writers were academics). Modernism was out of key with the welfare state, its claim to make 'good' culture accessible to everyone, and its purported concern with the ordinary person; in the Movement writer's jazz-playing, 'beery "blokeish" ambience' (Hebdige, p. 51), there was a residual egalitarianism, deriving from service in the armed forces and the hopes of

1945, and presided over by the ambivalent ghost of Orwell. Modernist pretensions were at odds with the kind of person a writer or don (if the word was still appropriate) now seemed to be. Al Alvarez observed 'an attempt to show that the poet is not a strange creature inspired; on the contrary, he is just like the man next door – in fact he probably *is* the man next door' (*New Poetry*, p. 25).

Finally, an element of national consciousness, a preoccupation with Englishness, fuelled hostility to Modernism. Generally, Modernisim had been a European phenomenon, and in Britain it had been dependent upon immigrants, particularly from the United States. In the first quarter of the century, London had attracted writers and artists because it was at the centre of a massive empire and hence was a major cultural centre. There, Modernists could both repudiate and, in a typical paradox of avantgardism, participate in the cultural establishment. But with the passing of British imperial power, Englishness became, even more than before, a sensitive matter (see chapter 7). Younger literary intellectuals weren't very interested in the empire; they mostly deprecated the Suez invasion, the 'independent' nuclear 'deterrent' and hostility towards immigrants. But they were sensitive in their own way to Englishness, and saw Modernism as a foreign fashion that had had its day.

The reaction against Modernism in British writing was manifested also by writers of a slightly earlier generation, such as Anthony Powell, Angus Wilson, C. P. Snow, Pamela Hansford Johnson, Olivia Manning and William Cooper. On the left, Doris Lessing declared her commitment to 'the great realists' of the nineteenth-century novel (Maschler, p. 14); and in *Culture and Society* (1958) Raymond Williams discussed Lawrence and Eliot not as Modernist experimenters but as thinkers in an English tradition concerned with industrialism and community. So a new formation succeeded the 1940s literary establishment, but its ascendancy was to be brief. Modernism was being reinvigorated and recentred just where Englishness was most distressed: in the United States, the former colony to which world power had passed.

Modernism in the Global Village

While the ascendant British literature and criticism had reasons for forgetting about Modernism, US counterparts had reasons for reconstituting it. Economically, politically and militarily, the United States was taking over

in the 1940s roles that had belonged to European states; cultural centrality followed. Its mode was Modernism, led by Jackson Pollock and
Abstract Expressionism (also called Action Painting). This not only lacked
the 'subversive' tone of the public work supported by Roosevelt's New
Deal administration in the 1930s, it claimed the sophisticated tone and
hence prestige of European high culture; so New York stole the idea of
Modern Art.[4] In other forms similarly, techniques of and affiliations to
Modernism were developed from the late 1940s: Beat and confessional
poetry; novels by Vladimir Nabokov, John Barth and Thomas Pynchon;
the music of John Cage and Morton Feldman; modern jazz.

It was a cause of satisfaction that US Modernism was distinctively
'American'. In the *Evergreen Review*, which from 1957 published every
Modernist it could find, the poet Frank O'Hara rejoiced that Action Painting has 'given us as Americans an art which for the first time in our history
we can love and emulate, aspire to and understand, without provincial
digression or prejudice. The Europeanisation of our sensibilities has at last
been exorcised as if by magic' (1958; *Evergreen Review Reader*, p. 199). Beat
writing was both Modernist and 'American': in 1957, Allen Ginsberg's
Howl was defended against a charge of obscenity on the ground that it
resembled Whitman's *Leaves of Grass* and Pound's *Cantos*, and defended
and attacked on the ground that it continued the manner of Dadaism
(*Evergreen Review Reader*, pp. 135–7). It all added up: for instance, Paul
Carroll wrote in 1961: 'Singlehandedly Ginsberg has transfused into
American prosody the important discoveries of jazzmen like Charlie
Parker and the spontaneities of the Action Painters' (*Evergreen Review
Reader*, p. 399).

Of course, post-1940 Modernism was not uncontested in the United
States. It was at odds with middlebrow culture, for instance, and with
nostalgia for European classical culture, which remained potent; and an
alternative poetics of place was developed, from William Carlos Williams
to Elder Olson to Ed Dorn (the oppositional character of this line of
writing is evident in its exclusion from the *Faber Book of Contemporary
American Poetry*, edited by Helen Vendler in 1986). But US Modernism
gained great impetus from the claim that it not merely countered, but
threw into reverse, a longstanding anxiety that US culture was unso-
phisticated and provincial. John Cage remarked: 'Once in Amsterdam, a
Dutch musician said to me, "It must be very difficult for you in America to
write music, for you are so far away from the centers of tradition". I had to
say, "It must be very difficult for you in Europe to write music, for you are

so close to the centers of tradition" ' (Cage, p. 73). Modernist enthusiasm for experiment and innovation could be interpreted as freeing the US artist or writer from the authority of traditions which (it was felt) he or she only partly shared. One incident in the identification of current US work with established Modernism was the taking up by the New York art world of Marcel Duchamp (Tomkins, pp. 13–14), whose *Nude Descending a Staircase* (1912) is a key painting of modern art. Duchamp found that the United States had become fertile ground for Modernism. Perhaps partly tongue-in-cheek, he said European artists are

> up against all those centuries and all those miserable frescoes which no one can even see any more – we love them for their cracks. That doesn't exist here. You don't give a damn about Shakespeare, do you? You're not his grandsons at all. So it's a good terrain for new developments. There's more freedom, less remnants of the past among young artists. They can skip all that tradition, more or less, and go more quickly to the real. (Tomkins, p. 66)

The internationalist and cosmopolitan strand in Modernism was also congenial to US Modernism, for it could be related to the international predominance and consequent cultural eclecticism of the United States. In the first 30 years of the century, the cosmopolitanism of European Modernism was, often, a repudiation of the dominant structure in international power relations – the imperial nation state. When the European powers armed and fought against each other and took the rest of the world as terrain upon which to compete for the largest share of imperial spoils, internationalism and cosmopolitanism registered a significant protest. But after 1945, when geopolitical power had simplifed into two blocs, the obscuring of time, place and national difference customary in Modernism could be regarded as a proper and apparently natural incorporation, or effacement, of cultures less powerful than the United States. Cage notes the adoption of his 'silences' and 'chance operations' in contemporary European music, and comments: 'It will not be easy, however, for Europe to give up being Europe. It will, nevertheless, and must: for the world is one world now' (Cage, p. 75). Cage's 'one world' is, in actuality, a world dominated by the United States. US Modernism, thus understood, merges internationalist and chauvinist criteria, folding the two together so that world culture *is* US culture. At the moment when (I have argued) English literature, partly for chauvinist reasons, was repudiating Modernism, US culture, partly for similar reasons, was reinventing it.

Modernism as US chauvinism may be observed in the ideas of a Canadian, Marshall McLuhan, who received surprising intellectual respect among theorists of Modernism in the 1960s.[5] McLuhan's evocations, in *Understanding Media* (1964), of technology as the key to the 'modern condition' often invoke Modernist works and ideas. For instance: 'The advent of electric media released art from this straitjacket [of the printed world] at once, creating the world of Paul Klee, Picasso, Braque, Eisenstein, the Marx Brothers and James Joyce' (p. 185). The revealing ambiguity in McLuhan's vision concerns the words 'we' and 'our', as when he says: 'We are certainly coming within conceivable range of a world automatically controlled'; and 'Our new electric technology ... extends our senses and nerves in a global embrace' (pp. 37, 90). In such instances, 'we' may seem to be humanity, but in actuality we know that these powers are not possessed by most people, or even most businesses and governments. The distinction is further apparent in McLuhan's disdainful stereotyping of the rest of the world – Africa of course is backward and savage. As Christopher Brookeman puts it, 'McLuhan's image of a global village joined by a single universal technology of electric circuitry chimed in with America's world role in reconstructing and maintaining the world economic and political system' (Brookeman, p. 133). McLuhan actually compares 'our' control of media with 'our' knowledge about 'maintaining equilibrium in the commercial economies of the world' (p. 37). And the ultimate ratification of US world power is Modernistic artistic greatness: 'Our' means North American when McLuhan asserts: 'Our unified sensibility cavorts amidst a wide range of awareness of materials and colors which makes ours one of the greatest ages of music, poetry, painting, and architecture alike' (p. 133). McLuhan was consulted and financed by multi-national corporations, advertising, and the US and Canadian governments, and featured in the glossy journals of Western thought and commodity consumption.[6]

In McLuhan's writing it becomes obvious that the reworking of Modernism was feeding into the major Free-World ideologies of the Cold War and the free market. This may be illustrated neatly from a later but revealing text by Hugh Kenner. After many prominent books creating the idea of Modernism, Kenner produced a home-grown, 'American' version: *A Homemade World: the American modernist writers*, including such diverse figures as Faulkner, Fitzgerald, Hemingway, Carlos Williams, and even the Wright Brothers and Benjamin Lee Whorf. Indeed, it finally emerges that US Modernists were ahead of the rest: Faulkner 'left the "closed" novel behind' and has been followed by Nabokov, Pynchon and Barth; and if we now ask 'what are words for anyway?', 'in part it is because the American Modernists did their work thoroughly'. This may be so, but Kenner's argument about why the cultivation of experiment and innovation in Modernism is 'peculiarly adapted to America's sense of reality' is revealing. In the United States, he says, 'language is something arbitrary, something *external* both to the speakers who use it and to the phenomena they hope to denote. Its norms are not imposed by history, they are elected, and if they turn out to be misleading us we can elect some new ones' (p. 213). This is absurd both as a theory of language and in its evident allusion to the US ideology of free electoral democracy; in the wake of the Vietnam War and Watergate it seems especially deluded. But Kenner has more: 'The New World felt itself detached from European necessities. Two millennia's resources are simply available, for free election' (p. 218). The achievement of US freedom is extended from the US constitution to the ransacking of the world's cultures (even as the world's material resources are consumed in disproportionate degree by countries of the Western Alliance).

The establishment of US Modernism proceeded on two fronts: the production and identification of new work, and the appropriate inter-pretation of earlier work. The latter was undertaken mainly in universities, by New Criticism (an equivalent function to that of Leavisism in relation to British anti-Modernism; the two are often elided, I think mistakenly). I have shown already the dominance of New Criticism in the 1950s, and how its formalism was congenial to Cold-War ideology, since it discouraged political, economic and social ideas among writers and critics (pp. 104–5). This formalism developed the strand in Modernism that imagined the poetic text as autonomous, drawing upon Modernist critical suggestions such as T. S. Eliot's theory of 'impersonal' poetry and Ezra Pound's definition of the image as 'an intellectual and emotional complex in an instant of time'.[7]

Alienation

New Criticism was Modernist also in that it claimed, in the last analysis, that the literary text embodies a profound truth about the supposed human condition, often in the specific guise of the alienated 'modern condition'. So John Crowe Ransom states in his seminal essay 'Criticism

Inc': 'The critic should regard the poem as nothing short of a desperate ontological or metaphysical manoeuvre. . . . The poet perpetuates in his poem an order of existence which in actual life is constantly crumbling beneath his touch' (Lodge, p. 238). This kind of claim would appear to conflict with the idea of the literary text as autonomous, since it suggests that the poem makes metaphysical and existential reference, even if in some non-propositional form; but paradox was prized by New Critics. In practice, they shuffled inconsistently between the idea of non-referentiality and the idea of a profound insight into the supposed modern condition.

This 'modern condition' was the special contribution of Modernism to Free-World ideology, for it handled the discontent of writers and artists. In theory, I argued in chapter 6, art was a free activity and therefore best pursued in the Free World – of which, in fact, it was a defining feature. However, writers and artists found the free market uncongenial, and hence experienced a discontent which, in a Cold-War situation, it was difficult to identify or express. Modernism copes with this by inviting a generalized critique of the 'modern condition' – nothing you could pin down to one political alternative or another, but a pervasive *Angst* (the contribution of Camus' kind of existentialism here is obvious). An *Encounter* editorial of July 1955 asked: 'Is the artist diviner and forerunner of a new life? Or is he the eloquent victim whose sensibility reflects those acted-upon objects we have all become today? Or is he, perhaps, the victim who, diagnosing ills, also leads?' There seem to be choices here, but they are all from within the Modernist notion of the uniquely sensitive artist, registering the sorrows of humankind without being able to intervene in any way, certainly not descending to political analysis.

The Modernist artist's situation was encapsulated in the term 'alienation'. This Marxist term – the only one not 'driven from polite conversation', says E. P. Thompson (*Poverty*, p. 24) – was taken into existentialism by Sartre and then robbed of its political dynamic as existentialism was co-opted for Cold-War ideology. Max Kozloff notes the contribution of the Abstract Expressionists: 'They disengaged themselves from the typical Sartrian problem of the translation of personal to political liberty, but they showed great concern for his notion that one is condemned to freedom' (p. 47). Once capitalism was accepted as the necessary political organization, alienation was invaluable to explain and protect the distinctive position of the artist. Its presence defined the modern condition (Guilbaut, p. 158). So for Clement Greenberg, the apostle of

215

Abstract Expressionism, the situation of the United States as the most developed and therefore most alienating capitalist state enabled art to flourish:

> The American artist has to embrace and content himself, almost, with isolation, if he is to give the most of honesty, seriousness, and ambition to his work. Isolation is, so to speak, the natural condition of high art in America. Yet it is precisely our more intimate and habitual acquaintance with isolation that gives us our advantage at this moment. Isolation, or rather the alienation that is its cause, is the truth – isolation, alienation, naked and revealed unto itself, is the condition under which the true reality of our age is experienced.
> (Guilbaut, p. 169)

From such a stance, political critique is fundamentally disabled: the Free World produces art not despite the alienation endemic in its economic system, but because of it. The scandal, to artists, of the free market, disappears: it is the well-spring of creativity. Abstract Expressionism was a medium for the Cold War, and the role of the Central Intelligence Agency in promoting it, through the New York Museum of Modern Art, has been established. The museum's director commended 'symbolic demonstrations of freedom in a world in which freedom connotes a political attitude' (Hewison, *Too*, pp. 43, 312).

Despite a fundamental collusion with the prevailing order, the Modernist artist claimed to be some kind of rebel (Camus' term). Perhaps this made sense when the bourgeoisie was a more coherent and confident formation. In 1955 T. R. Fyvel recalled 'the well-to-do middle class, the *haute bourgeoisie*', which had governed in much of Western Europe for more than a century – with

> the gentlemen's club (and the soft club chair), amateur sport, and the long weekend, with French *cuisine* and finishing schools, German scientific *Tüchtigkeit* and German music, Italian and Viennese opera; it went with family holidays in Scotland and Switzerland and on the Riviera; with large *appartements*, parlourmaids, and the solid house-façades of Europe's middle-class cities.
> (Fyvel, *Insecure*, pp. 112–13)

While all this was in place, the artist's revolt could disturb it. But lately, as Christopher Butler points out, the middle class 'pays for avant-garde art, and it has in fact been immensely hospitable to experiment from modernism on.' So we have 'the anti-bourgeois bourgeois, who accepts society more or less as it is, while at the same time entertaining a set of intellectual and artistic notions which are contradicted by his actual behaviour' (pp. 120, 122). This is the dilemma of the idealist concept of art (discussed in chapter 3): artworks are rendered ineffectual by the terms in which they are apprehended.[8]

I may seem in danger of pressing too hard the idea of a collusion between Modernism and the ascendancy of US capital and culture; of course, quite diverse movements, artists and texts are involved. But the point is not the politics of certain early twentieth-century texts; it is the category 'Modernism' that puts them together, and I am concerned with the creation of that category. The selection of appropriate texts from the first 30 years of the century and defining of the concept began, to all intents and purposes, in the 1950s. The term 'Modernism' was not generally available, as we now use it, until about 1960;[9] as will appear shortly, key 1950s texts in the establishment of 'Modernism' were written without the benefit of a current word for it. Nor does it matter, for the moment, whether we prefer to distinguish some post-1945 work, or post-1960 work, as 'Postmodern', or whether it is all 'Modernist' (but see chapter 13). Both those ways of construing the situation may assert the ascendancy of postwar US work and both use 'Modernism' as a reference point.

As world hegemony passed to the United States, the principles and practices of global, i.e. US, Modernism were fed back into the canon and practices and principles of English studies. In the first edition of Cleanth Brooks's *Modern Poetry and the Tradition* (1939), modern and especially US poetry is promoted as a break with tradition ('One cannot participate fully in the poetry of John Crowe Ransom, for example, and continue to enjoy Shelley on the old basis'). But 25 years later, in a new introduction, Brooks regrets that he dismissed English Romantic poetry so briskly, for his critical strategy, after all, 'can be applied to the poems of a Wordsworth as well as to those of an Eliot, to those of John Keats as well as to those of a John Donne' (p. xii; no one is to escape). Bernard Bergonzi remarks: 'The emergence of modernism as a literary category coincided with the explosion of the academic study of modern literature' (*Myth*, p. xiv). He might have added that it coincided with the ascendancy of North American critics and institutions in English studies.

It was as a US construct – often recognized explicitly as such – that Modernism was recentred in Britain from the end of the 1950s. Cultural power normally follows economic, political and military power, and as with jazz, rock-'n'-roll, Coca-Cola and blue jeans, the 'American' way of doing things, of seeing things, seemed impossible to ignore. Lawrence Alloway's *Nine Abstract Artists* was published in 1954, and the 'Situation' exhibition at the RBA Galleries in 1960 showed a trend towards tightly argued abstraction. As Bryan Appleyard puts it, Abstract Expressionism arrived in Britain together with 'the Beat generation, rock'n'roll, teenage rebellion and street wisdom. It was a heady mixture, a culturally imperialistic drive which swamped the more feeble British revolt' (p. 30). Walter Lippmann's prediction of 1946 came true: 'America is from now on to be at the center of Western civilisation rather than on the periphery' (Guilbaut, p. 128). The United States possessed institutional power – wealthy and prestigious universities, foundations and publishers (in his book *Intellectuals Today*, 1968, T. R. Fyvel has two chapters where academics and writers discuss US opportunities); and it seemed more vibrant, modern and important. Alvarez believed that the European intelligentsia sensed that 'under all that turmoil and chic' – the reservation is a characteristic device for mediating US culture to British people – US artists were 'exploring and defining areas of experience which have not previously been expressed in the arts' (*Under Pressure*, p. 184). For while US influence obviously undermined the autonomy of British culture, it also promised release from traditional mores and local structures of wealth, class and cultural capital. As such, it might appeal even to writers and critics who had embraced, or might have been expected to embrace, a Movement/Leavisite orientation.

Conductors

Cultural change occurs in long-term, general and uneven ways, but it is manifested through a multitude of individual decisions. The reintroduction of Modernism to Britain in the late 1950s and early 1960s was advanced crucially by well-placed individuals, who were drawn towards US culture and served as conductors, feeding back its framework of perceptions.

There were hints of non-Movement, non-Leavisite attitudes in British literary and academic circles in the mid-1950s – aspects of the poetry of Thom Gunn and Ted Hughes and of the novels of Iris Murdoch and William Golding, Lawrence Durrell's *Alexandria Quartet* (1957–60), the vogue of Colin Wilson's *The Outsider* (1956), the successful production of

Waiting For Godot (1955; though the London theatre pursued its own trajectory and this was perhaps just Modernism 40 years late). Gunn went to live in California in 1954 and negotiated his release from the British situation by arguing with Yvor Winters (Gunn, *Occasions*, pp. 175–7). But these were separate phenomena, more connected with French existentialism than with a continuing sense of Modernism. US commentators reported back rather unsympathetically on the strange state of British literary life.[10] Fundamentally, Modernism was reintroduced into Britain from the United States, and the conducting agents were British writers and academics whose success – often in a Movement or Leavisite vein – had given them access to the US orbit. I shall discuss the contributions of Donald Davie (ex-Movement poet and academic), Al Alvarez (ex-Leavisite academic and literary journalist), Frank Kermode (professional academic) and Stephen Spender (established man of letters). The range of their accomplishments and institutional roles indicates the scope of the change they helped to effect.

Davie's book *Purity of Diction in English Verse* (1952), arguing for the values of lucid communication, became something of a manifesto for the Movement (Morrison, pp. 37–9); in *Articulate Energy* (1955) Davie sought to show what is at issue when we accept the symbolist proposition that in poetry syntax turns into music. At this time the term 'Modernism' was not current, such is the extent to which the concept was reinvented: 'symbolism' is one of its forerunners. By April 1956 Davie was displaying a divided attitude to Eliot's *Four Quartets*. On the one hand, he still hoped for 'quite a different sort of poem in the future, a sort of poem more in harmony with what was written in Europe before symbolism was thought of'; on the other hand, he admired Hugh Kenner's 'brilliant' exposition of the *Quartets* and acknowledged that it would be futile 'to pretend that the symbolist revolution never happened' (*Poet*, pp. 36–7, 41). By July 1957 Davie was writing of Pound's *Cantos* as 'this great poem', particularly because 'it has created and put into action a language which is literally international', unlike subsequent English poetry which, Davie now believed, 'has committed itself to the status of being no more than a marginal pleasure, a deliberately and self-confessedly *provincial* utterance' (*Poet*, p. 47). He disagreed with Amis and Larkin over their disparagement of 'culture' and 'tradition', and accused Leavis of leading the way into 'an extreme provincialism'. The capital, the metropolis, of course, is the United States. Poets there, if anything, have gone too far in the opposite direction, being too experimental and cosmopolitan (p. 52). So Davie went to be visiting professor at the University of California in 1957–8, and sought opportunity to write on 'Hugh Selwyn Mauberley' for the generally Leavisite Pelican Guide to English Literature (*The Modern Age*, ed. Ford, 1961). He believed that, without his intervention, 'Pound's achievement would go unremarked in Britain; and that 'Mauberley' 'registers the death of England as a live cultural tradition' and the shift to 'the English-speaking nations in North America' (*Poet*, pp. 90, 92). He had accepted the main tenets of US Modernism.

In 1973, in *Thomas Hardy and British Poetry*, Davie was still arguing the pros and cons, but his awareness of power relations was sharper. He reiterated his sense of the sheepishness of the line of poetry that runs through Hardy and Larkin, but suggested, on the other hand, that the 'wholesale appropriation of foreign authorities' in US poetry might reflect 'the imperious rapacity which created just those banana republics that American poets are ashamed of, and inveigh against.' He observed, also, that 'the Englishman supposes he is trying to operate in some highly specific historical situation, conditioned by manifold contingencies . . . whereas the American poet . . . is sure that he is enacting a drama of which the issues are basically simple and permanent' (pp. 185–6). Davie does not quite say that the former approach is that of a culture that is aware of its subordination, whereas the latter represents the difficulty of a dominant culture in appreciating the relativity of its own perceptions.

Alvarez had been associated with the Movement in the early 1950s, and he retained Leavisite principles.[11] But by 1956 he had been for two spells in the United States, and in *The Shaping Spirit* (1958 – written with a grant from the Rockefeller Foundation) he appeals particularly to R. P. Blackmur (New Critic and modernist – the book is dedicated to him), and also to Hugh Kenner. Alvarez regrets 'the current sense of depressed limitation in poetry' in England (p. 76) and declares: 'English literature now, in the 1950s, is safely back on the track that seemed to have been abandoned when *Prufrock and Other Observations* appeared in 1917; it is back in the old way of traditional forms, traditional language and more or less traditional sentiments' (p. 87). Alvarez appeals instead, in a preface to *The Shaping Spirit*, to US Modernism – now identified, provisionally, as such: ' "modernism" – in inverted commas – has been predominantly an American concern, a matter of creating, almost from scratch, their own poetic tradition. It has affected English poetry peculiarly little' (p. 9). The special US conditions are those we have already heard of: freedom from tradition (pp. 12–13, 46, 50–6, 164–5) and the 'profound sense of alienation' with which 'artistic imagination in the States works' (p. 188).

In his introduction to the Penguin anthology *The New Poetry* (1962) Alvarez reiterated his analysis, accusing most English poets, and especially Larkin, of being in retreat from the 'new areas of experience' opened up by 'the great moderns' and rendered even more pressing by two world wars, concentration camps, genocide and nuclear war – all bundled together to form the modern condition (pp. 21, 26). Alvarez was far more optimistic about US poets such as Robert Lowell and John Berryman and about Sylvia Plath (see chapter 10). However, by 1967 Alvarez saw signs (long present, I think) that this line of US poetry had 'resurrected traditional experiments' and therefore was 'harmless'; and that 'the cosmopolitan bias in American poetry has been abandoned in favour of something altogether more chauvinistic' (*Beyond*, p. 4)

We recognize Frank Kermode's drift in *Romantic Image* (1957) from his opening exposition of two interlinked beliefs: in the autonomy of poetry and the artist's alienation – 'in the Image as a radiant truth out of space and time, and in the necessary estrangement or isolation of men who can perceive it' (p. 2). Strikingly, although Kermode has not yet the term 'Modernism', he presents a Modernist canon and critical principles as already agreed and beyond question:

> The one thing nearly everybody seems to be agreed upon is that the work of art has to be considered as a whole, and that considerations of 'thought' must be subordinated to a critical effort to see the whole as one image; the total work is not about anything – 'a poem should not mean but *be*' – which is simply a vernacular way of saying what modern critics mean when they speak of it as 'autotelic'. (p. 154)

Kermode's assumption that Modernism was, in 1957, the only way of thinking about literature is partly, I dare say, a strategy, a way of helping to produce that state of affairs (a performative utterance). But it occurs mainly because his frame of reference, outside the historical texts of Romanticism, Symbolism and Modernism, is almost entirely North American. He indicates no awareness of *Scrutiny* or the Movement (though he was personally acquainted with Wain as early as 1951).[12] The contemporary critics to whom he appeals include M. H. Abrams, R. P. Blackmur, Cleanth Brooks, John Crowe Ransom, Allen Tate, Philip Wheelwright and W. K. Wimsatt, Jr; to represent the position that he considers now untenable he chooses not Leavis but Yvor Winters.

Being primarily an academic, Kermode is more concerned with past writing than are the other conductors discussed here, and is specially committed to reading English literary history in the light of Modernist principles. He offers as anticipators of the poetic image not only the late-romantic and symbolist poets we would expect, but also Wordsworth, George Eliot and Matthew Arnold. And the 'next step', he promises, is to recover 'poetry of the past which has been excluded', including that of Spenser and Milton (*Romantic*, p. 165).

I disagree with Frank Lentricchia's view of *Romantic Image* as a book that hastened the death of New Criticism. True, Kermode did relativize New Criticism and Modernism by showing their historical origins, and he did propose integrating 'the poetic imagination with general human intellectual capacities' (Lentricchia, pp. 3–7). But demanding a general relation between literature and the 'modern condition' is, I have shown, a Modernist move; and by merging explicitly New Criticism and Modernism Kermode gave new coherence and authority to both. Further, and crucially, Kermode's historicizing is never radical; there is always an excess of profundity, bespeaking a deeper significance than the historical moment could produce or contain. This is characteristic of Modernism and of critical comment from within its orbit: history may be invoked, but it yields, implicitly, to a further, unspecified mode of truth. It is, in Eliot's phrase, a nightmare from which one is trying to awake.

Kermode's preoccupations made him a good choice to succeed Spender as co-editor of *Encounter* in 1966. His appointment was marked by an article by him on 'Modernisms', asserting a continuity but also a falling off between early and current work (some enthusiasts of US Modernism drew back when they saw it producing Pop Art and other mid-1960s phenomena). The scandal about CIA funding was about to break, and Kermode resigned in 1967. He recoiled from this episode to a new intellectual base, again involving interwoven literary, academic and general intellectual strands, in continental Europe – in the *nouveau roman*, structuralism and semiotics. These movements were also compatible with Modernism; how far they served to sustain US cultural hegemony is matter for another book.

Spender was never involved in the mood that sustained Leavisism and the Movement in 1950s Britain. As an established man of letters, he did not have to find new ground on which to make his stand, but a way of rescuing what he could from past engagements; and his distinction gave him access to the US cultural apparatus. Modernism suited both his Cold-War cultural theory and his personal predilections. Modernists had made individual protests against the oppressive norms of the high bourgeois society of his childhood; they had established the importance of literature in itself; they had eschewed social realism and hence, he believed, left-wing commitment; yet they had conducted a critique of the 'modern condition', and hence could not be declared irrelevant.[13]

Spender worked out his position in *The Creative Element* (1953): 'The creative element is the individual vision of the writer who realises in his work the decline of modern values while isolating his own individual values from the context of society', and this had been done pre-eminently by 'the great experimenters in writing at the beginning of this century' (pp. 11, 14). By the time he published *The Struggle of the Modern* in 1963 (deriving from lectures at Berkeley and Washington in 1959 and 1961), the academy and intellectual journals were ready for the term 'Modernism' and the distinction between 'moderns' and 'contemporaries' – which in fact had been made by Alvarez in *The Shaping Spirit*.[14] Spender finds the current British scene dominated by contemporaries who reject Modernist profundity; they are reacting against experimental writing and, dangerously to Spender's Atlanticist perspective, they are suggesting that 'Pound and Eliot were an alien incursion of American influence into English poetry' (*Struggle*, p. 216). And Leavisites are claiming that foreign visits '– to America for example – are simply excursions into an area of modern damnation called the "new and the unprecedented" ' (p. 231). These attempted assertions of British cultural independence may well strike us as ill-considered and futile, but Spender's determination to head them off is excessive. The reason, I believe, is that contemporaries and even Leavisites are likely to relate culture to politics – and Spender has in view by this date John Osborne, Doris Lessing, Alan Sillitoe, Arnold Wesker and Raymond Williams, as well as the Movement. He denigrates recent novels as 'weighed down with sociology and written by class-conscious young people concerned not with inventing values of life, but with communicating information about their working-class origins, or the Red Brick University' (*Struggle*, p. 130). The 'values of life' mustn't be too specifically located. That could lead (I show in chapter 11 that it did lead) to distrust of the Free World and the Western Alliance – to the Campaign for Nuclear Disarmament, for instance, which a number of prominent 'contemporaries' supported, though Spender doesn't mention it.

The Politics of English Studies

The conducting of reinvented Modernism into British culture was resisted mainly on reactionary grounds. Leavis fulminated against 'the rapid assimilation of this country to America' and 'the American literature that American wealth is bestowing on the world', and disputed the superiority of US criticism (*English Literature*, pp. 33–4). The case was put more thoughtfully by Graham Hough, another Cambridge don, in lectures in Washington in 1959. Hough had a traditional education in the classics, and found offensive the 'tasteless hewing up of gobbets' in Modernism (*Reflections*, p. 109). He saw that the ascendancy of Modernism derived from a shift in power from Britain to the United States (p. 98). He granted that cosmopolitanism and internationalism suit US people because of their geography and history (p. 93), but was unconvinced by the work of Kermode and Davie (pp. 11, 102). Hough didn't welcome the social and political inflection in writing of the late 1950s either (p. 166); he wanted to conserve the purity of a tenuous minority culture at Cambridge and Oxford.

By the end of the decade the specific mood of the early and mid-1950s had collapsed, and most younger people (including Amis and Wain, but not Larkin) quickly made terms with Modernism and US culture. Wain, while deprecating what he saw as the formlessness and lack of settled tradition of the United States, readily acknowledged 'the exhilaration' (*Sprightly*, p. 227). Since then, 'experimental' styles of writing, painting and film and an internationalist outlook have become commonplace, and Movement writing and its principles now seem a deflection from the main current of twentieth-century literature. Larkin remains acceptable, though rather quaint, because he is reckoned the best, and Amis is acknowledged as a good, old-fashioned comic novelist; the others have changed direction or slipped from prominence. Instead, a sophisticated eclecticism has become *de rigeur* if one is to get serious attention (consider John Fowles, the later Doris Lessing, Patrick White, William Golding, D. M. Thomas, Anthony Burgess, Salman Rushdie, Martin Amis). Already by 1970 the received story was being rewritten, as Bernard Bergonzi, Malcolm Bradbury and David Lodge found two strands in the postwar British novel, with the non-Modernist as the less significant.[15]

Mainly to the distress of Davie, Kermode and Spender (that was not what they meant at all), the news travelled from high art into the Pop Art and 'Underground' poetry of the 1960s and then into middle-class youth

counter-culture (consider record sleeves). The experimental displace-
ments, allusions, puns, self-references and shifts of register that once
provoked an affrighted and affronted bourgeoisie into censorship,
ostracism and even riot, became common currency in advertisements,
and now fit conveniently around 'Children's ITV', 'Coronation Street' and
'News at Ten'. At the same time, the classic Modernist texts of the early
part of the century have been widely distributed, through innumerable
gramophone records and tapes, reproductions of paintings and copies of
Penguin Modern Classics. I trace this sequence in chapter 13 and the use
of the term 'Postmodernism' to locate it.

In academic English, attention edged away from the eighteenth- and
nineteenth-century realist novels and seventeenth-century witty poetry
preferred by Leavisites, and towards Modernist texts and others that could
be treated as if they were Modernist texts. Since Modernist-New-Critical
method could be applied to virtually any writing, and seemed not
altogether unlike Leavisism, the shift in power and the change in the
political role of criticism were obscured. Even Terry Eagleton remarks no
significant break between Leavisism and New Criticism: 'New Criticism is
generally taken to encompass the work of Eliot, Richards and perhaps also
Leavis and William Empson, as well as a number of leading American
critics . . .'.[16] As the postwar consensus about the benefits and necessity
of welfare-capitalism drew to an end in Britain, in the 1970s, and the
political construction of English studies came into question, it was
discussed not in terms of its implication in a cultural framework deriving
from and tending to centre on the United States, but in terms of Englishness, class power, imperialism and Leavisism. English studies has been
considered, in other words, as it stood in the 1950s. But since that time it
has been informed only residually by Leavisism; its Englishness has been
pressured not by imperial ambitions but by economic, political, military
and cultural deference to the United States.

I write, as I say, of what Modernist texts have been made to mean –
Modernism and Postmodernism are not just there in the world, they are
concepts which construct us, even as we or our forebears have constructed them. In fact, the most vital challenge of some 'Modernist' texts
may well have been their racism and sexism: this really disconcerts
students unprepared by Modernist-New-Critical premises for such vivid
political commitment. But overall, the effective politics of Modernism
have been as Lionel Trilling proposed in 1966. To him, Modernist texts
were 'anti-social', 'anti-cultural', 'subversive'. But 'when the term-essays

come in, it is plain to me that almost none of the students have been taken aback by what they have read: they have wholly contained the attack.' Of course, it is drawing Modernism into the academy that helps to destroy its challenge; by doing this, Trilling himself has contributed to the effect he laments. And he feared, indeed, that '*the* modern element in modern literature' is its susceptibility 'to being made into an academic subject'.[17] Modernism, in English studies, had merged into the ideological wallpaper. However, this too began to break up in the 1960s.

Journalism and Literature

The review of Doris Lessing's *Five* in *The Times* (11 July 1953) called it 'a thoroughly competent reporting of social evils of all kinds which comes near to journalism' (Taylor, J., p. 3). The opposition between literature and journalism is one structure through which the notion of literature as transcending the local and the temporary is sustained. And, as with Lessing, it is likely to be brought into play when writing seems to be becoming left-wing. Alvarez used it when explaining why Auden did not measure up to the standards of Modernism: the journalist's task is 'to observe accurately, to present succintly and to comment. . . . His business is with the surface of things, not with their real nature' (*Shaping*, p. 94). The 'real nature' is deeper than politics, it is lodged in the human condition or the modern condition. It was not always so. Shakespeare, Swift, Johnson, Dickens, Shaw and Wells felt that they could write, and about the main issues of their time, without even having to think whether they were being profound about the 'human condition'.

The issue was fought out at the turn of the century as part of the process by which what we now call Modernism established itself. In E. M. Forster's *Howards End* 'the dividing line between journalism and Literature' is started as a conversational hare (p. 70); Helen is committed to Literature (p. 60). Henry James and Virginia Woolf attacked the approach of such as Wells and Bennett, demanding a finer attention to structure and detail and a generally more rarified atmosphere. In effect, this was to demand also a more conservative kind of writing – one that would not plunge into issues as they occurred. The journalistic tradition did not make for artistic refinement, and it often took a progressive view of human potential. In 'The Function of Criticism' (1923), as part of his case for 'the accumulated wisdom of time', 'literary *perfection*' and an 'impersonal' art that would not 'serve ends beyond itself', T. S. Eliot attacked 'Whiggery' (Lodge, pp. 78, 81). By the latter, he meant all kinds of meliorism – all political views, from liberalism to Marxism, that hold that the lives of people might, if we tried very hard, be made better. Journalists often (though not necessarily) write from such a position, hoping that their writing will encourage reform, whereas anti-meliorists prefer to lose present troubles in the soaring harmonies of art.

The distinction was reasserted as part of the recycling of Modernism. Spender declared that writers with social concerns were:

> publicists and not quite artists. Wells, though priding himself on being a social prophet, cultivated the manner of a travelling salesman for the scientific culture. Like Shaw, Bennett and Galsworthy he thought of his public personality as anti-aesthetic, lowbrow. He was forever explaining that he was a journalist who breathed a different air from that of characters in the novels of Henry James. (*Thirties*, p. 147)

Academic criticism exercized itself to identify and set to one side the 'contemporary references' of writers such as Shakespeare and Dickens, so that the formal perfection and universal appeal of their work could emerge. Even living writers had to be subjected to the same analysis. The introduction to a collection of essays about J. D. Salinger notes that he has been related to social criticism such as David Riesman's *The Lonely Crowd*, but is pleased to discover 'not the critique of a period or a particular situation but of the human condition'. After all, 'the Lonely Crowd is mankind' (Grunwald, p. xiii). Recently Susan Sontag has defended Naipaul against Peter Kemp's charges of a limiting preoccupation with lonely isolated characters and themes of political catastrophe: this, she says, is what we should expect of 'a great writer with a tragic sense of the human condition and of contemporary history'. She adds: 'Perhaps Kemp takes Naipaul to be some kind of journalist'; what should be kept in mind are 'the standards appropriate for judging literature'.[18]

The obvious and unashamed modern journalist is Orwell, who influenced Movement and Angry writers. They were much closer to journalism than most twentieth-century writing that gets called 'literature'. Wain has been an enduring crusader for Johnson and Bennett; Amis champions science fiction. Their cultivation of the common person was more than an affectation; their books did try to address current experience, and they have been genuinely popular. To that extent, they represented a positive possibility, but it was displaced before it could gain much political sophistication or much purchase on the literary and educational apparatus. By so much as literature is constituted as a rarified phenomenon, by so much it loses immediate force in the culture at large. And journalism is impoverished as well, as lower standards are expected and produced. The critical edge of our intellectual culture is blunted, its seriousness diminished.

In so far as art and literature have been alleged to manifest the 'modern condition', there is surely a sleight of hand: the condition is a presumptive, we might say presumptuous, construction of a few white male intellectuals in Europe and North America, on behalf of millions of other people whose concerns are quite different. What we actually suffer under is corporate capitalism, produced by economic, political and military power, and by choices made by people in history. By investing the alleged modern condition with a romanticism of extremity, writers and critics discourage political analysis. Modernism is offered as standing at the brink, daring to stare into the abyss so that the rest of us can only gasp. The situation is too urgent for such self-indulgence.

Notes

1 See Mulhern; Baldick; Eagleton, *Literary*; Hawkes, *Shakespeherian*. See also Chapters 4 and 6 above.
2 Larkin, *All What*, pp. 11, 17, 119; Wain, *Sprightly*, pp. 208–9; Gunn, *Occasions*, p. 174; see also pp. 79–81 and 158–63 above. Harry Ritchie argues that hostility to Modernism is a major determinant of Amis's writing and attitudes (pp. 91–105).
3 See Green, *Children*, pp. 406–65; Morrison, pp. 63–5; Hewison, *In Anger*, chs. 2–4. Amis's iconoclasm took in academic English. Reviewing a Penguin translation of Beowulf in the *Spectator*, he called *Troilus and Criseyde* 'that footling rigmarole', and said the *Faerie Queene* and *Paradise Lost* are 'remote and frigid . . . ultimately sterile' (5 April 1957, pp. 282–3).
4 See Guilbaut; Brookeman, pp. 190–2; pp. 102–3 above. Abstract Expressionism became influential in Britain through exhibitions in the 1950s (Hewison, *In Anger*, pp. 186–90).
5 For instance, in *Innovations*, edited by Bernard Bergonzi in 1968 (see pp. 15–19, 134–49, 175–9).
6 See Brookeman, pp. 124, 133; Fekete, pp. 184–5.

7 See Russell, C., p. 242; Bruss, pp. 10 13; Fekete.

8 Commentators now often propose a distinction between Modernism, which seeks to exalt art and render it autonomous; and the avant-garde, which seeks to destroy the distinction between art and other kinds of cultural production and intervene politically: see Bürger; Russell, C., ch. 1; Huyssen, pp. vi–vii, 3–4, 162–4. See also pp. 284–6 and 290–4 below.

9 See Faulkner, pp. viii–ix; Bergonzi, *Myth*, p. xiii; note 14 below.

10 See Karl; O'Connor; Rabinovitz.

11 On Alvarez and the Movement, see Morrison, pp. 43, 45, 46, 137. For Alvarez's Leavisism, see for instance Alvarez, *Shaping*, pp. 51, 54–5, 151, 163, 189.

12 Kermode, review of Morrison: *London Review of Books*, 5 June 1980, p. 6. In this review Kermode still finds little positive to say of the Movement. See also Morrison, p. 26. But cf. Kermode, *History*, part 1.

13 On Spender's Cold-War aesthetic, see Chapter 6. He opposed the idea of the artwork as autonomous because he wanted art to 'transform' life, but the idea tends to creep back when he has to deal with the 'reactionary' politics of Modernist writers; at least they 'put literature before politics': see above, pp. 30 and 103–4.

14 Spender, *Struggle*, pp. 71–8. Alvarez had written that Auden is 'much more "contemporary" than "modern", with all that last word, in its best sense, implies of profound originality' (*Shaping*, p. 93). Alvarez's use of 'modernism', in quotation marks (p. 9), is the next I have come across after Riding and Graves (1927). On the importance of Spender's *Struggle*, see Bergonzi, *Myth*, p. xi.

15 See Stuart Laing, 'Making and Breaking the Novel Tradition', in Gloversmith.

16 Eagleton finds in New Criticism and Leavisism alike 'the ideology of an uprooted, defensive intelligentsia': this locates the inceptions but doesn't address the subsequent histories (*Literary*, pp. 46–7). However, Eagleton does suggest that New Criticism was attractive to 'liberal intellectuals disoriented by the clashing dogmas of the Cold War' (p. 50). Cf. Hawkes, *Structuralism*, pp. 151–6; Widdowson, pp. 3, 121–2, 154–7.

17 Trilling, pp. 26, 4. See Bruss, pp. 12–13; Russell, C., p. 242; chapter 13 below.

18 Letter from Sontag to *Times Literary Supplement*, 28 August 1987, p. 925.

10
Women writing: Sylvia Plath

Got myself a crying, talking,
Sleeping, walking, living doll . . .
Gonna lock her up in a trunk, so no big hunk
Can steal her away from me.

(Cliff Richard and the Shadows, 'Living Doll' by Lionel Bart, August 1959)

> Naked as paper to start . . .
> A living doll, wherever you look.
> It can sew, it can cook . . .
> My boy, it's your last resort,
> Will you marry it, marry it, marry it.
>
> (Sylvia Plath, 'The Applicant', *CP*.182, October 1962)

What Happened to Feminism

Why feminism was generally in abeyance in Britain and the United States until the late 1960s is one of the commonest and most reasonable questions asked by students of the period. For the subordination of most women in modern Western societies – both when they seek paid employment and when they attempt to fill the expected family roles – is surely apparent enough. Such a powerful disjunction, between what now seems obvious and only 30 years ago did not, is a vital illustration of one leading proposition of this book: the cultural construction of the whole framework of understanding within which thoughts and actions take place.

In part, feminism was believed to have been successful and hence no longer necessary (like trades unions). A central assumption of welfare-capitalism was that the good state had in principle arrived, and only details needed attention. Women could indeed vote and be educated, and had some sort of access to most careers. In the early 1950s 'equal pay' was won in the civil service and teaching. A few women were high achievers, and some were rich and famous. So even progressive women believed that 'the cause of reasonable feminism' had been virtually won. 'Earlier' kinds of feminism came to seem old-fashioned; Sheila Rowbotham thought of feminists as older women who wanted to stop you doing things. Elizabeth Wilson concludes: 'Feminism led an underground or Sleeping Beauty existence in a society which claimed to have wiped out that oppression'.[1] Nevertheless, the situation was disturbed and anxious.

It may well be that many people wanted to get back to home and family after the disruption of the war; what is striking is the extent to which they had, apparently, to be exhorted to do so, through the propagation of an ideology of domesticity. A *March of Time* newsreel film of February 1948 (vol. 14, no. 7) expressed disquiet about the divorce rate, which it attributed to women earning their living and hence becoming economically able to end their marriage. Viewers are told:

> Catastrophic social forces have propelled American women away from femininity and into careers at terrific cost to themselves and society. Abandoning their feminine role has made women unhappy because it has made them frustrated; it has made children unhappy because they do not have maternal love; and it has made their husbands unhappy because they do not have real women as partners.

However, the speaker is a woman (Dr M. F. Farnham, 'noted physician and co-author of the best seller *Modern Woman: the lost sex*'), and we see her standing in her white coat in her consulting room, giving dictation to a female stenographer with a female nurse passing busily through. The career activities of these women receive no comment in the film.

That such insistence on domesticity was problematic may be observed in the awkward arguments of social scientists. Sociologists found that the particular kinds of gender and family relations that were supposed to occur in Britain and North America were proper and natural. The dominant approach was functionalist: all parts of the social organism were held to make their appropriate contribution. As Kate Millett puts it, functionalism 'examines the status quo, calls it phenomena, and pretends to take no stand on it' (p. 232). So women were alleged to be 'expressive' and men 'instrumental' – a convenient ratification of conservative sterotypes. British sociology was more empiricist, but it too found the family to be working well in modern society.[2] Michael Young and Peter Willmott attended so exclusively to families in *Family and Kinship in East London* (1957), at the expense of other kinds of relationship, that it is hard to imagine how husbands and wives ever met (perhaps they were all cousins). A new pattern of symmetry and complementariness between wife and husband was said to be developing, and there was a relative change. But women in paid employment still took (and take) primary responsibility for housework and childrearing (Marwick, *British*, pp. 64–71).

The dominant psychological notions were Freudian (or one variant thereof). In the 1950s, despite evidence of other kinds of family structure in Europe and other parts of the world, Freudians made the ideology of domesticity appear natural.[3] In Britain this attitude appeared in popular works by John Bowlby (*Child Care and the Growth of Love*, 1953) and D. W. Winnicott (*The Child and the Family*, 1957 – based on radio talks of 1944–45). Both studies insisted on the crucial role of the mother.

The typical intellectual slither in this work is evident in a key statement by John Bowlby: 'In Western communities today it is the tradition that "normal home life" is provided by a child's mother and father, which is conveniently described as the child's "natural home group" ' (p. 85). The sentence begins with a recognition that its subject is relative to time and place; then dignifies it with the term 'tradition'; but then calls it 'normal'; and finally, *for convenience*, 'natural'. Nurture is transformed, before our eyes, to nature. Winnicott, in similar vein, tells us: 'In the children's play there is the game "Mothers and Fathers" and, as you know, father goes off in the morning to work, while mother does the housework and minds the children' (p. 84). Observe the awkwardness: mothers are supposed to 'know' – being mothers, appropriate knowledge comes naturally; yet Winnicott has to tell them. Even so, Bowlby and Winnicott helped to soften what had often been harsh family regimes. Looking back, the 1950s were a good time for many children in Britain: they were treated more kindly, as by and large they are now, but had the advantage of expecting a relatively secure future.

The exclusive importance of the family was assumed also by people on the left. Peter Townsend, for instance, asserted: it is 'the chief means of fulfilment in life'. Sheila Rowbotham has recorded the difficulty she experienced, as a left-winger in the 1960s, in seeing anything wrong with the position of women; even when Simone de Beauvoir's *The Second Sex* appeared in paperback translation in 1960, Rowbotham found it 'very inaccessible'.[4]

It is not obvious why the ideology of domesticity was produced. There was an initial anxiety about the birth rate, but it was soon dispelled by a postwar 'baby boom' and a declining mortality rate. Again, initially at the end of the war women were urged to surrender jobs to men; but there was soon a labour shortage and women were drawn back in (the Ministry of Education appealed to married women teachers to return to the profession in 1955).[5] As I argued in chapter 3, the propagation of an ideology doesn't indicate what people were doing and thinking; if anything, insistent ideological work witnesses to uncertainty and contradiction. Domesticity was at issue because women were likely to resist it.

Placing the topic in a larger perspective, we are looking at an inflection in the historic exploitation of female labour – comparable with exploitation of the working class and the subjects of imperialism. Women, like men, are engaged in the reproduction of capitalism and patriarchy, and this involves reproducing both labour power and ideological structures. Women generally do this in three ways. Many are employed and paid workers (though usually in lower-paid, part-time, less interesting and less influential work than men); many are employed and unpaid workers, sustaining the labour force by servicing the households of men who are paid to work; and many are engaged in socializing the next generation of the labour force – bearing and rearing children (men also do the latter, but their role is usually much smaller). Many women engage in all three kinds of reproduction, quite often at the same time. The scope and balance of these three roles change continually. It is crucial that they should, for women above all are made to constitute that reserve army of labour, identified by Marx, that capital can call upon or dismiss to help it cope with its cycles of stagnation and over-production.[6]

This is not to say that people form families in order to maintain the social order; rather, as Michèle Barrett argues, following Roy Bhaskar, this is the unintended effect, since those affective relationships are formed and developed, inevitably, within the framework of capitalism and patriarchy.[7] Nor is it unworthy to love your husband and children; but the conditions within which many women choose to do those things, or not, are exploitative in our society.

In fact, powerful forces were running counter to domesticity in the 1950s. Both the war and the postwar boom encouraged women to take employment outside the household. The proportion of married women in paid work rose from 10 per cent in 1931 to 21 per cent in 1951, 32 per cent in 1961 and 47 per cent in 1972 (Wilson, E., p. 41). This tendency was accommodated by the limitation of family size, the development of social security and welfare services, changes in the structure of taxation, and the growing notion that the husband-father will contribute more to child-rearing. It is because all this undermined male control of public affairs and the household, and seemed to threaten women's roles in servicing the workforce and rearing children, that conservative institutions and individuals urged women back into the home. And that is why support facilities for women in paid work were (and remain) inadequate. The heavy ideological work around domesticity indicates, as usual, that they are telling us contradictory stories: the enticements to women to earn money and consume conflict with the demand to stay in a homely role.

Much of the incitement to consume was targeted on the housewife and mother. 'Advertisers who want a better motivated women's magazine for family selling should look at this week's issue of *Woman's Realm*', proclaimed an advertising director. Women were told to buy things to make ideal homes for their families, but to afford this they had to go out to work, and therefore could devote less time to children and household tasks. This, of course, was the opportunity for the quick-food industry – but again, you needed more money for that. Women were liable to feel guilty whatever they did.[8] And they were even more overworked. These strains had long been present for many lower-class women. They became an acknowledged 'problem' – requiring endless ideological work, trying the story this way then that to get it to fit – because they now affected the middle classes (the virtual disappearance of servants was much discussed). It was said that new household gadgets were compensating, but many women didn't have these aids and, apart from washing machines, they helped relatively little with looking after infants.

The insistence on domesticity was a confusing pressure upon a situation that was already disturbed and complex. Many women who were in paid work or higher education, in Britain and the United States, were uneasy about their roles. Those who were employed rarely said they had any 'right to work'; only a third of women in professional jobs stated that they wished to continue their careers after marriage.[9] Women in college said they regarded career achievement as masculine, unfeminine, and hence unattractive, and that their role was to establish a home for husband and children. They performed below their abilities for fear of disconcerting the fragile male ego.[10] They were fortunate to be there at all – there were moves to build up the scope of 'domestic science' (revealing term) in school syllabuses, and the press questioned whether higher education for women was a waste of time and money.

The boundaries of male and female roles became uncertain and disputable, problematizing marriage and the heterosexual relation in all aspects. Notice, for instance, how the emphasis on motherhood marginalizes fathers. Winnicott's whole theme is mothers, and he has to devote a chapter to explaining why fathers are needed. Bowlby says near the start of his book: 'Little will be said of the father–child relation; his value as the economic and emotional support of the mother will be assumed' (pp. 15–16). But, of course, it couldn't be assumed. Ideologies of gender roles help to keep men also in their place (albeit a better one). In our culture men have to be persuaded to go to work and contribute to the support of children. Hence the dignifying of their efforts with the term 'breadwinner' ('bread' implying that the whole continuance of life depends upon him, 'winner' masking the humiliation, often, of the daily grind). Where the woman was in paid work, her earnings were regarded as 'pin-money' – supplementary, subsidiary, helping, useful for 'extras', so preserving the image of the male breadwinner (Klein, V., pp. 26–7).

In part, focus upon motherhood started in wartime (see Riley, pp. 88–90, 95–6) and was carried through into the different conditions of the 1950s. The ideas of Bowlby and Winnicott originated during the war, and their attention to the mother surely reflects the fact – which because of their normative idea of the family they could hardly admit – that the presence of the father could not be relied upon. The new social security system also acknowledged this fact. In one respect the 'abnormality' of service life persisted through the 1950s, since all young men were required to undergo two years' military training. As the advertisement said, 'it's a man's life in the army'; but such reinforcement of masculinity was accompanied by rumours of prostitution and homosexuality (consider Amis's 'I Spy Strangers', Wesker's *Chips with Everything*, Arden's *Serjeant Musgrave's Dance*, Caute's *At Fever Pitch*).

Confusion and anxiety in male roles is evident in attitudes to homosexuality in the period (see Chapter 5). In the United States the man who failed to marry and support 'his' family was stigmatized, in psychiatry and popular culture, as 'immature' and possibly homosexual (Ehrenreich, ch. 2), while the Kinsey Reports suggested that homosexual behaviour was far more common than had been supposed. There was a persistent anxiety that husbands were no longer 'real men' (cf. Kimmel). Usually, this was ascribed to 'unnatural' female independence; Betty Friedan reversed the argument, declaring that the emasculating factor was the ideology of domesticity – she attributed 'the homosexuality that is spreading like a murky smog over the American scene' to over-intense mother-son relationships (pp. 274–6). A tendency to blame men for not living up to the claims made for them occurs elsewhere in proto-feminist work, for instance in Doris Lessing's *The Golden Notebook* (pp. 395, 470).

The 1950s produced few feminists, therefore, but gender relations were by no means untroubled and the ideology of domesticity was a response to anxiety and uncertainty. I would trace to this date both 1960s 'permissiveness' and the Women's Movement: both were fuelled by the contradictions I have outlined. Diverse kinds of discontented writing by women began to appear. Alva Myrdal and Viola Klein published *Women's Two Roles* in 1956, attacking the 'cult of Homemaking and Motherhood' as 'fostered by press and propaganda', and even casting doubt on John Bowlby's adequacy (pp. 146, 125–6). They saw middle-class women as subject to dilemmas over family and employment (ch. 8). Hannah Gavron's sociological research of 1960–1 found frustration and depression and resulted in her Penguin book *The Captive Wife* (1966). In the United States Betty Friedan wrote *The Feminine Mystique* (1963), labelling the frustration of US women 'the problem that has no name'. Novels on such themes included *The L-Shaped Room* by Lynne Reid Banks (1960), *The Golden Notebook* by Doris Lessing (1962) and *The Pumpkin Eater* by Penelope Mortimer (1962).

The rest of this chapter will explore these discontents through the figure of Sylvia Plath. In a way this colludes with a tendency to take her as the token woman poet, but one consequence of that tendency is that she has been very extensively discussed and is very well documented. All the main positions have been taken through her, and therefore she is a key point at which to attempt an intervention; also, she impinges upon diverse other concerns of this book, and I find her fascinating. Of course, she is not representative, but she points up aspects of the situation of the writer-woman through the complexity of one person's engagement with its contradictions. It will be noticed that in this chapter I have found it appropriate to use evidence from Britain and the United States with only occasional discriminations. It was to be the same with the Women's Movement: US developments were taken up immediately in Britain. Plath lived and worked in the United States and in England, and appropriations of her by Modernism, academic English and the Women's Movement have also been international.

The Politics of Madness

The institutions of literary culture want Sylvia Plath to be mad to protect themselves and readers from the implications of her life and work. For 'madness' seems to be individual. Richard Ohmann locates as a specific myth of the modern United States the 'illness story': deep social contradictions are transformed into an individual crisis, and the resolution – usually a hesitant one – involves the disordered person 'coming to terms' through some personal therapy with social reality. But this is the reality that initially discomposed them, and it remains untransformed – is imagined as untransformable. As Ohmann insists, such individual 'cures' cannot address the causes of the illness.[11]

Ohmann cites Plath's *The Bell Jar* as an instance, and in part it is one. But Plath violated the story of adjustment by going on to write violent and vengeful poetry and killing herself. Therefore, often, she is put down as pathological, schizoid, hysterical, so that we need not take seriously her ideas and attitudes.[12] David Holbrook makes the strategy explicit. He objects to Plath's 'rejection of certain kinds of femininity', finding in the poems 'forms of moral inversion which are absurd, or even deranged' (Holbrook, p. 2). We should use a knowledge of 'psychology' (by which Holbrook means normative gender roles) to 'defend ourselves against her falsifications' (p. 5). So the problem appears to be Plath herself and, by so much, it is not political.

The other way of disempowering Plath's politics is to represent her as a mad genius, supersensitive to the general horror of the modern world, inspired by a poetic furor that drove her ever onward to desperate expression and death. This notion fitted well with the concurrent recycling of Modernism (see Chapter 9). It is the dominant view of Plath, enunciated vividly and authoritatively by A. Alvarez (who knew her and recognized her ability) in *The Savage God* (1971). Stephen Spender, within a few sentences, actually manages both to disqualify Plath as a hysterical woman *and* to subsume her into the 'modern condition'. He compares her to Wilfred Owen as a poet who warns: 'But being a woman, her warning is more shrill, penetrating, visionary . . . her femininity is that her hysteria comes completely out of herself, and yet seems about all of us.'[13] Such an account leaves no space for gender politics.

That 'irrational' behaviour may be read to reveal social pressures was well understood by Plath. In *The Bell Jar* Esther decides not to marry Buddy, and tells him she will never marry (p. 97). In his vanity and conformity, he finds this incomprehensible, and brightly reminds Esther how she said she wanted to live both in the country and the city, thus exhibiting what he has been told is neurotic behaviour. By this, Buddy means to set aside Esther's refusal to marry him as a typically irrational whim. But she responds vigorously: 'If neurotic is wanting two mutually exclusive things at one and the same time, then I'm neurotic as hell. I'll be flying back and forth between one mutually exclusive thing and another for the rest of my days' (p. 98). Even so, Buddy refuses to take No for an answer, and thus provokes the skiing accident in which she hurls herself towards him, as she is expected to do but not in this manner, 'through year after year of doubleness and smiles and compromise' (p. 102). Esther's behaviour makes sense in terms of the pressures upon her. However – and this is the drawback with 'hysterical' behaviour – the situation is still there: 'Piece by piece, as at the strokes of a dull godmother's wand, the old world sprang back into position.' Moreover, 'A queer, satisfied expression came over Buddy's face' (p. 103). This is because Esther has demonstrated her irrationality once more, and spoilt her moment of independence by disabling herself.

What should be obvious is that putting everything down to emotional instability is of a piece with the customary stereotyping of women. If the writing of Sylvia Plath seems violent and hysterical, our task should be to follow that to its structural grounding in the concepts of gender that informed Plath and, indeed, in great part still inform ourselves. Not to recognize the representative nature of her difficulties – the extent to which 'many women may have died smaller unnoticed, spiritual deaths'[14] – is to deprive her once more of the sisterhood that might have been her support.

Women Writing

Writing was implicated in the attack on non-domesticity. At Plath's graduation from Smith College, Adlai Stevenson (liberal presidential candidate) observed: once women 'wrote poetry. Now it's the laundry list. Once they discussed art and philosophy until late into the night. Now they are so tired they fall asleep as soon as the dishes are finished.' But this was as it should be, Stevenson felt, given the profound responsibilities of the housewife: 'I could wish you no better vocation than that' (Friedan, pp. 60–1). However, women writers did resist the ideology of domesticity, and the Women's Movement probably owes more to that repression and resistance than to the 'permissive society' of the 1960s. Adrienne Rich recalls how in the early 1950s she found writing and domesticity barely compatible; but writing seemed 'more real'. In Cora Kaplan's intellectual-academic family, writing was positively encouraged, and so it was for Sylvia Plath, who recorded 'the home urge to study and do well academically'.[15] Writing and academic study were not impossible for women – just difficult, strange and ambitious. Alice S. Rossie found, in a sample of women graduating in 1961, that for themselves they wanted to become the mothers of highly accomplished children and the wives of very prominent husbands. But the women they admired were those who achieved scientific, scholarly, literary or artistic distinction (p. 126). Judith Hubback found that writing was the most common occupation after part-time teaching for wives who had been to college; 6 per cent were getting paid for it (pp. 48–9).

The historic silencing of women has not been a matter of inability to put pen to paper, or even of not publishing. The other work they have to do may be almost overwhelming, and the care of young children is uniquely demanding. That, said Edna O'Brien in 1965, is why 'modern women read as screams' (in Dunn, p. 59). But many men are exhausted by their work. Actually, the majority of eighteenth-century novels were written by large numbers of women – they were a way of exploring changes in social relationships under capitalism; in the nineteenth century writing was the form of public discourse in which women were most able to participate.[16] As I have shown, there were many prominent women writers in the 1940s and early 1950s (p. 63), and in other chapters I discuss fiction by Bowen, Heinemann, Lehmann, Lessing, Murdoch, Pym and Thirkell.

The 'silencing' of women is a matter of ideology, not output. First, women writers have difficulty seeing the scope of their oppression and finding ways of articulating it (this is true of homosexual men also, who have published a lot but only sometimes articulated their oppression). Second, it is difficult to gain serious notice for women's writing, and specially when it implies a critical stance on gender politics. This has worked most potently in the institutions of literature; the issue there is not why women write less literature, but how literature has been defined so as to marginalize, or present from male points of view, women's lives and gender politics (Russ; Olsen).

To the distress of critics, who prefer to believe that literature rises above such considerations, Plath regarded writing as a career. Indeed, there is something rather direct about her approach when she tells herself in July 1953: 'First, pick your market: *Ladies' Home Journal* or *Discovery*? *Seventeen* or *Mlle*? Then pick a topic. Then think' (*Journals*, p. 86). Plath disconcerts both literature and gender ideology by pursuing writing, not as a hobby or contribution to art, but as a career. In an interview in October 1962 she said she had been 'a bit of a professional' since her first published poem at the age of eight (Orr, p. 167). Ted Hughes says she wanted to be 'a professional with a real job in the real world' (Plath, *Johnny*, p. 12).

Plath's letters to her mother and Nancy Hunter Steiner's memoir (about the Smith College period) give the impression that Plath's personality was dominated by a need to conform. She was anxious socially at Smith, partly because most of the other students came from upper-class families (in *The Bell Jar* Esther remarks that she didn't have time to learn bridge 'at college, the way all the wealthy girls did'; p. 220). But her earnestness about her studies was not conformist, for although such colleges had been established to enable women to achieve high academic standards, they had fallen prey to the ideology of domesticity and were turning into smart finishing schools. Friedan found this at Smith in 1959. Unlike her own time there (she graduated in 1942), academic work and intellectual affairs were no longer taken seriously, careers were not considered, and finding a man to marry was the main preoccupation.[17] Plath was delighted when she talked her way into the class of the writer Alfred Kazin: he warmed to her when he found she was not 'just another pampered Smith baby like the rest' (*Letters*, p. 147).

Plath's determination to work as a writer was boldly nonconformist. Her mother (who came from an immigrant family, was widowed, and had to fend for herself) yearned for Sylvia to establish herself financially, either by marrying an appropriate man or by taking sensible career steps. But she did neither: she rejected college teaching to live as a writer, and married an Englishman from the lower classes who also declined to take regular employment. She noted in May 1958 her mother's 'guarded praise at our getting poems published, as if this were one more nail in the coffin of our resolve to drown as poets and refuse all "secure" teaching work' (*Journals*, p. 223). In June 1958 she wrote to her brother:

> I can talk to you freely about our plans, if not to mother. She worries so that the most we can do is put up an illusion of security–security to us is in ourselves, and no job, or even money, can give us what we have to develop: faith in our work, and hard hard work which is Spartan in many ways. (*Letters*, p. 342)

The Scriptor Scripted

Emphasis upon writing as career ran counter to the ideology of domesticity, but the institutions of writing were nonetheless immersed in that ideology. Friedan found that women's magazines such as the *Ladies' Home Journal* and *McCall's* had at the end of the 1940s ceased to publish articles on politics and general matters, and whereas in 1939 the typical heroine had been a happy career woman who loved and was loved, the 1950s stories presented housewife-and-mother as the only acceptable role for women. Increasingly, these magazines were written and edited by men, and women contributors found themselves denying the lives they themselves actually led (Friedan, pp. 38–57). 'If we get an article about a woman who does anything adventurous, out of the way, something by herself', a *Ladies' Home Journal* editor told Friedan, 'we figure she must be terribly aggressive, neurotic' (p. 52). It was the same in Britain. Mary Grieve, editor of *Woman*, declared that the magazine's fiction was inspired by 'a unanimous acceptance that to be loved and loving is better than to be brainy, rich, or nobly born' (Hopkins, p. 328).

Plath wrote 'Day of Success' in 1961–2 with an eye to the woman's magazine market.[18] Ellen's husband Jacob, a writer, is taken out to lunch by a (presumed) exotic woman radio producer. Ellen is uneasy, accuses herself of being jealous, fears that she is 'homespun, obsolete' (p. 197). And her anxiety is increased by her friend Nancy, whose marriage broke up after her husband's success as a playwright, and who advises Ellen to make herself look attractive. Ellen tells herself that Jacob is different, but gets herself up in 'an exquisite whispery, sapphire-sheened piece of finery', perfumes herself and does her hair (p. 202). She almost forgets the baby, but they have a wonderful bathtime. Jacob returns: 'Now that's what I like to see when I come home after a hard day!', he says, 'Wife and daughter waiting by the fireside to welcome the lord of the house.' He perceives her perfume as baby food and cod-liver-oil, takes her garment as a new bed-jacket and thinks with her hair up she's fresh from the tub. He 'obviously saw her as the wife and mother type, and she couldn't be better pleased' (p. 203). Finally Jacob says the producer is too high-powered for him, 'a career woman with a mind of her own', and announces that he has made the down-payment on the country cottage they both want.

In outline, 'Day of Success' fits the ideology of domesticity: Ellen has no career (she is not a writer), and the successful producer is imagined as destructive and antipathetic to the wife and mother. However, the story is disturbing. Ellen's anxiety that her husband will be attracted by the producer is very intense – almost the whole substance – and as such it witnesses to a basic insecurity of the domestic role, namely that it may be less compelling for the husband than it should be. And this anxiety is not unfounded, for look what happened to Nancy. 'Men won't admit it', she says, 'but they do want a woman to look *right*, really *fatale*' (p. 200). There is also an excess in Jacob's inability to recognize Ellen's attempts to vary her role. Whatever she does, it seems, he will insist that there is only one way for her to be. And the happy-ending country cottage will trap her more securely.

Plath used her experience very directly in her writing: she was led to frame herself within the current notions of women's roles. In 'Day of Success' she simplifies the opposition between home and career by making Ellen not a writer, but the fact that the story is written from Ellen's point of view points towards the woman writer who cannot be written. We may say she was scripted by the kinds of magazine for which she wrote. But she allows the reader to see the strain.

'I would really like to get something in *The New Yorker* before I die, I do so admire that particular, polished, rich, brilliant style', Plath wrote in January 1956 (*Letters*, p. 207). This was the other goal of Plath's career, and not an impossible one – in *55 Stories from The New Yorker* (1952) a third were written by women. Plath published nine poems there between August 1958 and September 1962; in February 1961 she was invited to give the journal a 'first reading' option on future poems (*Letters*, p. 411). The poems she wrote for it are, in effect, those published in *The Colossus* (1960), and their manner should be related to the requirements of the *New Yorker* as much as to Plath's supposed psychological or artistic needs. 'The Net-Menders' she saw as a '*New Yorker* poem'.[19] Three Spanish women are set into a landscape of concrete detail:

> On the road named for Tomas Ortunio, mica
> Winks like money under the ringed toes of the chickens.
> The houses are white as sea-salt goats lick from the rocks.

Not only well observed, well informed. The poem moves towards a larger perspective, placing the women symbolically as well as geographically: 'The moon leans, a stone madonna, over the lead sea/And the iron hills that enclose them.' But the enlarged significance is at the expense of the actuality of the women's lives. The concluding lines offer to share their prayer:

> *Tonight may the fish*
> *Be a harvest of silver in the nets, and the lamps*
> *Of our husbands and sons move sure among the low stars.*

The physical detail of the setting is precise, but the attributed thoughts and feelings are general. It is a tourist's vision.

The *New Yorker* story was shrewd, polished and self-conscious. Dwight Macdonald placed it in 1953 as tailored – 'a definite genre – smooth, minor-key, casual, suggesting drama and sentiment without ever being crude enough to actually create it – which the editors have established by years of patient, skilful selection the same way a gardener develops a new kind of rose' (Rosenberg and White, p. 65). Typically, it was of individual experience and adjustment to recalcitrant circumstances – in the manner identified by Richard Ohmann (p. 209 above). This powerful ideological framework was applied by Plath to her own experience: *New Yorker* stories wrote her, she lived them. The *55 Stories* anticipate both her fiction and her biography – they include the attempted seduction of a 15-year-old girl by an Italian man, a girl recalling a difficult relationship with her mother, a man thinking about his relationship with his psychiatrist, a man who shoots himself on a beach, an immigrant mother drowning herself because her son prefers to spend the vacation with a friend.[20]

In February 1958 Plath declared: 'My identity is shaping, forming itself – I feel stories sprout, reading the collection of *New Yorker* stories.' So she devised 'another story for *The New Yorker*' – and it is from her own life, her seventeenth summer, when a man drew her into a barn and kissed her. In May 1959, after reading Salinger's *Seymour: an Introduction* in the *New Yorker*, Plath dreamed that she found a story like that one ('with the would-be Salinger child in it') on the front page of the magazine, with a title anticipating another of her stories.[21] The *New Yorker* was telling her own story to her. She specially admired Salinger. In his 'Franny' (*New Yorker*, 1955), Franny travels from a college like Smith to meet a vain and obtuse Ivy-League boy-friend like Buddy in *The Bell Jar*, and like Plath's boy-friend Dick Norton as she describes him (*Journals*, pp. 38–9). Franny is evidently having a breakdown: she is upset by everyone trying to *get on* (Salinger, *Franny*, pp. 28–9). These Plath-like themes are developed in 'Zooey' (*New Yorker*, 1957), where Franny's brother Zooey talks to their mother – a woman not unlike Plath's mother: Zooey warns her not to get a psychoanalyst to make Franny 'gloriously normal' (*Franny*, p. 88). Eventually Zooey gets through to Franny, and convinces her that she should become involved in life, do things well, respect all people . . . in fact, make an individual adjustment to society.

Salinger, Plath and the *New Yorker* are writing Plath's story because they are all constructed within the current organization of gender relations, and this effect is enhanced by Plath's need to accommodate herself to dominant literary models. People generally are scripted by the prevailing stories, but the effect is specially marked for subordinated groups. Susan Gubar has drawn attention to stories in which Pygmalion-like men manufacture dolls that come to life. Often the woman is envisaged as a blank page, as when Othello asks, of Desdemona, 'Was this fair paper, this most goodly book,/Made to write "whore" upon?' (IV.ii.73–4). The doll in Plath's poem 'The Applicant' is 'Naked as paper to start', but after 25 years of marriage

> she'll be silver,
> In fifty, gold.
> A living doll, everywhere you look.
> (*CP*.182, p. 221)

Correspondingly, writing is figured by men as sexual – the pen(is) writing on the virgin page. Gubar suggests that this is why to women 'artistic creation often feels like a violation, a belated reaction to male penetration rather than a possessing and controlling.' Plath writes: 'The blood jet is poetry.'[22]

In so far as she chose to tell her story through the *Ladies' Home Journal* and the *New Yorker* – to herself and to her readers – Plath collaborated with patriarchy in the scripting of herself and other women. This is how cultural production works: we read our experience in the stories that we know. But the stories are contradictory and the point of intersection at which Plath was situated was particularly fraught. In so far as she allows us to see the strain she contributes to political understanding.

TH

The apparent resolution of Plath's contradictory insertion in ideology was TH. This is, of course, Ted Hughes, whom she met in Cambridge in February 1956 and married the following June. He was the father of her two children, and they separated in October 1962 as a consequence of his relationship with another woman. I use the initials TH not out of coyness, but because it was the *idea of a certain kind of man* that seemed to answer Plath's demand, and the relation between that idea and the historical Ted Hughes can only be speculative. Plath wrote in April 1953: 'Let's face it, I am in danger of wanting my personal absolute to be a demigod of a man, and as there aren't many around, I often unconsciously manufacture my own' (*Journals*, p. 79).

TH had to be a demigod because a mere mortal could not accommodate Plath's contradictory and challenging negotiation of current ideology. The journals from 1950–2, the early years at Smith, show her distrusting the great part of that ideology. She observed:

Most American males worship woman as a sex machine with rounded breasts and a convenient opening in the vagina, and as a painted doll who shouldn't have a thought in her pretty head other than cooking a steak dinner and comforting him in bed after a hard 9–5 day at a routine business job. (*Journals*, pp. 21–2)

She asked, 'Why should they [women] be relegated to the position of custodian of emotions, watcher of the infants, feeder of soul, body and pride of man?' (p. 30). She envied 'the man his physical freedom to lead a double life – his career, and his sexual and family life' (p. 35). She was reading Margaret Mead's *Male and Female* (Wagner-Martin, pp. 76–7), but there was little else in her culture to help Plath extend and validate such insights.

She would not reject marriage. She lacked other credible models – the older independent women she met at university and as a student editor on the journal *Mademoiselle* seemed disqualified by their apparent neglect of domesticity. Anne Stevenson observes that spinsterhood has suited writers rather well – Austen, Emily Brontë, Dickinson, Mew, Moore, Stevie Smith, Bishop. But now, Stevenson believes, it should be possible to be 'a fulfilled woman and an independent writer without guilt' ('Writing as a Woman', in Jacobus, p. 163). For Plath also, being a woman poet meant being in relation with a man (or so she told her mother) – 'one of the few women poets in the world who is fully a rejoicing woman, not a bitter or frustrated or warped man-imitator' (*Letters*, p. 256). So, invoking D. H. Lawrence, she demanded a marriage that would meet her wider aspirations (Lawrence seemed to other proto-feminist writers, including Lessing, to have identified a fuller womanhood). Plath repudiated the idea that she should be confined to an inner circle of 'home, other womenfolk, and community service, enclosed in the larger circle of my mate'. She wanted 'two overlapping circles . . . *both* with separate arcs jutting out in the world' (*Journals*, p. 43, May 1952).

The call for a man sufficiently strong and sympathetic to cope with her aspirations produced TH. In June 1958 Plath wrote of him as so 'big, creative in a giant way, that I imagine I made him up' (*Journals*, p. 240). TH had to be like that to cope with her demands: he had to be manly in the way that was currently envisaged and yet accommodate her determination to be a writer. She believed that their marriage defied the US 'expectancy of conformity'; she felt 'horrified at voicing the American dream of a home and children' and declared: 'I have my own dream, which is mine, and not the American dream. I want to write funny and tender women's stories' (*Journals*, p. 254). A friend, Wendy Campbell, thought 'Sylvia had found a man on the same scale as herself' (in Newman, p. 184).

But unfortunately, TH was not so far after all from the ideology of the women's magazines (this tended to happen if you started partly from Lawrence): Plath's image had not escaped the dominant structures. Indeed, in April 1958 she decided, after a couple of days in bed with a cold reading *McCall's* and the *Ladies' Home Journal*, that the articles and stories there were based on a passionate and spiritual love, and that the relationship with TH was that (soon, of course, she was thinking of writing it up for the magazines).[23] In the letters and journals, claims of independence and free creativity occur immediately alongside expressions of dependency and exaltations of routine domestic roles.

One outcome was the remarkable 'Ode to Ted', written in April 1956 (*CP*.10, pp. 29–30):

> From under crunch of my man's boot
> green oat-sprouts jut;
> he names a lapwing, starts rabbits in a rout
>   . . . how but most glad
> could be this adam's woman
> when all earth his words do summon
> leaps to laud such man's blood!

There are three strains here. One is the status of this Adam's woman. In particular, TH names the animals, as does Adam, and this suggests male domination of language (Daly, p. 8). But the poet also is a writer, and thus likely to trespass upon Adam's prerogative. Second, TH's creativity appears violent:

> hefting chalk-hulled flint
> he with rocks splits open
> knobbed quartz; flayed colors ripen
> rich, brown, sudden in sunglint.

Such violence is traditionally male, but nonetheless dangerous. The third problem is whether such a powerful creature may be contained within the confines of one relationship; can a single Eve match such prolific fertility?

> For his least look, scant acres yield:
> each finger-furrowed field
> heaves forth stalk, leaf, fruit-nubbed emerald;
> bright grain sprung so rarely
> he hauls to his will early;
> at his hand's staunch hest, birds build.

The terms in which Plath has created TH raise the prospect of his infidelity. After all, that is how the mythic demigods were.

Rabbit Catcher

The first poem in which Plath expresses a thorough revulsion from the TH figure is 'Rabbit Catcher' (*CP*.164), dated 21 May 1962. Plath intended to publish it in her *Ariel* volume but, like several of the bitter and accusatory poems that follow (*CP*.169, 171, 174), it was not published until the collection of 1981. 'Rabbit Catcher' rewrites the violence of 'Ode for Ted':

> I felt a still busyness, an intent.
> I felt hands round a tea mug, dull, blunt,
> Ringing the white china.
> How they awaited him, those little deaths!
> They waited like sweethearts. They excited him.
>
> And we, too, had a relationship –
> Tight wires between us,
> Pegs too deep to uproot, and a mind like a ring
> Sliding shut on some quick thing,
> The constriction killing me also.
>
> (p. 194)

The erstwhile Eve identifies herself with the rabbit, now the victim of TH's strong fecundity. The intimacy of domesticity, the hands round the mug, becomes a trap. Plath imaged a strong man in TH, believing he would afford her the space for her diverse needs. But the strong man is defined, conventionally, by his dominance over women. This is probably the significance of 'The Moon and the Yew Tree' (*CP*.153).

The Bell Jar was written in 1961–2 – in the period leading up to 'The Rabbit Catcher'. Plath may have aspired to the smooth competence of the *New Yorker* story, but her novel is fractured by partial consciousness of the strains in the TH image. It is written in the first person and past tense, but with a persistent uncertainty as to how innocent, or shrewd, Esther is supposed to be.[24] Some of the time we are silently invited to observe her naivety. In chapter two, for instance, when she and Doreen are picked up by the disc-jockey Lenny, Esther seems not to understand that the second man is intended for her, or the courtship behaviour between Doreen and Lenny. At other times Esther is much sharper and wiser, sharing Plath's later consciousness. When Buddy tells her of a drug given to women in labour to make them forget their pain so they will 'go straight home and start another baby', she thought 'it sounded just like the sort of drug a man would invent' (p. 68). And when she meets Marco, she recognizes him at once as a 'woman-hater' and explains: 'I began to see why woman-haters could make such fools of women. Woman-haters were like gods: invulnerable and chock-full of power' (p. 113). Yet, contrariwise, Esther's subsequent sexual liaisons are generally naive.

Finally Buddy asks: 'Do you think there's something in me that *drives* women crazy?' (p. 252). Esther bursts out laughing, seeing a double meaning, and we realize that Buddy has asked two questions in one: does association with him produce insanity? and is he irresistible to women? The reader may ponder the relation between the two – whether strong sexual attraction to a man, within the current organization of hetero-sexual relations, is bad for at least some women. Is TH what Esther needs, or would he make things worse? The novel leaves it open. Throughout, there are two levels of awareness of TH: the innocent Esther has as yet hardly glimpsed him, whereas the smart Esther has already seen through him. These disjunctions occur because, in the biographical sequence upon which *The Bell Jar* is founded, TH was the immediate resolution; whereas by the time of writing, TH had become an ambiguous figure. Consequently, a resolution to the novel is shadowed forth but not allowed to stand. Marriage is anticipated as part of the return to normal (pp. 254, 257), but all the men have been inadequate, and all the sexual experience futile or unpleasant. TH is the absent centre of the novel. We know, from page four, that Esther has a baby. But the father is never hinted at; he is the missing link.

The separation of Plath and Hughes released her from the pressure to find virtue in TH. She rejected her mother's insistence that the world needs 'cheerful stuff . . . about happy marriages. Let the *Ladies' Home Journal* blither about *those*' (*Letters*, p. 473). This repudiation encompasses a manner of writing, an ideology, and an identity. (Male) literary models have been proposed for the later poems (Lowell, Roethke, Stevens, Yeats, Hughes). But the change, above all, is release into compusively vivid insights about the entire gender politics of the period.

Plath tried to find specific strengths as a woman. Since she decided to have a baby, in spring 1959, she had been purposefully reading women writers – Adrienne Rich, Anne Sexton, Elizabeth Hardwick, Jean Stafford, Eudora Welty, Katharine Anne Porter, Mavis Gallant, May Swenson, Elizabeth Bishop, Marianne Moore, Iris Murdoch, Stevie Smith. However, we cannot make a satisfying story of Plath celebrating womanhood, for at this time especially it was difficult to conceive the idea of woman without seeing her as the counterpart of man. As Susan Gubar puts it, 'To celebrate uniquely female powers of creativity without perpetuating destructive feminine socialisation is the task' (in Showalter, p. 308). In poems written after the separation, Plath retains TH as the absence that defines what is left: woman alone. It is an identity founded in loss, as in 'For a Fatherless Son' (*CP*. 172): 'You will be aware of an absence, presently,/Growing beside you, like a tree' (p. 205). In 'By Candlelight' (*CP*.192), a mother nurses her son, but his toy is a model of the demigod that held up the world:

> He is yours, the little brassy Atlas –
> Poor heirloom, all you have,
> At his heels a pile of five brass cannonballs,
> No child, no wife.
>
> (p. 237)

Both the child and Atlas are deprived when the family is split.

We are seeing once more an effect of the oppositions through which ideology often works: in repudiating the dominance of one term, we move to validate the other – but that is to occupy the space that is defined and permitted by the dominant. So in an attempt to re-establish herself through the idea of fertility and motherhood, Plath fell into the trap – identified by Adrienne Rich as one through which patriarchy seeks to divide and control women – of derogating the 'Childless Woman' (*CP*.211; Rich, pp. 249–53). It has been argued, by Julia Kristeva and others, that 'the feminine' constitutes an area of carnival that repudiates patriarchy. But, as Juliet Mitchell replies, this validates 'just what the patriarchal universe defines as the feminine, the intuitive, the religious, the mystical, the playful, all those things that have been assigned to women.'[25] We should not make the argument too absolute either way: 'the feminine' is not as such resistant to the dominant, being constituted within its overall domain; yet because the manner of that constitution in particular conditions is so complex, the feminine, and other such subordinate constructions, may offer ground for resistance.

Feminist critics have admired Plath's sequence of bee poems (*CP*.176–80).[26] It represents a gain in confidence, as the poet moves from anxious observer to controller of her own hives. But no distinct model of gender relations emerges. Rather, the imagery is an exploration, in which

the poet tries on different identities, reviewing the shapes of power –
victim, worker-drudge, provider, queen. The queen is the centre of the
hive, but she has only one brief nuptial flight (which proves the death of
the male privileged to mate with her); in 'Stings' she may be dead,
sleeping, or 'flying/More terrible than she ever was' (p. 215). Mostly her
task is to preserve herself and so the hive. Only the females survive
the winter; this is the theme of the last of the sequence, 'Wintering'
(*CP*.180):

> Winter is for women——
> The woman, still at her knitting,
> At the cradle of Spanish walnut,
> Her body a bulb in the cold and too dumb to think.
>
> (p. 219)

The *Ariel* volume that Plath intended was to conclude with this poem
and its anticipation of spring; it would have given a more positive image
than the volume actually published after her death. However, the fact
that Plath didn't make it through the winter indicates that bee analogies
could rework but not resolve the absence of TH; the queen still has to
mate.

The critical force of Plath's late poems is in what they do with violence –
bees signify danger as well as honey. 'Letter in November' (*CP*.204), where
a woman walks around her territory alone, is one of the most positive late
poems. Even so, male violence appears at the last moment, extending the
final line as if an unanticipated thought breaks in:

> O love, O celibate.
> Nobody but me
> Walks through the waist-high wet.
> The irreplaceable
> Golds bleed and deepen, the mouths of Thermopylae.
>
> (p. 254)

Atlas in 'By Candlelight' is represented with 'five brass cannonballs'
(p. 237). In 'The Swarm' (*CP*.179) TH is the beekeeper; he is Napoleon,
and the swarming bees are the peoples of Europe who think to rise against
him. He plays with them as if they were 'chess people', 'The mud squirms
with throats' (p. 216), and he is only apparently defeated:

The man with gray hands smiles –
The smile of a man of business, intensely practical.
They are not hands at all
But asbestos receptacles.
Pom! Pom! 'They would have killed *me*'.

(p. 217)

Plath invokes Napoleon because she had been reading a biography of the Empress Josephine, and related Josephine's marriage to her own. Napoleon is transmuted into 'a man of business' because she had been profoundly disturbed by articles in *The Nation*, 'all about the terrifying marriage of big business and the military in America' (*Letters*, p. 437). She spoke to Elizabeth Sigmund 'with bitter anger of the involvement of American big business with weaponry' (Butscher, p. 100). Plath was reaching towards the idea that her experience with TH was of a piece with the violence and oppression that are produced generally in patriarchy.

The Case for Extremism

Plath's anxieties about war, militarism and state violence were by no means sudden. Despite what most critics say, she had long expressed political commitment. She was opposed to the Korean War and McCarthyism (Wagner-Martin, pp. 58–9, 90), and horrified by the electrocution of Ethel and Julius Rosenberg as alleged Soviet spies in June 1953. The latter combined Cold-War pressure and gender politics, since Ethel Rosenberg was attacked as the unnaturally dominant partner (*Journals*, p. 82). The reference to the Rosenberg at the start of *The Bell Jar* links up with other caustic remarks about the American dream in the opening pages, and with Esther's ECT treatment: failure to conform is punished electrically. In 1955 Plath thought of working overseas 'to counteract McCarthy and much adverse opinion about the U.S. by living a life of honesty and love' (*Letters*, p. 163). In November 1956, at the time of the Suez invasion and Soviet occupation of Hungary, she shared British left-wing attitudes. She argued to her mother that soldiers should refuse to fight, that the principles of Christ and Socrates should be followed, that mothers and children had nothing to gain from men fighting. 'I wish Warren [her brother] would be a conscientious objector', she wrote.

Like many up-and-coming British writers, Plath responded strongly to the Campaign for Nuclear Disarmament (see Chapter 11). Active CND supporters were nearly as likely to be women as men; Peggy Duff and Pat Arrowsmith were key figures; a deputation received by Harold Macmillan in 1962 included Alix Meynell, Janet Aitken, Diana Collins, Jacquetta Hawkes, Dorothy Hodgkin, Marghanita Laski, Dorothy Needham, Antoinette Pirie and Mary Stocks. Plays of the time present the woman as the one sensitive to the nuclear issue.[27] In April 1960 Plath found the annual CND march 'an immensely moving experience'; she told her mother that 40 per cent of the marchers were housewives, and complained of the poisoning of babies' milk by the release of strontium 90 through weapon testing. She would not attend the church near her Devon home because of the anti-CND views of the rector. In published pronouncements during 1962 she declared that she was a political person and poetry should be relevant to issues such as the military – industrial complex, Hiroshima and Dachau.[28]

So Plath had the basis for seeing connections between the personal defection of TH, her long-standing resentment of male attitudes, and state violence. In her radio poem 'Three Women' (CP.157, March 1962) one woman says:

> And then there were other faces. The faces of nations,
> Governments, parliaments, societies,
> The faceless faces of important men.

> It is these men I mind:
> They are so jealous of anything that is not flat!
>   They are jealous gods
> That would have the whole world flat because they are.
> I see the Father conversing with the Son.
> Such flatness cannot but be holy.

(p. 179)

Recognition of a pattern of male violence in patriarchy informs 'Daddy' (CP.183, October 1962). The poet scornfully identifies her father with the devil, God, Nazis, torturers of early modern times, and TH – in the marriage ceremony she said 'I do':

> I made a model of you,
> A man in black with a Meinkampf look
> And a love of the rack and the screw.
> And I said I do, I do.

(p. 224)

They are all instances of male power. And in 'Lady Lazarus' (*CP*.198) she identifies her body with the abused remains of gassed Jews – 'my skin/ Bright as a Nazi lampshade' (p. 244).

It is a bold move – 'monstrous, utterly disproportionate', declared Irving Howe, the voice of ex-radicalism in the United States. In the last poems, Howe found, Plath illustrates 'an extreme state of existence'. She couldn't illustrate 'the general human condition' because she was 'so deeply rooted in the extremity of her plight'. This is not a new accusation for the woman writer: Matthew Arnold found Charlotte Brontë's *Villette* 'disagreeable' because 'the writer's mind contains nothing but hunger, rebellion and rage'.[29] The reasonable man finds Plath's last poems extreme; my project is to look at the social construction of that writing and that judgement.

Plath is saying – and I don't claim it is fully articulated, which is not surprising since it was a thought struggling into consciousness, scarcely anticipated in its period; she is saying that Jews and women, both, have been among the victims of institutionalized violence in Western civilization. Certainly those oppressions differ. Nazi persecution of Jews, as with other scapegoatings, was focused, systematic and directly lethal. Other oppressions have been more long-term and uneven, and that is generally the case with the subjection of women. Nonetheless, the treatment of women through the centuries of Western man constitutes one of the great offences. 'Society as we know it fears and tries to destroy "the Other" ', writes Mary Daly – with the Jews, women, and the Vietnamese in mind; Daly links rape, genocide and war as the most unholy trinity (pp. 62–3, 114–22). If, as Plath suggests, 'Every woman adores a Fascist' ('Daddy', p. 223), it is because there is indeed a continuity between the patriarchal structures that legitimate state violence and violence against women. TH is male power in western society; and this is an extreme view.

Furthermore, Plath writes of violence against men. 'I've killed one man, I've killed two' ('Daddy', p. 224); 'I eat men like air' ('Lady Lazarus', p. 247). 'Purdah' (*CP*.197), spoken from within a harem, conjures Clytemnestra, slayer of the hero Agamemnon:

I shall unloose –
From the small jeweled
Doll he guards like a heart –

The lioness,
The shriek in the bath,
The cloak of holes.

(p. 244)

Men in our culture are generally anxious about female power, which Adrienne Rich identifies as 'first of all, to give or withhold nourishment and warmth, to give or withhold survival itself.' And this produces male fear: 'the hatred of overt strength in women, the definition of strong independent women as freaks of nature, as unsexed, as frigid, castrating, perverted, dangerous; the fear of the maternal woman as "controlling", the preference for dependent, malleable, "feminine" women' (Rich, pp. 67, 70). Hence, Rich says, the domestication of women: domesticity is supposed to contain female power. But in Plath's poems domesticity and hostility to men tangle together, threatening that containment. This is specially true of the last poem in the published *Ariel*, 'Edge' (*CP*.224), which invokes Medea, who revenged herself on the man who deserted her, the heroic Jason, by killing their children. By such an action, the poem says, 'The woman is perfected'. Now her children are hers alone, 'She has folded/Them back into her body as petals' (pp. 272–3); at last she is entire in her motherhood, free of TH. Adrienne Rich, telling of a woman who killed her children, asks what woman, caring single-handed for her children or struggling to retain her personhood against the idea that she must be only a mother, 'has not dreamed of "going over the edge", of simply letting go, relinquishing what is termed her sanity, so that she can be taken care of for once' (Rich, p. 279). It is not for a man to reply.

Of course, Plath failed to transcend the violence that she identified. She was unable to live in her own instance the vision that made her support CND and want her brother to be a conscientious objector. The conditions for that were scarcely available, so mystified was the whole topic. In part the customary idea of woman as victim rather than assailant triumphed, and she turned her violence upon herself. Yet she also turned it upon TH: I believe that the poems, and the suicide that showed she really meant it, were partly vengeance on TH. As such, they were not unsuccessful, though they could be recuperated through male myths about the monstrous independent female (Robert Lowell wrote in introduction to the US *Ariel* of Plath's voice as that of 'the vampire – a Dido, Phaedra, or Medea'). But the violence is not just Plath's: it is the violence of patriarchy, unleashed out of manipulation and entrapment in a woman who had taken on the contradictory demands of patriarchy at their widest and deepest. Plath had tried to tell the acceptable stories and realized their stresses in herself. Now she turned upon their prime scriptors.

The L-Shaped Room, The Pumpkin Eater and *Franny and Zooey* are not extreme because they fit the woman back, albeit uncertainly, into the social order. For moderation, maturity and good sense are defined normatively, by patriarchy. I drew attention in chapter 3 to Nancy K. Miller's argument that plausibility is normative: that which is not conventionally thought to be the case will seem incredible and perhaps extreme ('Emphasis Added', in Showalter). Miller quotes Freud's belief that men's daydreams are ambitious, egoistic and erotic, whereas women's are mainly erotic (since, of course, that is where their ambitions are supposed to reside). But, Miller asks, if women have ambitious daydreams, how do they appear? As 'a fantasy of power that would revise the social grammar in which women are never defined as subjects' (p. 348). That is what we see in 'Daddy' and 'Lady Lazarus': a fantasy of power reversal, which appears extreme not only to many readers, but to Plath herself. The violence and extremity indicate the scale of social change that would have to occur for Plath to become acceptably powerful. For, Miller argues, verisimilitude and the 'truths' of 'human' experience to which it appeals are male in our culture, and that is why words such as 'extravagant' suggest the feminine (p. 357). Speaking as a woman, of women's oppression, is extreme because the language – the credible stories – are written by patriarchy. Plath's extremity is a necessary and necessarily limited strategy of the oppressed.[30]

The same argument applies to 'hysteria'. Juliet Mitchell locates hysteria as 'the woman's simultaneous acceptance and refusal of the organization of sexuality under patriarchal capitalism. It is simultaneously what a woman can do both to be feminine and to refuse femininity.'[31] If Plath's poetry appears hysterical, that is because the power of naming is Adam's, and women (and other subordinated groups) who want to tell a different story must either adapt to prevailing discourses or force a way through. The latter produces hysteria – as a discursive feature and, indeed, in the writer herself, scripted by her stories.

Afterlife

After her death in February 1963, as individual late poems were published, Plath became a figure of excited comment, and when *Ariel* came out in 1965 it sold more than 5000 copies in ten months. This too was not unscripted: Salinger's Seymour shot himself leaving poems for his brother to publish, and the latter comments: 'The suicide poet or artist, one can't help noticing, has always been given a very considerable amount of avid attention' (Salinger, *Raise*, p. 164). Even so, Plath had to get past the condescension of established commentators. 'She steers clear of feminine charm, deliciousness, gentility, supersensitivity and the act of being a poetess. She simply writes good poetry', says Alvarez on the back of the *Colossus* volume. She's 'hardly a person at all, or a woman, certainly not another "poetess" ', wrote Lowell introducing the US *Ariel*. The price of admission to the male construct 'significant poet' is the waiving of the disqualification of being female.

Plath's 'extremism' was welcomed, by some, as a timely witness to the inevitability of Modernism; as I have noted, Alvarez was a key scriptor in both stories – Plath and Modernism. 'In Sylvia Plath's last poems', declared A. E. Dyson, 'we are reminded that the Modern Movement, as Kafka himself exemplified it, is not dead, but still with us'; George Steiner called 'Daddy' 'the "Guernica" of modern poetry'. Within this framework, Plath's work was linked with that of Lowell and Berryman as a 'poetry of confession'; and Alvarez developed the idea that writing now had to be 'extreme', manifesting 'a progressively more inward response to a progressively more intolerable sense of disaster'.[32] History, politics and society disappear into a mash of profound psychic disturbance and generalized horror, with vague reference to Nazis and atomic weapons; it's the 'modern condition' (see Chapter 9). Charles Newman actually disparages Plath's reading about the military – industrial complex as an unlikely source of 'materials for the imagination'. He says: 'In absorbing, personalising the socio-political catastrophes of the century, she reminds us that they are ultimately metaphors of the terrifying human mind' (Newman, pp. 33, 53).

Such criticism transmutes the extremism of the poems into an existential *Angst* that offered no threat to literary intellectuals; on the contrary, it made them seem rather important. Most revealingly, it tends to conclude that Plath's aggressive poetry was actually 'celebratory'. Certainly that poetry may be positive in effect, once the social pressures upon it are opened up to discussion, but mystified notions – such as destruction paradoxically transforming itself into creation, or Plath bodying forth the death within her – only inhibit understanding. These formulations betray a wish to retrieve at any cost the Arnoldian – Leavisite notion of literature as 'life-enhancing'.

Another route to the same goal is often taken by academic criticism, whose mission is generally to discourage disturbance of the status quo, and especially the status of the academy. Rather than celebrate Plath's extremism, it tries to talk it away. 'These poems are whole and structured when imagined as *speeches*, soliloquies, if you will, or monologs'; 'It is the form of the expression, and not the neurosis from which it may or may not issue, which concerns us, and which we can evaluate, celebrate'; 'There is a unity, an integrity, and an integrity of the imagination – and whatever the hammer-splittings of the self, behind the sad mask of the woman is the mind and heart of someone making transcendent poems.'[33] Gender, in fact any disturbance, evaporates in 'transcendent poems'.

Such diverse retellings of Plath's story are only what we should expect, for this is how culture is produced: texts are read, writers are discussed, in ways that advance particular viewpoints within the contest that makes up the current political conjuncture. Most importantly, Plath has been formative for the Women's Movement. Even as Plath's story was written for her, so other women have found her in their own lives and work. For them it was an exciting new script, an alternative to the dominant ideology. 'Though I never met Plath', says Sandra M. Gilbert, 'I can honestly say that I have known her most of my life.' Gilbert read and wondered at the gender politics of an early story, and actually became a guest editor of *Mademoiselle* four years after Plath. Working under 'Jay Cee' (as she is called in *The Bell Jar*), she too found the career women on the staff disconcerting. When the story of Plath's life (much of it) and death was told, 'all of us who had read her traced our own journey in hers.' Again, Anne Stevenson tells of her own life, remarking how thousands of women have followed a similar trajectory; when she wrote her partly autobiographical sequence of poems *Correspondences* (1974), she found that her character Kay is a blend of her own experiences and Plath's Esther.[34] Alicia Ostriker, in her book *Writing Like a Woman* (1983), records how she read Plath's work while her husband and babies were asleep, guiltily because of her domestic duties and college responsibilities (p. 64): even while reading Plath she replicated Plath's situation. Susan Bassnett describes how Adrienne Rich, Paula Rothholz and Rose Leiman Goldemberg have drawn upon the Plath myth in their writing (ch. 6).

The importance of work on Plath and gender politics may be gauged by the resistance to it. Feminist literary criticism has produced its own versions to counter the ones I have mainly been quoting; I have referred to some of them. They are admitted to academic attention, but as a special case; often they are placed as partial, immature and lacking balance – not addressing the full human complexity (which of course is male).[35] The patronization and victimization that afflicted Plath are still there for women who address her political import.

The same ideology, though in the register of the gutter-press, informs a three-page article in the *Mail on Sunday* (1 February 1987, pp. 31–3). Three (male) journalists pretend to reveal 'closely guarded secrets', but their article is contrived from already printed material, some of which they pretend is told personally to them, and is innovative only in its inaccuracies (e.g. Plath was 'rich' and her father fled Germany just before the war). The article is offensive in its personal intrusion, its gender stereotyping and its whole tone. But the ultimate target is 'the feminist movement', which is accused of 'an obsessive campaign', 'a passion approaching hysteria', 'extreme feminist logic' and 'terrible hatred'. If the story of Sylvia Plath's life and writing is powerful in our society, so are the structures within which she struggled.

Notes

1 Rowbotham, *Woman's*, p. 13. Wilson, E., p. 187, also pp. 2–4, 48, 162–5, 181–7; Birmingham, Hopkins, pp. 320–3. Judith Hubback denied that 'reasonable feminism' is 'egalitarian', asserted that 'modern feminists are not unpractical idealists', and urged educated women to work out individual solutions to their difficulties (pp. 83–7). See Pearson Phillips, 'The New Look', in Sissons and French. Despite the title of Dale Spender's *There's Always Been a Women's Movement This Century* (London, Pandora, 1983), Spender's interviews show a hiatus in the 1950s (see pp. 35–6, 131, 161–2).

2 See Parsons and Bales, pp. 45–7; Wilson, E., pp. 60–74. See Friedan, ch. 6; Poster, *Critical*, pp. 78–84; Veronica Beechey, 'Women and Production', in Kuhn and Wolpe.

3 Poster, *Critical*, esp. ch. 7; Mitchell, *Women*, p. 43; Millett, pp. 176–220; Friedan, ch. 5; Barrett, ch. 6.

4 Townsend, 'A Society for People', in MacKenzie, pp. 119–20; Rowbotham, *Woman's*, p. 21 and ch. 2. See Riley, pp. 175–88. On women and the Communist Party, see Davis. For a similar response to Friedan's *Feminine Mystique*, see Pat Garland and Christine Buchan, in McCrindle and Rowbotham, pp. 291, 328–9.

5 Titmuss, *Essays*, pp. 89, 94; Birmingham, p. 58; Klein, V., pp. 9–12; Myrdal and Klein, ch. 4; Wilson, E., pp. 26–9, 41–7, 187–8; Riley, chs. 5, 6. On refusing motherhood, see Steedman, pp. 83–97. One consequence of relative female financial independence was that it became more feasible for the man to desert the family, producing single-parent families as the largest group, along with the elderly, living in poverty (Ehrenreich, pp. 171–5).

6 Marx, *Capital*, II, pp. 701–8. See in Kuhn and Wolpe: Veronica Beechey, 'Women and Production'; Mary McIntosh, 'The State and the Oppression of Women'. Also Elizabeth Wilson, *Women and the Welfare State* (London: Tavistock, 1977); Barrett, chs. 5–7.

7 Barrett, pp. 36–7, and chs. 1, 5. As Barrett points out, because they work well together it does not follow that patriarchy is peculiar to capitalism. See also Rich, ch. 2; Roisin McDonough and Rachel Harrison, 'Patriarchy and the Relations of Production', in Kuhn and Wolpe; Althusser, pp. 123–8.

8 Hopkins, pp. 335–6, and see Friedan, ch. 9; Myrdal and Klein, pp. 143–9; Light.

9 Birmingham, pp. 51–4; Wilson, E., pp. 33–6, 51–4; Myrdal and Klein, p. 152; Klein, V., pp. 13–14; Friedan, pp. 159–67; Hubback, ch. 10.

10 Myrdal and Klein, pp. 138–41; Klein, V., p. 13; Hubback, pp. 125–8; Oakley, *Subject*, pp. 125–6 and ch. 6; Oakley, *Housewife*, pp. 197–8 and ch. 8; Hopkins, pp. 324–8; Rossi; Ehrenreich, pp. 1–2; Friedan, chs. 3, 7; Mead, pp. 316–24.

11 Ohmann, pp. 210–19. Ohmann instances *Catcher in the Rye, Franny and Zooey, Portnoy's Complaint, One Flew Over the Cuckoo's Nest, The Crying of Lot 49, Something Happened. The L-Shaped Room, The Golden Notebook* and *The Pumpkin Eater* also fit the pattern.

12 In Butscher: Irving Howe, 'The Plath Celebration: a Partial Dissent'; Marjorie J. Perloff, 'On the Road to *Ariel*', pp. 127–8, 142 (but cf. Perloff, 'Sylvia Plath's "Sivvy" Poems', in Lane, G., pp. 156–7, after she has read *Letters*). In Lane, G.: Hugh Kenner, 'Sincerity Kills', pp. 42–3; David Shapiro, 'Sylvia Plath: Drama and Melodrama'; Murray M. Schwartz and Christopher Bollas, 'The Absence at the Center'. In Alexander: Elizabeth Hardwick, 'On Sylvia Plath', p. 100. For alternative views, see the biographical accounts of Elizabeth Sigmund, 'Sylvia in Devon: 1962' and Clarissa Roche, 'Vignettes from England', in Butscher.

13 Spender, 'Warnings from the Grave', in Newman, pp. 202–3. See Ellmann, p. 85, Wagner-Martin, p. 99.

14 Wilson, E., p. 138. And see Oakley, *Subject*, pp. 65–9; Kaplan, C., *Salt*,

pp. 290–1; Bassnett, pp. 63–4; Carole Ferrier, 'The Beekeeper's Apprentice', in Lane, G., pp. 203–4, 215.

15 Rich, *Of Woman*, p. 25; Kaplan, C., *Sea*, pp. 219–22; Plath, *Journals*, p. 20. Cf. Juhasz, chs. 1, 6.

16 Mitchell, *Women*, pp. 288–9; Cora Kaplan, 'The Indefinite Disclosed', in Jacobus, pp. 64–5; also Jane Tomkins, 'Sentimental Power' and Annette Kolodny, 'Dancing Through the Minefield', in Showalter.

17 Friedan, pp. 76, 70–1, 150–5, 357–61. Friedan's research even anticipates the scene in *The Bell Jar* where Jay Cee asks Esther about her career intentions (pp. 33–5). And a *Mademoiselle* editor tells Friedan that college guest editors (which is what Plath and Esther were) now have no career plans (p. 56).

18 *Letters*, pp. 401–2; *Johnny*, pp. 17–18; it was published in 1976 in *Johnny*, from which it is quoted here.

19 *CP*.108, p. 121; *Letters*, p. 387; the poem was published in *The New Yorker* on 20 August 1960. She says she wrote 'Water Color of Grantchester Meadows' (*CP*.96) 'bucolically "for" them' (*Journals*, p. 301).

20 The stories are 'Down in the Reeds by the River' by Victoria Lincoln; 'The Middle Drawer' by Hortense Calisher; 'The Second Tree from the Corner' by E. B. White; 'A Perfect Day For Bananafish' by J. D. Salinger; 'Pigeons en Casserole' by Bessie Breuer (*55 Short Stories*).

21 For these *New Yorker* aspirations, see *Journals*, pp. 191–2, 305–6; the experience of the man kissing her is on pp. 5–8. On Salinger, see further *Letters*, pp. 114, 249; *Journals*, p. 156; Wagner-Martin, pp. 187, 237.

22 Gubar, ' "The Blank Page" and the Issues of Female Creativity', in Showalter, p. 302; Plath, 'Kindness', *CP*.220, p. 270. For similar imagery, see 'A Life', *CP*.132; 'Tulips', *CP*.142; 'Fever 103°', *CP*.188; 'Lyonesse', *CP*.190.

23 *Journals*, p. 212, 214. For independence alongside dependence, see *Letters*, p. 270, 276; *Journals*, p. 154.

24 This is noted by Robert Scholes, 'Esther Came Back Like a Retreaded Tire', and Vance Bourjaily, 'Victoria Lucas and Elly Higginbottom', both in Alexander. They take it as Plath's purposeful control of her material. The image of TH deteriorated quite gradually. Stories and poems about marital problems are written or planned from 1957 (Bassnett, pp. 102–9); a quarrel of December 1958 about sewing on buttons leads Plath to envisage a story about 'his deep-rooted conventional ideas of womanhood, like all the rest of the men, wants them pregnant and in the kitchen' (*Journals*, p. 277). See also *Journals*, p. 292.

25 Mitchell, *Women*, p. 291. See Ann Rosalind Jones, 'Writing the Body', in Showalter.

26 See Mary Lynn Broe, ' "Enigmatical, Shifting My Clarities" ', in Alexander; Carole Ferrier, 'The Beekeeper's Apprentice', in Lane, G.; Sandra M. Gilbert, 'A Fine, White Flying Myth', in Gilbert and Gubar, *Shakespeare's*.

27 Driver, p. 90; Wilson, E., pp. 177–80; for such plays, see pp. 275–6 below.

28 *Letters*, pp. 282, 284, 378, 434, 449; *Johnny*, pp. 98–9; Orr, pp. 169–70.

29 Howe, 'The Plath Celebration', in Butscher, pp. 233–5. Arnold is quoted by Mary Jacobus, 'The Buried Letter', in Jacobus, p. 43. 'Hers is extremist poetry, to be sure' (Newman, in Newman, p. 52).

30 For similar reasons, Sandra M. Gilbert argues that women find themselves writing extravagant, mythic, gothic and fairy-tale plots (Gilbert and Gubar, *Shakespeare's*, pp. 248–60). See also Alice Ostriker, 'The Thieves of Language', in Showalter.

31 Mitchell, *Women*, pp. 289–90; also pp. 293–4. Mitchell traces 'hysteria' back through the invalid lady of the Victorian period to medieval witchcraft (pp. 117–20). See also Olsen, p. 224 and *passim*; Russ; Elaine Showalter, *The Female Malady* (New York: Pantheon Books, 1985).

32 In Newman: A.E. Dyson, 'On Sylvia Plath', p. 210; George Steiner, 'Dying Is an Art', p. 218; M. L. Rosenthal, 'Sylvia Plath and Confessional Poetry'. See Alvarez, *Savage*, pp. 260 and 257–83. Alvarez' views were known well before *The Savage God*: see Alvarez, 'Sylvia Plath', in Newman, p. 56. On reception, see Mary Kinzie, 'An Informal Check List of Criticism', in Newman; Paul Alexander, 'Introduction' and Katha Pollitt, 'A Note of Triumph', in Alexander, pp. 94–5; Marjorie G. Perloff, 'On the Road to *Ariel*', in Butscher, pp. 125–7; Juhasz, pp. 85–7.

33 J.D. O'Hara, 'Plath's Comedy', in Lane, G., p. 77; Newman, in Newman, p. 24; Stanley Plumly, 'What Ceremony of Words', in Alexander, pp. 24–5 (see also p. 47).

34 Gilbert and Gubar, *Shakespeare's*, pp. 245–7; Stevenson, 'Writing Like a Woman', in Jacobus, pp. 166–72.

35 E.g. Gary Lane, 'Introduction', and Jerome Mazzaro, 'Sylvia Plath and the Cycles of History', in Lane, G., pp. xiii, 238; Paul Alexander, 'Introduction', and Elizabeth Hardwick, 'On Sylvia Plath', in Alexander, pp. xiii, 110–11; Charles Newman, in Newman, p. 43. See also Holbrook, p. 2.

11
The rise of Left-culturism

Class and the Establishment

Are the requisites all in the toilet?
  The frills round the cutlets can wait
Till the girl has replenished the cruets
  And switched on the logs in the grate.
                              (Betjeman, p. 243)

John Betjeman's poem 'How to Get On in Society' followed an article in *Encounter* by Nancy Mitford (September 1955; taken up by Evelyn Waugh in the December number). It illustrates one preoccupation of mid-1950s intellectual culture: how to distinguish 'U' or 'non-U' (upper or non-upper) forms of English speech and behaviour.

Such yearnings for the class distinctions of pre-1939 English society were obstructing the attempts of younger intellectuals, in diverse fields, to produce distinctive work and make their mark; I wrote of the sexual politics of this moment in Chapter 5. But, generally, they aspired to rise in society rather than to change it. Blake Morrison sums up the stance of 'Movement' writers as 'an uneasy combination of class-consciousness and acceptance of class division; an acute awareness of privilege, but an eventual submission to the structure which makes it possible' (p. 74). So *Lucky Jim* (1954) features both subversive irreverence and a fantasy of social advance. When John Wain was invited to present Movement poetry on the Third Programme he remarked: 'This was a chance to move a few of the established reputations gently to one side and allow new people their turn' (*Sprightly*, p. 168). Aspiring film-makers such as Lindsay Anderson, Karel Reisz and Tony Richardson couldn't break in because cinemas were controlled by two or three combines, and these preferred heavy dramas about how a stiff upper lip won the war, and Ealing comedies projecting a fantasy of community spirit within traditional structures. Anderson wanted a film art 'neither exclusive and snobbish, nor stereotyped and propagandist – but vital, illuminating, personal and refreshing'.[1] Meanwhile Kenneth Tynan was complaining in *The Observer* that, 'apart from revivals and imports, there is nothing in the London theatre that one dares discuss with an intelligent man for more than five minutes' (Tynan, p. 148). The idea in founding the English Stage Company at the Royal Court Theatre in 1956 was to discover new, youthful talent.

Although professional blockage rather than political outlook was the issue, class feeling came in as well because, as I showed in Chapter 4, the intellectual establishment was perceived as upper-class in outlook, and some of the aspirants were quite lower-middle class. Donald Davie wrote in December 1957 of himself in such terms, as winning his way to university 'rather than going there as a matter of course as in the case of products of more privileged classes, such as Spender, Auden, Lehmann and Connolly and almost every writer of previous generations that you can think of.'[2]

Established writers appreciated that they were being challenged through class and culture together. In *Encounter* Spender wrote of 'a rebellion of the Lower Middle Brows' (November 1953), and Evelyn Waugh complained about 'the new wave of philistinism . . . grim young people . . . coming off the assembly lines' (December 1955). Somerset Maugham, in the *Sunday Times* in the same month, attacked grant-aided students such as the protagonist of *Lucky Jim*: 'They have no manners, and are woefully unable to deal with any social predicament. . . . They are scum.' Tynan quoted and repudiated this in May 1956 when he celebrated *Look Back in Anger* as 'all scum and a mile wide'. Most of the reviewers of *Look Back* sought to put down Jimmy Porter in class terms, describing him as an 'oaf', a 'bore', 'uncouth, cheaply vulgar', one who should be 'sentenced to a lifetime cleaning latrines'.[3] The contest for cultural space was encapsulated in the coining of the term 'the establishment' (initially over the cover-up for Burgess and Maclean) to specify the informal structure through which the already-powerful maintain their dominance.[4]

The sense of 'establishment' hypocrisy and incompetence was validated, for the discontented, by the Suez invasion of 1956. Prime-minister Eden was confessedly still fighting the battles of the 1930s (he compared Nasser with Hitler); the issue was represented, dishonestly, as to do with 'the rule of law'; and the invasion of Egypt was fumblingly executed. Further, it was halted because US opposition caused a run on the pound, so British impotence was humiliatingly exposed.

Even so, most noted writers did not see or want, until the late 1950s, a political dimension in their work. The May 1957 issue of John Lehmann's *London Magazine* asked various writers how far they were concerned in their writing with fundamental current issues – such as 'atomic weapons and the levelling down of classes through discriminatory taxation'! Writers from Enright and Wain to Golding and Colin Wilson produced either equivocations or conservative responses: only Osborne and Plath spoke up for political commitment. This was owing partly to the notion that the welfare state had instituted all the changes necessary for the good society (including the education of the likes of themselves); and partly to the difficulty in discerning a left position not contaminated with Stalinism.

However, a stronger political development was to follow, based partly on class. A principal concession to the wartime egalitarian spirit, and to the needs of an advanced modern capitalist society (these two imperatives were of course contradictory and mutually disabling), was enhanced opportunity for social mobility through education. To the 'unsuccessful', this 'meritocratic' tendency suggested that their class inferiority derived from natural incapacity, and this was both tranquillizing and obscurely frustrating. For the upwardly mobile, there were distinctive anxieties; the class background of intellectuals became an issue.

The preoccupation with upward mobility through education was a story that society, or parts of it, wanted to tell itself, not a record of experience. The initial novels of the upwardly mobile young man (women figured in so far as they impeded or facilitated his rise) were actually based on the experience of writers who had finished their education before 1944, and the theme isn't grasped at all precisely. Philip Larkin's *Jill* is set in the war years and published in 1946; *Lucky Jim* is vague about Dixon's class background and *Look Back in Anger* says little about education. Even in Richard Hoggart's *The Uses of Literacy* the theme is articulated only towards the end and relatively briefly (pp. 291–300); it took off from here, in 1957. Hoggart wrote of the 'scholarship boy' who becomes a 'declassed' expert: he has succeeded at the price of separation from lower-class culture and unease in his new sphere. He is at 'the friction-point of two cultures' (p. 292).

These diverse writings were read through a preoccupation with education and social mobility which developed along with the growth in salaried middle-class employment in teaching, social work, technical work, local government, media and management. The offspring of manual workers were channelled through the education system towards such occupations,[5] throwing up a typical proportion of aspirant writers and artists. Traditionally, it had not proved difficult to assimilate into intellectual circles, on certain terms, a few bright young lower-class men (very rarely women). But because the leisure elite on which high culture depended was weakened anyway, an issue was perceived and a sequence of novels, social studies and television plays appeared. Michael Young's popular satire *The Rise of the Meritocracy* (1958) was predicated on the idea that educational selection would become ever more efficient, to the point where the lower orders revolt out of their inextinguishable humanity. In 1960 Raymond Williams was able to publish *Border Country*, the first draft of which had been finished in 1947. Dennis Potter returned several times to the theme: by the time he wrote *Stand Up, Nigel Barton* (1965), Barton's appeal to his working-class background could be met with the cocktail-party remark: 'There's nothing unique about that. It's been well documented in Jackson and Marsden's book.'[6]

Of course, the tendency towards 'meritocracy' was overstated – it was part of an ideology of 'equality of opportunity' which supposedly justified the system. Most upward movement was not because the class system was weaker but because there were more middle-class jobs, and it was probably within a fairly narrow 'buffer zone' between the middle class and working class proper. Generally, family circumstances remained the major determinant of educational and hence occupational attainment. The Robbins Committee found in the early 1960s that there were more lower-class students only because the number of students had doubled: the proportion was the same as in 1939. By 1972 the effect of parental class on education had actually risen since 1945, as the importance of examination success had increased.[7]

The relation between social mobility and political outlook was complex. Early studies suggested that the new middle classes were narrow, selfish and conservative – Hoggart's achiever is anxious and conformist. In *Education and the Working Class* (1962) Brian Jackson and Dennis Marsden found that many of the newly middle class were embarrassed about their origins and much less inclined than their parents to vote Labour (pp. 174–8, 183–9, 192). But this changed. The impetus of such studies was itself mostly leftwards, and their publication helped to promote the awareness and confidence through which young people could challenge rather than conform. In *Stand Up, Nigel Barton* Potter's protagonist truculently asserts (to the standard upper-class girl-friend): 'The days of the timid, kow-towing little runt of a scholarship boy are long since over' (p. 44). By 1963 surveys were showing students generally to be to the left of their parents, and the longer they spent in higher education the further left they became.[8]

Socialism with a British Face

We have come to think of the European left as highly diversified, but the Cold War made all left-wing thought appear implicated in Stalinism, and Orwell's *1984* seemed to have clinched the argument. E. P. Thompson observed in 'Outside the Whale' (1960): 'What must be seen to have "failed" is the aspiration itself: the revolutionary potential – not within Russian society alone – but within *any* society, within man himself.'[9] That is why Jimmy Porter could discern no good brave causes.

Stalin died in March 1953, and the new regime seemed inclined to liberalization. Khrushchev talked of different roads to socialism, and made peace with Tito in Yugoslavia. In July 1955 Soviet and NATO leaders met and talked. Then at the Twentieth Party Congress in February 1956 the Soviet leadership criticized the cult of personality and lack of collective leadership, and admitted that Party members had confessed to crimes they hadn't committed and been condemned to death or sent to labour camps in their thousands. The speech was given in secret but it leaked out. In Poland in June 1956 a workers' demonstration was fairly gently controlled, and in October a liberal regime not challenged. However, an uprising in Hungary followed, and a new popular government called for the removal of Soviet troops and withdrawal from the Warsaw Pact. This was too much for Moscow, and Budapest was brutally occupied by Soviet tanks on 4 November 1956.

British left-wingers had committed themselves to the Soviet Union in the 1920s and 1930s, when it seemed a beleaguered but exciting instance of a communist state, and for many this enthusiasm had been reinvigorated during the war, when Russia was seen widely as a heroic ally. To sustain this commitment in the face of rumours of the repressiveness of Stalin's regime, western communists cultivated diverse and sometimes devious mental reservations. The 'liberalization' of 1953–6 stimulated optimism about a more humane, open kind of communism.

This mood is exemplified in Doris Lessing's novel *Retreat to Innocence*, set in 1955 and published in 1956. Jan Brod is a Czech, a Jew, a communist and an exile. He is reluctant to return to Czechoslovakia, but insists on the positive potential of the Russian Revolution and the communist movement ('We were strong. Everything that was ugly belonged to the past, everything beautiful to the future'; p. 88). He has written a book that explains Stalin as a great man who had faults, who became understandably bitter at the hostility he aroused in his enemies (p. 318). As the Czech regime liberalizes, Jan's brother (who is an official) appeals to him to contribute to the development of that society (pp. 309–10). Jan abandons the book and returns to Czechoslovakia, where he will perhaps write funny satires on 'the secret police of the world' (p. 325).

We might take the title *Retreat to Innocence* to imply a placing of Jan's idealism, but it seems to refer mainly to the inability of British people to address the modern world. Young people particularly are shown as ignorant of and uninterested in national and international politics – getting their idea of communism from Cold-War accounts in a corrupt and malicious press, and unmoved by the labour tradition. As elsewhere in Lessing, lack of vigour in heterosexual love-making figures a general failure of human intensity. Though British preparedness to live and let live effects a critique of the Soviet Bloc, corruption and violence in the British state is exposed: 'When it comes to the point, you'd do all the things you blame *them* for, and laugh' (p. 266).

The alleged lack of intensity in British experience enables Lessing to recuperate Soviet communism in terms of the suffering of its adherents. Jan asserts:

> When people formed themselves together in the Party, for the first time in history, without God, without excuses, relying on themselves, saying: We accept the responsibility for what we do, we accept all the good and evil of the past, we reject nothing – then for the first time in history man became free; he became free because he rejected nothing. (pp. 228–9)

The corrupt activities of communists are heroic because, transcending the ethics of bourgeois hypocrisy, they stand on the moral frontier of the twentieth century. This is the existentialist argument that Sartre relates to the actions of the Resistance (*Existentialism*, pp. 18–41). In Lessing's book it is surely a desperate move: what should have been a material, historical triumph has to be defended on a supposed larger framework than history, that of the 'modern condition'. It leads away from socialism and towards a vague, apocalyptic Modernist vision (see chapter 9); Lessing's later work took this path.

The changing Cold-War temperature may be registered in Lessing's *Going Home*, which she wrote in early 1956. Lessing writes as a communist, but remarks that she doesn't expect people in Britain to take easily to communism until it 'has proved itself to be as genuinely democratic as it has been claiming to be'. She is optimistic about this, expecting communist countries to become freer and more democratic while the West does the opposite.[10] As the book goes to press, however, Lessing adds an anxious note about Hungary, affirming that in any event, in the three years since the death of Stalin, 'the great words liberty, freedom and truth have again become banners for men to fight under – in all countries of the world' (p. 297). Twelve years later, in the edition of 1968, Lessing avers that Soviet liberalization had turned out to be only a safety valve (p. 312).

The suppression of the Hungarian revolt, following on the hopes of liberalization, caused an exodus from the British Party, and often this is represented as a destruction of left-wing activity in Britain. The opposite is the case: there was a release from the crippling ideological manoeuvring which allegiance to Stalinism had imposed, and very gradually from the Cold-War stigma. This work was done notably by left-wing historians, who had been challenging Communist Party discipline. Edward Thompson and John Saville started the *New Reasoner* in summer 1957, and in 1960 that merged with *Universities and Left Review* (set up in Oxford in 1957) to form the *New Left Review*. A special project for historians was to uncover an indigenous British or English radicalism, a story of utopian ideals and resistance to oppression that predated the Soviet revolution. In *Out of Apathy* (1960) Thompson invoked 'a revolutionary tradition' of Levellers, Peterloo, Chartists and dockers: 'It is a tradition which could leaven the socialist world.'[11] This work had been begun in the 1940s, but as it developed it had the advantage of evading the embarrassment of Stalinism.

At this point an independent left became feasible. I use three main terms to describe it: 'the New Left' refers to the distinct phase of left-wing activity in the late 1950s and early 1960s – not just in *New Left Review* and among prominent intellectuals, but in a whole constituency, mainly of younger people; a 'left-liberal class fraction' identifies the main social basis of the New Left; and 'middle-class dissidence' (see pp. 41–3) alludes to a longer and more general radical tradition.

CND and a New-Left Intelligentsia

I have argued that middle-class dissidence may take diverse political slants, but that in the early 1950s it was often reactionary – lamenting that the old system was under threat (Chapters 4 and 5). Left-liberal dissidence had found its crowning achievement in the welfare state, but that very success seemed to render it redundant. Angus Wilson wrote in 1950 of 'Such Darling Dodos' – Oxford dons still pursuing earnest causes among right-wing students. Michael Frayn saw the Festival of Britain (1951) as their last flourish; he called them 'herbivores':

> The radical middle-classes – the do-gooders; the readers of the *News Chronicle*, the *Guardian*, and the *Observer*; the signers of petitions; the backbone of the BBC. In short, the Herbivores, or gentle ruminants, who look out from the lush pastures which are their natural station in life with eyes full of sorrow for less fortunate creatures, guiltily conscious of their advantages, though not usually ceasing to eat the grass.[12]

However, not everyone in the 1950s was conservative. In 1951, when the Labour Party lost (or abandoned) office, it received more votes than the Conservatives, and more than in 1945 and 1950. Opinion polls through the 1950s show between 25 and 40 per cent of people opposed to the extension of conscription (during the Korean War), to increases in 'defence' expenditure and to the Suez invasion; and favouring unilateral nuclear disarmament (Marwick, *British* pp. 105–6). Just when most commentators were declaring that ideology had ended and consensus politics could contain all aspirations, there was the Campaign for Nuclear Disarmament.

CND should perhaps require less explanation than British investment in nuclear weaponry: the latter was part of the fantasy of 'great power' status (Leys, pp. 62–3). From this point of view it was actually counter-productive, because it deformed the UK economy. During the 1950s Britain was spending between 8 and 10 per cent of its gross national product, a third of its tax revenue, on 'defence', while Germany and Japan were spending virtually nothing (Lewis, P., *Fifties*, pp. 104–5); naturally enough, the economic success of those countries was ascribed elsewhere – to the docility of their workforces. For CND supporters, the Bomb was of a piece with other 'establishment' complacency and hypocrisy. The reassurances of political leaders were undercut by the announcement in 1957 of a policy of 'massive nuclear retaliation' to *any* attack from the Soviet Union; by the testing of weapons in the atmosphere, which was poisoning people, animals, crops, the land and the sea; by the rearmament of Western Germany; and by leaks about the deep bunkers from which the protected leaders would exercise martial law. There was to be a four-minute warning of nuclear attack on Britain – 'Well, I would remind those doubters', says the Civil Defence lecturer in *Beyond the Fringe*, alluding to the record broken by Roger Bannister, 'that some people in this great country of ours can run a mile in four minutes' (Bennett, Cook et al., p. 79).

CND was initiated largely by middle-class dissidents – people such as J. B. Priestley, Bertrand Russell, Michael Foot, A. J. P. Taylor, Sir Richard Acland, Jacquetta Hawkes, Canon John Collins, Kingsley Martin, Fenner Brockway, Benjamin Britten, Michael Tippett, E. M. Forster, Barbara Hepworth, Henry Moore. It was rooted in liberal humanism; Bertrand Russell acknowledged the capacity of 'Man' for 'cruelty and suffering', but appealed to 'potentialities of greatness and splendour'. The problem with this humanism is that it disregards the actual structures of power in class and patriarchal society. It takes at face value the 'humanism' of capitalist society, accepting the bourgeois universalization of itself as the human, and appeals to the current order to ameliorate 'man's inhumanity to man'.[13] *March to Aldermaston*, a film made mainly by Lindsay Anderson in 1958, shows nicely spoken CND marchers watched by ordinary people who are variously passive, mystified, cheerful, curious and deriding.

However, CND was not limited by its origins. It rapidly became a focus for the other discontents I have discussed. First, it was supported by many newly prominent writers – Lessing, Osborne, Arnold Wesker, Iris Murdoch, Christopher Logue, John Silkin, Adrian Mitchell, David Campton, John Arden, Robert Bolt, John Berger, Bernard Kops, Shelagh Delaney, David Mercer, Alan Sillitoe. To them it seemed an obvious extension of their distaste for the prevailing system; even John Braine said he was Labour and against Suez and the Bomb (Allsop, p. 84). Second, it became a focus of left-wing activity. The CND leadership (as in the 1980s) hedged on how far Britain should 'depend' on the US 'nuclear umbrella' (a clever but tellingly confused media phrase), but many, including *New Left Review* editors Thompson and Stuart Hall, entertained the thought that Britain might subscribe neither to NATO nor to the Soviet Bloc. And Labour Party activists in the constitutencies and trades unions responded to CND as an issue on which to attack the right-wing leadership. Thompson describes the temporary capture of Labour for CND as 'the authentic expression of a tradition, deeply rooted, not only in an intelligentsia but in the trade unions and constituency parties'.[14] And third, CND recruited strongly among the upwardly mobile who depended upon educational attainment for their access to welfare and cultural professions. To them it offered a political commitment not implicated in traditional labourism – typically, they affirmed a clutch of humanitarian issues but were doubtful on traditional socialist matters such as trades unions and nationalization.[15]

This moment saw the formation and consolidation of a distinct class fraction: a younger-generation, left-liberal intelligentsia, with a quite specific subcultural formation. In his *Declaration* essay of 1957, Tynan discerned among some young people an 'instinctive Leftism' that needed only 'a rallying-point, social and political' (Maschler, p. 128). CND was to be one such; others were Royal Court drama, higher education, folk song and jazz. Already in his review of *Look Back*, Tynan discerns major components of this nascent formation: he links the play to grant-aided students, a 'non-U intelligentsia', jazz, and progressive political attitudes. This was the group likely to share the discontent of Jim Dixon and Jimmy Porter. As T. R. Fyvel remarks, the expansion in higher education made it much larger than the group which wrote and read left-wing poetry in the 1930s (*Intellectuals*, p. 16).

This new left-liberal fraction entered into contest with, and gradually replaced, the remnants of the leisure-class elite. It was to spearhead and endorse more and less radical change through the 1960s. Probably the moment of its hegemony, in the 1960s, was also the start of its decay, due to the failure of the welfare-capitalist assumptions upon which it generally relied.

Of course, the effect was uneven. I have shown how general dissatisfaction at establishment stuffiness and the slow yielding of the old guard was one stimulus, and consequently the politics were often only relatively left-wing. In particular, not only upwardly mobile young people were involved: Oxbridge students and other graduates from privileged backgrounds experienced career frustration and found that they could identify here. A. S. Byatt recalls fellow Cambridge undergraduates following the *Lucky Jim* fashion and rejecting images of 'varsity privilege'.[16] The temperamentally conservative resisted. Byatt herself, in her novel *Shadow of a Sun* (1964), has the evident purpose of showing that there are still, around 1960, thriving traditional upper-middle-class families (with Edwardian-type long hot summers and echoes of Woolf's *To the Lighthouse*). The novel's young man of alleged working-class origins (we don't see them) is clever, but rude and insensitive. He says he's 'an outsider' and 'angry', and insists on 'commitment' and 'life as it is lived' (pp. 81–2, 84, 89). So the upper-middle-class people dislike him, and the novel abets them by making him the only character not presented through his own self-perceptions and not shown in any of his own milieux (though he does have a speech of self-justification). However, he is sexually vigorous, despite his unprepossessing manner, and captures two of their womenfolk. Byatt was to become, according to the *International Who's Who* (1987–8), a 'broadcaster, reviewer and judge of literary prizes' – carrying on the crusade against barbarians (such as myself) within the gates of literary sensitivity.[17]

Left-culturism

Middle-class dissidents had often proclaimed the importance of culture, and the Frankfurt School saw 'mass' culture as a threat to liberty and civilization (see pp. 106–9). For the New Left, culture almost filled the political vision, producing the virtual expectation that society can be transformed through cultural change. Nor was this a limited phase: Perry Anderson, who helped replace the original editorial board of *New Left Review* in the name of a stricter Marxism, celebrated in 1965 the Hoggart-Williams 'original critique of the capitalist organisation of culture' and credited F. R. Leavis's claims for the intellectual centrality of his kind of literary criticism.[18]

The fact that 'mass' culture appeared to derive from the United States was convenient, for it meant that working-class culture had been interfered with and was not guilty of its own corruption. Williams observed, 'In

Britain, we have to notice that much of this bad work [synthetic culture] is American in origin. . . . To go pseudo-American is a way out of the English complex of class and culture, but of course it solves nothing' (*Communications*, p. 102). The left joined wholeheartedly in the attack on rock music (discussed in chapter 8); Williams dismisses 'the horror film, the rape-novel, the Sunday strip-paper and the latest Tin-Pan drool' (*Long*, p. 364).

Culture and Society (1958) was the key book. In the concluding chapter Williams argued from a left-wing perspective the general relevance of the tradition of high culture and middle-class dissidence. this was not straightforward, for that tradition was often reactionary and had made only occasional connections with the working class.[19] Yet it had an aesthetic and moral force (generally, and for Williams) that could not easily be jettisoned; it was the aspiration and often the vehicle of the upwardly mobile; and it was a British, non-Stalinist, tradition. So Williams refuses the idea of 'proletarian' art, asserting: 'The body of intellectual and imaginative work which each generation receives as its traditional culture is always, and necessarily, something more than the product of a single class' (pp. 307–8). This, I would note at once, is true, for cultures are characteristically put together out of elements from diverse quarters. But their organization and transmission may nevertheless be dominated by one class fraction (see pp. 39–43). However, Williams's first point, and the sequence of wise men discussed in *Culture and Society* supports it, is that the received 'good' culture is for everyone.

Hence Williams's attack on the concept of 'masses', and his insistence that the extension of education had not caused a deterioration of culture (pp. 287–97). Even so, within such a framework the working-class contribution seems slight. Williams tries to cope with this by offering a second definition of culture as 'a whole way of life' and by positing, as well as 'the body of intellectual and imaginative work which each generation receives', two class cultures, each defined by its 'way of life'. Working-class culture manifests an ethos of co-operation in community, whereas middle-class culture is competitive and individualistic. By this distinction, at a stroke, Williams combats the capitalist spirit of individual success and discovers a specific working-class cultural contribution (pp. 312–18). If working people have been able to produce few enduring texts and artefacts, they have shown us how to live. However, these two cultural contributions are not in balance: while middle-class individuals produce great works, the working class contributes only generally.

In an essay written shortly after, Williams addresses the difficulty from another angle: 'We use the word culture in these two senses: to mean a whole way of life – the common meanings; to mean the arts and learning – the special processes of discovery and creative effort' (MacKenzie, pp. 75–6). But this formulation uses the opposition between the 'common' and the 'creative' that Williams needs to avoid, and because 'the special processes of discovery and creative effort' sound individualistic, specially when opposed to 'common', the distinction seems to correlate with the two class cultures: workers have a whole way of life and middle-class people the special creative processes. So these two ways of using the word 'culture' reinforce class hierarchy. This, I think, is unavoidable while the notion of 'the arts', more or less as defined in dissident middle-class culture, is retained. And generally it was retained on the left, and still is.

It is not merely, as Terry Eagleton has said, that the Marxist tradition was weakened in the 1950s (*Criticism*, pp. 23–7, 34). The idea that high culture transcends material conditions, such as class, has a good socialist lineage. As Williams noticed (anticipating later work), Marx fell over himself trying to explain the continuing appeal of Greek art and literature.[20] Trotsky doesn't suggest that we should understand art in any distinctively socialist way; he says it has made us more complex and flexible, and can nourish and educate our feelings. If we repudiated it, 'we should at once become poorer spiritually' (pp. 305–13). The Communist Party in the 1950s promoted Britishness and good culture as against the imperialist inroads of a debased US commercial culture. The Party literary journal *Arena* stated its belief in 'human values' and 'the artist's prophetic function', and lamented the undermining of national cultural standards by existentialism and Hollywood (Taylor, J., p. 31). Sam Aaronovitch, fulltime Party-worker on cultural matters, said there is 'a British cultural heritage which we Communists should unite to defend along with millions of people of the most varied political and social opinions.' It included Chaucer, Shakespeare, Milton, Fielding, Blake, Burns, Shelley, Byron, Dickens, Morris, Hardy, Lewis Grassic Gibbon and Shaw. All this was under threat from the capitalist culture of the United States, which was different from the true US people's culture of Emerson, Whitman, Dreiser, Paul Robeson and Howard Fast; the Party orchestrated a campaign against 'horror' comics (Barker, *Haunt*, ch. 3).

These attitudes I call 'left-culturism'. They were quite compatible with the approach of Matthew Arnold and F. R. Leavis, which in schools and colleges was helping to ratify class mobility by entangling it with the acquisition of a superior culture. They were fundamentally those of middle-class dissidence, and were virtually unquestioned by the New Left. Lindsay Anderson declared: 'By his nature, the artist will always be in conflict with the false, the narrow-minded and the reactionary.' Stuart Hall wrote in *Encore* in 1959: 'The political intellectual is concerned with the institutional life of the society: the creative artist with the attitudes, the manners, the moral and emotional life which the individual consummates within that social framework.' Wesker saw it as an essential part of socialism that art gives 'people the feeling that they are part of a whole group, which is humanity'.[21] Such statements strive to politicize art; their vagueness indicates that it was not easy.

The appeal of left-culturism was basically fourfold. First, it amplified the ideology of welfare-capitalism announced in the 1940s: that everyone should have opportunity to share the good things that the upper classes had customarily enjoyed. These included economic security, education, health-care, decent housing – and 'good' culture. Mechanisms designed to achieve the last named were in place by 1950: the Arts Council, the 1944 Education Act, the BBC (including the Third Programme), local authority responsibility for the arts. In effect, new-left cultural policy was a demand that the implied promise of welfare-capitalism be fulfilled. And this was parallel to concurrent demands from Richard Titmuss, Peter Townsend, Brian Abel-Smith and the Robbins Report about social security, health-care, housing and education. Williams's endorsement of co-operation as against individualism has the same drift: more welfare, less capitalism.

Second, there was a particular appeal for those who were class-mobile through education. In Britain, to advance in educational and occupational terms was, is, normally to be drawn into some kind of middle-class culture. If the choice was between the Schlegels and the Wilcoxes; between *Lady Chatterley's Lover* and the prosecuting counsel who asked the jury if they would allow their servants to read the book (Rolph, p. 17); between Jackson and Marsden and the mean-minded aspirants they wrote about; then the former seemed humane, responsible, anti-establishment, even socialist.

More specifically, writers and humanities students were drawn into the orbit of F. R. Leavis and *Scrutiny*, where a claim for a serious high culture, independent of the leisured elite, had long been made. Simon Raven remarked in 1955; 'Dr Leavis' adherents are largely state-aided young men who cannot afford a claret and Peacock approach to literature. They come from poor homes where books are a luxury and must be taken seriously.'[22] And in so far as left-culturism claimed that 'good' culture should be for everyone, adherents were not deserting their class but leading the way into a fuller humanity. Many tried to go back and bring the others along too, especially through teaching. Hoggart, Williams and Thompson had all been working in adult education. Wesker's *Roots* became a popular school text because it witnessed to the cultural development of the lower-class Beatie. In so far as this is made to occur, at the end, individually and spontaneously, the play supports the 'progressive' view that the student needs only the right encouragement to reveal her or his personal sensitivity.

Third, left-culturism contributed to the repudiation of Stalinism, for literature and the arts were believed to involve both personal experience and an essential humanity. Stalinism was seen as hostile to those values, both generally and by giving priority to economic determinants in its cultural theory (though actually Stalin was knowledgeable and enthusiastic about literature). Williams and Thompson argued that cultural, social and economic activities should be studied together, in their interrelations, without giving priority to one factor.[23] Christopher Hill says he began studying the seventeenth century because T. S. Eliot got him interested in the metaphysical poets (Kaye, p. 101); Hill's *Puritanism and Revolution* (1958) includes essays on Andrew Marvell and Samuel Richardson.

Left discourse invoked literature all the time. In 'Outside the Whale', for instance, to identify the ideology of Natopolis, Thompson returned to Wordsworth and the French Revolution, reviewed the writing of Auden and Orwell, and deprecated the influence of T. S. Eliot and *Lord of the Flies* (in *Poverty*). Left-inclined social sciences aspired to the condition of literature. Studies in the Fabian tradition of intervention in social policy, especially from the Institute for Community Studies, dwelt upon personal experience in the way that novels were understood to do. Richard Crossman, reviewing Peter Townsend's *The Family Life of Old People* (1957) in the *New Statesman*, enthused: 'A novelist's eye for detail and power of description is nicely balanced by a passion for scientific analysis.' Townsend said his experience of old people in the East End produced 'a deeper respect for people like Charles Booth and Mayhew and also for D. H. Lawrence and George Orwell'.[24]

Fourth, left-culturism addressed two perceived political failures: the absolute failure of the proletarian revolution in the West, and the relative failure of welfare-capitalism. The revolution hadn't occurred in advanced industrial societies, and the apparent economic and ideological success of welfare-capitalism made it seem no longer likely. The substantial case for socialism had been that capitalism doesn't work – it produces extremes of income and is subject to periodic slumps in which even the wealthy suffer. But the postwar boom seemed to show that the trade cycle could be controlled through Keynesian demand management, people rendered happy through consumption, and the poor cared for by the welfare apparatus. At the same time, there was not the spirit that should accompany socialism. The very processes that made welfare-capitalism effective – mass production, consumerism, advertising – seemed to be 'what D. H. Lawrence described as "anti-life" '.[25] The revolution hadn't occurred because the fundamental oppression of working people was being obscured, and affluence was destroying their dignity and resistance. It all seemed a failure at the level of culture.

The State and the Left

Most left-culturists believed that commerce was the problem and state funding the answer. In *The Long Revolution* Williams argues for more purposeful state education so that people can make responsible choices, and for public ownership to place the cultural aparatus into 'responsible hands' (pp. 363–75). In *Communications* (ch. 5) he develops these proposals, demanding education in cultural discrimination, a series of public authorities to regulate and intervene in the distribution of culture, and public money to hold cultural institutions in trust for the cultural workers who will know best how to use them.

Williams initiated here a whole phase of work on culture, including the present study. But two aspects of his early programme may still give us pause. One is the extent to which control is to be exercised by 'qualified' professionals – artists, writers, broadcasters and film-makers, and expert panels. This chimes in very well with the concerns of the meritocratic, displaced, dissident intelligentsia, and I shall argue in Chapter 12 that what was actually produced was a new-left subculture, by and for that class fraction.

The other problem, we may now see, is the belief that the state will shield us from capital. That is surely improbable. Frank Parkin identifies the state as the institutional embodiment of the industrial, legal, educational and political sectors of society, with the distinctive function of mobilizing collective force in defence of those institutions (*Class*, pp. 26–8). As such, it is obviously committed to the prevailing power arrangements. The issue is fundamental, for it affects the implied balance between the state and capital in welfare-capitalism (to which I return in Chapter 13). Within the Labour Party, Harold Laski had argued after the collapse of the Labour Government in 1931 that the state could not be neutral in a society founded on class relations. In a phase of expansion it might be tolerant, but in crisis 'all the gifts of political and social reform were called into question' and the interpretation of the unwritten constitution was likely to be 'strict and authoritarian'.[26] During the relative affluence of the 1950s and 1960s it was easy to forget all that, as Williams subsequently observed:

> Not only was there an extraordinary blindness to the coercive powers of the state, but there was even a kind of complicity with it, in that no clear distinction was ever made on the left between the notion of public power and the organisation of the capitalist state, or indeed of any possible state. Thus the major transfer of further kinds of power to an increasingly centralised state after the war was partly a function of the needs of the capitalist system itself, but it was partly also the realisation of the programme of the British left. (*Politics*, p. 416)

The hopes of the New Left were soon tested. There are moments when 'the whole basis of political leadership and cultural authority becomes exposed and contested' (Hall, Critcher et al., p. 217); at such moments, as E. P. Thompson observes, significant political change might be introduced with general enthusiasm, or at least consent (at other times, the main task is to prepare so that opportunities won't be wasted).[27] 1945 was such a moment, and so, in my view, were the early 1960s; the ferment of the late 1960s, represented in the idea of 1968, resulted from the failure of legitimate institutions to respond to the opportunity of 1964. This was a turning point for British social democracy.

The last years of the Macmillan-Home Conservative administration (1959–64) were accompanied by increasing impatience, especially among younger people. The dissident mood associated specifically with intellectuals and the New Left spread outwards. The economy, notoriously, was growing at only about half the rate attained in West Germany and Japan, and the government was resorting to 'stop-go' (cautious expansion cut back when it threatened a balance of payments deficit and the exchange rate). There seemed to be new social problems – a rising crime rate, juvenile delinquency, racial discrimination; and too many strikes. And the sufficiency of welfare provision, the fairness of the education system, and the 'quality of life' were under question. Michael Shanks's *The Stagnant Society* (1961) initiated a sequence of 'What's Wrong' books (Booker, pp. 153–60).

At the same time, it was felt that things might be improved – the other precondition for a positive attitude towards change. Despite anxiety about the economy, most people were in work and manifestly better off (and from a low base – it made more difference to get an inside lavatory than to get a video-recorder). New opportunities seemed to be opening up, in education, occupations, cultural choice, personal relationships, holidays. Hugh Carleton Greene, Director-General of the BBC from 1960 to 1969, said he 'wanted to open the windows and dissipate the ivory-tower stuffiness' (Hewison, *Too*, p. 26). And the 'natural' authority of the Tory Party was undermined by scandals and incompetence.[28] *Beyond the Fringe* was followed by satirical television programmes and the magazine *Private Eye*. These were often frivolous, but they were exuberant and irreverent, and indicated that there was a constituency for change. *That Was The Week That Was*, in a sketch looking back over the year 1962, summed it up as 'a year in which principles went by the board. A year of incompetence. A year of mendacity. A year of lying.'[29] Such treatment marked a decisive decline in the respect accorded the official political system.

The extent of public readiness to reconsider established alignments was apparent in October 1962 when the United States threatened the Soviet Union with nuclear war over missile bases in Cuba (which the Soviets thought only comparable with those in Greece and Turkey). The stance of the Soviet leadership and the efforts of CND were making Cold-War ideology less persuasive, and only the Beaverbrook newspapers clearly supported the United States. A public opinion poll a fortnight after, asking with whom 'on the whole Britain should side', produced 47 per cent for the United States, 1 per cent for the Soviet Union, and 44 per cent for neither. The *Daily Telegraph* suppressed the poll.[30]

The New Left allowed its hopes to be raised by the campaign of the Labour Party, led by Harold Wilson, for the 1964 election; CND declined as people looked towards the possibility of an effective parliamentary politics. 'Paradoxically, this difficult and chaotic situation is far more promising than the earnest hope of 1945', Tom Nairn believed, partly because 'great sections of the intelligentsia once buried entirely in the tribal rites of Oxford or literary London have responded to the critical plight of British society.'[31] Labour won with a tiny majority, and this allowed it the benefit of the doubt until the election of 1966, despite its support for US bombing of North Vietnam, immigration legislation, the conservative assumptions of the National Plan, a series of nibbling deflations, and the shelving of steel nationalization (Foot, ch. 9). The White Paper on the Arts of 1964 was cautiously endorsed by Williams; Arts Council budgets were boosted (from £3.2 million in 1964–5 to £9.3 million in 1970–1); and the Open University was founded. However, by May 1967 Williams was thoroughly disenchanted – Harold Wilson encouraging Lord Thomson to take over more newspapers was the last straw.[32] *May Day Manifesto* (1967; edited initially by Williams, Thompson and Stuart Hall) signalled the disillusionment of the left-intelligentsia. However, a younger generation, not overshadowed by Stalinism, had already begun a new investigation of Marxist theory.

The failure of the Wilson administration to respond to the opportunity for significant change derived partly from its roots in 1950s rebelliousness. Like 'Angry' writing, Wilson presented 'the effete establishment' as the problem: 'We are living in the jet age but we are governed by an Edwardian establishment mentality' (Wilson, H., p. 9). This took up the mood of the time, but did not move it on towards radical analysis or change. Paul Foot identifies 'no more than a meritocrat's irritation with an incompetent and amateur aristocracy: the cry of the scholarship boy angrily knocking at the bolted door of the bourgeoisie' (pp. 327–9). The major question that remains is: how much more was possible? Williams records in *Politics and Letters* how it had been assumed that 'a Labour government with a strong majority would be able to overcome the limitations of social-democratic parliamentarianism.' 1945–51 didn't count because of special circumstances after the war, but 1966 was conclusive – 'It was to do with the whole character of the party machine and the nature of the capitalist state' (pp. 414–5). Paul Foot observes that when social democratic governments seem likely to achieve reform they are stopped: in Austria in 1934, Spain in 1936, Greece in 1967 (pp. 338–9); and since he wrote, add Chile and Australia. It has been alleged that British secret service agents conspired to undermine the Wilson government in the 1970s.

The point was taken in the spate of extra-parliamentary activity that we associate with 1968 – industrial disputes, student disturbances, squatters and claimants' organizations, demonstrations against the Vietnam War. Even so, looking back, I would remark less the degree of disaffection than the persisting trust in the system. When you pushed and shoved to break through the police cordon in front of the US Embassy, what was the purpose? Suppose you had reached the building, what would you have done: scratched at the walls with your fingers? The underlying assumption still, for most people, was that if you made enough fuss they would take notice (like a child with kind parents). In effect, there was a persisting faith in social democracy, a belief that the state would respond to just demands once they were sufficiently urgently expressed. I pursue such topics in chapter 13.

For all this, left-culturism was far from ineffectual. It gained a powerful position in the academic and professional social sciences and humanities; all kinds of contributions became best-sellers. Its attitudes filtered into the education system, and key texts went rapidly onto secondary-school syllabuses and stayed there. Left-culturism helped to modernize and hence sustain the public-service concept of broadcasting in Britain: the Pilkington Committee, considering how to deploy a third TV channel, came under the influence of Hoggart and sharply criticized commercial television. So strong did the case appear that the Conservative Government set up BBC 2; it began broadcasting in 1964 (the same year as the off-shore pirate station Caroline).

The significance of *Look Back in Anger* and the Royal Court was partly institutional: the principle that the state should finance 'good' culture was reinforced and extended, specially in theatre. Fifteen theatres were built across the country between 1958 and 1970, all with public money; the National Theatre began work in 1963 and the South Bank complex was designed to house it. The Royal Shakespeare Company's trajectory is exemplary. Until 1960 it mounted a brief, self-financing season of Shakespeare at Stratford. Under Peter Hall it took over the Aldwych Theatre in London to produce Royal-Court-type work, made a large loss, and challenged the Arts Council to let the venture die. Already left-culturism was strong enough to prevent that. So RSC subsidy was doubled and redoubled through the 1960s and (as I have shown elsewhere) the company claimed well into the 1970s to be pursuing a 'radical' policy, while actually effecting a compromise between traditional and new-left notions of 'good' culture.[33]

The left-liberal intelligentsia achieved a brief ascendancy and established its claim to define 'good' culture. It made a distinctive attempt to hold welfare-capitalism to its promises, and set the agenda that is now disputed by the Thatcher Government (see Chapter 13). Its programme is still reiterated by left-wing cultural workers. Steve Gooch of the Half

Moon Theatre, for instance, called in 1984 for 'the abolition of the market-place and the instant return of its culture to the population as a whole', asserting, 'subsidy is therefore not just a piecemeal necessity but an across-the-board prerequisite of any genuine culture' (Gooch, pp. 69–70).

However, the assumption on the left that 'good' culture is likely to be that funded by the public sector has distorted attempts to produce radical cultural work. Certainly the state may behave benignly in some of its aspects for some of the time, but so may private capital. Both state or market institutions may, in appropriate circumstances, be bent to radical purposes. But when under pressure, both are likely to succumb. In the early 1980s the Greater London Council pursued a socialist cultural policy, and the government abolished it. Williams's instance, in 1962, of a good state institution was the University Grants Committee (*Communications*, pp. 155–6); in the 1980s it became the agent for a politically motivated assault on the intellectual, financial and institutional integrity of higher education and then was abolished. Trevor Griffith's play *Oi For England* (1982), about a punk band and race riots, found diverse sponsors and venues and diverse audiences and responses: it was produced first on commercial television, then in youth clubs, then at the Royal Court (perhaps at the last, though, it reached its proper left-culturist abode).[34]

Conversely, what was ignored almost entirely on the left, until the Rock Against Racism movement of 1976–81,[35] was the possibility of working with – politicizing – actual popular cultures, 'commercial' though they are. The idea, always, was to replace them with 'good' culture. It was a historic missed opportunity.

Notes

1 Quoted in Sussex, p. 32; see Hewison, *In Anger*, pp. 150–5; Laing, pp. 112–16.

2 Morrison, p. 58. See also George Scott, in Feldman and Gartenberg, p. 246; Morrison, pp. 55–9; pp. 79–80, 184 above.

3 Ritchie, H., pp. 72, 66–74 and ch. 5; Tynan, p. 177; Sinfield, *Society*, p. 177.

4 On the establishment, see Thomas; Hewison, *In Anger*, p. 166–74.

5 Hopkins, pp. 157–60; Parkin, *Class*, pp. 49 and 49–60; Fyvel, *Intellectuals*, p. 54; Heath, *Social*, pp. 75–7; pp. 53–7 above.

6 Potter, *Stand*, p. 97. On Potter returning to this theme, see *Glittering*, pp. 71–2 and ch. 5; and Laing, pp. 166–7. Osborne's *A Patriot For Me* (1965) is also

about this, despite the play's remote setting. Related texts are discussed in Chapter 12.

7 Parkin, *Class*, p. 56; Laing, pp. 24–5; Halsey, p. 184; Jackson and Marsden, ch. 1.

8 Parkin, *Middle*, pp. 170–1. Parkin attributes the radicalism of late 1950s intellectuals to awareness 'of class pressures and status distinctions, arising from their exposure to two different value systems' (*Middle*, p. 102). Cf. Potter, *Glittering*, pp. 79–80, 88–9, 95–103.

9 In Thompson, *Poverty*, p. 11. Cf. Amis, 'Socialism and the Intellectuals', in Feldman and Gartenberg; and chapter 6 above.

10 p. 102. See also Lessing in Maschler; Taylor, J., introduction; John Berger, *A Painter of Our Time* (1958); Margot Heinemann, *The Adventurers* (1959), pp. 302–19; David Mercer, *The Birth of a Private Man* (1963); Edward Upward, *The Spiral Ascent* (1977).

11 Thompson, *Out*, p. 308. See Thompson, *William Morris* (1955) and *Making* (1963); Christopher Hill, *Puritanism and Revolution* (1958), especially on the Norman Yoke; Eric Hobsbawm, *Labouring Men* (1964) and, with George Rudé, *Captain Swing* (1969); Rodney Hilton and H. Fagan, *The English Rising of 1381* (1950). Not all these historians left the Party, but they shared an independent attitude to it; see Hobsbawm. On this history, see Kaye; Johnson, 'Culture and the Historians', in Clarke et al.; Samuel, *People's*, pp. xv–xxxix. Also, there was a shift away from collective discipline, leading to the long-term dispersal of the radical left (Samuel, 'Lost', 'Staying').

12 'Festival', in Sissons and French, p. 331. See Donnison; Inglis, ch. 7; Wilson, A., *Such*; Thompson, *Poverty*, pp. 1–2; Lessing, *Each*.

13 Russell, B., *Has Man*, p. 121; Barthes, pp. 137–42.

14 'Peculiarities', in *Poverty*, p. 68. See Driver, pp. 78–82; Foote, pp. 293–6; Robert Taylor, 'The Campaign for Nuclear Disarmament', in Bogdanor and Skidelsky; Anderson, 'The Left', pp. 10–13.

15 Parkin, *Middle*, pp. 17, 39–44, 166–74; Driver, p. 60.

16 Quoted in Ritchie, H., p. 209; for another instance, see Allsop, p. 129; and Hartley, p. 49.

17 See, for instance, A. S. Byatt, 'Insights *ad nauseam*', *Times Literary Supplement*, 14 November 1986, p. 1274 (reviewing Sinfield, *Alfred Tennyson*).

18 Anderson, 'Problems', in Anderson and Blackburn, p. 287; 'The Left', p. 17; 'Components of the National Culture', in Cockburn and Blackburn, pp. 268–77. See also Barnett; and, in Samuel, *People's*: Richard Johnson, 'Against Absolutism' and E. P. Thompson, 'The Politics of Theory'.

19 Critics have argued that Williams traps himself by the selection he makes. See Thompson's review of *Long Revolution, New Left Review*, nos. 9 and 10, May–June and July–August 1961; Eagleton, *Criticism*, pp. 25–6. See also

Richard Johnson, 'Three Problematics', in Clarke et al., pp. 214–19; Peter Sedgwick in Widgery, *Left*, p. 137.

20 In *Culture and Society* Williams speaks shrewdly of Marx's comments on literature as 'those of a learned, intelligent man of his period' (p. 258); cf. Williams, *Marxism*, p. 52. See Eagleton, *Marxism*, pp. 10–13.

21 Anderson, 'Get Out and Push', in Maschler, pp. 177–8; Hall quoted by Hewison, *In Anger*, p. 181; Wesker interviewed in Marowitz and Trussler, p. 88.

22 Quoted in Ritchie, H., p. 110. See Mulhern, pp. 318–23; p. 184 above.

23 Williams, *Long*, p. 62; Thompson, *Making*, 1963, p. 213; see Abelove et al., p. 7; Kaye, ch. 6. However, Thompson complained that Williams had scanted concepts like 'ideology' and 'mode of production' ('The Politics of Theory', in Samuel, *People's*). On Stalin, see Snow, *Variety*, pp. 172–4.

24 Townsend, 'A Society for People', in MacKenzie, p. 108. Crossman's review is quoted on the Pelican cover of Townsend's book, 2nd edn, 1963. See also Young and Willmott; Jackson and Marsden; Klein, J.; Frankenberg. On the genre, see Platt; Chas Critcher, 'Sociology, Cultural Studies and the Post-war Working Class', in Clarke et al.; Laing, ch. 2. In *Border Country* and *Second Generation*, Williams has scholars abandon their research because it is too removed from experience.

25 Hoggart, p. 340. Critcher remarks the crisis 'of a group of social-democratic intellectuals faced with the contention that capitalism works' ('Sociology', in Clarke et al., pp. 15–16).

26 Foote, pp. 154–9. See Held, in McLennan et al., pp. 352–61; Panitch, 'Development', pp. 124–6; Wright, ch. 5; Leys, ch. 12; Hall, Critcher et al., pp. 201–6.

27 Thompson, 'Peculiarities', in *Poverty*, p. 67.

28 Levin, B., chs. 2–5; Booker, chs. 6–8.

29 Cardiff and Scannel, p. 170; see Booker, pp. 46, 171–2, 180, 187, 215–16, 219, 265–6, 199–200; Hewison, *Too*, pp. 27–30, 34–5.

30 Mander, *Great*, ch. 2; Driver, p. 142. On readiness for change, see Ryder and Silver, pp. 280–8; McKie and Cook, pp. 2–3.

31 In Anderson and Blackburn: Nairn, 'The Nature of the Labour Party', pp. 212–13; and 214–17; Williams, 'Towards a Socialist Society', p. 368. See Williams, R., *Politics*, pp. 366–7. However, Peter Sedgwick, from a Trotskyist point of view, attacked the New Left's collaboration with meritocratic ideas and its socio-cultural preoccupations ('The Two New Lefts', Widgery, *Left*, pp. 138–9).

32 *Communications*, appendix B and postscript; *Politics*, pp. 369–71.

33 See Dollimore and Sinfield, ch. 9. RSC subsidy went from £5,000 in 1961 to £57,000 in 1963, £152,000 in 1966, £205,500 in 1967 and £280,670 in 1970; in 1965 the Barbican complex was planned (Sinfield, *Society*, pp. 189–95;

Addenbrooke). See also Hewison, *In Anger*, p. 55; Stuart Laing, 'The Production of Literature', in Sinfield, *Society*, pp. 138, 141–4; Hutchison.

34 Sinfield, 'Culture'. For the collapse of an attempt by Jonathan Dollimore and myself to edit a 'Cultural Politics' series with Manchester University Press, see 'University Press Blocks Gay Book', *New Statesman*, 12 August 1988, p. 7.

35 Widgery, *Beating*. See Kipnis, pp. 33–4; Hall, 'Notes on Deconstructing "the Popular" ', in Samuel, *People's*, p. 239.

12
Intellectuals and workers

What About The Workers?

Stuart Laing has shown in his *Representations of Working-class Life, 1957–1964* the preoccupation with working-class culture at this date. Through every medium and discourse – novels, plays, autobiography, sociology, political analysis, film – it was suddenly vital, especially on the left, to write about the working class. These representations constitute rival attempts to interpret political and cultural possibilities. In respect of political analysis, if the working class could credibly be shown as retaining a valid culture and political consciousness, then the original Marxian show could still take the road. If, however, working people seemed content, affluent, and rescued from the horrors of the industrial revolution and the depression by wise consensual political management, there was no call for 'more socialism'.

There were reassertions of working-class political consciousness, but they were largely overwhelmed by claims that the class struggle was, or should be, over. On the right of the Labour Party it seemed (not for the first time) that a rethink was required if its leaders were to enjoy the satisfactions of office. In *The Future of Socialism* (1956) Anthony Crosland proclaimed that adequate social change was well on the way already:

> Traditional socialism was largely concerned with the evils of traditional capitalism, and with the need for its overthrow. But today traditional capitalism has been reformed and modified almost out of existence. . . . Instead of glaring and conspicuous evils, squalor and injustice and distressed areas, we have to fuss

about the balance of payments, and incentives, and higher productivity; and the socialist finds himself pinioned by a new and unforeseen reality. (pp. 97, 99)

Crosland's idea of socialism was the spread of affluence and the decline of evident class distinctions. Therefore he thought the United States the example of a society that was attaining a good attitude to social equality. This was not because there was 'a more equal distribution of incomes' or more 'vertical mobility', but because 'Americans *believe* in the "office-boy to president" mythology' (pp. 251–2). The italics are Crosland's: they betray his wish not for social justice, but for *the popular belief that it is occurring*; in other words, for a people governable by benevolent technocrats.

In 'The Transition from Capitalism', in Richard Crossman's *New Fabian Essays* (1952), Crosland showed this more starkly:

The feeling among workers of an eternal and irreconcilable conflict between wages and profits, capital and labour: their feeling too of non-participation in the control of the firm for which they work, and so of non-responsibility for its well-being: the acute sense of class that goes with different accents: the knowledge that differentials in education mean differentials in opportunity – these are all signs that Britain still is, and feels itself to be, a class society.

The purpose of socialism is quite simply to eradicate this sense of class, and to create in its place a sense of common interest and equal status. This will require not only more measures on the economic plane, directed to the greater equalisation of living standards and opportunities, but also measures on the socio-psychological plane. (p. 62)

The problem, according to Crosland's first sentence here, is the 'feeling' that workers have – about conflict between capital and labour, about non-participation, about class, about educational opportunities. Crosland cannot allow that these feelings might derive from fundamental injustice, since he denies that this occurs any more. But they are a nuisance, so 'the purpose of socialism' is to change them – 'to eradicate this sense of class'. And that will require not just economic 'measures' (measured measures, no doubt), but also measures on 'the socio-psychological plane'. In other words, we must be persuaded that our 'sense' of inequality is mistaken, and adopt a genial myth like that attributed to US people.

It became general wisdom that as the working classes were better paid they took on a middle-class outlook and lost political militancy. Commentators wrote of the 'affluent worker' and his 'embourgeoisement'. Hugh Gaitskell believed: 'The changing character of labour, full employment, new housing, the new way of life based on the telly, the frig., the car and the glossy magazine – all have their effect on our political strength.'[1] So the Labour Party leadership set out to produce a new 'image' (as the advertisers began to say).

The New Left mounted some resistance. Leon Rosselson parodied the attitude to the tune of 'The Red Flag' (which the Labour leadership has to sing once a year at Conference):

> The cloth cap and the working class
> As images are dated
> For we are Labour's avant-garde
> And we were educated.
> By tax adjustments we have planned
> To institute the promised land.
> And just to show we're still sincere
> We sing *The Red Flag* once a year.
>
> (Collins et al., p. 44)

In *Chips with Everything* (1962) Wesker showed air-force conscripts led into resistance by the upper-class Thompson, but his revolt collapses when his 'motive is discovered':

Power. Power, isn't it? Among your own people there were too many who were powerful, the competition was too great, but here, among lesser men – here among the yobs, among the good-natured yobs, you could be king. KING. Supreme and all powerful, eh? Well? Not true? Deny it – deny it, then. We know – you and I – we know, Thompson. (p. 63)

This might well be the upper-class leadership of the Labour Party. Wesker's conscripts do achieve a spontaneous revolt, inspired by the illtreatment of one of their number, but it is defused with the help of Thompson, now to be an officer. He has learnt the kind of management of people that is appropriate for modern times (p. 70).

The New Left was both reluctant and ready to believe the Crosland – Gaitskell story – I showed in Chapter 11 the importance it attached to 'good' culture ('left-culturism'). Potter, in *The Glittering Coffin*, warns of the need to avoid contempt for working people – 'they are not the morons described so contemptuously by advertising agent Mark Abrams' (Abrams was to be commissioned to run Wilson's 1964 election campaign). But on the next page Potter writes of 'the dull and listless vacuity of so much leisure activity, and the absence of roots stretched into any form of reality or regional identity' (pp. 47–8).

The agenda was set by Hoggart in *The Uses of Literacy* (1957). His argument is 'that we are moving towards the creation of a mass culture; that the remnants of what was at least in parts an urban culture "of the people" are being destroyed; and that the new mass culture is in some important ways less healthy than the often crude culture it is replacing' (p. 24). The deficiencies in Hoggart's account have been much discussed. One is that despite his claims for working-class culture, he makes it all sound narrow, conformist and quiescent. Summarizing what remains, he finds marriage and the home, tolerance, the personal, scepticism and nonconformity, a fundamental ethical rudder, the ability to keep on 'putting up with things', cheerfulness and self-respect (pp. 324–5). Perhaps that was right. After all, events had been discouraging – the industrial revolution, poverty and powerlessness, the 1914–18 war, the failure to realize socialism or even significant trades unionism, unemployment and then the war of 1939–45. That a more resistant subordinate culture is feasible in modern society may now be inferred from recent development (such as roots reggae music on illegal radio stations) among ethnic and sexual minorities.[2]

At the same time, Hoggart almost certainly underestimates elements of organized and maverick resistance, critical analysis and strategic adjustment. He admits that he has not discussed the 'earnest minority' (pp. 319–21), and this slants the whole project. Also, there is a great deal about home and almost nothing about work – because young Richard didn't see the work situation, he got educated instead. This crucially skews the political implications, for it is at work that most explicit working-class politics takes place (the same effect occurs in *1984*). Finally, Hoggart leaves unresolved the question about the strength of the cultural resources with which the working class may resist consumer capitalism. It is uncertain when he is talking about currently active virtues and when he is lamenting the past – he appeals to his own experience, but that was mainly before 1939 (he was born in 1918). The outcome is a running ambiguity about how far the rot has gone.

A key issue in much of this work was taken to be 'community'. In the early 1960s Josephine Klein and Ronald Frankenberg reviewed a sequence of studies sharing this preoccupation. Klein boldly disputed the virtues of community (I, chs. 1–5). But Frankenberg, more convention-ally, adapted Marxist terminology to Merton's functionalist approach and argued that decay of community produces 'alienation' – not from the product of one's labour, but from 'cultural goals' (pp. 276–8). And this, Frankenberg believed, explains deviance, delinquency and anomie. Among conservatives, anxiety about community amounted to anxiety that the ideology of welfare-capitalism was failing to produce working-class commitment to 'good' values. For community may help to keep people static and inward-looking. Perry Anderson argued that the qualities discovered by Hoggart, and indeed Williams, were the problem rather than the solution: 'It is, precisely, the entrenched, immobile, corporate, class-consciousness of the English working class – a world steeped in precedent and tradition and archaism, that mimics the traditionalism of the whole society.'[3]

For left-culturists, preoccupation with community could amount to a justification of their activity. Lindsay Anderson wrote, in respect of his film about the people of Covent Garden: 'Those good and friendly faces deserve a place of pride on the screens of their country; and I will fight for the notion of community which will give it to them' (Maschler, p. 177). Community, in this version, requires the New-Left intellectual to conceive and bestow it on the workers.

Most work in this vein – social studies by Willmott and Young, plays by Wesker and Shelagh Delaney, novels such as *Weekend in Dinlock* and *A Kind of Loving*; the films based on all that, and so through to 'Coronation Street' and the television plays of Potter and David Mercer – represents working-class culture either negatively or as quiescent; or, if positively, as something that is being lost. Williams's analysis, which I discuss later, was the most intricate. Socio-linguistics contributed: from 1958 Basil Bernstein developed the idea that middle-class children were socialized into an 'elaborated' language, working-class children into a 'restricted' one. Bernstein was upset when critics said the restricted code implied a humiliating uniformity, obscuring the diversity and imaginative potential of cultural forms (Bernstein, p. 19 and *passim*): he had run into the culturist debate.

Women were stereotyped around the traditional image of 'Mother', which, according to Hoggart, 'can make the most unpromising and unprepossessing young woman arrive at a middle-age in which she is, when in the midst of her home and family, splendidly "there" and, under all the troubles, content' (p. 50). Alternatively, women were supposed to be moving into a new, genial middle-class partnership in marriage.[4] Sarah Kahn in Wesker's *Chicken Soup* is the bearer of socialist values – to her they overlap with the woman's role as provider of food and drink. Only Beatie in Wesker's *Roots*, in the writing that came to prominence, shows signs of breaking out of the roles conventionally proposed for working-class women.

Vigour and intelligence were sometimes shown in working-class culture, but less often. Williams's *Second Generation* (1964) includes a strike in a car factory, though it ends in defeat. The educated young man suggests that the workers 'won't see' how they are exploited. But his shop steward father replies: 'See it? They see it all right. But what's the use of seeing it? All they see's where the power is, and they curse and accept it. They have to go where the money comes from, and anything else is just silly bloody talk' (p. 330). In this view people were not so much deluded by affluence as coerced by the ancient methods.

Alan Sillitoe's *Saturday Night and Sunday Morning* (1958) finds an anarchic vitality in the outlook of young Arthur Seaton and people in his neighbourhood. To be sure, there have been improvements in material life-style, including television, but Arthur retains a spontaneous suspicion of everything official. However, along with this goes distrust of any kind of political organization, and it is unclear how far we are to envisage Arthur's marriage at the end as defusing his rebellion. Also, as in Hoggart, there is a blurring of the present with an earlier date (the 1940s),[5] and this too makes it hard to see what scope is proposed for current working-class attitudes. In *The Loneliness of the Long-Distance Runner* (1959) the rebellion is individual and anarchic. More damagingly, it takes on standard aspects of 1950s writing. Individual psychological motivation (the death of Smith's father) is supplied; and there are hints of an existential revolt ('as far as I was concerned this feeling was the only honesty and realness there was in the world'; p. 39). Both tend to make Smith's rebellion less political.

Margot Heinemann's novel *The Adventurers* (1959) reasserts the cultural and political vigour of the working class; but the author derived from an earlier, Marxian generation. There is community in the Welsh mining valley and the final scene affirms it with a party, but this is not the book's preoccupation. On the contrary, we repeatedly see people disagreeing – about how far they should compromise their rights to support the war effort or the Labour Government, how far they should settle for minor improvements or fight for really decent conditions, whom they should support in union elections. They are reasonable people with specific concerns: community is a place where people work out difference. Militancy depends on activists, some of them communists, some middle-class: pit closures are successfully resisted, despite the sluggishness of the local Labour Party and the national union, because activists stimulate understanding and feeling and make their case convincingly. The miners respect effective leadership; without it they may be influenced by industrialists, management, the media and complicit unionists. There is no simple recipe: new techniques of 'efficiency' may prove as inhuman as the old coal-owners, the wrong man is elected to national office because of media intervention, and the TUC Conference is undemocratic. However, at the end it is probable that a good regional leader will be elected: the struggle continues. This is the most positive and astute representation of working people that I have seen in the period; it is rarely discussed.

New-Left Subculture

New-Left intellectuals, of diverse origins, tended not to share the working-class culture that preoccupied them. Even writers who were not explicitly separated from a working class background by education and occupation were separated from it by virtue of their writing. Wesker, Delaney and Sillitoe are instances. In Clancy Sigal's *Weekend in Dinlock* the miner Davie cannot work as an artist without leaving the pit village and its way of life. For whatever the writer's background or allegiance, she or he is called upon to reach some accommodation with the current conception of what it is to be a writer – partly because it is difficult to think of yourself *as* a writer otherwise, partly because the institutions that mediate writing to publics require it.[6]

This effect was enhanced in the 1950s as it became easier for people from lower-class backgrounds to gain public recognition. Sillitoe, writing in 1959, includes as 1950s 'proletarian' writers Osborne, Delaney, Kops, Selvon, Braine and himself. He is apparently pleased that 'the proletarian novel' is evolving from 'a wail of the underprivileged ... into a solid branch of literary art', but regrets that it is 'read mostly by a middle-class audience' ('Proletarian'). He seems not to notice a connection between the two tendencies.

Sillitoe registers the issue in his fiction. As Stuart Laing observes, the narrative point of view of *Saturday Night and Sunday Morning* wanders, because Sillitoe cannot settle upon how much to attribute to Arthur Seaton's consciousness. It is the difficulty (Sillitoe says) of how 'to write a book about a man who has never read a book' (Laing, pp. 69–70). *The Loneliness of the Long-distance Runner* is written from the point of view of Smith, but seeks to account for this by having him remark that he's read a book or two lately. This wouldn't explain publication, so he adds: 'I'm going to give this story to a pal of mine and tell him that if I do get captured by the coppers he can try and get it put into a book or something' (p. 48). The fact of publication suggests that he did get 'captured': so success in writing is linked to set-back in the lower-class revolt.

D. H. Lawrence suddenly became very important. He could be celebrated for his working-class origins and portrayal of the alienation of working-class life, but he also featured in the Leavisite crusade to render high culture earnest, appeared progressive on sexual relations and had been persecuted by 'the establishment'. He seemed to bridge the gap between the New Left and the working class. A *Times* article of January 1960 remarked: 'If anyone is making a list of authors who will come into their own in 1960, then D. H. Lawrence claims to be the favourite.' And he indeed inspired a fine selection of dissident intellectuals – including, crucially, Hoggart – to defend *Lady Chatterley's Lover* against the charge of obscenity. Penguin wrote in their blurb for the book: 'It was not just a legal tussle, but a conflict of generation and class.'[7] But the class was mainly the dissident middle class.

Reading Lawrence was not the same as living in a Nottingham pit village. Nor were working-class people likely to feel at home at the Royal Court, though the wish for a wider audience was announced repeatedly. Peter Townsend admitted in *Conviction*: the left-wing intellectual 'wants to stand apart from the crowd, to be original, to wear an outrageous shirt, condemn the mass media and talk of commitment, positivism and free cinema.' So 'he runs the risk, in his thoughts and actions of alienating himself from ordinary people.'[8] More seriously, there was distress that working-class culture was hostile to progressive attitudes. Hoggart mentions, awkwardly, a network of prejudices, including 'intolerance' towards Jews and Roman Catholics (p. 94). Potter says:

> Much of what is indiscriminately labelled 'working class' is hostile by defin-
> ition to any form of progressive thought, and is little but a narrow, bitterly

defensive reaction to the abuses of capitalism, the consequences of stunted under-privilege rather than social vigour and optimism. This is inevitable, and not a condemnation of working-class culture at all. (*Glittering*, p. 12)

The reservations running all through this statement signal anxiety, but hardly deal with it.

For all their concern with working-class culture – indeed partly *through* that concern – left-liberal intellectuals were actually engaged in making their own subculture. I argued in Chapter 11 that a youthful left-liberal intelligentsia cohered around CND, Royal Court drama, some literature, folk music and jazz. Of course, those discourses were not exclusive to this class fraction, nor it to them, but they constituted a distinctive *bricolage*. They amounted to a New-Left subculture. Phil Cohen doubts that there can be middle-class subcultures, because subcultures are produced by subordinate groups.[9] But middle-class dissidence is a subordinated part of the dominant class, and new-left activities are best understood in terms of subculture.

New-Left subculture found it hard to avoid evaluating working-class culture against a high-cultural norm. In *Roots* Beatie's mother can be persuaded to clap her hands to Bizet, so all may not be lost (p. 129). Hoggart remarks that milk bars exhibit:

in the nastiness of their modernistic knic-knacks, their glaring showiness, an aesthetic breakdown so complete that, in comparison with them, the layout of the living-rooms in some of the poor homes from which the customers come seems to speak of a tradition as balanced and civilised as an eighteenth-century town house. (pp. 247–8)

I doubt that the people who skivvied in eighteenth-century town houses found them very balanced and civilized. All through *Education and the Working Class*, Jackson and Marsden indicate their disapproval of snobbery in the upwardly mobile; so, in conclusion, they deny that 'our central culture' and 'middle class values' are the same thing. They ask: 'is it at all true, as the head-teachers say, that the working class (three-quarters of the "nation") bring nothing of their own to meet the cultural inheritance?' (p. 222). But notice how 'the cultural inheritance' is said to be waiting there in the school for the lower-class pupils to 'meet' it. The question is introduced by an appeal to Arnold and Leavis, and the best Jackson and Marsden can manage is to leave it open.

The theatre, jazz and folk song were the characteristic New-Left cultural forms. That *Look Back in Anger* was one starting point illustrates once more that subcultures appropriate what they want from a text (see Chapter 8). Jimmy Porter was too busy displacing his frustration onto his wife to develop a socialist analysis. The play's political limitations derive also from its dependence on Orwell, who ranked high with the New Left because he seemed right on Stalinism and imperialism and had reported on poverty and popular culture, and because atomic weapons offered the prospect of a *1984*-type war economy. *Look Back* takes up Orwell's analysis of 'the decay of ability in the ruling class' in *England Your England* (1941) – hence Jimmy's rage about Alison's gang and Nigel the chinless wonder from Sandhurst, and his complaint that they have been plundering their countrymen (p. 20) – Orwell's expression. Orwell posits ex-colonial blimps and the intelligentsia as the two groups most affected by the decline of the ruling class, and this gives us Jimmy and Alison's ex-India father. If Jimmy Porter sounds negative and querulous, offers the irresponsible carping of one who never expects to be in power, and would be more ashamed of standing to attention during the national anthem than of stealing from a poor box – all that is exactly what Orwell says about left-wing intellectuals.[10]

It wasn't the intention of the English Stage Company to promote left-wing plays. Its council tried to stop such plays (Osborne's *The Entertainer*, for instance) and the director, George Devine, distrusted political commitment and valued most his theatre's work with Samuel Beckett. Nevertheless, the Royal Court and *Look Back* became points around which New-Left perceptions were organized – and this came to include demands for a more purposeful politics.[11] Tynan's review of *Look Back*, right at the start, improves on the play's politics: 'One cannot imagine Jimmy Porter listening with a straight face to speeches about our inalienable right to flog Cypriot schoolboys. You could never mobilise him and his kind into a lynching mob, since the art he lives for, jazz, was invented by Negroes' (Tynan, p. 178). This credits the play with more than it says: Jimmy doesn't talk about Civil Rights or the British occupation of Cyprus, but in Tynan's view he could have.

The political import of *Look Back* and the Royal Court was augmented by the Hungarian revolt and the Suez invasion. Now Jimmy Porter had a cause to talk about, and plenty of excited people to talk with – Lindsay Anderson says a friend in the audience wanted to jump up and call out: 'What about Suez?' (Maschler, p. 164). *The Entertainer*, which opened at the Royal Court in April 1957, is set during the Suez operation, and juxtaposes it with Osborne's view of England as a run-down music-hall act. When the soldier Mick is killed, Frank sings, sardonically:

> Those playing fields of Eton
> Have really got us beaten.
> But ain't no use agrievin'
> 'Cos it's Britain we believe in.
>
> (p. 74)

The song was both booed and cheered on the opening night, and dropped for the West End transfer.[12]

Arnold Wesker's *Chicken Soup with Barley*, produced at the Royal Court in 1958, was important because it revisits the communist commitment of the 1930s. When Mosley's Blackshirts tried to march down Brick Lane the issues were clear: 'They shall not pass!'. The postwar period produces confusion and dispersal and Ronnie, the boy who went through grammar school, is beset with a sense of pointlessness. Stalin and Hungary are the last straw, but the mother insists: 'You've got to care or you'll die' (p. 75). Despite this merely gestural ending, the play was exciting for its assumption of a communist perspective; for younger audiences, this history was news, and afforded a context for their own commitment.

The combative significance of left-wing plays was enhanced by the attempts of old-style reviewers to put them down. *The Times* asserted, of Wesker's *Roots*, 'Since all its characters are inarticulate they are not, for the most part, given anything interesting to say'; the *Sunday Times* pronounced Arden's *Serjeant Musgrave's Dance* 'another frightful ordeal'. Meanwhile, the ethos of the leisure class made its last stand in the Lord Chamberlain's censorship function (until 1968). Theatre became a place where new-left attitudes could be explored. The magazine *Encore* was founded to develop the connection, and the work of Joan Littlewood and Theatre Workshop, marginalized hitherto for its socialist policy, was celebrated. The formally educated were hugely over-represented at the 'new drama': it was the same fraction that supported CND, and a number of plays focused on the demands of activism.[13]

I discussed in chapter 8 the appropriation of jazz as a music of rebellion by literary intellectuals seeking a serious cultural form that was not associated with established high culture. This was, in large part, the new-left constituency also. Like lower-class rock-'n'-roll, jazz was rebellious and fun, but it was an acceptable form of US culture – a node of opposition at the centre of the capitalist giant (in *The Long Revolution* Williams begins his derogation of commercial entertainment by granting that 'jazz is a real musical form'; p. 364). Free Cinema films nearly always used jazz sound-tracks; *Momma Don't Allow* (1956) was set in a club with the Chris Barber Band playing.

Key jazz figures on the left included Humphrey Lyttelton, Johnny Dankworth and George Melly. Eric Newton, reviewer and author of *The Jazz Scene* (1959), is New-Left historian Eric Hobsbawm. Ken Colyer's purist band marched with CND, and so did many others – after all, one of the functions of New Orleans bands was, and still is, to walk with street festivals and funerals. Anderson's *March to Aldermaston* includes youngsters dancing in the evening to jazz; the voice-over says: 'It's no use being against death, if you don't know how to enjoy life when you've got it.' Christopher Logue (who had written some of the commentary for the CND film) read his 'protest' poems with jazz music at the Royal Court.[14] Tynan, in his *Declaration* essay, tells a young man needing to know where the political action is: 'Go first of all to the jazz clubs' (Maschler, p. 128). Ken Worpole was one such: he describes how his initiation into Youth CND was to the accompaniment of records of Shostakovitch, *Porgy and Bess*, the Red Army Choir, Josh White, Paul Robeson, and jazz of all kinds.[15]

Furthermore jazz – and the same was true of folk music – was regarded as an authentic music of oppressed people – of Blacks and the lower classes before they were spoilt by Hollywood, advertising, rock-'n'-roll and the record industry. It offered the ideal imaginary resolution of the gap between New-Left and lower-class culture: it was the 'good' music which the working class would have been performing if it hadn't been got at; and, of course, there were working-class jazz fans.

In *Look Back in Anger*, Jimmy's jazz trumpet helps to define an oppositional identity. Harold Hobson saw it as part of the attack on Alison and, through her, on a stultifying social order. George Melly says he was one of many jazz enthusiasts who found *Look Back* 'a play about the chaps' and thought of the Royal Court Theatre as their kind of place from that time.[16] In *The Entertainer*, Osborne uses a black woman singer to trigger release from the inauthentic self (this is reminiscent of Sartre's *La Nausée*; the motif recurs in François Sagan's *Aimez-vous Brahms*, 1959). The role of jazz is enhanced in the film of *Look Back* (1959). Behind the initial credits we see Jimmy (Richard Burton) in a jazz club, sitting in with the Barber band: this sets the keynote for the film, not the dreary English Sunday of the play. And walking home through the dark wet streets Jimmy re-hears the jazz and blows, or imagines he blows, answering riffs; so the lonely, anguished, rebellious figure is established through the jazz idea. Later on, the dialogue about Alison's father and the old Edwardian brigade is set in the club, with the band behind Jimmy representing, it seems, the contemporary situation. Jimmy plays a military bugle call, and then turns it blue: the Raj gives way to the solo trumpeter whose personal malaise mingles with nostalgia – but in the mode of imperial subjects rather than imperial rule. The band starts up again cheerfully, and people jive: as Jimmy says, we are in the 'American Age'. However, there is a further gesture linking jazz with ordinary English people: ex-servicemen, late middle-aged, stroll through the market busking, playing banjo and cornet.

The acoustic guitar was immensely convenient as a portable signal of commitment. In the United States there had long been an association between the left and folk music, linked to the poverty and oppression of Blacks and the rural people of regions such as the Appalachians and Arkansas, and the political songs of the Wobblies labour movement. Some left-wing performers were still active in the late 1950s, despite Cold-War harassment – Pete Seeger, Paul Robeson and Josh White, for instance; Woodie Guthrie was strongly present on record and through other performers of his songs. Seeger, who was convicted in 1961 of 'UnAmerican Activities' and blacklisted by the media, described himself as a 'cultural guerilla': he sang pre-Cold-War labour songs such as 'Union Maid' and 'If I Had a Hammer'. Black music was focused by the Civil Rights Campaign: Josh White, following Billie Holiday, sang Lewis Allan's poem 'Strange Fruit', about lynching in the South: 'Here is a strange and bitter crop'. 'We Shall Overcome' and 'We Shall Not Be Moved' became universal protest songs.[17]

This was for the New Left an acceptable US culture, though some British performers held it a political imperative to sing only British songs – the true culture of the people. Ewan MacColl and A. L. Lloyd specialized in songs about working people and victims of the penal system. But it became acceptable to write your own songs in an approximation to the folk idiom (the origin of the performer-composer, now dominant in rock music). MacColl sang powerfully about people who had recently been unjustly killed by the state (Timothy Evans, Derek Bentley); Pete Seeger adapted 'Where Have All the Flowers Gone?' (about war), wrote 'Little Boxes' (about conformity), and sang Idris Davies's poem 'The Bells of Rhymney' (about the Depression in South Wales). MacColl, Peggy Seeger and Charles Parker devised a sequence of 'Radio Ballads' (1958–63), interspersing songs in the folk manner with the recorded speech of working people (hardly heard before on BBC radio: MacColl says it was like talking to Piers Plowman or the biblical Joshua). They managed to fight off BBC feeling that the employers' point of view should be presented as well.[18]

This is the milieu that welcomed Bob Dylan. To be sure, 'Blowin' in the Wind' and 'Times They Are a-Changing' are remarkably vague as political songs; so even is 'It's a Hard Rain's a-Gonna Fall', written during the Cuban missile crisis. But 'The Lonesome Death of Hattie Carroll' (1964) is not. 'And she never done nothing to William Zanzinger'.

Of course, this political orientation of folk and jazz was as appropriative as the other uses I described in Chapter 8. Dylan, like Guthrie before him, had to seek out the alternative scene of New York in order to gain attention. Tony Palmer notes of Dylan, 'To young blacks or the poor of any colour, he said not a word. In spite of his declared dislike of the bourgeoisie, his was a middle-class music' (p. 86). Jeff Nuttall remarks the 'pragmatic contradiction' whereby jazz and folk performers copy the awkwardness of the unrehearsed recording and the quaverings of the cracked voice 'in order to be as authentic and sincere as they could possibly contrive' (p. 39). In fact enthusiasts were not unaware of this (there was a lot of humour and self-awareness among the earnestness), and the occasional contradiction seemed an acceptable price for involvement in the scene.

Wesker made sustained attempts to proclaim New-Left subculture as a universal culture. In *Chips with Everything* an airman, under the influence of the upper-class Pip, recites 'This ae Night' by Robert Burns, so challenging the Wing Commander's belief that dancing to rock music shows the airmen's congenital inferiority. Then the airmen menace the officers with 'The Cutty Wren', an old peasant resistance song (Act I, scene 7). It is improbable that they would know this song, but New-Left folk singers might.

More significantly, Wesker tried to alter the cultural apparatus. He set up Centre 42 to raise non-commercial finance from trades unions, and organized six festivals for working people in 1962. The programme was variously criticized, for being up-market, patronizing, poorly executed, vulgar (Laing, pp. 102–3). In fact it was pure New-Left subculture. The Nottingham Festival consisted of exhibitions of trades-union life and local and children's art, folksinging (the programme hails trades unionists as 'the rightful custodians of that tradition'), Bernard Kops's play *Enter Solly Gold* (a Jewish comedy about an East-End confidence trickster), folk-ballads by Charles Parker, poetry and jazz, Stravinsky's *The Soldier's Tale*, Wesker's music drama *The Nottingham Captain* (about Luddites), Christopher Logue's poetry read in factory canteens, a National Youth Theatre performance of *Hamlet* (billed as 'Shakespeare's Jimmy Porter') and a jazz concert with a trophy for the best dancing. The back of the programme prints a poem by D. H. Lawrence: 'If you make a revolution, make it for fun.' This was new-left subculture exactly: relatively political and hopefully accessible instances of high culture together with bits of current student subculture and uncertain gestures towards the creativity of working people. But Wesker was only trying to do what many people spoke about – and what is still the proclaimed policy of many cultural workers on the left.

New-left subculture defined itself against both high culture and working-class culture. If the working class appeared passive, losing its cultural cohesion, reactionary and infatuated with trivial consumer goodies, then upwardly mobile intellectuals were justified in leaving it. They could properly criticize it and campaign for arts centres and 'serious' television programmes; they could make their way into educational and arts institutions, and from there propagate a left-culturist outlook. Williams remarked that the Marxism of 1930s literary intellectuals was partly 'the old Romantic protest that there was no place in contemporary society for the artist and the intellectual.' New-Left intellectuals were not quite so remote from this model as they hoped.[19]

However, to point out that the New Left produced a subculture, rather than a universal culture or an objective evaluation of other cultures, is not to disqualify it. It is true that a principal attraction of CND was the friendliness and solidarity of the march, but that was not irrelevant politically; such feelings were a feature of the war years that welfare-capitalism had failed to sustain. It is true that going to the Royal Court isn't going to change society, and that folk music wasn't really the music of the people. But political identity does not derive directly from class or gender or racial position, or sexual orientation; or simply from personal choice. It derives in large part, and this is not sufficiently remarked, from involvement in a milieu. So an individual discovers a certain kind of selfhood in relation to others, learns to inhabit certain preoccupations and forms. A subculture sets the framework of understanding – makes alternative stories plausible. That is not, in itself, political action, but it has implications for how we set out to produce political action.

The Working Class Revisited

The impetus to 'better' yourself by moving away was a major component in working-class culture, but it existed in uncertain juxtaposition with a suspicion that the aspirant might be 'getting above' himself (it was usually himself). The most sensitive moment was his return, and it figures repeatedly in representations. These are offered mostly from the point of view of the upwardly mobile, the one who writes. He looks to place the family and neighbourhood in their proper supporting role in his story. The resulting interaction is fraught, for it seems to justify or impugn his class-mobility.

The narrator in *Weekend in Dinlock* visits Dinlock as an outsider; Sigal, from the United States, follows the model set by Orwell. But most of these writers were revisiting former home territories, trying to establish relationship (the pub in 'Coronation Street' is called The Rover's Return). Willmott and Young admit to only professional concern in *Family and Kinship*, but the note at the front of the book says Peter Willmott served an apprenticeship in engineering, worked in the mines and was a student at Ruskin. Jackson and Marsden acknowledge that they are revisiting: 'We were formed by the grammar school world of Marburton, and for some years our natural line of interest has led to constant discussion around questions of social class and state education' (p. 3). So they invite readers 'not so much to observe with us the people of Marburton, as to observe us observing them' (p. 14). This is how all such writing should be regarded. The working-class people are not a given, they are items in the story of the revisitor.

The revisitor often seeks personal ratification: by attending the death-bed of Mrs Tanner, Jimmy Porter seems to confirm his ability to relate across class and hence his humanity (there is often a deathbed – it perhaps bespeaks the extremity of the issue, the plight of working-class culture and the guilt of the revisitor). But usually the occasion is laden with class anxiety. In *The Entertainer* Jean rapidly gets at cross-purposes with her family; so does Beatie in *Roots*. We may sense an element of self-justification when Hoggart says: 'The minority who become conscious of their class-limitations and take up some educational activity – so as to "work for their class" or "improve themselves" – tend to be ambiguously regarded' (p. 84). 'Class-limitations' shows Hoggart's slant; he is on the side of 'educational activity' (passivity sounds bad). Again: 'There is bound to be occasional friction, of course – when they wonder whether the boy is "getting above himself", or when he feels a strong reluctance to break off and do one of the odd jobs a boy is expected to do' (pp. 295–6). The controlling perspective is the boy's: that is why the parents' words are in quotation marks. His 'strong reluctance' is personal, as against the conventional expectation.

The sharpest version of the revisiting fable is in Heinemann's *The Adventurers*. Here the young man who leaves the pit valley via a working men's college intends at first to speak for the people who remain (p. 43). But he becomes an industrial journalist and is used by right-wingers to provide information for smear campaigns in union elections; his revisits are treacherous. He is told: 'You went away from Abergoch, fair enough; you couldn't do much with your brains there. But if you went you should have stayed away, see. You can't be the boy now to tell the world what we're thinking' (p. 287).

The protagonist in Williams's *Border Country* returns because his father is dying, so the question of closeness and distance is sharply set. Through a double time scheme, the lives of the father, Harry, and the son, Matthew, are juxtaposed. Harry, a railway worker, was solid with the miners in 1926 and is uncomfortable with his friend Morgan's business venture, but he wants his son to do well at school and go to college. Williams believed, or wanted to believe, that this might involve little strain – he wrote in *Conviction*: 'Learning was ordinary; we learned where we could. Always, from those scattered white houses, it had made sense to go out and become a scholar or a poet or a teacher' (MacKenzie, p. 76). In *Culture and Society* he complains that education is interpreted as a ladder of individual attainment, acknowledging that it 'has produced a real conflict of values within the working class itself' (pp. 317–18); but he cannot suggest how, within the current arrangements, that is to be avoided.

In *Border Country* there is a sequence of awkward conversations with diverse people, both as Matthew is growing up and when he returns. More seriously, we see his aspiration depending upon the parson, Pugh, who admits that it is through the chapels, not his Anglican ministry, that local people express and consolidate neighbourliness: 'The chapels are for people to meet, and to talk to each other or sing together. Around them, as you know, moves almost the whole life of the village' (p. 214). In other words, getting to college means working outside the very institutions of co-operation in community that Williams presents as the working-class contribution to culture. In 1977 he was to observe that educational advance there was tied in with the hegemony of England over Wales (*Politics*, p. 25).

Despite this, the novel revolves around Matthew's key assertion: 'Every value I have, Morgan, and I mean this, comes from him. Comes only from him' – from Harry, the father (p. 275). But this is not easy to see, because Harry has always been a man of few words and his illness actually prevents him from speaking. He is presented mainly through the viewpoint of Matthew, who is educated to write. So it is difficult to see Harry's life standing for itself; his presence is, so to speak, muted. And the fact of writing, which makes Harry available to the reader, bespeaks the distance between father and son.

Border Country wants Harry to be the strong man; Williams wants to repudiate the idea that working-class culture lacks vitality and commitment. But Harry may alternatively be viewed as a victim – of his employers, the trades unions (who failed to press the National Strike), and even of the conservative community ethos. And above all he is the victim of the class and education system, which ordains that Harry will encourage his son to express his talents, and hence must lose him. *Border Country* ends with the assertion that the revisiting has produced 'the feeling of exile ending. For the distance is measured, and that is what matters. By measuring the distance, we come home' (p. 334).

So it is said. But in *Second Generation* (1964), Williams's protagonist thinks about how his education does not enable him to serve the people he comes from: 'It was really as if, oppressed by an enemy, a people had conceived its own liberation as training its sons for the enemy service. And they would even boast how well they were doing, how much the enemy thought of them' (pp. 137–8). In *Modern Tragedy* (1966) Williams offers a personal instance: 'the life of a man driven back to silence, in an unregarded working life. In his ordinary and private death, I saw a terrifying loss of connection between men, and even between father and son' (p. 13). A class society produces a class culture, and its distances are not often bridged, even by generosity and commitment. Human freedom has gained immeasurably from the books of Raymond Williams but, revisiting Pandy, I met Mrs Smith, the retired postmistress who remembers him as a boy; she told me she has never read one of them.

The development of television as a popular form was a further challenge for the New Left. In 1950, 4.3 per cent of homes had sets; it was 49.4 per cent by 1956, and over 90 per cent by 1964 (Ryder and Silver, p. 255). Hoggart begins his *Conviction* essay 'Speaking to Each Other' by figuring the classroom where the pupils talk to their friendly, ex-scholarship-boy teacher about last night's programmes; he has no set (MacKenzie, p. 121). Television was the medium through which working-class people were most likely to find out what was being said about them. Commercial television (from 1955) was aggressively 'popular', and since it was organized regionally companies felt they should look for regional material.[20] Through programmes such as 'Coronation Street', limited versions of lower-class cultures came into public visibility.

Though most left-culturist writers preferred the Royal Court, the more adventurous felt that television might be the place to work. David Mercer regretted television's impermanence and lack of cultural status, but acknowledged that theatre 'becomes a consumer object for a restricted audience – a middle-class, theatre-going audience – whereas in television fifteen million people can, at least, switch on for free, and if they want they can switch off. You couldn't get more democratic than that.'[21] For new-left writers, television was a way of revisiting working-class homes with your revisiting story.

Alun Owen's *Lena, Oh My Lena*, shown in ABC Television's ambitious Armchair Theatre series in 1960, represents the difficulties experienced by a student, Tom, who takes a job in a warehouse because he wants to work with 'people' for a change (p. 125). He is revisiting – he complains that his father, a foreman, has cut him off from his class roots by getting him educated. In this play the working people have a fair share of the point of view, and their life-style is adequately complex, reasonable and humane (though there is a touch of *Carmen* or *Porgy and Bess* in the straightforward sexuality ascribed to them). Even Tom's humanitarian concern for the simple Derek ('after all, he's a human being'; p. 122) appears shallow in comparison with the foreman's care for Derek. Tom repeatedly mis-understands the language and what is going on, but the writing cleverly contrives that the viewer (or at least this viewer) will not misunderstand; so we are aligned with the workers. Tom's revisit, it emerges, has been used in the relationship of Lena and Glyn; he, we might say, is part of their story. This reverses the usual arrangement, say in *Roots*, whereby the visited contribute to the story of the revisitor. Even so, the working people end the play more or less where they began, whereas Tom will learn from his experience: this locates the play's concern finally with him.

Mercer's *Where the Difference Begins* (BBC, 1961) was aimed originally at the stage. It has two revisiting sons, both anxious about class mobility.

Richard has married and divorced a wealthy but vulnerable woman (as in *Look Back*) and has lost confidence in his work as an artist; Edgar has a bitter, failed marriage, is ultra-conservative, and helps to research nuclear weapons. Richard says: 'I'm wondering if we haven't become the image of everything they [their parents] lacked the insight to despise!' (p. 23). The revisitors are highly articulate, in the manner of Jimmy Porter, and this intensifies all the oppositions. But the railwayman father, Wilf, has a good deal to say (here it is the mother that is dying). In the last part of the play Wilf asserts the value of his life and of socialism as he has understood it, but laments that he has lost touch with his sons. However, this crediting of working-class experience is positioned so as to illuminate the sons: the 'difference' of the title is between them, and is said to derive from how they value Wilf's life (p. 56).

Potter's *Stand Up, Nigel Barton* suggests how parents may have felt at having the likes of themselves broadcast in order to justify their offspring. A sequence of awkard relations between the undergraduate Barton and his family and neighbourhood climaxes in Barton's appearance in a television documentary about class in modern Britain – it is shown while he is visiting his parents:

> Here [at Oxford], books are not regarded as muddles. Here, you can discuss things without letting it turn into a bad-tempered argument. Back at home – in the village, in the working man's club, with people I went to school with – well, I'm so much on the defensive, you see. They suspect me of making qualitative judgments about their environment. (pp. 72–3)

The parents are offended and hurt. This is more or less what happened to Potter: after writing an article about class mobility in the *New Statesman* he was interviewed for a TV programme in 1958 and his remarks were taken up by the Labour paper *Reynolds News* under the headline 'Miner's Son at Oxford Ashamed of Home. The Boy who Kept his Father Secret' (*Glittering*, pp. 71–2). Williams had a comparable experience when he wrote a story about nonconformist narrowness, while at Cambridge, and it got back to Pandy – 'all hell broke loose' (*Politics*, p. 31). Jackson and Marsden were told by one of their upwardly mobile interviewees:

> There was a programme on television which said something about not being able to converse with your parents after you'd been educated. And we were all sat round the television set, my father, my mother, some aunts and an

uncle – and they all said the same thing, just the same reaction – 'snobbish-ness!' But it was right, we all knew it was right, because that's how it was with us. (p. 188)

Barton castigates himself for exploiting people, but he blames his narrow upbringing and the action confirms his story: we see him having experiences such as he complains of, and his parents have no coherent response to his accusations. By thus arranging the representation of working people to alleviate the guilt of the class-mobile, the play re-enacts the exploitation that it appears to criticize. The revisiting is shot through with guilt and self-justification.

These texts were all autobiographically rooted. Their similarities witness to the way a culture organizes itself: those writers who can engage with a current anxiety come to notice. Their differences witness to a contest about how that anxiety should be understood. We should not assume literal truth. Mercer remarked later that Wilf was idealized to establish the story he wanted to tell (Jarman, p. 47). Williams says, in *The Country and the City* (p. 359), that Harry in *Border Country* was only one half of his actual father. These texts offer representations of possible relations between the New Left and an idea of the working class. Typically, it is a story of loss but also of connection: New-Left intellectuals felt them-selves neither part of the working class, which in any case was debilitated (typified by the elderly), nor separate from it.

Cultural Work

The texts discussed so far in this chapter embody, generally, two assumptions: that the working class should be the locus of socialist values, and that intellectuals as a category scarcely exist (they appear as unfortunate individual by-products of the working class and the education system). To conclude this chapter I consider the structure and potential of intellectual dissidence, and two relationships in particular: between intellectuals and the left, and between intellectuals and other classes and groups.

Since the early 1960s there has been much attention to the category 'intellectuals', as numbers in higher education and cultural production increased, new-left thinkers became aware of themselves and their forbears, students became a prominent dissident group, and the work of

Antonio Gramsci and Nicos Poulantzas was published and translated (especially by *New Left Review*).[22] One immediate consequence was profound dissatisfaction with the dominant English tradition, with the role of literature and with Leavisism (they were taken, virtually, to be all the same thing): they seemed to have afforded only the disabling illusion of a radical critique of capitalism.[23]

Gramsci afforded a good starting point because he acknowledges that all people are intellectuals, but goes on to specify as a social category people who perform the professional function of intellectuals (pp. 7–8). His distinction between traditional and organic intellectuals is less applicable now because the vast majority of intellectuals are no longer leisured gentlemen, but are employed. Modern societies produce a continual ideological barrage; we are 'saturated with signs and messages' (Jameson, p. 139). This requires numerous cultural workers – we have the news every hour on the hour lest we wander away from the proper stories. Foucault relates the change in the occupational position of intellectuals to a change in the kind of authority-claim they may make. Before, they spoke as arbiters of truth and justice, as expounders of the universal; now their effect is exercised through the circumstances of their work (*Power/Knowledge*, pp. 126–33).

Not all today's cultural producers would normally be called 'intellectuals', for that term often has status implications. Konrad and Szelényi argue that 'intellectual' is not a structural position but a badge of distinction which intellectuals confer on one another (p. 8). If we are to use the term 'intellectuals' as a social category, it is crucial not to include evaluative connotations – recognizing that, as with other social categories, it will contain ineffectual instances (there are incompetent, lazy and reactionary intellectuals). With this in mind, we may adopt Tom Bottomore's definition as 'those who contribute directly to the creation, transmission and criticism of ideas', including writers, artists, scientists, philosophers, religious thinkers, social theorists and political commentators, through into teachers and journalists (p. 70). However, at the same time, people who are employed in other ways, or unemployed, may make key contributions, especially locally and within minority groups (Escoffier, pp. 127–30). We might think of them as part-time intellectuals, or use the wider term 'cultural producers' to indicate the extent to which this work occurs outside conventional occupations.

Intellectuals, cultural producers, are important because they help to maintain or undermine belief in the legitimacy of the prevailing power arrangements. They help to set the boundaries of the thinkable. They confirm or change the stories through which we tell ourselves who we are. In Colin Sumner's view, the relations of production may even become so delicately poised that intellectual institutions may tip the balance by favouring one version (p. 237). Richard Crossman attributed the Labour victory of 1945 to the way the ground had been prepared by 'the "disloyal intelligentsia" '.[24]

The persisting question is whether or how far intellectuals are pre-disposed to radicalism. Alvin Gouldner puts intellectuals together with the technical intelligentsia as a 'new class', alienated from the prevailing system when its upward mobility is blocked. He attributes to intellectuals a 'culture of critical discourse' – meaning that 'there is nothing that speakers will on principle refuse to discuss or make problematic' (p. 28). This locates well the ethos within which intellectual enquiry is now generally conducted – in political and social matters, and in science and technology, for experts in all those fields are expected to show themselves ready to consider new theories and techniques; and in the arts too (it evokes the probable stance of a Royal Shakespeare Company audience). A critical discourse is surely what we require. However, it may be only a manner of speaking, and need not produce a radical analysis. It may mask manipulations, evasions, concealments and lies.

Others hold that intellectuals in Western Europe and North America are by definition incorporated or ineffectual. I have noted the belief of Orwell and others that intellectual freedom depended upon a leisure class in a *laissez-faire* economy (pp. 41–7). Pursuing this vein, Konrad and Szelényi hold that state monopoly capitalism now prevails in the West and has destroyed the independent intellectual, or confined him or her to one of a set of ghettos (the artistic, the radical grouplet, academic life; pp. 63–4). The incorporation of modern Western intellectuals withholds even 'the consciousness-raising experience which their Eastern European counter-parts' derive from state opposition (pp. 63–4, 81). This argument has been developed, especially in North America, in relation to the concentration of intellectual work in three principal venues: the academy, television, and right-wing think tanks funded by business or government.[25]

Those three institutional developments produce diverse dangers, but also some opportunities. In my view it is a mistake to suppose that the scope and political outlook of intellectuals is fully determined, either way, by their social position (the same is true of workers, Blacks, women). The swing to the right in many countries, associated with the world recession, the focusing of cultural power through multi-national corporations, and advances in expensive technological facilities, certainly affords every reason for renewed vigilance and effort. However, it often enhances political perceptions, even while restricting the means of intervention. In fact, to be more closely tied into the central processes of business and the state is to be more vividly subject to their contradictions. Employed intellectuals share many of the experiences of other employed people – subject to unfair and stupid decisions, to dismissal – their labour alienated (see Foucault, *Power/Knowledge*, p. 126). At the moment of writing we may not be winning, but the conditions of struggle are far clearer than before.

Current conditions of cultural production are discussed further in Chapter 13; here, together with the question of intellectuals and the left, I want to consider the relationship between intellectuals and other classes and groups. It is with this in mind that I have tried to establish the concept 'middle-class dissidence', to identify a fraction of the middle class partly hostile to the dominant ideology. I pointed out in chapter 4 that middle-class dissidents are often intellectuals, and that they may be right-wing, left-wing or liberal: they may imagine a 'return' to traditional structures, attempt an alliance with the working class or other oppressed groups, or try to find a compromise between radical intuitions and the prevailing system. Characteristically, they have universalized their perceptions and claimed the right to adjudicate 'good' culture.

Middle-class dissidence has not always been left-wing, therefore, far from it; but it is a space in which socialism, feminism and anti-imperialism have been found (Marx, the Suffragettes), disputed and developed. Disappointed at the tendency of the Russian labour movement towards trades unionism in the 1890s, Lenin endorsed Kautsky's beliefs that socialist consciousness requires study, and 'the vehicle of science is not the proletariat, but the *bourgeois intelligentsia*: it was in the minds of individual members of this stratum that modern socialism originated.' Perry Anderson admits middle-class dissidence among the main currents that have fed the British left: working-class consciousness, classical English liberalism, and moral and aesthetic criticism.[26] There is no reliable political tendency in middle-class dissidence (or in other classes or groups). There is potential for development.

This analysis is relevant to Eric Hobsbawm's argument that the failure of the Labour Party to win elections is due to the shrinking and changing character of the working class (see Jacques and Mulhern). The Labour

Party has always been a coalition with working-and middle-class elements and, as Raymond Williams has shown, it could never depend on a unified proletarian vote (*Towards*, pp. 54–7, 153–7). In fact there is still a socialist/social-democratic majority against the Conservatives, but the current situation produces splits and indecisiveness (Gamble). Labour's failure is due to its inability to generate a persuasive analysis to replace welfare-capitalism: an analysis that will relate traditional concerns to new and wider initiatives, and activate diverse commitments of class, gender, race, nation and sexual orientation.

The 1950–60s New Left were mainly middle-class dissidents, but reluctant to identify themselves as such – hence left-culturism and the anxious revisiting. The shame-facedness of middle-class activists has persisted, and it weakens their effect. Where there is a specific, active identification with another community, on the ground, perhaps, of race, gender, nation, sexual orientation or location, middle-class dissidents may be able to work within that. But generally they should stop trying to disavow their specific constitution, and stop trying to speak for other classes and groups. They should acknowledge, for instance, that other people's cultural activities may do better outside 'the arts'. Then alliances may be possible. Alliance does not suppose vanguard: when middle-class dissidence is recognized as itself, it won't need to justify itself as the voice of others. Revisiting working-class England, Beatrix Campbell finds powerful evidence of political consciousness and purpose, especially among young women. She calls her book *Wigan Pier Revisited*, being conscious of 'an awkward relationship with my own class' (p. 5), but she rejects the Orwellian assumption that the working class needs the intellectual visitor. It is the same in Black communities and among gay men and lesbians.

Middle-class dissidence has to recognize its own traditions, concerns and modes of operation, not to imagine itself as universal or as a misplaced version of someone else's politics and culture. It has to examine and build upon its characteristic resources; thus it may lose its apologetic tone and secure a basis for effective political analysis and action. A socialist society will draw upon economic and cultural modes developed in the dissident middle class, as well as those from oppressed classes and groups.

Notes

1 Laing, p. 3 and ch. 1; the theory was virtually disproved by Goldthorpe et al. See also J. H. Westergaard, 'The Withering Away of Class', in Anderson and Blackburn; Ryder and Silver, pp. 233–9. On Labour Party revisionism in the 1950s, see Foote, ch. 10.

2 See Sparks; Critcher, 'Sociology', in Clarke et al., pp. 17–20; Swingewood, ch. 3; Phil Cohen, 'Subcultural Conflict and Working-class Community', in Hall, Hobson et al.; John Clarke and Tony Jefferson, 'Working Class Youth Cultures', in Mungham and Pearson; ch. 8 above. On the resistance of Black unemployed, see Hall, Critcher et al., pp. 357–8, 362–8; on Blacks and the arts, see Khan.

3 Anderson, 'Problems of Socialist Strategy', in Anderson and Blackburn, p. 265. See also J. H. Westergaard, 'The Withering Away of Class', in Anderson and Blackburn, pp. 107–8.

4 See Klein, J., I, pp. 155–93, 283–302; Wilson, E., pp. 61–9; Campbell; Steedman; pp. 203–8 above.

5 See Laing, pp. 66–7; Jonathan Dollimore, 'The Challenge of Sexuality', in Sinfield, *Society*, pp. 69–70.

6 See Bourdieu, 'Symbolic Power', p. 116; Konrad and Szelényi, p. 6; Ohmann, p. 219; Orwell, *Essays*, II, p. 58; Morley and Worpole, pp. 67–71, 97–9; Sinfield, 'Power'; pp. 39–40 above.

7 Rolph; Sutherland, *Offensive*, pp. 18, 23–4; Dollimore, in Sinfield, *Society*, pp. 52–61. For new-left admiration of Lawrence, see Potter, *Glittering*, pp. 27, 118; Thompson, *Poverty*, p. 30; Thompson, *Out*, pp. 286, 291, 296–7.

8 'A Society for People', in MacKenzie, p. 119; endorsed by Potter, *Glittering*, pp. 47–8.

9 'Subcultural Conflict', in Hall, Hobson et al., p. 85.

10 Orwell, *Essays*, II, pp. 88–95. On the reasons for Orwell's left-credibility, see Williams, R., *Orwell*, pp. 84–5.

And *Look Back* is closer than is usually reckoned to Terence Rattigan, who had also written about discontented young men. In *The Deep Blue Sea* (1952) Freddie is ex-air force and unable to settle to the responsibilities of ordinary life, work and relationships. In *Separate Tables* (1954) John is an emotionally unstable political journalist. He admits to being boorish, speaks up for striking dockers, warns a wealthy old lady that the Labour Party will introduce a capital levy, attributes to class difference his violence against his wife, and makes speeches about it all – 'Goodness, John, how you do go on', says his wife (pp. 12, 19, 20, 26, 28). She, like Alison, is persuaded to blame herself.

11 Wardle, p. 191 and chs. 13, 14; Marowitz, Milne and Hale, pp. 52–6 and *passim*.

12 Allsop, pp. 119–20. Harry Ritchie, looking at the popular press and 'the public' generally, says Suez had little to do with the Angries, (pp. 31–2). But from the point of view of the building of the New Left over the following five years it was otherwise. Cf. Hartley, pp. 73–5.

13 Sinfield, *Society*, pp. 177–80; Marowitz, Milne and Hale, pp. 115–16 and *passim*; Goorney. *Each His Own Wilderness* (Doris Lessing, 1958), *The Tiger and the Horse* (Robert Bolt, 1960) and *A Climate of Fear* (David Mercer, 1962) were about the appeal of anti-bomb commitment to humane middle-class women (see p. 223) – and included problematic class-mobile young men. *O What a Lovely War* (1963), by Theatre Workshop and Charles Chilton, was crucial. There were also CND plays by David Campton: see Taylor, J. R., *Anger*, pp. 162–9.

14 Nuttall, p. 47; Sussex, p. 39; Hewison, *In Anger*, p. 183.

15 Maschler, p. 128; Worpole; Newton, pp. 87–8.

16 Hobson, in Taylor, J. R., *John*, p. 48; Melly, *Owning*, p. 200.

17 See Rodnitzky, p. 15 and ch. 1; Frith, *Sound Effects*, pp. 27–30; Palmer, ch. 11. For some of the songs mentioned here, see Collins et al., pp. 21, 40, 60.

18 'Folk on 2', BBC Radio 2, 29 June 1988; Laing, pp. 163–5.

19 Williams, R., *Culture and Society*, p. 263. See John Hill, 'Ideology, Economy and the British Cinema', in Barrett, Corrigan et al., pp. 127–9.

20 Stan Barstow, 'Desert Island Discs', BBC Radio 4, 29 August 1986. 'Coronation Street' began in December 1960: on it and 'Z Cars' see Laing, pp. 169–92.

21 In Jarman, p. 55. Dennis Potter says he had by 1964 a yearning 'for there to be at least the possibility of a common culture . . . and that because of the tyranny and treachery of words, which are dependent upon education, which in itself is dependent upon class, in England, one of the ways of jumping over the hierarchies of the print culture was television' ('Arena', BBC 2, 30 January 1987).

22 See this combination of circumstances in Cockburn and Blackburn, especially in Gareth Stedman Jones's chapter, 'The Meaning of the Student Revolt'.

23 See Nairn, 'English'; Anderson, 'Components of the National Culture', in Cockburn and Blackburn, pp. 268–76.

24 Crossman, 'The Lessons of 1945', in Anderson and Blackburn, p. 146. See John Rex, 'Capitalism, Elites and the Ruling Class', in Stanworth and Giddens, p. 214; Harris, *Beliefs*, p. 52. Marcuse suggested that intellectuals have 'a decisive preparatory function, not more' ('Liberation from the Affluent Society', in Cooper, p. 188). See pp. 30–7 above.

25 See Jacoby on academia; Postman, Debray on television; Blumenthal, Peschek, Edsall on the think tank; Escoffier. Chomsky furiously attacks intellectuals who collaborated with the Vietnam War (pp. 62–3, 249–53).

26 Lenin quoting Karl Kautsky, in *What Is to Be Done?*, in Lenin, *Marx-Engels-Marxism*, p. 127; Anderson, 'Problems of Socialist Strategy', in Anderson and Blackburn, p. 283. Compare Sartre's point, against Stalin, about the role of reflection in producing consciousness (see pp. 87–8 above). See Parkin, *Class*, p. 101.

13

The ways we live now

I have attended closely to the 1940s and 1950s in the belief that distinctive political and cultural assumptions and institutions were established then, prompted by the fears of the 1930s and inspired by the hopes and suffering of the 1940s. Those arrangements, as they were developed in the postwar international political and economic system, are still substantially in place, embedded in the social structure, though in almost all respects under threat. They proved inherently unstable, and we live now in the period of their disintegration. Nevertheless I have discussed major conceptual breaks, quite suddenly in the Women's Movement and among gays and lesbians, and through a diverse body of work on the left and within ethnic groups. This last chapter analyses the failure of welfare-capitalism and then concomitant changes in ideas about cultural production. Finally I consider some ideological manoeuvrings of the New Right and the implications for current opportunities for cultural intervention.

The Failure of Welfare-Capitalism

The idea of welfare-capitalism, I have maintained, is that the state attempts an unprecedented pact with the people, almost all the people, to protect us from the manifest disadvantages of capital; which are, in brief, cyclical recessions that throw people into poverty and despair, and disregard for poverty and suffering however caused. Keynes argued that capitalism is self-regulating only in the medium term: but by promoting investment and controlling consumption, the state might maintain employment and so, with the resources from that enhanced efficiency, afford welfare. On this basis governments tried 'to build consensus, to bring the whole nation within the wide circle of citizenship (with the exception of a residual dross of deviants, who were needed to mark the boundaries)' (Wilson, E., p. 2).

I have noted already, in relation to left-culturism, the tendency on the left to regard the state as a bulwark against capital (pp. 245–50); this led people, some of them on the left, to imagine that welfare-capitalism is socialism; or, at least, that it tends towards socialism. But welfare-capitalism is a kind of corporatism. In *laissez-faire* capitalism the state stands back while industrial, commercial and labour interests fight to produce the survival of the stronger, the destruction of the weaker, and allegedly a general increase in wealth. In corporatism the state takes on the running of the economy and responsibility for social justice, and seeks, through a network of influence and control, to reconcile capital and labour by drawing them into the process of government.

Corporatism was not produced arbitrarily, by intrusive governments, but by the logic of capitalism. For *laissez-faire* capitalism self-destructs, as the attempt to maintain profits leads to merger and monopoly, and hence to the undercutting of the initiative and incentive that made it once effective: 'Left unchecked, the capitalist economy may well make the perpetuation of the capitalist system impossible' (Bauman, p. 131). State intervention appeared necessary to regulate the terms of trade, facilitate growth and restrain inflation. In 1940 the question was urgent, for *laissez-faire* apparently produced social conditions favourable to the growth of communism and fascism. Keynesian economics seemed to show how the state might release capitalism from the 1930s role of villain, to become the producer of wealth which the state will redistribute where necessary.[1]

Corporatism is not socialism, but an attempt to rescue capitalism. Probably it works best with social democratic governments, because then workers can be persuaded by their 'own' party (Warren, p. 25), but it became the orthodoxy of postwar British 'consensus' politics. Aubrey Jones in 1950 proposed it as a programme for conservatives, denying that conservatism demands economic liberalism and individualism (Jones, A., p. 7). He believed things were better before the rise of liberalism, when wealth accepted obligations and people knew their place; the decay of that system produced trades unions, which became 'infected with the doctrine that the struggle of the classes was something inevitable'. Now the state must intervene to make labour 'feel that it has the same purpose as capital'. Labour must be consulted (but not too much! – 'a master there must be'). Rivalry should be 'subordinate to a unity. That, after all, is 'the first condition of a healthy society' (pp. 24–31). Conservative leadership between 1951 and 1979 veered between liberal and corporatist policies; they often said the former, but effected mainly the latter. Harold Wilson made Jones chairman of his Prices and Incomes Board, and the Labour governments of 1964–70 tried hard to make corporatism work. But they found an increasing need for coercion: compulsory wage restraint was followed by a wage freeze, then legislation was proposed to weaken the bargaining power of organized labour. The legislation was called 'In Place of Strife': the title revises that of Aneurin Bevan in his book calling for a fairer postwar society, *In Place of Fear*, and expresses the corporatist project of smoothing away conflict. The fact that 'strife' was to be removed by law indicates how, in that project, force will rarely be far away. Indeed, the proposal produced explicit political conflict and had to be withdrawn (Panitch, *Social*, chs. 5–7).

Of course, welfare-capitalism is more likely to work in countries that are better placed in the international league table of capitalist growth or better insulated from its consequences. But in Britain it was doomed almost from the start because it requires a powerful commitment to social justice to secure popular co-operation. The problem was acknowledged at the start. Beveridge quoted from the *Banker's Magazine* the argument that because of 'human nature' and international competition, 'fears of losses and bankruptcy, and, yes, fears of unemployment and poverty' are necessary for industrial discipline. Beveridge's reply was that sufficient social justice would have to be created to ensure 'the co-operation of work-people'.[2] But that degree of social justice was attempted only briefly (Beveridge believed that price controls would be needed and that 'abolition of private property' might prove necessary; pp. 201–3, 23). The Conservative governments of the 1950s defined the possible 'good society' of welfare-capitalism in terms of individual striving and consumer goods, with a manifest rejection of egalitarian redistribution and only a subsidiary and apologetic role for community provision. Then the exuberance and disrespect for traditional authority of the 1960s produced, among other things, a property boom and a more frantic chase for satisfaction through consumption. Capitalist enterprise was liberated from the fig-leaf decencies of old-style Toryism – Thatcherism is one outcome of that liberation. Consider those unconventional entrepreneurs who began as 1960s buccaneers: the unlucky ones went to prison, others evolved into 1980s take-over wizards.

So the compromise of welfare-capitalism became a contradiction. George and Wilding sum up: 'Individualism and welfarism live, at best, in an uneasy truce situation, at worst, in open warfare. So far, individualism has clearly been the winner in most conflicts' (p. 125; and pp. 117–29). Indeed, it has been argued that an ethos of collective benefits was never really generated around the welfare state: welfare provision remains popular, despite support for new-right policies in other areas, but that is because it is perceived in terms of individual need (Taylor-Gooby, pp. 112–14).

Since the ethos of collective benefits has failed to develop and counter-balance the competitive individualism of capitalism, the burden of justifying the system falls largely upon its ability to buy off all sectors with continual increases in consumption. This produces three problems. First, there must always be something further to desire, in order that acquiescence will be sustained, and thus the consumer society creates, systematically, frustration and restlessness. Second, there must be, all the time, more resources; and that requires a good rate of growth and therefore courts economic disequilibrium. The relative decline of the British economy has been crucial because the whole project of welfare-capitalism, and hence the stability of the social order, has been made to depend upon economic growth. Third, as money-making becomes virtually the sole criterion of social satisfaction, so it becomes virtually the sole legitimate mode of recalcitrance. Consequently the economic system is troubled by its use to express more fundamental needs. André Gorz suggests that the majority of wage claims are

revolts against the systematic mutilation of the worker's personality, against the stunting of his professional and human faculties, against the subordination of his nature and content of his working life to technological developments which rob him of his powers of initiative, control and even foresight. Wage claims . . . express a demand for *as much money as possible to pay for the life wasted, the time lost, the freedom alienated* in working under these conditions. . . . In short, the worker – even the highly-paid worker – tries to sell himself as dearly as possible because he cannot avoid *having* to sell himself.[3]

The principal tasks of government become to achieve economic growth and to explain why all sectors cannot be satisfied immediately. Even so, the aspirations that are aroused advance more rapidly than the means to meet them. The state cannot arrange sufficient rewards to obtain the cooperation necessary to produce the economic growth and social stability that will fund the rewards. Governments become preoccupied with the manipulation of public opinion and this becomes apparent. The likely outcome is continual social friction and eventually a legitimation crisis.[4]

Hence the persistent, though incoherent, strain of disaffection and aggression in postwar British society. We may observe it in youth cultures, in disputes and lack of co-operation at work and in education; in vandalism and other abuses of the environment; in indifference towards the official political system (including trades unions); in hostility to minorities such as Blacks, Asians and gays; in lack of consideration towards the disabled, the sick and the elderly; in drug abuse and civil disorder. Raymond Williams saw some of the signs already in 1958: 'If people cannot have official democracy, they will have unofficial democracy, in any of its possible forms, from the armed revolt or riot, through the "unofficial" strike or restriction of labour, to the quietist but most alarming form – a general sullenness and withdrawal of interest.'[5] The media and politicians tend to treat these signs of discontent as individual malfunctions, or as pretexts for moral panics or laments on the 'modern condition', making it hard to recognize a fundamental political unease. And because of a tradition of tolerance and courtesy, and perhaps deference (Marwick calls it 'secular Anglicanism'; British, p. 16), disaffection has only gradually become assertive and violent. Now the tolerance has been abused and hence eroded.

Older people, A. J. P. Taylor has remarked, look back on the war as 'the brief period when the English people felt that they were a truly democratic community' (Calder, p. 400). This, as I showed in chapter 2, is partly a myth, but it displays an aspiration upon which the postwar settlement might have built. Peter Townsend, in his essay 'A Society for People', recalls two wartime impulses: one of trust, generosity and goodwill, and one of self-denial and readiness to share (MacKenzie, p. 95). CND and other demonstration cultures – Greenham Common, The Right to Work, Gay Rights – have transmitted similar values, and they may feature also during industrial action and at football matches and rock concerts. Bauman remarks that recent urban riots have often been unaccustomed exercises in racial co-operation (p. 179). Solidarity is an aspiration in postwar culture, but always it is forced to the margins of or into conflict with the economic and political system.

Under favourable circumstances, welfare-capitalism might fudge along for many decades (though lately it has been in difficulty almost everywhere). But Britian has been in relative economic decline, whatever governments do, ever since its remarkable imperial over-extension at the end of the nineteenth century. Three further, particular factors have proved overwhelming. One is the inability to cope with racial attitudes exacerbated by the disintegration of empire. When London dockers marched in favour of immigration controls in 1968 they sang 'Bye Bye Blackbird' and 'I'm Dreaming of a White Christmas' – drawing, with characteristic resourcefulness, upon texts embedded in working-class culture (Hoggart, p. 160). A growth in popular support for neo-fascism was headed off in the late 1970s by the rise of Thatcherism. A second factor is the inability to cope with the long-standing resentments of Roman Catholics in Northern Ireland. There, a large minority was kept in subjection, so state legitimacy was very weak, but the attempt in the 1960s to develop welfare-capitalism meant the erosion of Protestant ascendancy: it was a programme for confrontation (Cairns and Richards, pp. 141–2). Yet even in Ireland civil rights demonstrators were astonished, initially, when police beat them off the streets: they had expected better of duly constituted authority.[6] This illustration of the readiness of the state to use force, and of the nasty consequences, has cast a long shadow across the rest of the United Kingdom. It has, in the eyes of many, discredited 'the peculiar missionary nostalgia and phoney *grandeur* of Britishism' (Nairn, *Break-up*, p. 79), and techniques of surveillance and control are seeping back into mainland policing. 'Terrorism' is replacing the Cold War as the reason why we must all submit to strenuous government. The third overwhelming factor was the inability to cope with the recession following the oil-price rises of 1973–4. According to Keynesianism, recessions should be headed off by counter-cyclical economic policies, but when this was tried on a large scale, it didn't work. Postwar economic confidence had been based on a delusion, and for welfare-capitalism in Britain it was the last straw.[7]

The failure of hopes in the Wilson governments produced the political crisis of 1968, when a considerable proportion of people became sceptical about the viability of social-democratic institutions (see chapter 11). Through the 1970s, the Wilson move from collaboration to coercion was repeated under Labour and Conservative governments (Leys, ch. 6). Edward Heath, as prime minister (1970–4), proposed new-right economic and industrial policies, but performed a 'U-turn' when unemployment rose to one million; he would not risk the consequences of repudiating welfare-capitalism. The key economic crisis, the one that showed the game was up, came in 1976. The Callaghan – Healey government was already giving priority to controlling the money supply (this was not a new-right invention; Riddell, pp. 57–60), but it also was trying to maintain a 'social contract' with trades unions in the face of rising unemployment. So the ambitions of welfare-capitalism were at full stretch. Sudden pressure on the pound caused Chancellor Denis Healey to accept from the International Monetary Fund a package, devised in the US Treasury, which slashed social spending. The attempt to create sufficient growth to maintain a social system that would produce an enthusiastic workforce fell to pieces.

It is because of those perceived political and economic failures that Margaret Thatcher has been elected and re-elected: people came to distrust the endless manipulations practised by 'consensus' politicians in their attempts to keep all the balls in the air at once (see Gamble). The old stories failed. Many people no longer believe in the capacity of governments to deliver on the pact of welfare-capitalism. Whether it could be established on more fruitful grounds is a crucial question.

The Failure of 'Good' Culture

As the Wilson administrations took welfare-capitalism to its furthest stretch in the 1960s, the cultural assumptions that had been generated in the late 1940s were strained and broken. I argued in chapter 11 that a left-liberal intelligentsia displaced the old leisure elite and demanded that welfare-capitalism live up to its promises, especially in respect of culture; and government responded (though not to the satisfaction of the left). Arts Council grants tripled; public sector broadcasting was developed and maintained. And inequalities in education were addressed: secondary education was largely comprehensivised, producing eventually a notable rise in achievement, and student numbers in higher education doubled. Education spending rose to overtake 'defence' – but this was only in line with the increase in numbers of young people, and dissatisfaction persisted.[8] Despite such attention to left-culturist priorities, the early 1960s exuberance and readiness for change far outdistanced the ethic, funding and resourcefulness of state-sector cultural production. By 1966 Lord Goodman, chairman of the Arts Council, was warning that 'the pop groups are winning the battle' against the arts and their intuition of 'the worthwhile things in life' (Hewison, *Too*, pp. 126–7). The moment of left-culturism was also the moment of its supersession, and of the disintegration of the assumptions about 'good' culture which it had inherited and developed.

'The 1960s' is of course a myth; but that is an important thing to be, since what we think and do depends on the stories we tell ourselves:

> Fashions changed, changed again, changed faster and still faster: fashions in politics, in political style, in causes, in music, in popular culture, in myths, in education, in beauty, in heroes and idols, in attitudes, in responses, in work, in love and friendship, in food, in newspapers, in entertainment, in fashion. What had once lasted a generation now lasted a year, what had lasted a year lasted a month, a week, a day. There was a restlessness in the time that communicated itself everywhere and to everyone. (Levin, B., p. 9)

It wasn't quite bliss to be alive, but it made a change. Thom Gunn associates London in 1964–5 with the Beatles: 'They stood for a great optimism, barriers seemed to be coming down all over, it was if World War II had finally drawn to its close, there was an openness and high-spiritedness and relaxation of mood' (*Occasions*, p. 180). Others were horrified. Donald Davie said the government was 'Financing, out of foreign loans,/Welfare and the Rolling Stones' (*Collected Poems*, p. 265). Roy Fuller, speaking as Oxford professor of poetry, decided he was a Leavisite after all (*Professors*, ch. 1). But such resistance added to the fun, to the sense that something significant was happening. The dam of established authority broke, weakened by the loss of empire and an outmoded class structure.[9]

The conception of 'good' culture generated in welfare-capitalism, I have shown, took much from the residual leisure elite. Movement and Angry writers eschewed self-consciously artistic modes and presented 'down-to-earth' attitudes on class and sexuality, but their conception of 'good' culture was not very different – they adopted jazz as a protest but also as an art. The New Left actually revalidated 'good' culture and 'responsible' institutions. All this came into question as the rebellion of middle-class and higher-educated young people impatient with the reticence of their parents coincided, briefly and almost uniquely, with the rebellion of lower-class young people, built upon the rock-'n'-roll and skiffle subcultures. There were new kinds of employment in cultural production for the upper-middle-class young, and unaccustomed people invaded the old kinds.[10] These young people had acquired the confidence not to compromise with 'good' culture but to challenge it with new modes. Robert Christgau writes of an unprecedentedly widespread 'nonslumming bohemianism', typified by the 'unpretentious and declassé' Rolling Stones, deriving from their immersion in mass culture, state education (especially art school) and consumer capitalism (in Miller, J., pp. 185–6). Through Pop Art, happenings, Artaud and fringe theatre, Underground poetry, and the new respect shown to television and popular music, traditional notions of cultural authority fell into confusion. 'Art', 'literature' and 'poetry' looked like grafitti, advertisements, comics and pop songs, and the kind of attention usually given to 'good' culture was lavished on popular and commercial forms.

The authority and consensual significance of 'art' and 'literature' collapsed together with other kinds of authority and consensus. Irreverent attitudes invaded such citadels as the Church of England and the BBC – for instance in Bishop John Robinson's *Honest to God* and Edmund Leach's 1967 BBC Reith Lectures (Robinson was headlined as declaring 'Our image of God must go'; Leach questioned whether there is something intrinsically virtuous and natural about law and order, argued that moral rules are conventional and cultural, and suggested that the current 'anarchic' temper of young people was a healthy attack on the class system). Bernard Levin related upheavals in the arts to a general failure of deference:

> Not only was Jack as good as his master, but sound was as good as music; nay, the simultaneous blaring of six random-tuned radio sets (a work by John Cage) was as good as Mozart if not better (because less bourgeois), and a papier-maché thumb four feet high (the centre-piece of the I.C.A. exhibition at which Jennie Lee [Minister for the Arts] had made her impassioned defence of the new art) more real than Titian. (p. 317)

Levin's scepticism did not protect him from the infection – he goes on to quote Bob Dylan's 'It's a Hard Rain' in its entirety, admiring its 'genuinely poetic quality' (p. 321).

Despite raids into the state sector (the Royal Shakespeare Company promoted work based on Artaud, and the Arts Council cautiously funded fringe theatre),[11] the aura that was cultivated was recklessly commercial – in magazines, clothes, the music business, love-ins, psychedelic lightshows and drugs. Left-culturists were disconcerted by the combination of commerce and rebelliousness. They had accepted the notion of art as opposed, by definition, to commerce (see pp. 28–9, 245–6). They were uncertain what to think, for instance, about pirate pop radio stations: the Wilson government dithered between its image of enterprise and youth (it awarded the Beatles the MBE), and its feeling that state control and BBC culture should be maintained (Turnstile; Hood). In chapter 8 I described jazz and rock fans' fascination with the United States, and in chapter 9 how a revived Modernism, starting from Abstract Expressionism, became a vehicle of US cultural ascendancy by seizing the concept of art. Now the stylistic juxtapositions of Modernism were combined with the danger of US popular culture and a glossy or throw-away consumerist manner: this was regarded as 'American', and was cultivated as a way of resisting the patronizing and nannying (as it was perceived) of establishment institutions of 'good' culture. Pop Art, which began in Britain and the United States in the 1950s, played upon these motifs.

Pop Art was stimulated partly by the new respectability of Modernism: it used some of the same stylistic strategies, but refused the romantic intensity of Abstract Expressionism and its supporters (though it wasn't always clear which was which in the exuberance of the mid-1960s). Scandalously, it broke down the division, which Modernism had sustained, between art and commercial imagery. Pop Art knows that art is a commodity, and doesn't care; or, perhaps, it despises earlier art for pretending that it could escape. It refuses the exalted isolation of art and the solemnity of the gallery, and seeks to draw representation back into social reality. Roy Lichtenstein specified 'the use of commercial art as subject matter in painting' as the key to Pop Art – 'an involvement with what I think to be the most brazen and threatening characteristics of our culture'.[12] By playing with a plurality of styles and using self-consciously the methods and motifs of popular culture and the market, Pop Art makes manifest the conditions of its own production and consumption. Andy Warhol's Marilyn Monroe and Campbell Soup prints are paradigmatic instances: by using images of the mass media and advertising and repeating them symmetrically, and in prints rather than a unique painting, Warhol proclaims a relationship with mass-produced representations. The scandal is that he doesn't indicate what the relationship is. He refuses the produndity and responsibility of Modernism: 'If you want to know all about Andy Warhol, just look at the surface of my films and paintings and me, and there I am. There's nothing behind it' (Gidal, p. 9).

So art became like advertising and advertising became like art: you could buy poster copies of great masters and there was a soup advertisement alluding to Warhol. Avant-grade techniques, visual and verbal, became standard fare in advertising and pop music; it is hard to tell where art begins and ends. To be sure, the cultural apparatus was not circumvented. According to Lichtenstein, the idea had been 'to get a painting that was despicable enough so that no one would hang it' (Russell and Gablik, p. 92). In 1958 the authorities refused to hang Rauschenberg's *Bed* at Spoleto, but in 1964 he won the prize at the Venice Biennale and drew the largest crowds ever at the Whitechapel Gallery in London. New works were sold for large sums before they reached the dealers.[13] However, this has further damaged the pretensions of 'art', tending to confirm the sceptics' opinion that visual art has fallen prey to a commercial racket.

The success of Pop Art was to render large areas of cultural production 'Pop-ish' – overruling conventional distinctions of genre and status. Groups such as The Who and the Beatles were said to be influenced by it (the cover for *Sergeant Pepper*, 1967, was designed by Pop artists Peter Blake and Jan Howarth; *The Who Sell Out*, 1968, has between the songs the commercials and jingles of commercial radio). The cultural establishment lost its bearings. The Royal Academy exhibition of 1963 featured a painting in the Pop manner which turned out to be a *Private Eye* hoax. The Beatles' chord progressions were compared with Mahler's in *The Song of the Earth* by the music critic of *The Times*; their refrains were admired by Wilfred Mellers, in lectures at York University, as 'vocalised regression, emulating the cry of the newborn babe (which may also be the chuckle or hum of the deity), attempting to re-enact the primal relationship of mother and child' (Mellers didn't forsake his Leavisite principles, though – he found 'a basic, life-affirming human experience'). The guest of honour at the Foyle's literary luncheon to celebrate the 400th anniversary of Shakespeare's birth was John Lennon.[14] The state censored and banned plays at theatres that it was subsidizing.

Pop facilitated a mid-1960s break-through into political work, both by its disrespect for the dignity of art and its collage methods (always crucial for political pamphlets) – particularly in British pop poetry and fringe theatre – and in relation to the Vietnam War (from *US* at the Royal Shakespeare Company in 1966 to the 'Angry Arts Week' at the Roundhouse in 1967). In the 1970s explicitly political theatre became possible and exciting, especially through the Women's Movement. However, the strategy of routing protest against economic and political conditions through a protest at the conventional concept of art lost power through familiarity. Pop Art is still disputed, not quite safely pigeon-holed. But once the status of art as non-commodity was finally blown, the effect couldn't be repeated: you cannot have an avant-garde without an established tradition to confront.[15] Once there is a big constituency ready to welcome the new and challenging – sufficiently big to be massaged by colour supplements in Sunday newspapers – it becomes hard to be new and challenging. And it becomes hard to see where art goes next.

Literature was comparably affected, especially through the attitudes of Englit. students in higher education. The growth in their numbers was one outcome of the welfare-capitalist programme of making 'good' culture widely available – to all who could become qualified, according to the Robbins Report on higher education (1963). But cultures don't mean the same when you switch them from one social group to another. Deriving from the culture of the leisure class, albeit modified by Leavisism, literature was an acquired culture for the new students rather than part of their customary ambience. Graham Hough was remarking by 1964 that Englit. was turning out to be just a 'subject', the acquisition of 'a set of special tricks' ('Crisis', pp. 99, 103–5).

At first, in the 1950s, scholarship boys and girls deferred to the syllabus: they thought the lower-class cultures they were abandoning to be narrow, and that they were moving into 'good' culture. From the early 1960s the syllabus was, for many, an academic study, one of the rival subcultures they inhabited. In June 1965 the Albert Hall hosted a symptomatic occasion: a reading of Beat and Underground poetry for 6,000 people in an atmosphere, according to Jeff Nuttall, of 'pot, impromptu solo acid dances, of incredible barbaric colour, of face and body painting, of flowers and flowers and flowers, of a common dreaminess in which all was permissive and benign.' Nuttall wrote to a friend: 'London is in flames. The spirit of William Blake walks on the water of Thames. sigma has exploded into a giant rose. Come and drink the dew.'[16] Such novelties undermined not just the literature recommended in lectures but also the New Left subculture that had reaffirmed the imaginative seriousness of literature. The Albert Hall audience was still recognizably continuous with the youthful left-liberal intelligentsia that had cohered around CND (Adrian Mitchell's Vietnam poem 'To Whom It May Concern' was as well received as the more Blakean contributions), but the next stage was the development of a student version of popular culture. Student culture and popular youth culture converged.

Folk music had been edging round, partly through the influence of Dylan, towards 'folk rock' (Miller, J., pp. 206–21), leading on towards singer-songwriters and 'progressive rock'. The Beatles' *Sergeant Pepper* album and the best-selling Penguin Modern Poets volume *The Mersey Sound*, both in 1967, consolidated these tendencies towards a poetry that sounded like rock lyrics and a rock music that was more thoughtful (or pretentious, depending on your viewpoint). Here students found, as previously with jazz but more directly (there was to be jazz – rock too), cultural forms that responded to their class and educational backgrounds, to their intellectual and artistic aspirations. On the whole the wish to make rock into art by drawing upon classical music was a British (rather than a US) phenomenon; John Rockwell attributes it to 'class divisions and the crushing weight of high culture' (in Miller, J., p. 322). The effect was further to confuse categories that had been distinct.

Most pop and Underground poetry was written to be read aloud, and its immediacy and impermanence was intended partly as a critique of the solemn practices of the literary establishment. But its subversive power derived from the way it claimed the imaginative excitement that was supposed to belong to canonical literature. To justify his 'Children of Albion' Michael Horovitz quoted Leavis: 'Poetry matters because of the kind of poet who is more alive than most people, more alive in his own age. He is, as it were, the most conscious point of the race in his time' (Horovitz, p. 373). It was plausible, to young people, that Dylan and Underground poets met this demand. Englit. students began to call for comparable 'relevance' in their courses. The fact of this call signalled irreparable damage to cultural authority, because 'great art' should be relevant by definition – that's how you know it's great. The universal culture, it appeared, was not universal – not even for those selected as specially suited to its study.

Meanwhile, the pretensions of literature were being tested in secondary schools also. Progressivists sought to make literature relevant at all ages and levels of study, and inevitably, therefore, drew away from canonical texts and towards the students' experience. Humanities programmes were devised partly for the same reason – to present issues in accessible ways. By 1980, on British examination syllabuses, Shakespeare was becoming the one remaining witness to the universality of the canonical literary text; absurdly, he is made to represent a category of which he is the only undoubted instance (Dollimore and Sinfield, ch. 3).

Hough believed that literary education had been founded in 'an ideal of intellect and character combined, an ideal of general personal development' ('Crisis', p. 97). But university teachers of Englit. became increasingly professionalized – partly because they themselves were not leisure class, partly because the changing character of the students undermined their traditional rationale, partly through the influence of the United States. The language was already there: the technical stance of I. A. Richards, the cleverness of William Empson, the quarrelsomeness of F. R. Leavis – these were not gentlemanly discourses. Nor, even, were the scholarship and earnestness of Muriel Bradbrook and Helen Gardner quite ladylike. New Criticism was very appropriate for professional exploitation (as it was for teaching). Any number of 'explications' of 'the text' could be offered, and the more arcane they were the better they suggested professorial mystique. Also, interpretation might achieve relevance: often it strove to make texts deriving from distant moral, social and political assumptions acceptable in the modern world. Of course, it was all depoliticized – the meanings discovered were in terms of the 'human condition'.

The fragility of these procedures made it inadvisable to raise general issues – the cat might get out of the bag. For the same reason, I suspect, quarrels about the relative quality of authors and texts faded away, and it became unprofessional even to dispute others' readings. Such disputes might expose the fact that there was no coherent basis on which they could have been resolved. It all became very boring; Elizabeth Bruss remarks a tendency 'to render literature ever more vacuous as it became more precious'.[17]

So when calls for relevance were given systematic political force by women, lower-class students and Blacks, sections of the left-liberal intelligentsia readily forsook traditional modes. Literary studies diversified (in Britain often implicitly and mainly in 'new' universities and polytechnics) into American Studies, Women's Studies, Cultural and Media Studies, Black Studies. Texts were contextualized historically, and modern writing became the focus (rather than, as hitherto, an embarrassment). Englit. became self-conscious about its own history and construction. The Women's Movement was particularly important, for women formed the larger part of Englit. students and feminist awareness problematized virtually every canonical text. First it was suspected that much 'literature' might be sexist; then, as more and more writing by women was republished, the canon began to look like a conspiracy to deprive women of intellectual and artistic status (see Chapter 10). Literary theory was developed partly to sort out the muddle, but mostly, I think, because the existing arrangements were exhausted, especially for clever young graduate students. And to some of us it became apparent that the cultural apparatus is political.

All this is seen by traditionalists as the wilful destruction of 'good' culture. In one sense that is wrong: the institution has rarely been livelier. There are more and more books and articles, now with a diversity of embattled approaches. But the fact that the profession seems able to accommodate everything does not guarantee its vitality; perhaps the opposite. The category 'literature' lacks coherent content (this book witnesses to the difficulty: it reconsiders what is called literature and relates it to marginal cases, other writing and other forms, but without attempting clear demarcations). For all the theory, Englit. is founded now in confusion and absence, and could collapse quite suddenly.[18]

Postmodernism and Standards

A major right-wing response to the collapse of cultural authority is to reassert a traditional notion of literary study. The fashionable version at the time of writing is Allan Bloom's rambling opus *The Closing of the American Mind* (1987). But the previous arrangement collapsed because its social basis fell away and its consequent incoherence became glaringly obvious. T. S. Eliot declared that 'good' culture should be grounded in a class; otherwise the cultural elite 'will consist solely of individuals whose only common bond will be their professional interest: with no social cohesion, with no social continuity' (*Notes*, p. 42). In a class society, Eliot is right: without a social location and allegiance, a subculture can gain little purchase on the rest of society, let alone set 'standards' for it. Bloom laments the absence of an aristocracy (p. 89), and even admits the intellectual incoherence of the 'Great Books' programme he wants to reinstate (p. 344). The only authority he can propose is the say-so of professional academics.

The crucial property that cannot be restored is universality. While the leisure elite felt confident enough in its superior civilization to univer-salize its culture, it could propose its readings as centrally human; when welfare-capitalism claimed literature for everyone, critics could read on behalf of us all. So the key assumption of criticism, that you examine the text and say what it means, could continue. But once it is noticed that texts mean differently for different groups, criticism is revealed as an authority claim tending to disqualify inappropriate readers. If a lower-class person, woman, student, person of colour, lesbian or gay man does not 'respond' in an 'appropriate' way to 'the text', it is because they are reading wrongly – i.e. not from the position that has traditionally been privileged in the literary-critical apparatus (white, adult, male, middle-class, heterosexual). To be sure, almost anyone may be coached to internalize and produce an 'appropriate' response, but that will be at the expense of the person they thought they were.

This is not to say that Englit. is a pointless place to be. It is a mistake to suppose that there is, somewhere else, an untainted site of intellectual or political engagement. Englit. is one of a range of current intellectual practices, all more and less unsatisfactory. However, there is a fundamental challenge to the skills of textual analysis once we accept that instead of the 'right' reading we must ask: for whom? For that leads towards a sociology and politics of readers, and for this, most in-post teachers have few skills and little knowledge. Actually, the hitherto disqualified readers are in an overwhelming majority in the world, but they have been denied power by the authority claims of the institution. From this knowledge there may be forgiveness but, surely, no return.

Another response to the collapse of cultural value is to call it Post-modernism. That much-canvassed term is often defined as the fading of cultural authority – the disintegration of hierarchy among texts. In this light, the postwar revival of Modernism appears as a last-ditch attempt to salvage 'good' culture by declaring the artwork autonomous, independent of a wicked world; and avant-gardes such as Surrealism and Pop Art appear as the principal alternatives to that – attempts to rediscover a political role for art in the world (though it is not easy to distinguish them in the 1960s, when diverse tendencies tangled together exuberantly). Post-modernism proclaims the end of both: that there are now no effective hierarchies in cultures, no depths beneath surfaces, no totalities through which to organize fragments; and no political theories adequate to the dispersal of significance in the postmodern world.[19] When Leavis and Adorno complained that 'good' culture was threatened by commercial culture, they thought they knew which was which. The 1960s realization was that market structures were organizing all cultural production. Harry Levin wrote: 'The development of the arts is registered through a series of shocks to the public – which, after all, in buying cars or clothes, accepts the principle of planned obsolescence' (p. 225); and Harold Rosenberg drew attention to 'the belief that the most recent art condemns earlier modes to obsolescence, as the latest model of a kitchen appliance renders earlier oncs out of date.'[20]

I have discussed the marketing of painting. Literature since the 1960s has also looked increasingly like a commodity (with, for instance, a 'top ten' like pop records). Books may be conceived not by authors, but by publishers who commission the work they believe they can sell. Big profits are possible, so more books are published though there are only a few more readers, and the competition to attract media attention becomes greater. The moderately successful book may be squeezed out. Publishers and retailers are subsumed into conglomerates often not concerned primarily with books. The idea of literary quality is used as a manifest marketing ploy – in literary prizes such as the Booker (with the final announcement live on television), in the promotion of book 'clubs', and in the selling of films and television serials through their derivation from a 'literary classic' – and then the book through its connection with the screen version. For instance after Conrad's tale 'The Duel' had been made into the film *The Duellists*, a new paperback novel of the film, called *The Duellists*, was produced.[21]

It is a question, though, how far the situation is new. Novels have always been published for profit – hence the complex attitude to money in many of them (Lovell, pp. 28–35), and the struggle of Henry James, Virginia Woolf, Leavisites and others to claim 'the novel' as an art form. I have remarked early 1950s anxieties about literature and the market (pp. 105–9). Fredric Jameson argues that capitalism has for a long time been absorbing all cultural production and making art into one more market activity (Jameson, pp. 136–7). Rachel Bowlby locates the latter part of the nineteenth century as the point when business shifted from production to selling – from the satisfaction of staple needs to the invention of new desires (ch. 1). At that moment (the moment that produced Veblen's analysis of conspicuous consumption) art and commerce converged. Of course, art is not generally understood in such terms; on the contrary, it is believed to be the one thing that resists consumer capitalism. I have already argued that art and literature (as they have been conceived) depend on the contrasting 'commercialization' of 'mass' culture to establish their authenticity (see Chapters 3, 8).

It is precisely the claim to rise above use value that makes art the ideal commodity. Having supplied all the useful goods that it is interested in supplying, capital seeks a further range of useless items that people can be persuaded to buy, and art affords excellent opportunities. The ultimate item of consumption is something you didn't know you wanted, but which appears supremely necessary when it comes into view. So the market shares the programme of welfare-capitalism: making as many people as possible want 'good' culture (and some forms have flourished in the market and state system equally – literature for instance). However, as the number of people who can afford to buy something beyond immediate needs has increased, the market has spoilt its own strategy by overworking it. The idea of art depends partly on rarity, elitism and exclusion, and the wider dissemination of texts, performances and objects allows it to be seen that art is (among other things) a commodity. This undermines cultural hierarchy, and is called Postmodernism.

Though Postmodern discourse seems to locate itself beyond the failure of art, it remains remarkably preoccupied with art. Even Leslie Fiedler, who seized upon Postmodernism in 1970 as *'subversive*: a threat to all hierarchies', wants to retrieve the exalted artistic experience: 'Literature becomes again prophetic and universal – a continuing revelation appropriate to a permanent religious revolution, whose function is precisely to transform the secular crowd into a sacred community' ('Cross', p. 294). Like the Absurd with God, Postmodern discourse is structured by the absence it claims to transcend. Though it repudiates the *Angst* of Modernism, it often gives off an air of bravado or loss; Charles Russell observes paranoia and entrapment (pp. 260–4). Look again at the left-culturism of Richard Hoggart, in 1961:

> Culture becomes a commodity . . . the products of art become an eclectic shiny museum of styles. . . . You may buy by subscription and renew, as often as you renew the flowers in your sitting room, examples of Aztec art or African art or Post-Impressionist painting or the latest book (probably about the horrors of mass-society). . . . And all have the same effect as the latest instalment of the television magazine. . . . Culture has become . . . a thing to be consumed, like the latest cocktail biscuit.[22]

Postmodern discourse often amounts only to a reorganization of this anxiety, still thinking in its terms even while renouncing its distaste, bravely asserting that there is no cause for alarm. It is informed, still, by the yearning for a point beyond commodity relations; whereas actually there is, and has been, no such point. Meanwhile the institutions of art remain in place – galleries and print shops, concerts, prestige publishing, serious reviewing, literary prizes, features on television, literary criticism and theory in higher education; in Britain, the Arts Council and BBC as well. Often they are discussing Postmodernism which, I suspect, is keeping 'good' culture going around the assertion that it cannot be kept going.

This suspicion is fed by the attention given to television – an ancient ground of mass-cultural consternation among traditionally-minded intellectuals. They find it no consolation that television in Europe is establishing itself as a vehicle of serious culture (a number of features and films broadcast in Britain are drawn upon in the present study). The movement of intellectuals and fiction writers into television – including the development of the 'telenovel' (designed for televisual realization) – spoils the dignity of 'good' culture.[23] Jean Baudrillard, expounding Postmodernism in an essay called 'The Ecstasy of Communication', declares television 'the ultimate and perfect object for this new era – our own body and the whole surrounding universe become a control screen' (in Foster, p. 127). 'It is well known', he asserts, 'how the simple presence of the television changes the rest of the habitat into a kind of archaic envelope, a vestige of human relations whose very survival remains perplexing' (p. 129). Like McLuhan, Baudrillard imagines that television is undifferentiated electronic flickering, and that it displaces utterly other kinds of cultural production. This is contradicted by numerous studies showing that people watch selectively and place what they see in relation to ideas about 'human relations' from diverse sources. While it is now common for humanities students and teachers in Britain to watch a soap opera, they won't watch *any* soap opera (it is the same with rock music). The improved status of television is so disconcerting to traditional intellectuals that it seems to prove that anything goes. But it has occurred largely through traditional means: employing good writers on interesting topics. Of course, this happens only some of the time and often outside peak hours; as with print, you select.

The fading cultural hierarchies (if they are indeed fading) correspond to political hierarchies. I considered in Chapter 7 the humiliation of European humanism when it was learnt that colonial subjects dispute its superiority; lower-class subcultures have constituted a similar threat to elitist intellectual assumptions.[24] One project of Modernism was the containment of such diverse others within a Eurocentric, high-cultural framework:

Jerusalem Athens Alexandria
Vienna London
Unreal.

Unreal, but realized in Eliot's 'Waste Land'. When such containment becomes implausible, the discourse of Postmodernism registers the return of the repressed; and this is so disquieting to an introverted intellectual elite that it is represented as a universal collapse of value.

The tendency of Postmodern discourse to claim sway over other discourses, including those of politics, has manifest political implications. Modernism claimed to describe 'the modern condition', but part of that condition was the gap between high culture and the social order; so a space was produced that might be used for criticism. The totalizing, apocalyptic vision most often proposed in Postmodern discourse depoliticizes culture by imagining it as flowing, necessarily, with the stream of consumer capitalism. No position is envisaged from which to speak that is in advance of, even outside, the general situation. Hal Foster calls this 'the postmodernism of reaction' and proposes 'a postmodernism of resistance', but he acknowledges that the former is 'far better known'.[25] One theme of this book has been that cultures are intertwined with social and political arrangements. If this is so, it is likely that the fading of certain kinds of hierarchy is producing the compensatory strengthening of others. If moral and intellectual power are now more diffused in the arts, they are very much in place elsewhere. Any notion that Postmodernism signals a general dispersal and weakening of power in the social system is extraordinary in the decade of Reagan and Thatcher. Before considering the prospects for a positive cultural strategy I attempt an analysis of aspects of New Right cultural policies that set the conditions for its activity.

New-Right Cultural Production

In the view of the New Right, the postwar attempt to rule by consent must be replaced by a regime based on discipline. The monetarist cure for inflation is mass unemployment: then the workforce will have to reduce its expectations. Unemployment, in Britain, is not just the unfortunate consequence of recession, for the increase has been greater than in other countries; of the rise between 1979 and 1983, 40 to 50 per cent has been variously estimated as due to government policies (Riddell, pp. 91–2). The number on or below the poverty line increased from 5.9 million in 1979 to 8.8 million in 1983, and to around 10.2 million in 1988. These people are consigned indefinitely to payments that were supposed to be for emergencies and anomalies.[26] An underclass returns, and it will be kept in order by stronger policing. At the same time, the beneficiaries of tax cuts have been the already well-off, who also receive state handouts through mortgage relief and pension funds (Riddell, pp. 230, 270).

These policies are rendered inevitable to a majority of the electorate by the failure of welfare-capitalism, and attractive to many by an ideology of 'law and order', family, 'individualism', race and nation. As Stuart Hall says, we would be unwise not to acknowledge the strength of new-right ideology. Its themes are made the more insidious by the way they vary certain radical themes: the libertarian impulse (for instance, not to be harried by a bureaucratic state) is reorganized as aggressive individualism; the wish for a collective identification is parodied by racist ideology; the idea that the personal is the political is shrivelled to belief in 'the family'.

Even so, we need to keep in mind the precariousness of all ideological manoeuvres. As I observed in Chapter 3, people hold divergent attitudes without needing to reconcile them, and progressive and reactionary elements may be tangled in together. The jingoism at the time of the Falklands/Malvinas expedition, for instance, was not the one true attitude of British people exposed, but one layer of sentiment that could be brought to the surface and exploited in particular circumstances. Nor was it unalloyed: older people not specially to the left remembered with sadness the departure of troop ships in World War II, and expressed more trepidation than enthusiasm. Ideology is not a block of beliefs that the cultural apparatuses propagate and you either do or do not hold. Rather, there is a continual contest to render this or that story of reality more persuasive.

Some people who are manifestly suffering from New Right policies are persuaded to support them. Other excluded people, and some who partly support the right, become disaffected. The disharmony and disruption that the inclusive ideology of welfare-capitalism was intended to contain grows stronger. As Edward Heath put it in 1986: 'If a significant number of our fellow citizens come to feel that they have no realistic expectation of sharing in prosperity, then alienation is inevitable. . . . And alienation brings with it the prospect of crime and social breakdown. Why obey the rules if obedience offers one nothing?' (Deakin, p. 181).

What is surprising, reading New Right books, is how innocent the authors are of social thinking, so taken are they with their simple economic theory. The principal strategy is to talk a lot about 'individual freedom'. In books with titles such as *Capitalism and Freedom* (by Milton Friedman, 1962), *Freedom and Reality* (by J. Enoch Powell, 1969), *The Machinery of Freedom* (by David Friedman, 1973) and *The Recovery of Freedom* (by Paul Johnson, 1980), the latest threat to capitalist freedom is said to come not from the Soviet Union (see Chapter 6), but from creeping socialism within. This has been specially the error of Western Europe, but with Lyndon Johnson's 'Great Society' policy it infected the United States too. Generally though, we are told, political and economic freedom have been exemplified in the United States. This is proclaimed in *Free to Choose* by Milton and Rose Friedman (1980), who discover a 'golden age' in the nineteenth century. However, the Friedmans have to begin by 'omitting' the Amerindians and 'excepting' slavery! (pp. 2–3). As well as being insulting, such an unrealistic notion of freedom gains little purchase on the power relations of complex societies (see Hindess, pp. 122–6).

The question about why people should 'obey the rules' has reached the Home Secretary, Douglas Hurd, who has taken to making 'thoughtful' speeches. At Tamworth in 1988 he reflected upon disturbances in public order – and not just by Blacks, whom he evidently expects to be a nuisance, but by people who are 'white, employed, affluent and drunk'. He wonders why teachers, churches and parents haven't instilled 'a sense of responsibility and values' and warns: 'The fruits of economic success could turn sour unless we can bring back greater social cohesion to our country.' So an ideological difficulty is admitted: 'social cohesion' has to be created. Hurd insists, though, that we shouldn't try again the welfare-capitalist idea of social justice – 'Social cohesion is quite different from social equality.' He wants 'social cohesion alongside the creation of wealth through private enterprise: these are the two conditions of our future progress.' That the two might be incompatible seems not to strike him; on the contrary, he says it worked for the Victorians (overlooking that this is the period of the rise of socialism), and took Britain through the 1914–18 war (overlooking that aggressive capitalism brought Britain into that war). He doesn't mention the 1939–45 war, which was won by state intervention and the promise of more.

That the New Right has a problem with 'social cohesion' is acknowledged by the 'neo-conservative' former editor of *Encounter*, Irving Kristol. He doubts that 'a capitalist system produces the morality needed to sustain it', and fears that 'the free market has a tendency to subvert traditions, having a turbulent effect upon culture and morality.' So it is necessary to search for a way 'of connecting the free market with an attitude towards life that is not economic but derived from religion or at least from traditional values' (Graham and Clarke, p. 86; see Kristol, pp. 169–76). Kristol perceives that Hurd's economic theory undermines his social theory.

Margaret Thatcher's calls for a return to 'Victorian' values are intended to deal with this difficulty by evoking a time when aggressive competition co-existed with tradition, family, religion, respectability and deference. In an interview in the *Daily Mail* (29 April 1988), she represents the 1950s as 'old-fashioned . . . clean and orderly', and blames 'Sixties culture' for spoiling British manners:

> Permissiveness, selfish and uncaring, proliferated under the guise of the new sexual freedom. Aggressive verbal hostility, presented as a refreshing lack of subservience, replaced courtesy and good manners. Instant gratification became the philosophy of the young and the youth cultists. Speculation replaced dogged hard work.

(Ominously for some of us, she says 'this business of breaking the rules began in universities, where most of these theoretical philosophies always start.') Thatcher's story gives her a problem though, for aggression, selfishness, discourtesy, speculation and even freedom are linked in at least some people's minds with economic individualism. So she asserts that the 1960s repudiated individualism, producing 'the block mentality; tower blocks, trade union block votes, block schools' – the country 'had gone quite Socialist in its addiction to welfare, nationalisation and trade union dominance'. But this doesn't sound like permissiveness, instant gratification and lack of subservience; it seems that the 1960s were both individualist and not individualist! She tries to deal with the contradiction: 'All individualism was despised, unless it was an arrogant and selfish individualism' – not a very clear distinction (especially coming from that quarter).

The underlying issue is the same as that in Hurd's speech. New-right economic policy encourages selfish social attitudes, but community feeling cannot be invoked or acknowledged because it is liable to sound like socialism – which has to be stigmatized as 'the block mentality'. Thatcher's difficulty in specifying the right kind of individualism makes it all the more necessary to harp on about Englishness, respectability, family and nation. Belief in them might restore the social stability that is lost with the idea that everyone may join the good society.[27]

This is not to say that Thatcherism is easily challenged. The contradiction between its components may appear not as a disqualification but as a capacity to get you whichever way you move. Unemployment need not be attributed to the government or capitalism: Thatcherism says, 'You have lost your job because women are taking men's jobs'; or 'because all those immigrants are taking the jobs'; or 'because the trade unions maintain such high wages' (Mouffe, p. 96). Like other powerful stories, it partly creates the reality that it expounds, setting limits to 'what will appear as rational, reasonable, credible, indeed sayable or thinkable' (Hall, S., p. 44).

The arts seem an obvious place for the New Right to discover and develop tradition, Englishness, elitism and social stability. But this also is ideologically complex, for 'good' culture has been defined by its uneasy relationship with the market. The arts have always been assumed to need special funding, first by the lesiure elite, then from state subsidy. That, I have argued, has marked their status and, conversely, the funding of 'good' culture has seemed to justify, successively, the elite and the state. Major arts institutions which developed under welfare-capitalism are dependent upon state funding (the national drama companies still derive under half their income from box office and sales; Myerscough, p. 41). But the New Right is unwilling to grant that there is any flaw in market organization, any call for special funding. Thatcherite policy on the arts is like that on other institutions developed by welfare-capitalism in the public domain: they should be 'returned' to the private sector. They should either pay their way or attract business sponsorship.

This attitude is taking root. A 1988 report from the Policy Studies Institute makes an uncompromising commercial case for the arts. They are found to have similar economic dimensions to the motor industry, plastics and chemicals, and agriculture, and can act as a catalyst for urban renewal (Myerscough, pp. 35, 76–9). They come high in the league table of overseas invisible earnings (the proportion of overseas visitors in London theatre audiences has risen rapidly to 37 per cent; I think the fact that English is not, for many of them, their first language, explains a good deal about current productions).[28] The role envisaged for government is specific and like that proposed on the right for other industries: to encourage 'research and development' through 'pump-priming' with 'incentive funds, soft loans or grant-aid' (pp. 158, 163).

Business sponsorship produces money for the arts, but without infringing the market ethos. Company executives believe that the arts 'create the right atmosphere in which business can operate', that they 'turn the region into a better business address', that sponsorship produces 'image enhancement' (Myerscough, pp. 134, 142). So no cultural value need be acknowledged that requires the breaking of market rules, and companies are obliged to declare as much in their programmes and publicity. Jameson remarks that for US business society 'culture' has become 'par excellence the most trivial and non-serious activity in the "real life" of the rat race of daily existence' (p. 139).

But if the arts lose the status that goes with special funding, and become merely up-market entertainments, can they retain the authority of tradition, Englishness and elitism? Sponsorship is not just an alternative mode of funding, it undermines the received idea of the arts and their dignity. After all, the attempt of conservative academics to reinstate 'standards' and 'Great Books' is scarcely compatible with unfettered capitalism; Allan Bloom complains that the current school system has an 'utter inability to distinguish between important and unimportant in any way other than by the demands of the market' (p. 59; also 76–7, 209–10). In the arts the New Right puts at risk properties it needs because, to secure them alongside and in support of competitive individualism, it must contest the received ideological and institutional arrangement of the arts. In brief, those are the arrangements I have been tracing: residually, the high culture of the old leisure class, which the New Right associates with old-style conservatism; the welfare-capitalist belief that good culture should be shared by everyone; and the left-culturist assumption of authority in the arts, with its explicit insistence on a progressive culture for everyone and its effective creation of a New Left subculture. The New Right has to wrest the arts away from these formations. Chancellor Nigel Lawson asserts that Shakespeare is all about order and conservatism (see p. 147), but he still has to persuade much of the accredited Shakespeare apparatus. The interchange between cultural and financial value when Shakespeare's image appears on banknotes and credit cards still strikes many people as incongruous.[29] Far more is at issue than the cost to the state (which is tiny): the granting or refusal of public funding stakes out an ideological position.

This battle has been fought partly through Clause 28 of the Local Government Act (1988), which makes it illegal for a local authority intentionally to 'promote homosexuality'. The clause threatens, among other things, local authority theatres and libraries that present or stock works by Marlowe, Tennessee Williams, Forster, Genet, Mann, Ginsberg, Plato. It provoked strong but unsuccessful resistance from the arts lobby.

Many people seem to believe it an unfortunate oversight that the arts are caught up in Clause 28. Surely, it is implied, the government wants only to stop helplines that might keep gay men and lesbians from suicide; that's fair enough, but they can't really be meaning to interfere in that noble, disinterested realm, the arts? But homosexuality and the arts are already connected: I showed in chapter 5 the link in the 1950s between high culture and a leisure class that was perceived as 'effeminate', 'queer'. Since then anxiety about the issue has abated in artistic circles, but the link is still there. The prevailing idea of the arts in modern English society is defined against the supposed masculine properties of empire builders, industrialists, bankers – the realists who manage the real world. The arts are to do with poetry, ballet, the spirit, sensitivity, taste, camp; and in our culture all that shades into 'effeminacy', and hence gays. Meanwhile, the ethos of the leisure class survives in old-style conservatives – the Tory 'wets' who still want to make welfare-capitalism work – who are concerned, sensitive, tasteful; probably, it is imagined, homosexual.

Furthermore, the removal of some of the legal restrictions on homosexuals in 1967 was a typical 1960s reform designed to bring an excluded group into the consensus; Gay Rights is a left-liberal cause, and homosexuals are perceived as hostile to 'the family'. So for the New Right Clause 28 and the arts bracket a whole bloc of targets, a major ideological project. In the Cold War, communist homosexual treachery was witch-hunted close to the heart of the high-cultural establishment (see chapter 5). This image was reactivated for our age in a *Times* leader of 22 November 1979, which took Anthony Blunt (professor of art history and Soviet spy) and John Maynard Keynes as pivotal Bloomsbury figures, linking welfare-capitalist economic and social policy with 'a homosexual culture', 'the cult of personal relations', 'one of the highest expressions of our culture' and treason. However, *The Times* betrayed itself: 'absolute standards' was misprinted as 'obsolute standards', suggesting a repressed yearning for the 'wrong' word, 'obsolete', and epitomizing the newspaper's sagging standards.

There was a barely perceptible confrontation when Margaret Thatcher talked on television about her 'Favourite Things' with the late Russell Harty – a major media representative of the arts establishment and concurrent victim of a gutter-press campaign around his alleged homosexuality. Thatcher kept her distance from the sensitive, 'effeminate' image of the arts by praising a ceramic of butch marines waving a flag on the Falklands/Malvinas. Harty had the nerve to remark that he hadn't heard of the artist before – surely a great put-down of the premier's choice by an arts authority. But Thatcher kept him in his place by glaring pointedly at him when she spoke of the importance of having children. It is the Schlegels versus the Wilcoxes once more: the arts and 'effeminacy' are set against imperial adventure and the family in a contest over representation and 'good' culture.

Dismantling 'the Culture'

Foucault has observed that for a long period the 'left' intellectual 'was heard, or purported to make himself heard, as the spokesman of the universal' (*Power/Knowledge*, p. 126). This claim is now made mainly by conservatives – Allan Bloom, for instance, thinks our highest task is to ask ourselves, 'What is man?' (p. 21). 'Man' is a powerful concept, but I cannot regret its loss to the left. A divided society should have a divided culture: an (apparently) unified culture can only reinforce power relations. In many situations it may be necessary, now, to defend the arts, as they have been inherited from welfare-capitalism, against new-right assault. But the idea of a universal 'good' culture is mystifying and oppressive, and a medium-term project should be to validate instead a range of subcultures. These are already in place, producing alternative stories, contributing to the solidarity and self-understanding of the groups that sponsor them. It is not a time for universals, but for rebuilding from that base.

At first sight, the 'Man' of European and North American humanism, in whose name 'good' culture was allegedly produced and has usually been read, seems to include everyone; that is why this seemed the culture for welfare-capitalism and left-culturism to proclaim. But in practice 'Man' always has a centre and a boundary. The function of the concept, after all, is to distinguish man from not-man, and this means that someone is marginal and someone gets left out; I showed in Chapter 7 how colonial subjects have been used in European stories. Subordinated groups are, by definition, those whose claim to be 'Man' is weaker, who are less likely to be credited as speaking for the universal.

This argument is specially provocative for gays. Partly because of the history described in Chapter 5, many have learnt to pride themselves on gay contributions to 'culture' (the campaign against Clause 28 was conducted in these terms). However, the arts in general are overwhelmingly heterosexist. Much more than nine to one, the representations they propagate assume that gay men and lesbians do not exist (if they do, they are usually stereotyped). One gay man recalls how he combed the literary canon, hoping to find among these respected stories a place for the feelings that were disturbing him. 'I read of awful stereotyped "queers", objects of derision, pathetic characters, bitchy, mentally unbalanced, sick, criminal almost by definition, at best to be pitied, sad and lonely' (Banks and Weitsch, p. 18). Even writers, painters and choreographers whom we have reason to think of as homosexual have very often adopted a heterosexual point of view in their work. It is because they wouldn't have been published, shown or performed otherwise; and/or were persuaded to believe that their work should be 'universal' – that is, heterosexual!

Terence Rattigan couldn't have the Major in *Separate Tables* (1954) convicted of homosexual soliciting because the London theatre censor wouldn't allow it, so he had him nudging a woman in a cinema. When invited to restore the Major's homosexuality for the New York production, Rattigan said: 'the play might have been construed as a thesis drama begging for tolerance specifically of the homosexual. Instead it is a plea for the understanding of everyone' (Darlow and Hodson, p. 228). In this view heterosexual men who harass women count as 'everyone', whereas gays are too peculiar to be 'Man'. It is sometimes suggested that the struggle for discreet emotional expression was good for the literary imagination – that it produced impressive and even subversive ambiguity (e.g. Meyers, pp. 1–3). To be sure, we can and should uncover the underlying gay implication in discreet writing, but that very act tends to reinforce a notion that gay creativity must be covert. Decoding the work of closeted homosexual artists produces not a cause for congratulation, but a record of oppression and humiliation.

When gay activists remind the world that homosexual men have produced a notable proportion of what is called art and literature, they are pushing at an open door. The world knows that; indeed, it is likely to regard anyone 'cultured' as gay. So far from making us respected and liked, the link with high culture enables them to despise us. Gay men and lesbians gain more self-respect, more community feeling and a better self-understanding by insisting on their own explicit subculture – history, fiction, music. The same, I think, is true for other subordinated groups.[30]

Fredric Jameson has written:

> The only authentic cultural production today has seemed to be that which can draw on the collective experience of marginal pockets of the social life of the world system: black literature and blues. British working-class rock, women's literature, gay literature, the *roman québecois*, the literature of the Third World; and this production is possible only to the degree to which these forms of collective life or collective solidarity have not yet been fully penetrated by the market and by the commodity system. (p. 140)

This is not quite what I have in mind. First, as I have argued (Chapter 8), the yearning for an 'authentic' culture somewhere beyond the commodity system has to be abandoned (certainly if we are to include working-class rock and gay writing, to go no further). Radical cultural production may occur in any sector; I have suggested that the scandal of rock music, which may give it paradoxical political force, is the way it overstates key market motifs. We need a stronger sense of how texts are negotiated in reception, for it is what you do with a book or record that counts: it is easy to be insensitive and reactionary about *King Lear* (as the history of criticism shows) and possible to be subtle and progressive about a soap opera. Furthermore, it is sentimental to imagine that the conditions in which subcultures are produced guarantee the power or goodness of the work done there. Rather, they are places where issues may be contested and identities discovered and consolidated.

Jameson's call for authenticity suggests that part of his purpose is to retrieve 'good' culture (it would be ironic if the peoples that have been excluded by it were to rescue it). He specifies Black, women's and gay literature, but the term 'literature' is of doubtful value to subcultures because of the normative expectations with which it is still laden (for instance preferring complexity and 'quality' to accessibility and commitment). Hence the adjective in a term such as 'Black literature': literature has to be qualified before it can be Black. The Federation of Worker Writers and Community Publishers resists the Arts Council category 'Community Arts' for this reason (Morley and Worpole, p. 56). In her study of 'ethnic minority arts' Naseem Khan shows that activists have to choose between sustaining community cohesion and demonstrating that Blacks, Asians, Cypriots and Poles have as much to contribute to 'the arts' as other people. She herself veers between the two, while making shrewdly the point that the Cypriot Theatro Technis is no more of a 'minority' interest than is the Hampstead Theatre Club, though in 1976 the former received £250 from Camden Borough Council, the latter £14,000 (p. 10).

My emphasis on subcultures is in part defensive, a strategy for bad times. The fading of the welfare-capitalist notion that everyone might eventually join the good society has made it far more acceptable, in the press and legislation, to scapegoat and victimize subordinate groups. The subcultural sense of shared identity and purpose is necessary for self-preservation. However, subcultures may also return to trouble the dominant. Tony Bennett argues, following Ernesto Laclau, that a project for intellectual work is to 'interrupt, uncouple and disrupt the prevailing array of discourses through which subject identities are formed' (Bennett, p. 68). Subcultures may exercise a leverage upon the dominant, denying it a monopoly of credibility; and for two reasons.

First, they are not just collections of texts, but practical milieux which people inhabit and, as I argued in Chapter 13, it is through involvement in a milieu that one discovers an identity in relation to others and perhaps a basis for political commitment. In the terms I proposed in Chapter 3, a subculture promotes its own stories and renders them plausible by making them work in that bit of the world where the subculture is effective. It creates a distinctive circle of reality, partly alternative to the dominant. In your subculture you can feel that Black is beautiful, gay is good. At the same time, and this is the second reason why they may unsettle the prevailing order, subcultures are by no means independent of the dominant. On the contrary, they are formed partly by and partly in reaction to it. They redeploy its cherished values, downgrading, inverting or reapplying them, and thereby demonstrate their incoherence. Their outlaw status may exert a fascination for the dominant, focusing fantasies of freedom, vitality, even squalor. So they form points from which its repressions may become apparent, its silences audible.

Consider as an example the women's theatre movement, which from the mid-1970s became one distinctive place, along with books and journals, where British feminism was thought through, by such companies as the Women's Theatre Group and Monstrous Regiment and such writers as Caryl Churchill, Pam Gems, Michelene Wandor and Claire Luckham. I read this as a major new stage in the New Left subculture that I identified in Chapter 12. The point is not that the plays propagated any precise embodiment of feminism (the writers generally did not start from a worked-out position), but that being at such performances afforded opportunity for women to live for a while in a challengingly female subculture – among the audience and in the whole ambience, as well as in the fictional world of the play. In that context, an alternative reality was being made plausible, and the implications were deeply troubling for customary attitudes. It was suddenly apparent that women might not see things in the same way as men, and that women's perspectives have been suppressed – in that they have not been considered as a legitimate audience response, and in that plays hitherto have almost all assumed a male outlook. The whole hierarchy of theatre and the arts was discomposed: suddenly there is no universal (male) human subject for the artist to address and the critic to invoke, but a choice for the playwright to make as to which group she is going to organize her work for. The next step was to ask whether women's theatre groups should include men and whether men should be allowed to attend performances. The reactions of many men to such unaccustomed marginality showed how a subcultural alternative can get under the skin of the dominant. (However, the limits upon women in conventional theatre largely remain.)

Marcuse warned that abandoning the universal claim of art leaves 'the traditional culture, the illusionist art behind unmastered' (*Essay*, p. 53). But the failure of welfare-capitalism has rendered that culture less persuasive, making space for subcultures to develop alternative forms and institutional bases (such as the women's theatre groups) – venues, audiences, criteria of competence, mediating agents, publishing outlets.

The restriction of subsidy and changed attitude of the state under the Thatcher governments have shown the need for alternative outlets – independent of big business and public funding. To be sure, these are subject to desperate insecurity, needing large efforts by few people. It is not so much that economic viability is impossible; on the contrary, independents have the flexibility and commitment to introduce new forms (in health-foods and feminist publishing for instance), but when their potential becomes apparent they are exploited by big business, draining off personnel and resources (Landry et al., pp. 96–9). However, they are important in keeping the idea of socialism actively present during a bleak period. Small-scale independents selling their work to cover costs and finance further output, creating organizations of a scale to be responsive to the wishes of their constituencies, are a very satisfactory socialist way to arrange cultural production.[31] We should be able to learn from the co-operatives and small-scale enterprises being developed in Yugoslavia, Hungary and now the Soviet Union.[32]

Once more, there is no absolute rule – no intrinsically radical organization or formal principle. If you can get some money from business sponsorship, the Arts Council, a university or the BBC, go right ahead. For a while key institutions may be allowed to pursue a positive cultural policy, much as television did when it felt able to produce plays by Trevor Griffiths, and the Greater London Council (before it was abolished). Do Shakespeare if you can make it work for you. But don't come to depend on the authority and resources of business, the state or the arts. Subcultural work is validated, rather, by the vigour of its engagement with its constituency. It may even witness to the possibility of a workable socialism whose fuller achievement is not at the moment in sight. 'In a perfect world we'd all sing in tune, / But this is reality so give me some room' – Billy Bragg, 'Waiting for the Great Leap Forwards'.

Freedom Once More

In his book *Why Not Trust the Tories?* Aneurin Bevan told how, when Churchill and Ernest Bevin went to watch soldiers boarding ships from which to launch the D-Day invasion of France, the question the soldiers asked was: 'When we have done this job for you are we going back to the dole?' And both leaders replied: 'No, you are not' (p. 49).

The dole queues disappeared for 20 years, though because of a consumer boom rather than the continuation of the wartime spirit of community. But eventually the perpetual chase of affluence after consumption and consumption after affluence accelerated to the point where all sectors could no longer be bought off through shuffles, adjustments and negotiations (pay bargaining, productivity agreements, conciliation and arbitration, royal commissions, incomes policies, pay pauses, social contracts, indexation; race-relations acts and equal-pay acts). When all these fail, the governing elite pulls back into pre-1940, pre-Keynesian attitudes. Now the claim is no longer that everyone is included in the good state, or very soon will be – that capitalism will soon produce enough wealth for welfare to get round to the remaining pockets of deprivation. Now the claim is that there is no alternative. The system is not going to deliver for very many people, and it cannot be helped. The lower classes are divided into those in work, perhaps doing quite nicely, and the others, the underclass. It is adequate, now, to keep a majority content; the pact of 1945 is abrogated.

Chronicling the breakdown of welfare-capitalism and its culture is not difficult (a soft target for the New Right). But, I repeat once more, welfare-capitalism was not introduced at whim, but to cope with the disastrous and threatening conditions of 1900 to 1940. As its ethos fades, we see the return of comparable repression and accelerating social disintegration. If capitalism is in crisis, we cannot assume that the outcome will be a move to the left.

Part of the ideology of 'consensus' was that governments would not go too far in imposing policies on the recalcitrant – there would be some eventual compromise with groups that indicated settled opposition. But the New Right has never been afraid to attack democracy. Frederick Hayek, who opposed welfare-capitalism from the start, said he had no intention 'of making a fetish of democracy', adding that 'there has often been much more cultural and spiritual freedom under an autocratic rule than under some democracies' (p. 52). Despite his idea of leaving things to the spontaneous operations of the market, Hayek recommended coercion when it suited capital and the state – for instance, if trades unions were to resist attempts to lower wages after the war (pp. 153–4).

The Thatcher governments, at three elections, have each time attracted only about 43 per cent of the poll; 1983 was the Conservatives' lowest postwar figure apart from 1945 and 1974 (Gamble, pp. 7–9). But they have systematically assaulted institutions associated with welfare-capitalism, the labour movement and middle-class dissent – trades unions, big-city local authorities, council housing estates, nationalized industries, education, the BBC. They have abandoned, without disguise, the consensual 'arm's-length' understanding on which local authorities, universities and quasi-governmental bodies were run. Now the BBC, the Arts Council, even the Sports Council (Hargreaves, pp. 187, 193–6) are packed with political appointees. Civil liberties have been undermined through use of the Official Secrets Act, further restrictions on citizenship and immigration, removal of trades union rights of teachers and some civil servants, abolition of academic tenure and interference with television and radio news and features (Riddell, pp. 243, 274–5). Colin Leys distinguishes five changes in police powers and operational tactics: the bureaucratization of the police and elimination of democratic control, the shift from community- to 'fire-brigade' and 'pre-emptive' policing, the deployment of new technology, the expansion of political surveillance, and the use of the army for domestic political control (pp. 299–309). New-right 'freedom' is accompanied by authoritarian restrictions; the rolling back of the state is proclaimed, but it becomes ever more intrusive. Labour governments, labelled bizarrely as totalitarian, never dreamt of acting so determinedly.

Now the war is invoked not to figure the promise of a fair society, nor even the desirability of all pulling together, but the need to outlaw sections of the population (disadvantaged sections, of course). On 2 August 1984 *The Times* editorialized on the miners' strike over the closing of their pits and communities:

> There is a war on. It is an undeclared civil war instigated by Mr Scargill, his squads of pickets, and his political associates against the rest of society. The enemy within dares insurrection against legitimate authority. The challenge can be met in only one way if the values of liberal democracy and liberty under the law are to prevail – by enforcing the surrender of Mr Scargill and the national executive of the mine-workers' union. (Corrigan and Sayer, p. 1)

The banners under which we are marshalled there – legitimate authority, liberal democracy, liberty under the law – all took their characteristic modern nuances in the 1940s. But now they are invoked to resist just the kinds of disturbance that welfare-capitalism was supposed to render unnecessary.

And, of course, the excluded are blamed. They tried to cash the implicit promise of fair living and working conditions, and therefore it cannot be kept. Deviants are always used to define the boundaries of the permissible, but the ideology of welfare-capitalism was that eventually everyone could be included. The New Right has no wish to diminish social division, it finds it too convenient. Now that not everyone has to be rendered acquiescent, out-groups who seem not to fit the required ideology can be stigmatized and victimized. Blacks and 'scroungers' bear much of the brunt of such scapegoating in modern Britain, and powerful discourses are mobilized around them to handle unemployment, violence and disaffection (see Hall, Critcher et al). The homosexual community is an obvious target (Dollimore, 'Homophobia'); the arrival of AIDS delighted the gutter press, which made Clause 28 possible (at least it disproves the complacent Postmodernist view that all cultures are now equal: one subculture is not allowed). The larger danger of Thatcherism lies not in its moments of triumph, but in its eventual failure to satisfy or control the emotions it arouses. The rhetoric of law and order and victimization of subordinate groups, with which it attempts to make plausible its social and economic policies, provoke forces of retribution and stimulate expectations that may find terrible kinds of satisfaction.

Specific new-right policies are not popular. In July 1988 opinion polls, as earlier in the decade, are showing big majorities against privatization, the poll tax and a two-tier health service. Asked to choose between sets of 'socialist' and 'Thatcherite' values, there were majorities for the former. 49 per cent of people questioned said they would prefer 'a mainly socialist society in which public interests and a more controlled economy are most important'; 43 per cent wanted 'a mainly capitalist society in which private interests and free enterprise are most important' (Howe). The Thatcher government, nevertheless, has popular support. This, I believe, is not because the Labour Party presents itself badly (people are not stupid), but because people cannot see a way of actualizing their wish for a society based on sharing. The changes of the late 1940s occurred because the war had shown that it could be done, and in 1964 that mood was reactivated. Now we lack such evidence, and Thatcherism is founded on that absence. And because it might just discover a newly persuasive story, the left is derided vehemently at every turn by all established institutions.

There is some work to do before we reach such a point, and this rehearsal of the story so far has been designed to help it forward. The postwar hope for socialism in Britain now seems to have been amazingly hubristic. The formal opposition was underestimated, and so was the danger from the persistence of old ideas embedded inside the best of new intentions. Not only was welfare-capitalism interpreted in the most optimistic light, so was the power of Britain to make it work. The source of the hubris, I now think, was a scarcely recognized sense, on the left, of Britain as a great capitalist power, a victor in the war and somehow imperial even in the decline of empire. This produced the hope that socialism might be introduced, through substantially parliamentary means, in one small island country. But even if the system could have approached this point, 'they' would never have let it happen. Now the perspectives have shifted. It seems that the European Economic Community is to become the major regional administrative structure for relaying the power of international capital – a power that disdains national boundaries, and can bring any economic or political experiment to almost instant crisis. It is a demanding time, even a frightening one, but the enforced uncoupling of left-wing thought from some of its traditional assumptions may yet prove fertile.

Notes

1 Panitch, 'Development'; Panitch, *Social*; Foote, chs. 7, 8; Middlemas, ch. 13; Harris, N., *Competition*, pp. 203–6, 249–54 and *passim*; Bauman, chs. 5–6; Grahame Thompson, 'Economic Intervention in the Post-war Economy', in McLennan et al; Wright, pp. 157–60. Corporatism was claimed by fascism, but improperly, since actually conflict is there repressed rather than negotiated.

2 *Full*, pp. 194, 206; see p. 148 above. W. Arthur Lewis made the same point in *The Principles of Economic Planning* in 1949 (Bauman, pp. 122–4, 173–7). See Panitch, *Social*, pp. 8–9; Bowles and Gintis, pp. 6–7.

3 'Work and Consumption', in Anderson and Blackburn, p. 319; see Bauman, pp. 98, 109–112.

4 Habermas, pp. 61–8; Bauman, ch. 5; Wright, pp. 157–60; Panitch, *Social*, pp. 252–3; David Held, 'Power and Legitimacy in Contemporary Britain', in McLennan et al., pp. 321–38; Middlemas, pp. 369–70, 375–7. For the detailed machinations through the 1950s, see Keith Middlemas, *Power, Competition and the State: Britain in search of balance*, 1940–61 (London: Macmillan, 1986); on the failure to achieve growth in the 1960s, see Peter Sinclair, 'The Economy: a Study in Failure', in McKie and Cook; Leys, ch. 5.

5 *Culture and Society*, p. 303. See Westergaard, p. 38; Held, in McLennan et al.; Corrigan and Sayer, pp. 197–9. On increasing political violence, see Clutterbuck.

6 Bernadette McAliskey, speaking on 'The Year of Dreams', part 5: 'Ireland: the Spark that Lit the Bonfire', Radio 4, 17 February, 1988; see Hall, Critcher et al., pp. 259–60.

7 Rory MacLeod, 'The Promise of Full Employment', in Smith, H. L.; Grahame Thompson, 'Economic Intervention in the Post-war Economy', in McLennan et al., pp. 92–104; Bowles and Gintis, pp. 56–9.

8 See Brian MacArthur, 'The Education Debate', in McKie and Cook; Ryder and Silver, pp. 285–7. On broadcasting and the Arts Council, see p. 249 above.

9 Booker, p. 80 and *passim*; Nuttall, pp. 114–25; Hall, Critcher et al., pp. 235–60; Hewison, *Too*.

10 Fyvel, *Intellectuals*, pp. 54–8; Booker, pp. 20, 45, 80, 86–91, 135–6; Nuttall, pp. 114–16 – citing 'The Goon Show' as a bridge; Melly, *Revolt*, pp. 104, 111–14.

11 Charles Marowitz, 'Notes on the Theatre of Cruelty', in Marowitz and Trussler; Addenbrooke; Sinfield, *Society*, pp. 167, 190–5; Hewison, *Too*, pp. 89–94, 197–225.

12 Russell and Gablik, p. 92; see the introduction by John Russell; and Melly, *Revolt*, pp. 13–16, 127–31; Hewison, *Too*, pp. 41–52. Some commentators now propose a distinction between Modernism, which seeks to exalt art and render it autonomous, and the avant-garde, which seeks to destroy the distinction between art and other kinds of cultural production and intervene politically. See Bürger; Russell, C., ch. 1; Huyssen, pp. vi–vii, 3–4, 162–4. Russell (pp. 242–5) and Huyssen (ch. 8) credit movements of the 1950s and 1960s as a political avant-garde; but Bürger doesn't (p. 61).

13 Tomkins, pp. 204, 181, 184; Hewison, *Too*, pp. 52–5.

14 Melly, *Revolt*, pp. 104, 111–15, 127–8, 172–80; Booker, pp. 199, 221, 235, 245–6; Hewison, *Too*, pp. 61–70, 142–4; Mellers, pp. 28, 33; Fiedler, 'Cross'.

15 See Fyvel, *Intellectuals*, chs. 1, 2, 6, 16; Russell, C., pp. 31–3, 242–8; Huyssen, pp. 21–4 and ch. 9; Kaplan, E. A., chs. 1, 6; Butler, C., pp. 119–24; Graff, 'Myth', pp. 248–9; pp. 189–90 above.

16 Nuttall, pp. 182–3, and 160–206. See Horovitz, pp. 316–28, 336–42; Hewison, *Too*, ch. 3; Melly, *Revolt*, pp. 205–15; Sinfield, *Society*, pp. 109–14, 163–9.

17 Bruss, p. 13, and 12–18; Graff, 'Myth', pp. 245–7 and *Professing*, ch. 14; Eagleton, *Function*, ch. 5; Sinfield, 'Against'.

18 Hohendahl; Graff, *Professing*, pp. 240–62; Eagleton, *Function*, pp. 94–106; Culler, chs. 1, 2; Nowell-Smith.

19 See Eagleton, 'Capitalism, Modernism and Postmodernism', in *Against*; Foster; Kipnis; Russell, C., ch. 8; Kaplan, E. A., ch. 6; Nowell-Smith.

20 Rosenberg, *Anxious*, p. 252 and chs. 2, 20, 22. See Melly, *Revolt*, pp. 131–55, 172–3 and *passim*; Marcuse, *Essay*, chs. 2, 3; Marcuse, *One*, pp. 58–65.

21 Stuart Laing, 'The Production of Literature', in Sinfield, *Society*, pp. 122 35; Sutherland, chs. 3, 4, 9, 10; Lane, M., chs. 6, 8, 9, 12, 13; Morley and Worpole, pp. 37–9; Debray, pp. 107–23; Ohmann, p. 208. I owe the point about 'The Duel' to Cedric Watts.

22 'Mass Communications in Britain', in Ford, *Modern*, p. 462; David Hill drew my attention to this quotation.

23 See Debray on intellectuals; on telenovels, Sutherland, *Fiction*, ch. 12.

24 See Craig Owens, 'The Discourse of Others: Feminists and Postmodernism', in Foster, pp. 57–9; Kipnis; Nowell-Smith.

25 'Postmodernism: a Preface', in Foster, pp. xi–xii. See Russell, C., pp. 268–70; Graff, 'Myth', p. 243.

26 Deakin, p. 157; Leys, p. 90–6; W. G. Runciman, 'Diary', *London Review of Books*, 23 June, 1988, p. 21; Campbell; Ehrenreich, pp. 171–5.

27 Hall, S., pp. 38–9; Laclau and Mouffe, pp. 169–76. Richard Johnson has argued that in the nineteenth century the dominant ideology combined liberal and traditional themes ('Barrington Moore', in Hall, Hobson et al., p. 66).

28 Myerscough, p. 81. Terry Hands, artistic director of the Royal Shakespeare Company, says US tourists make up 20 per cent of summer audiences at the Barbican, and in 1986 the RSC lost £1 million because they didn't come to Britain for fear of terrorism. In 1988 the exchange rate threatens the same, and the RSC is looking to Europe. So titles must be 'classical', well known in Europe; you couldn't put David Edgar's *Maydays* into the main auditorium now, Hands instances ('PM', Radio 4, 13 January, 1988).

29 Graham Holderness discusses the £20 note in Holderness, pp. xi–xiii; the 'bard-card', using Shakespeare's image to guarantee credit-worthiness, has just been announced. See also, in Holderness, ch. 1, and John Drakakis, 'Ideology and the Institution'.

30 See pp. 175–8 above; Culler, ch. 2; Kipnis; Escoffier. And, as I have said, middle-class dissidents should work on their own subculture (pp. 273–4). On gay culture and Rattigan, see Sinfield, 'Who's for Rattigan?'; on Blacks and the arts, see Khan; on 'community intellectuals', see Escoffier, pp. 127–30; on gay history, see Dollimore, 'History'.

31 See Landry et al.; Morley and Worpole; Taylor, H. In the first six months of 1980, for instance, 90 new record labels appeared in Britain (Frith, *Sound*, pp. 155–7). Local Black radio stations may even become legal – here the government's wish to 'deregulate' is likely to have progressive consequences.

32 See Nove, parts 3, 5; Vanek; Hindess, pp. 147–51. Western politicians infer that the Soviets are groping towards a capitalist economy, but actually they may be developing new institutions that will acknowledge a broad range of human needs and potential.

List of books and articles cited

Abelove, Henry, Blackmar, Betsy, Dimock, Peter and Schneer, Jonathan, *Visions of History* (Manchester UP, 1983).

Ackerley, J. R., *My Father and Myself* (London: Bodley Head, 1968). [*My Father*]

——, *We Think the World of You* (1960; Harmondsworth: Penguin, 1971).

Addenbrooke, David, *The Royal Shakespeare Company* (London: William Kimber, 1974).

Addison, Paul, *The Road to 1945* (London: Cape, 1975).

Adorno, Theodor, *Prisms*, tr. Samuel and Shierry Weber (London: Neville Spearman, 1967). [*Prisms*]

Alexander, Paul (ed.), *Ariel Ascending* (New York: Harper and Row, 1985).

Allsop, Kenneth, *The Angry Decade* (London: Peter Owen, 1958).

Althusser, Louis, *Lenin and Philosophy and Other Essays*, tr. Ben Brewster (London: New Left Books, 1971).

Altick, Richard D., *The English Common Reader* (Chicago UP, 1963).

Alvarez, A., *Beyond All This Fiddle* (London: Allen Lane, 1968). [*Beyond*]

——(ed.), *The New Poetry* (1962; rev. edn, Harmondsworth: Penguin, 1966). [*New Poetry*]

——, *The Savage God* (1971; Harmondsworth: Penguin, 1974). [*Savage*]

——, *The Shaping Spirit* (London: Chatto, 1967). [*Shaping*]

——, *Under Pressure* (BBC talks broadcast in 1962–4; Harmondsworth: Penguin, 1965).

Amis, Kingsley, 'Editor's Notes', *The Spectator*, 7 Oct., 1955, p. 459.

——, *Lucky Jim* (1954; Harmondsworth: Penguin, 1961).

——, *My Enemy's Enemy* (London: Gollancz, 1962).

——, *One Fat Englishman* (London: Gollancz, 1963).

——, *Take a Girl Like You* (1960; Harmondsworth: Penguin, 1962).

——, *That Uncertain Feeling* (London: Gollancz, 1955).

Anderson, Perry, *Arguments within English Marxism* (London: Verso, 1980).

——, 'The Left in the Fifties', *New Left Review*, 29 (Jan.-Feb. 1965), pp. 3–18. ['The Left']

Anderson, Perry and Blackburn, Robin (eds.), *Towards Socialism* (London: Collins, 1965).

Annan, N. G., 'The Intellectual Aristocracy', in *Studies in Social History*, ed. J. H. Plumb (London: Longmans, 1955).

Appleyard, Brian, *The Culture Club* (London: Faber, 1984).

Arden, John, *Serjeant Musgrave's Dance* (London: Methuen, 1960).

Ardrey, Robert, *African Genesis* (London: Collins, 1963).

Arnold, Matthew, *Lectures and Essays in Criticism*, Complete Prose Works 3, ed. R. H. Super (Ann Arbor: U. of Michigan, 1962).

Aron, Raymond, *The Opium of the Intellectuals*, tr. Terence Kilmartin (London: Secker, 1957).

Ashford, Douglas E., *The Emergence of the Welfare States* (Oxford: Blackwell, 1986).

Auden, W. H., *The English Auden*, ed. Edward Mendelson (London: Faber, 1977). [*English*]

——, *Forewords and Afterwords*, ed. Edward Mendelson (London: Faber, 1973). [*Forewords*]

——, *The Shield of Achilles* (London: Faber, 1955).

Austin, Allan E., *Roy Fuller* (Boston: Twayne, 1979).

Baldick, Chris, *The Social Mission of English Criticism, 1848–1932* (Oxford UP, 1983).

Balibar, Renée, 'An Example of Literary Work in France', in *1848: the sociology of literature*, ed. Francis Barker et al. (Colchester: U. of Essex UP, 1978).

Ballantyne, R. M., *The Coral Island* (London: Dean and Son, n.d.).

Banks, John, and Weitsch, Martina (eds.), *Meeting Gay Friends* (Manchester: Friends Homosexual Fellowship, 1982).

Banks, Lynne Reid, *The L-Shaped Room* (1960; Harmondsworth: Penguin, 1962).

Barker, Martin, *A Haunt of Fears* (London: Pluto, 1984). [*Haunt*]

——, *The New Racism* (London: Junction Books, 1981). [*New*]

Barnett, Anthony, 'Raymond Williams and Marxism: a rejoinder to Terry Eagleton', *New Left Review*, 99 (Sept.-Oct. 1976), pp. 47–64.

Barraclough, Geoffrey, *An Introduction to Contemporary History* (Harmondsworth: Penguin, 1967).

Barrett, Michèle, *Women's Oppression Today* (London: Verso, 1980).

Barrett, Michèle, Corrigan, Philip, Kuhn Annette and Wolff, Janet (eds.), *Ideology and Cultural Production* (London: Croom Helm, 1979).

Barthes, Roland, *Mythologies*, tr. Annette Lavers (St Albans: Paladin, 1976).

Bassnett, Susan, *Sylvia Plath* (London: Macmillan, 1987).

Bauman, Zygmunt, *Memories of Class* (London: Routledge, 1982).

Bell, Daniel, *The End of Ideology* (Glencoe, Illinois: Free Press of Glencoe, 1960).

Benjamin, Walter, *Illuminations*, ed. Hannah Arendt (Glasgow: Fontana, 1973).

Bennett, Alan, Cook, Peter, Miller, Jonathan and Moore, Dudley, *The Complete Beyond the Fringe* (London: Methuen, 1987).

Bennett, Tony, 'Texts in History: the determinations of readings and their texts', in *Post-Structuralism and the Question of History*, ed. Derek Attridge, Geoff Bennington and Robert Young (Cambridge UP, 1987).

Bennett, Tony, Muncie, John and Middleton, Richard, *Politics, Ideology and Popular Culture*, 1 (Milton Keynes: Open University Press, 1982).

Bennett, Tony and Woollacott, Janet, *Bond and Beyond* (London: Macmillan, 1987).

Berger, John, *A Painter of Our Time* (London: Secker, 1958).

——, *Ways of Seeing* (New York: Viking Press, 1973). [*Ways*]

Bergonzi, Bernard (ed.), *Innovations* (London: Macmillan, 1968).

——, *The Myth of Modernism and Twentieth Century Literature* (Brighton: Harvester, 1986). [*Myth*]

Bernstein, Basil, *Class, Codes and Control*, vol. 1, 2nd edn. (London: Routledge, 1971).

Betjeman, John, *Collected Poems*, ed. the Earl of Birkenhead (London: John Murray, 1958).

Bevan, Aneurin, *In Place of Fear* (London: Heinemann, 1952).

——, *Why Not Trust the Tories?* (London: Gollancz, 1945). [*Why*]

Beveridge, William, H., *Full Employment in a Free Society* (London: Allen and Unwin, 1944). [*Full*]

——, *Social Insurance and Allied Services* (the Beveridge Report) (London: HMSO, 1942). [*Social*]

Bhabha, Homi, 'Of Mimicry and Men: the ambivalence of colonial discourse', in *Politics and Sociology*, ed. James Donald and Stuart Hall (Milton Keynes: Open University Press, 1986).

——, 'The Other Question', *Screen*, 24, no. 6 (1983), pp. 18–36.

Biles, J. I., *Talk: conversation with William Golding* (New York: Harcourt and Brace, 1970).

Birmingham Feminist History Group, 'Feminism as Femininity in the Nineteen-fifties?', *Feminist Review*, 3 (1979), pp. 48–65.

Blackburn, Thomas, *The Price of an Eye* (London: Longmans, 1961).

Blishen, Edward, *Roaring Boys* (1955; London: Panther, 1966).

Bloom, Allan, *The Closing of the American Mind* (New York: Simon and Schuster, 1987).

Blumenthal, Sidney, *The Rise of the Counter-establishment* (New York: Times Books, 1986).

Bogdanor, Vernon, and Skidelsky, Robert (eds.), *The Age of Affluence, 1951–1964* (London: Macmillan, 1970).

Bold, Alan, *Gunn and Hughes* (Edinburgh: Oliver and Boyd, 1976).

Bolt, Robert, *The Tiger and the Horse* (1960; London: Heinemann, 1963).

Bond, Edward, *The Fool and We Came to the River* (London: Eyre Methuen, 1976).

——, *Lear* (London: Eyre Methuen, 1972).

——, *Saved* (London: Methuen, 1966).

Booker, Christopher, *The Neophiliacs* (Glasgow: Fontana, 1970).

Born, Georgina, 'Modern Music Culture: on shock, pop and synthesis', *New Formations*, no. 2 (Summer 1987), pp. 51–78.

Borzello, Frances, *Civilising Caliban* (London: Routledge, 1987).

Bottomore, T. B., *Elites and Society* (Harmondsworth: Penguin, 1966).

Bourdieu, Pierre, 'Cultural Reproduction and Social Reproduction', in *Knowledge, Education and Cultural Change*, ed. Richard Brown (London: Tavistock, 1973).

——, 'Symbolic Power', in *Identity and Structure: issues in the sociology of education*, ed. Denis Gleeson (Driffield: Nafferton Books, 1977).

Bowen, Elizabeth, *The Demon Lover and Other Stories* (1945; Harmondsworth: Penguin, 1966). [*Demon*]

——, *The Heat of the Day* (London: Cape, 1949).

Bowen, John, 'The Dialogue of Logic: Foucault and intellectual practice', *LTP [Journal of Literature Teaching Politics]*, 5 (1986), pp. 38–47.

Bowlby, John, *Child Care and the Growth of Love* (1953; 2nd edn. Harmondsworth: Penguin, 1965).

Bowlby, Rachel, *Just Looking* (New York and London: Methuen, 1985).

Bowles, Samuel and Gintis, Herbert, *Democracy and Capitalism* (London: Routledge, 1986).

Bradbury, Ray, *Fahrenheit 451* (1954; London: Corgi, 1969).

Braine, John, *Room at the Top* (1957; Harmondsworth: Penguin, 1959).

Branson, Noreen and Heinemann, Margot, *Britain in the Nineteen Thirties* (St Albans: Granada, 1973).

Brittain, Vera, *England's Hour* (1941; London and Sydney: Macdonald, 1981).

Brooke, Jocelyn, *The Image of a Drawn Sword* (1950; Harmondsworth: Penguin, 1983).

——, *The Orchid Trilogy* (1948–50; Harmondsworth: Penguin, 1981).

Brookeman, Christopher, *American Culture and Society since the 1930s* (London: Macmillan, 1984).

Brooks, Cleanth, *Modern Poetry and the Tradition*, with new introduction (Chapel Hill: U. of North Carolina Press, 1967).

Bruce, Lenny, *How to Talk Dirty and Influence People* (London: Granada, 1975).

Bruss, Elizabeth, *Beautiful Theories* (Baltimore and London: Johns Hopkins UP, 1982).

Bürger, Peter, *Theory of the Avant Garde*, tr. Michael Shaw, foreword by Jochen Schulte-Sasse (Minneapolis: Minnesota UP and Manchester UP, 1984).

Burgess, Anthony, *The Malayan Trilogy (Time for a Tiger*, 1956; *The Enemy in the Blanket*, 1958; *Beds in the East*, 1959; Harmondsworth: Penguin, 1972). [*Malayan*]

——, *The Novel Now*, 2nd edn. (London: Faber, 1971).

Burnham, James, *The Struggle for the World* (London: Cape, 1947).

Butler, Christopher, *After the Wake* (Oxford UP, 1980).

Butler, R. A., Inaugural Address to P.E.N. Congress, 1956, in *The Author and the Public* (London: Hutchinson, 1957).

Butscher, Edward (ed.), *Sylvia Plath: the woman and the work* (New York: Dodd, Mead, 1977).

Byatt, A. S., *Shadow of a Sun* (1964; London: Panther, 1966).

Cage, John, *Silence* (Cambridge, Mass.: MIT Press, 1961).

Cairns, David and Richards, Shaun, *Writing Ireland* (Manchester UP, 1988).

Calder, Angus, *The People's War* (St Albans: Granada, 1969).

Calvocoressi, Peter, *The British Experience, 1945–75* (Harmondsworth: Penguin, 1979).

Campbell, Beatrix, *Wigan Pier Revisited* (London: Virago, 1984).

Camus, Albert, *The Myth of Sisyphus* (1942), tr. Justin O'Brien, 1955 (Harmondsworth: Penguin, 1975).

——, *The Outsider* (1942), tr. Stuart Gilbert, with an introduction by Cyril Connelly, 1946 (Harmondsworth: Penguin, 1961).

——, *The Rebel* (1951), tr. Anthony Bower, with a foreword by Herbert Read, 1953 (Harmondsworth: Penguin, 1962). [*Rebel*]

Cardiff, David and Scannell, Paddy, 'Broadcasting and National Unity', in *Impacts and Influences*, ed. James Curran, Anthony Smith and Pauline Wingate (London and New York: Methuen, 1987).

Carew, Anthony, *Labour Under the Marshall Plan* (Manchester UP, 1987).

Carothers, J. A., *The African Mind in Health and Disease* (Geneva: World Health Organization, 1953).

Caute, David, *At Fever Pitch* (London: Deutsch, 1959).

——, *Communism and the French Intellectuals* (London: Deutsch, 1964). [*Communism*]

Chambers, Iain, *Urban Rhythms* (London: Macmillan, 1985).

Chetham Strode, Warren, *The Gleam* (London: Sampson Low, Marston, n.d.).

——, *The Guinea Pig* (London: Sampson Low, Marston, n.d.).

Chomsky, Noam, *American Power and the New Mandarins* (Harmondsworth: Penguin, 1969).

Churchill, Winston S., *The End of the Beginning: war speeches*, ed. Charles Eade (London: Cassell, 1943).

Clarke, John, Critcher, Chas and Johnson, Richard (eds.), *Working-class Culture* (London: Hutchinson and Centre for Contemporary Cultural Studies, 1979).

Clutterbuck, Richard, *Britain in Agony* (Harmondsworth: Penguin, 1980).

Cockburn, Alexander and Blackburn, Robin (eds.), *Student Power* (Harmondsworth: Penguin, 1969).

Cohen, Stanley, *Folk Devils and Moral Panics*, 2nd edn. (Oxford: Martin Robertson, 1980).

Cohn, Nik, *Awopbopaloobop Aloopbamboom* (London: Paladin, 1970).

Collins, Mal, Harker, Dave and White, Geoff (eds.), *Big Red Songbook* (London: Pluto, 1977).

Colville, Sir John, *The New Elizabethans* (London: Collins, 1977).

Connolly, Cyril, *Ideas and Places* (London: Weidenfeld, 1953). [*Ideas*]

——, *Missing Diplomats* (London: Queen Anne Press, 1952).

——, *The Unquiet Grave*, rev. edn. (London: Grey Arrow, 1961). [*Unquiet*]

Conquest, Robert (ed.), *New Lines* (London: Macmillan, 1956).

Conrad, Joseph, *Youth: Heart of Darkness* (London: Dent, 1965).

Cooper, David (ed.), *The Dialectics of Liberation* (Harmondsworth: Penguin, 1968).

Corrigan, Philip and Sayer, Derek, *The Great Arch* (Oxford: Blackwell, 1985).

Cox, C. B. and Dyson, A. E., *The Twentieth-century Mind*, III: 1945–1965 (Oxford UP, 1972).

Crosland, Anthony, *The Future of Socialism* (London: Cape, 1956).

Crossman, Richard (ed.), *New Fabian Essays* (1952; London: Dent, 1970).

Culler, Jonathan, *Framing the Sign* (Oxford: Blackwell, 1988).

Dabydeen, David (ed.), *The Black Presence in English Literature* (Manchester UP, 1985).

Daly, Mary, *Beyond God the Father* (Boston: Beacon Press, 1973).

Darlow, Michael and Hodson, Gillian, *Terence Rattigan* (London: Quartet, 1979).

Dart, Raymond A., 'The Predatory Transition from Ape to Man', *International Anthropological and Linguistic Review*, 1 (1953), pp. 201–19.

Davidson, Michael, *The World, the Flesh and Myself* (London: Quartet, 1977).

Davie, Donald, *Collected Poems, 1950–1970* (London: Routledge, 1972). [*Collected Poems*]

——, *The Poet in the Imaginary Museum*, ed. Barry Alpert (Manchester: Carcanet, 1977). [*Poet*]

——, *Thomas Hardy and British Poetry* (London: Routledge, 1973).

Davis, Tricia, 'What Kind of Woman is She? Women and Communist Party Politics', in *Feminism, Culture and Politics*, ed. Rosalind Brunt and Caroline Rowan (London: Lawrence and Wishart, 1982).

Deakin, Nicholas, *The Politics of Welfare* (London: Methuen, 1987).

Debray, Régis, *Teachers, Writers, Celebrities*, tr. David Macey, with an introduction by Francis Mulhern (London: New Left Books, 1981).

Delaney, Shelagh, *A Taste of Honey* (1958; London: Methuen, 1982).

Denneny, Michael, Ortleb, Charles and Steele, Thomas (eds.), *The View from Christopher Street* (London: Chatto, 1984).

Deutscher, Isaac, *Heretics and Renegades* (London: Cape, 1955).

Dibblin, Jane, *Day of Two Suns* (London: Virago, 1988).

Dollimore, Jonathan, 'Different Desires: subjectivity and transgression in Wilde and Gide', *Textual Practice*, 1 (1987), pp. 48–67. ['Different']

——, 'The Dominant and the Deviant: a violent dialectic' *Critical Quarterly*, 28, nos. 1–2 (1986), pp. 179–92. ['Dominant']

——, 'A History of Some Importance', *Gay Times*, 119 (August 1988), pp. 44–5. ['History']

——, 'Homophobia and Sexual Difference', in *Sexual Difference*, ed. Robert Young, special issue of *Oxford Literary Review*, 8, nos. 1–2 (1968) pp. 5–12. ['Homophobia']

——, *Sexuality, Transgression and Subcultures* (forthcoming).

Dollimore, Jonathan and Sinfield, Alan (eds.), *Political Shakespeare* (Manchester UP, 1985).

Donnison, David, 'Drawing Conclusions', in *Founders of the Welfare State*, ed. Paul Barker (London: Heinemann, 1984).

Douglas, J. W. B., Ross, J. M. and Simpson, H. R., *All Our Future* (1968; London: Granada, 1971).

Drakakis, John (ed.), *Alternative Shakespeares* (London: Methuen, 1985).

Driberg, Tom, *Ruling Passions* (London: Quartet, 1978).

Driver, Christopher, *The Disarmers* (London: Hodder, 1964).

Dunn, Nell, *Talking to Women* (London: Pan, 1965).

Durrell, Lawrence, *Bitter Lemons* (London: Faber, 1957).

Dyer, Geoff, *Ways of Telling* (London: Pluto, 1986).

Eagleton, Terry, *Against the Grain* (London: Verso, 1986). [*Against*]

——, *Criticism and Ideology* (London: New Left Books, 1976). [*Criticism*]

——, *The Function of Criticism* (London: Verso, 1984). [*Function*]

——, *Literary Theory: an introduction* (Oxford: Blackwell, 1983). [*Literary*]

——, *Marxism and Literary Criticism* (London: Methuen, 1976). [*Marxism*]

——, *The Rape of Clarissa* (Oxford: Blackwell, 1982). [*Rape*]

Edsall, Thomas Byrne, *The New Politics of Inequality* (New York: Norton, 1984).

Ehrenreich, Barbara, *The Hearts of Men* (London: Pluto, 1983).

Eliot, T. S., *The Idea of a Christian Society* (London: Faber, 1939). [*Idea*]

——, *Notes Towards the Definition of Culture* (London: Faber, 1948). [*Notes*]

Ellmann, Mary, *Thinking about Women* (1968; London: Virago, 1979).

Enright, D. J. (ed.), *Poets of the 1950's* (Tokyo: Kenkyusha, 1955).

Escoffier, Jeffrey, 'Pessimism of the Mind: intellectuals, universities and the left', *Socialist Review*, 18, no. 1 (Jan.–March 1988), pp. 118–35.

Evergreen Review Reader, 1957–1967 (New York: Grove Press, 1967).

Faas, Ekbert, *Ted Hughes: the unaccommodated universe* (Santa Barbara: Black Sparrow Press, 1980).

Fanon, Frantz, *Black Skin, White Masks*, tr. Charles Lam Markmann (New York: Grove Press, 1967). [*Black*]

——, *The Wretched of the Earth* (1961), preface by Jean-Paul Sartre, tr. Constance Farrington (Harmondsworth: Penguin, 1967). [*Wretched*]

Faulkner, Peter, *Modernism* (London: Methuen, 1977).

Fekete, John, *The Critical Twilight* (London: Routledge, 1977).

Feldman, Gene and Gartenberg, Max (eds.), *Protest* (London: Panther, 1960).

Fiedler, Leslie A., 'Cross the Border – Close the Gap' (1970), in *A Fiedler Reader* (New York: Stein and Day, 1977). ['*Cross*']

——, 'The Middle Against Both Ends', *Encounter*, 5 (Aug. 1955), pp. 16–23.

——, 'The Un-Angry Young Men', *Encounter*, 10 (Jan. 1958), pp. 3–12.

55 Stories from the New Yorker [1940–50] (London: Gollancz, 1952).

Firchow, Peter (ed.), *The Writer's Place* (Minneapolis: Minnesota UP, 1974).

Fish, Stanley, *Is There a Text in This Class?* (Cambridge, Mass., and London: Harvard UP, 1980).

Fitzgibbon, Constantine, *When the Kissing Had to Stop* (1960; London: Panther, 1978).

Foot, Paul, *The Politics of Harold Wilson* (Harmondsworth: Penguin, 1968).

Foote, Geoffrey, *The Labour Party's Political Thought*, 2nd edn. (London: Croom Helm, 1986).

Ford, Boris (ed.), *The Modern Age*, Pelican Guide to English Literature 7 (1961), new edn. (Harmondsworth: Penguin, 1979). [*Modern*]

——, (ed.), *The Present*, New Pelican Guide to English Literature 8 (Harmondsworth: Penguin, 1983). [*Present*]

Forster, E. M., *Howards End* (1910; Harmondsworth: Penguin, 1941).

——, *The Life to Come and Other Stories*, ed. Oliver Stallybrass (Harmondsworth: Penguin, 1975). [*Life*].

——, 'The New Disorder', in *Writers in Freedom*, ed. Hermon Ould (17th Congress of PEN Club, 1941; Hutchinson: London, n.d.).

——, *Two Cheers for Democracy* (London: Arnold, 1951). [*Two Cheers*]

Foster, Hal (ed.), *Postmodern Culture* (London: Pluto, 1985); also published as *The Anti-aesthetic* (San Francisco: Bay Press, 1983).

Foucault, Michel, *Language, Counter-memory, Practice* (Oxford: Blackwell, 1977). [*Language*]

——, *Power/Knowledge*, ed. Colin Gordon (Brighton: Harvester, 1980).

Frankenberg, Ronald, *Communities in Britain* (Harmondsworth: Penguin, 1966).

Freeland, Richard M., *The Truman Doctrine and the Origins of McCarthyism* (New York: Knopf, 1972).

Freud, Sigmund, *Case Histories II*, Pelican Freud Library 9, ed. Angela Richards (Harmondsworth: Penguin, 1979). [*Case*]

——, *Totem and Taboo*, tr. James Strachey (London: Routledge, 1960). [*Totem*]

Friedman, Betty, *The Feminine Mystique* (1963; London: Gollancz, 1965).

Friedman, Milton and Friedman, Rose, *Free to Choose* (London: Secker and Warburg, 1980).

Frith, Simon, 'Art Ideology and Pop Practice', in *Marxism and the Interpretation of Culture*, ed. Cary Nelson and Lawrence Grossberg (London: Macmillan, 1988). ['Art']

——, 'The Making of the British Record Industry', in *Impacts and Influences*, ed. James Curran, Anthony Smith and Pauline Wingate (London and New York: Methuen, 1987). ['Making']

——, 'Playing with Real Feeling: making sense of jazz in Britain', *New Formations*, no. 4 (Spring 1988), pp. 7–24.

——, *Sound Effects* (London: Constable, 1983). [*Sound*]

Frith, Simon and McRobbie, Angela, 'Rock and Sexuality', *Screen Education*, 29 (Winter 1978/9), pp. 3–19.

Fryer, Peter, *Staying Power* (London and Sydney: Pluto Press, 1984).

Fuller, Peter, *Beyond the Crisis in Art* (London: Writers and Readers, 1980).

Fuller, Roy, *Collected Poems, 1936–61* (London: Deutsch, 1962). [*Collected Poems*]

——, *Professors and Gods* (London: Deutsch, 1973). [*Professors*]

Fussell, Paul, *The Great War and Modern Memory* (London, Oxford and New York: Oxford UP, 1975).

Fyvel, T. R., *The Insecure Offenders* (Harmondsworth: Penguin, 1963). [*Insecure*]

——, *Intellectuals Today* (London: Chatto, 1968). [*Intellectuals*]

Gagnon, John H. and Simon, William, *Sexual Conduct* (Chicago: Aldine, 1973).

Galbraith, J. K., *The Affluent Society* (1958; Harmondsworth: Penguin, 1962).

Gamble, Andrew, 'Thatcher: the second coming', *Marxism Today*, 27, no. 7 (July 1983), pp. 7–14.

Gates, Eleanor M., *End of the Affair* (London: Allen and Unwin, 1981).

General Education in a Free Society, Report of the Harvard Committee (Cambridge, Mass.: Harvard UP, 1945).

Genette, Gérard, 'Valéry and the Poetics of Language', in *Textual Strategies*, ed. Josué V. Harari (London: Methuen, 1980).

George, Vic and Wilding, Paul, *Ideology and Social Welfare* (London: Routledge, 1976).

Getty, J. Arch, *Origins of the Great Purges* (Cambridge UP, 1985).

Gidal, Peter, *Andy Warhol* (London: Studio Vista, and New York: Dutton, 1971).

Giddens, Anthony, *Central Problems in Social Theory* (London: Macmillan, 1979).

Gilbert, Sandra M. and Gubar, Susan, *No Man's Land*, vol. 1: *The War of the Words* (New Haven and London: Yale UP, 1988). [*No Man's*]

——, *Shakespeare's Sisters* (Bloomington: Indiana UP, 1979). [*Shakespeare's*]

Gillis, John R., *Youth and History* (New York and London: Academic Press, 1974).

Ginsberg, Allen, *'Howl' and Other Poems* (San Francisco: City Lights, 1956).

Glendinning, Victoria, *Elizabeth Bowen* (London: Weidenfeld, 1977).

Gloversmith, Frank (ed.), *The Theory of Reading* (Brighton: Harvester, 1984).

Godbolt, Jim, *A History of Jazz in Britain, 1919–50* (London: Quarter, 1984).

The God that Failed, Arthur Koestler, Ignazio Silone, André Gide, Richard Wright, Louis Fischer and Stephen Spender (London: Right Book Club, n.d.). [*God*]

Goffman, Irving, *Stigma* (Harmondsworth: Penguin, 1968).

Golding, William, *Free Fall* (1959; Harmondsworth: Penguin, 1963).

——, *The Hot Gates* (London: Faber, 1965). [*Hot Gates*]

——, *The Inheritors* (1955; London: Faber, 1961).

——, *Lord of the Flies* (1954; Harmondsworth: Penguin, 1960).

Goldthorpe, John H., Lockwood, David, Bechofer, Frank and Platt, Jennifer, *The Affluent Worker*, 3 vols. (Cambridge UP, 1968–9).

Gooch, Steve, *All Together Now* (London: Methuen, 1984).

Goorney, Howard, *The Theatre Workshop Story* (London: Eyre Methuen, 1981).

Gosling, Ray, *Personal Copy* (London: Faber, 1980). [*Personal*]

——, *Sum Total* (London: Faber, 1962).

Gould, Tony, 'Shaky Do', *London Review of Books*, 10, no. 9 (5 May 1988), p. 18.

Gouldner, Alvin, *The Future of Intellectuals and the Rise of the New Class* (New York: Continuum, 1979).

Graff, Gerald, 'The Myth of the Postmodernist Breakthrough', in *The Novel Today*, ed. Malcolm Bradbury (Glasgow: Fontana, 1977). ['Myth']

——, *Professing Literature* (Chicago and London: Chicago UP, 1987). [*Professing*]

Graham, David and Clarke, Peter, *The New Enlightenment* (London: Macmillan, 1986).

Gramsci, Antonio, *Selections from the Prison Notebooks*, ed. and trans. Quintin Hoare and Geoffrey Nowell Smith (London: Lawrence and Wishart, 1971).

Green, Martin, *Children of the Sun* (London: Constable, 1977). [*Children*]

Greenblatt, Stephen, 'Psychoanalysis and Renaissance Culture', in *Literary Theory/Renaissance Texts*, ed. Patricia Parker and David Quint (Baltimore and London: Johns Hopkins UP, 1986).

Greene, Graham, *The Heart of the Matter* (London: Heinemann, 1948).

——, *The Ministry of Fear* (London: Heinemann and Bodley Head, 1973).

Grunwald, Henry Anatole (ed.), *Salinger: a critical and personal portrait* (New York: Harper and Roe, 1962).

Guilbaut, Serge, *How New York Stole the Idea of Modern Art*, tr. Arthur Goldhammer (Chicago UP, 1983).

Gunn, Thom, *My Sad Captains* (London: Faber, 1961).

——, *The Occasions of Poetry*, ed. Clive Wilmer (London: Faber, 1982). [*Occasions*]

——, *The Sense of Movement* (London: Faber, 1957). [*Sense*]

Gurevitch, Michael, Bennett, Tony, Curran, James and Woollacott, Janet, *Culture, Society and the Media* (London: Methuen, 1982).

Habermas, Jürgen, *Legitimation Crisis*, tr. Thomas McCarthy (London: Heinemann, 1976).

Half our Future (the Newsom Report) (London: HMSO, 1963).

Hall, Stuart, 'The Toad in the Garden: Thatcherism among the theorists', in

Marxism and the Interpretation of Culture, ed. Cary Nelson and Lawrence Grossberg (London: Macmillan, 1988).

Hall, Stuart, Critcher, Chas, Jefferson, Tony, Clarke, John and Roberts, Brian, *Policing the Crisis* (London: Macmillan, 1978).

Hall, Stuart, Hobson, Dorothy, Lowe, Andrew and Willis, Paul (eds.), *Culture, Media, Language* (London: Hutchinson, 1980).

Hall, Stuart and Jefferson, Tony (eds.), *Resistance Through Rituals* (London: Hutchinson and Centre for Contemporary Cultural Studies, 1976).

Hall, Willis, *The Long and the Short and the Tall* (1958); Harold Pinter, *The Dumb Waiter*; N. F. Simpson, *A Resounding Tinkle* (Harmondsworth: Penguin, 1964).

Halsey, A. H., *Change in British Society*, 3rd edn. (Oxford and New York: Oxford UP, 1986).

——, 'Towards Meritocracy? The case of Britain', in *Power and Ideology in Education*, ed. Jerome Karabel and A. H. Halsey (New York: Oxford UP, 1977).

Hampshire, Stuart, 'An English Intellectual', *New Statesman*, 28 April 1956, p. 457.

Hargreaves, John, *Sport, Power and Culture* (Cambridge: Polity, 1986).

Harris, Nigel, *Beliefs in Society* (Harmondsworth: Penguin, 1971). [*Beliefs*]

——, *Competition and the Corporate Society* (London: Methuen, 1972). [*Competition*]

Harrisson, Tom, *Living Through the Blitz* (Harmondsworth: Penguin, 1978).

Hartley, Anthony, *A State of England* (London: Hutchinson, 1963).

Hatch, David and Millward, Stephen, *From Blues to Rock* (Manchester UP, 1987).

Hawkes, Terence, *Structuralism and Semiotics* (London: Methuen, 1977). [*Structuralism*]

——, *That Shakespeherian Rag* (London: Methuen, 1986). [*Shakespeherian*]

Hayek, F. A., *The Road to Serfdom* (London: Routledge, 1944).

Heath, Anthony, *Social Mobility* (London: Fontana, 1981). [*Social*]

Hebdige, Dick, *Subculture: the meaning of style* (London: Methuen, 1979).

Hechter, Michael, *Internal Colonialism* (London: Routledge, 1975).

Heffner, Richard D., *A Documentary History of the United States* (New York: Mentor, 1952).

Heinemann, Margot, *The Adventurers* (London: Lawrence and Wishart, 1959).

Hewison, Robert, *In Anger* (London: Weidenfeld, 1981).

——, *Too Much* (London: Methuen, 1986). [*Too*]

——, *Under Siege* (London: Weidenfeld, 1977). [*Under Siege*]

Heyck, T. W., 'From Men of Letters to Intellectuals', *Journal of British Studies*, 20 (1980), pp. 158–83.

Higgins, Hugh, *The Cold War*, 2nd edn. (London: Heinemann, 1984).

Hillary, Richard, *The Last Enemy* (1942; London: Macmillan, 1950).

Hindess, Barry, *Freedom, Equality, and the Market* (London and New York: Tavistock, 1987).

Hobsbawm, Eric, 'The Historians' Group of the Communist Party', in *Rebels and Their Causes*, ed. Maurice Cornforth (London: Lawrence and Wishart, 1978).

Hoggart, Richard, *The Uses of Literacy* (1957; Harmondsworth: Penguin, 1958). [*Uses*]

Hohendahl, Peter, 'The Use Value of Contemporary and Future Literary Criticism', *New German Critique*, 4 (Winter 1976), pp. 3–20.

Holbrook, David, *Sylvia Plath: poetry and existence* (London: Athlone, 1976).

Holderness, Graham (ed.), *The Shakespeare Myth* (Manchester UP, 1988).

Hollis, Christopher, *A Study of George Orwell* (London: Hollis and Carter, 1956).

Holloway, John, 'New Lines in English Poetry', *Hudson Review*, 9 (1956–7), pp. 592–7.

Holroyd, Stuart, *Contraries* (London: Bodley Head, 1975).

Hood, Stuart, 'Dealing with the Pirates', *The Spectator*, 15 July, 1966, pp. 75–6.

Hopkins, Harry, *The New Look* (London: Secker and Warburg, 1963).

Horovitz, Michael (ed.), *Children of Albion: poetry of the Underground in Britain* (Harmondsworth: Penguin, 1969).

Hough, Graham, 'Crisis in Literary Education', in *Crisis in the Humanities*, ed. J. H. Plumb (Harmondsworth: Penguin, 1964). ['Crisis']

——, 'In Dark Times', *The Listener*, 23 May, 1968, pp. 661–3.

——, *Reflections on a Literary Revolution* (Washington, DC: Catholic University of America, 1960). [*Reflections*]

Howe, Stephen, 'Votes or Values?', *New Statesman and Society*, 15 July 1988, p. 21.

Hubback, Judith, *Wives who Went to College* (London: Heinemann, 1957).

Hughes, Donald, 'Recorded Music', in *Discrimination and Popular Culture*, ed. Denys Thompson (Harmondsworth: Penguin, 1964).

Hughes, Ted, *Lupercal* (London: Faber, 1960).

Hurd, Douglas, 'Tamsworth Manifesto', *London Review of Books*, 17 March 1988, p. 7.

de Huszar, George B. (ed.), *The Intellectuals* (Glencoe, Ill.: The Free Press, 1960).

Hutchison, Robert, *The Politics of the Arts Council* (London: Sinclair Browne, 1982).

Huxley, Aldous, *Brave New World Revisited* (London: Chatto, 1959).

Huyssen, Andreas, *After the Great Divide* (Bloomington and Indianapolis: Indiana UP, 1986).

Hyde, H. Montgomery, *The Other Love* (London: Granada, 1972).

Inglis, Fred, *Radical Earnestness* (Oxford: Martin Robertson, 1982).

Ionesco Eugène, *Notes and Counter-notes*, tr. Donald Watson (London: Calder, 1964).

Isherwood, Christopher, 'Success Story' (BBC Television, 1974).

Jackson, Brian, *Working Class Community* (London: Routledge, 1968).

Jackson, Brian and Marsden, Dennis, *Education and the Working Class* (London: Routledge, 1962).

Jacobus, Mary (ed.), *Women Writing and Writing about Women* (London: Croom Helm, 1979).

Jacoby, Russell, *The Last Intellectuals* (New York: Basic Books, 1987).

Jacques, Martin and Mulhern, Francis (eds.), *The Forward March of Labour Halted* (London: Verso, 1981).

Jameson, Fredric, 'Reification and Utopia in Mass Culture', *Social Text*, 1 (1979), pp. 130–48.

JanMohammed, Abdul, 'The Economy of Manichean Allegory: the function of racial difference in colonialist literature', *Critical Inquiry*, 12 (Autumn 1985), pp. 59–87.

Jarman, Francis, 'Birth of a Playwriting Man' (interview with David Mercer), *Theatre Quarterly*, 3, no. 9 (Jan.–March 1973), pp. 43–55.

Joad, C. E. M., *Decadence* (London: Faber, 1948).

Johnson, Paul, *Enemies of Society* (London: Weidenfeld, 1977).

Jones, Aubrey, *Industrial Order* (London: Falcon Press, 1950).

Jones, T. H., *Dylan Thomas* (Edinburgh: Oliver and Boyd, 1963).

Juhasz, Susanne, *Naked and Fiery Forms* (New York: Harper Colophon Books, 1976).

Kaplan, Cora (ed.), *Salt and Bitter and Good* (London: Paddington Press, 1975). [*Salt*]

——, *Sea Changes* (London: Verson, 1986). [*Sea*]

Kaplan, E. Ann, *Rocking Around the Clock* (New York and London: Methuen, 1987).

Karl, F. R., *A Reader's Guide to the Contemporary English Novel* (New York: Noonday Press, 1962).

Kaye, Harvey J., *The British Marxist Historians* (Cambridge: Polity, 1984).

Kenner, Hugh, *A Homemade World: the American modernist writers* (New York: Knopf, 1975).

Kermode, Frank, *History and Value* (Oxford UP, 1988). [*History*]

——, *Romantic Image* (London: Routledge, 1957). [*Romantic*]

Khan, Naseem, *The Arts Britain Ignores* (London: Arts Council, 1976).

Kimmel, Michael S., 'The Contemporary "Crisis" of Masculinity in Historical Perspective', in *The Making of Masculinities*, ed. Harry Brod (Boston and London: Allen and Unwin, 1987).

King, P. R., *Nine Contemporary Poets* (London: Methuen, 1979).

Kipnis, Laura, ' "Refunctioning" Reconsidered; towards a left popular culture', in *High Theory/Low Culture*, ed. Colin MacCabe (Manchester UP, 1986).

Klein, Josephine, *Samples from English Cultures*, 2 vols. (London: Routledge, 1965).

Klein, Viola, *Working Wives* (London: Institute of Personnel Management, 1954).

Koestler, Arthur, *The Yogi and the Commissar* (London: Cape, 1945).

Koestler, Arthur, Koestler, Cynthia and Harris, Harold, *Strangers on the Square* (London: Hutchinson, 1983). [*Strangers*]

Konrad, George and Szelényi, Ivan, *Intellectuals on the Road to Class Power*, tr. Andrew Arato and Richard E. Allen (Brighton: Harvester, 1979).

Kozloff, Max, 'American Painting during the Cold War', *Artforum*, 11 (May 1973), pp. 43–54.

Kristol, Irving, *Reflections of a Neoconservative* (New York: Basic Books, 1983).

Kuhn, Annette and Wolpe, Ann Marie (eds.), *Feminism and Materialism* (London: Routledge, 1978).

Laclau, Ernest and Mouffe, Chantal, *Hegemony and Socialist Strategy*, tr. Winston Moore and Paul Cammack (London: Verso, 1985).

Laing, Stuart, *Representations of Working Class Life, 1957–1964* (London: Macmillan, 1986).

Lamming, George, *In the Castle of my Skin* (1935; Trinidad and Jamaica: Longman Caribbean, 1970).

——, *The Pleasures of Exile* (London: Michael Joseph, 1960). [*Pleasures*]

Lancaster, Osbert, *The Life and Times of Maudie Littlehampton* (Harmondsworth: Penguin, 1982).

Landry, Charles, Morley, David, Southwood, Russell and Wright, Patrick, *What a Way to Run a Railroad* (London: Comedia, 1985).

Lane, Gary (ed.), *Sylvia Plath: new views on the poetry* (Baltimore and London: Johns Hopkins UP, 1979).

Lane, Michael and Booth, Jeremy, *Books and Publishers* (Lexington, Mass., and Toronto: Heath, 1980. *A Language for Life* (the Bullock Report) (London: HMSO, 1975). [*Language*]

Larkin, Philip, *All What Jazz* (London: Faber, 1970). [*All What*]

——, *High Windows* (London: Faber, 1964).

——, *Jill* (1946), 2nd edn. (London: Faber, 1964).

——, *The Less Deceived* (Hessle: Marvell Press, 1955).

——, *The Whitsun Weddings* (London: Faber, 1964).

Lasch, Christopher, *The Agony of the American Left* (London: Deutsch, 1970).

de Lauretis, Teresa, *Alice Doesn't* (London: Macmillan, 1984).

Lawrence, Erroll, 'Just Plain Common Sense: the "roots" of racism', in Centre for Contemporary Cultural Studies, *The Empire Strikes Back* (London: Hutchinson, 1982).

Leach, Edmund, *A Runaway World* (London: BBC, 1968).

Leakey, Richard, *The Making of Mankind* (London: Michael Joseph, 1981).

Leakey, Richard and Lewin, Roger, *People of the Lake* (London: Collins, 1979).

Leavis, F. R., *The Common Pursuit* (1952; Harmondsworth: Penguin, 1962).

——, *English Literature in our Time and the University* (London: Chatto, 1969). [*English Literature*]

——, 'Keynes, Spender and Currency-values', *Scrutiny*, 18 (1951–2), pp. 45–56. ['Keynes']

——, *Mass Civilisation and Minority Culture* (Cambridge: Minority Press, 1930).

——, *New Bearings in English Poetry*, 2nd edn. (Harmondsworth: Penguin, 1972).

——, '*Scrutiny*: a retrospect', *Scrutiny*, 20 (1963), pp. 1–24.

Lee, Hermione, *Elizabeth Bowen: an estimation* (London: Vision, 1981).

Le Grand, Julian, *The Strategy of Equality* (London: Allen and Unwin, 1982).

Lehmann, John, *The Ample Proposition: autobiography III* (London: Eyre and Spottiswoode, 1966). [*Ample*]

——, (ed.), *The Craft of Letters* (London: Cresset, 1956). [*Craft*]

——, *I Am my Brother: autobiography II* (London: Longman, 1960). [*I Am*]

——, *In a Pagan Place* (London: Gay Men's Press, 1985). [*In a Pagan*]

Lehmann, Rosamond, *The Echoing Grove* (1953; Harmondsworth: Penguin, 1958). [*Echoing Grove*]

Lekachman, Robert, *The Age of Keynes* (Harmondsworth: Penguin, 1969).

Lenin, V. I., *Marx-Engels-Marxism*, rev. edn. (Moscow: Progress Publishers, 1968).

Lentricchia, Frank, *After the New Criticism* (London: Methuen, 1983).

Leslie, David Stuart, *In my Solitude* (London: Hutchinson, 1960); republished as *Two Left Feet* (London: Pan, 1963).

Lessing, Doris, *Each His Own Wilderness* (1958), in *New English Dramatists*, ed. E. Martin Browne (Harmondsworth: Penguin, 1959). [*Each*]

——, *Five* (1953; Harmondsworth: Penguin, 1960).

——, *Going Home* (1957), 2nd edn. (St Albans: Granada, 1968).

——, *The Golden Notebook* (1962; London: Panther, 1973).

——, *The Grass is Singing* (1950; Harmondsworth: Penguin, 1961).

——, *Retreat to Innocence* (London: Michael Joseph, 1956).

Levin, Bernard, *The Pendulum Years* (London: Cape, 1970).

Levin, Harry, *Refractions* (New York: Oxford UP, 1966).

Levy, Carl (ed.), *Socialism and the Intelligentsia*, 1880–1914 (London and New York: Routledge, 1987).

Lewis, C.S., *A Preface to Paradise Lost* (London: Oxford UP, 1960).

Lewis, Peter, *The Fifties* (London: Heinemann, 1978). [*Fifties*]

——, *A People's War* (London: Thames Methuen, 1986). [*People's*]

——, 'The Radio Road to Llareggub', in *British Radio Drama*, ed. John Drakakis (Cambridge UP, 1981).

Lewis, Roy and Maude, Angus, *The English Middle Class* (London: Phoenix House, 1949).

Leys, Colin, *Politics in Britain* (London: Verso, 1986).

Lichtheim, George, *Imperialism* (Harmondsworth: Penguin, 1974).

Light, Alison, 'Writing Fictions: femininity and the 1950s', in *The Progress of Romance*, ed. Jean Radford (London: Routledge, 1986).

Lipset, Seymour Martin, *Political Man*, 2nd edn. (London: Heinemann, 1983).

Lodge, David (ed.), *20th Century Literary Criticism* (London: Longman, 1972).

Lorentz, Konrad, *King Solomon's Ring* (London: Methuen, 1952).

Lovell, Terry, *Consuming Fiction* (London: Verso, 1987).

Lukacs, Georg, *Marxism and Human Liberation*, ed. E. St Juan, Jr (New York: Dell, 1973).

McCauley, Martin, *The Origins of the Cold War* (London and New York: Longman, 1983).

McCrindle, Jean and Rowbotham, Sheila (eds.), *Dutiful Daughters* (Harmondsworth: Penguin, 1979).

MacCrone, I.D., *Race Attitudes in South Africa* (Oxford UP, 1937).

Macherey, Pierre, *A Theory of Literary Production*, tr. Geoffrey Wall (London: Routledge, 1978).

Macherey, Pierre and Balibar, Etienne, 'Literature as an Ideological Form', *Oxford Literary Review*, 3 (1978), pp. 4–12; also in *Praxis*, part 5 (1981), pp. 43–58.

MacInnes, Colin, *Absolute Beginners* (1959; London: Allison and Busby, 1980).

——, *City of Spades* (1957; Harmondsworth: Penguin, 1964).

——, *England, Half English* (London: MacGibbin and Kee, 1961). [*England*]

MacKenzie, Norman (ed.), *Conviction* (London: MacGibbon and Kee, 1958).

McKie, David and Cook, Chris (eds.), *The Age of Disillusion* (London: Macmillan, 1972).

McLennan, Gregor, Held, David and Hall, Stuart (eds.), *State and Society in Contemporary Britain* (Cambridge: Polity, 1984).

McLuhan, Marshall, *Understanding Media* (1964; London: Sphere, 1967).

McRobbie, Angela, 'Settling Accounts with Subcultures', *Screen Education*, 34 (Spring 1980), pp. 37–49.

McRobbie, Angela and Nava, Mica (eds.), *Gender and Generation* (London: Macmillan, 1984).

Malinowski, Bronislaw, *Sex, Culture and Myth* (London: Mayflower-Dell, 1967).

Mander, John, *Great Britain or Little England* (Harmondsworth: Penguin, 1963). [*Great*]

——, *The Writer and Commitment* (London: Secker, 1961). [*Writer*]

Mannheim, Karl, *Essays on the Sociology of Culture* (London: Routledge, 1956).

Mannoni, O., *Prospero and Caliban* (1960), tr. Pamela Powesland, 2nd edn. (New York and Washington, DC: Praeger, 1964).

Marcus, Greil, *Mystery Train* (New York: Dutton, 1975).

Marcuse, Herbert, *An Essay on Liberation* (Harmondsworth: Penguin, 1969). [*Essay*]

——, *One Dimensional Man* (Boston: Beacon Press, 1964). [*One*]

Marowitz, Charles, Milne, Tom and Hale, Owen (eds.), *The Encore Reader* (London: Methuen, 1965).

Marowitz, Charles and Trussler, Simon (eds.), *Theatre at Work* (London: Methuen, 1967).

Marshall, John, 'Pansies, Perverts and Macho Men: changing conceptions of homosexuality', in *The Making of the Modern Homosexual*, ed. Kenneth Plummer (London: Hutchinson, 1981).

Marshall, T.H., *Citizenship and Social Class* (Cambridge UP, 1950).

Martin, Kingsley, *London Critic's Diary* (London: Secker, 1960).

Marwick, Arthur, *British Society since 1945* (Harmondsworth: Penguin, 1982). [*British*]

——, *The Social Impact of World War II*, War and Society, video unit 9 (Milton Keynes: Open University Press, n.d.). [*Social Impact*]

Marx, Karl, *Capital*, tr. Eden and Cedar Paul, 2 vols. (London and Toronto: Dent, 1930; New York: Dutton, 1930).

Marx, Karl and Engels, Friedrich, *The German Ideology* (London: Lawrence and Wishart, 1965).

Maschler, Tom (ed.), *Declaration* (London: MacGibbon and Kee, 1957).

Mass Observation, *The Journey Home* (London: John Murray, 1944).

Matza, David and Sykes, Gresham, 'Juvenile Delinquency and Subterranean Values', *American Sociological Review*, 26 (1961), pp. 712–9.

de Mauny, Erik, 'The Literary Climate in France', *Encounter*, 3, no. 1 (1954), pp. 67–71.

Mead, Margaret, *Male and Female* (New York: William Morrow, 1949).

Mellers, Wilfred, *Twilight of the Gods* (London: Faber, 1973).

Melly, George, *Owning Up* (1965; Harmondsworth: Penguin, 1974). [*Owning*]

——, *Revolt into Style* (Harmondsworth: Penguin, 1972). [*Revolt*]

Mercer, David, *Where the Difference Begins* (broadcast 1961), in *Collected T.V. Plays Volume One* (London: Calder, 1981).

Meyers, Jeffrey, *Homosexuality and Literature, 1890–1930* (London: Athlone, 1977).

Middlemas, Keith, *Politics in Industrial Society* (London: Deutsch, 1979).

Miliband, Ralph, *Parliamentary Socialism*, 2nd edn. (London: Merlin, 1972). [*Parliamentary*]

——, *The State in Capitalist Society* (London: Weidenfeld, 1969). [*State*]

Miller, Christopher L., *Blank Darkness* (Chicago and London: Chicago UP, 1985).

Miller, Jim (ed.), *The Rolling Stone Illuminated History of Rock & Roll* (New York: Rolling Stone Press, 1976).

Millett, Kate, *Sexual Politics* (1969; London: Virago, 1977).

Mills, C. Wright, 'The Cultural Apparatus', *The Listener*, 26 March, 1959, pp. 552–6.

Mills, Sarah, 'Alternative Voices to Orientalism', *LTP* [*Journal of Literature Teaching Politics*], 5 (1985), pp. 78–91.

Minns, Raynes, *Bombers and Mash* (London: Virago, 1980).

Mitchell, Juliet, *Women's Estate* (Harmondsworth: Penguin, 1973).

——, *Women: the longest revolution* (London: Virago, 1984). [*Women*]

Modleski, Tania, *Loving with a Vengeance* (New York and London: Methuen, 1984).

Montgomery, John, *The Fifties* (London: Allen and Unwin, 1965).

Moore, Robert, *Racism and Black Resistance* (London: Pluto, 1975).

Morley, Dave and Worpole, Ken (eds.), *The Republic of Letters* (London: Comedia, 1982).

Morris, Desmond, *The Naked Ape* (London: Corgi, 1968).

Morrison, Blake, *The Movement* (London and New York: Methuen, 1986).

Morse, David, *Motown* (London: Studio Vista, 1971).

Mortimer, Penelope, *The Pumpkin Eater* (1962; Harmondsworth: Penguin, 1964).

Mouffe, Chantal, 'Hegemony and the New Political Subjects: toward a new conception of democracy', in *Marxism and the Interpretation of Culture*, ed. Cary Nelson and Lawrence Grossberg (London: Macmillan, 1988).

Mulhern, Francis, *The Moment of 'Scrutiny'* (London: New Left Books, 1979).

Mungham, Geoff and Pearson, Geoff, *Working Class Youth Cultures* (London: Routledge, 1976).

Murdoch, Iris, *The Flight from the Enchanter* (1956; Harmondsworth: Penguin, 1962).

——, 'The Novelist as Metaphysician' and 'The Existential Hero', *The Listener*, 43 (1950), pp. 473–6, 523–4.

——, *Under the Net* (1954; Harmondsworth: Penguin, 1960).

Myerscough, John, *The Economic Importance of the Arts in Britain* (London: Policy Studies Institute, 1988).

Myrdal, Alva and Klein, Viola, *Women's Two Roles* (London: Routledge, 1956).

Naipaul, V. S., *An Area of Darkness* (London: Deutsch, 1964).

——, *A House for Mr Biswas* (1961; Harmondsworth: Penguin, 1961).

——, *The Mimic Men* (London: Deutsch, 1967).

Nairn, Tom, *The Break-up of Britain* (London: New Left Books, 1977). [*Break-up*]

——, 'The English Literary Intelligentsia', in *Bananas*, ed. Emma Tennant (London: Blond and Briggs, 1977), pp. 57–83. ['English']

Nandy, Ashis, *The Intimate Enemy* (Delhi: Oxford UP, 1983).

National Deviancy Conference, *Permissiveness and Control* (London: Macmillan, 1979).

Naumann, Manfred, 'Literary Production and Reception', *New Literary History*, 8 (1976), pp. 107–26.

Newman, Charles (ed.), *The Art of Sylvia Plath* (London: Faber, 1970).

Newton, Eric, *The Jazz Scene* (London: MacGibbon and Kee, 1959).

New World Writing: seventh mentor selection (New York: New American Library, 1955).

Nicolson, Harold, *Diaries and Letters, 1939–1945*, ed. Nigel Nicolson (London: Collins, 1967). [*1939–1945*]

——, *Diaries and Letters, 1945–1962*, ed. Nigel Nicolson (London: Collins, 1968). [*1945–1962*]

Nove, Alec, *The Economics of Feasible Socialism* (London: Allen and Unwin, 1983).

Nowell-Smith, Geoffrey, 'Popular Culture', *New Formations*, no. 2 (Summer 1987), pp. 79–90.

Nuttall, Jeff, *Bomb Culture* (London: Paladin, 1970).

Oakes, Philip, *At the Jazz Band Ball* (London: Deutsch, 1983).

Oakley, Anne, *Housewife* (Harmondsworth: Penguin, 1976).

——, *Subject Women* (Glasgow: Fontana, 1982). [*Subject*]

O'Brien, Connor Cruise, *Camus* (London: Fontana, 1970).

O'Connor, William Van, *The New University Wits and the End of Modernism* (Carbondale: Southern Illinois UP, 1963).

Ohmann, Richard, 'The Shaping of a Canon: US fiction, 1960–1975', *Critical Inquiry*, 10 (1983), pp. 199–223; repr. in Ohmann, *Politics of Letters* (Middletown, Conn.: Wesleyan UP, 1987).

Olsen, Tillie, *Silences* (London: Virago, 1980).

Orr, Peter (ed.), *The Poet Speaks* (London: Routledge, 1966).

Orwell, George, *Burmese Days* (1934; Harmondsworth: Penguin, 1967).

——, *The Collected Essays, Journalism and Letters*, ed. Sonia Orwell and Ian Angus, 4 vols. (Harmondsworth: Penguin, 1970). [*Essays*]

——, *1984* (1949; Harmondsworth: Penguin, 1954).

Osborne, John, *A Patriot for Me* (London: Faber, 1966).

——, *The Entertainer* (London: Faber, 1957).

——, *Inadmissible Evidence* (London: Faber, 1965).

——, *Look Back in Anger* (London: Faber, 1957). [*Look Back*]

Ostriker, Alicia, *Writing Like a Woman* (Ann Arbor: Michigan UP, 1983).

Other People's Lives (London: Contact Publications, 1948).

Owen, Alun, *Three TV Plays* (London: Cape, 1961).

Palmer, Tony, *All You Need is Love* (London: Futura, 1977).

Panitch, Leo, 'The Development of Corporatism in Liberal Democracies', in *Trends Towards Corporatist Intermediation*, ed. Philippe C. Schmitter and Gerhard Lehmbruch (Beverly Hills and London: Sage, 1979). ['Development']

——, *Social Democracy and Industrial Militancy* (Cambridge UP, 1976). [*Social*]

Parkin, Frank, *Class Inequality and Political Order* (London: Paladin, 1972). [*Class*]

——, *Middle Class Radicalism* (Manchester UP, 1968). [*Middle*]

Parrinder, Patrick, *Authors and Authority* (London: Routledge, 1977).

Parsons, Talcott and Bales, Robert F., *Family, Socialisation and Interaction Process* (New York: Free Press, 1955).

Passmore, John, *The Perfectibility of Man* (London: Duckworth, 1970).

Patterson, Sheila, *Dark Strangers* (1963; Harmondsworth: Penguin, 1965).

Pearce, Frank, 'The British Press and the "Placing" of Male Homosexuality', in *The Manufacture of News*, 2nd edn., ed. Stanley Cohen and Jock Young (London: Constable, 1981; Beverly Hills: Sage, 1981).

Penrose, Barrie and Freeman, Simon, *Conspiracy of Silence* (London: Grafton, 1986).

Peschek, Joseph G., *Policy-planning Organisations* (Philadelphia: Temple UP, 1987).

Pinter, Harold, *The Caretaker* (London: Methuen, 1960).

——, *Plays: One* (London: Eyre Methuen, 1976).

——, *A Slight Ache and Other Plays* (London: Methuen, 1961). [*Slight*]

Plath, Sylvia, *The Bell Jar* (1963; London: Faber, 1966).

——, *Collected Poems*, ed. Ted Hughes (London: Faber, 1981). [*CP*]

——, *Johnny Panic and the Bible of Dreams* (London: Faber, 1977). [*Johnny*]

——, *The Journals of Sylvia Plath*, ed. Ted Hughes and Frances McCullough (New York: Dial Press, 1982). [*Journals*]

——, *Letters Home*, ed. Aurelia Schober Plath (London: Faber, 1975). [*Letters*]

Platt, Jennifer, *Social Research in Bethnal Green* (London: Macmillan, 1971).

Poster, Mark, *Critical Theory of the Family* (London: Pluto, 1978). [*Critical*]

——, *Existentialist Marxism in Postwar France* (Princeton UP, 1975). [*Existentialist*]

Postman, Neil, *Amusing Ourselves to Death* (London: Heinemann, 1986).

Potter, Dennis, *The Glittering Coffin* (London: Gollancz, 1960). [*Glittering*]

——, *Stand Up, Nigel Barton* (1965), in *The Nigel Barton Plays* (Harmondsworth: Penguin, 1967). [*Stand*]

Priestley, J. B. and Hawkes, Jacquetta, *Journey Down a Rainbow* (London: Heinemann, 1955).

Pym, Barbara, *A Glass of Blessings* (1958; Harmondsworth: Penguin, 1984).

——, *Excellent Women* (1952; Harmondsworth: Penguin, 1980).

Quiller-Couch, Sir Arthur, *On the Art of Writing* (1916; London: Guide Books, 1946).

Rabinovitz, Rubin, *The Reaction Against Experiment in the English Novel, 1950–1960* (New York and London: Columbia UP, 1967).

Rattigan, Terence, *The Deep Blue Sea: Harlequinade; Adventure Story; The Browning Version* (London: Pan, 1955).

——, *Separate Tables* (London: Samuel French, 1956).

Read, Herbert, *To Hell with Culture* (London: Kegan Paul, Trench, Trubner, 1941).

Report of the Committee on Broadcasting, 1960 (the Pilkington Report) (London: HMSO, 1962).

Rhodes, Richard, *The Making of the Atomic Bomb* (London: Simon and Schuster, 1986).

Rich, Adrienne, *Of Woman Born* (London: Virago, 1977). [*Of Woman*]

Richmond, Anthony H., *The Colour Problem* (Harmondsworth: Penguin, 1955).

Riddell, Peter, *The Thatcher Government*, 2nd edn. (Oxford, Blackwell, 1985).

Riding, Laura and Graves, Robert, *A Survey of Modernist Poetry* (London: Heinemann, 1927).

Rieff, Philip (ed.), *On Intellectuals* (New York: Doubleday, 1969).

Riley, Denise, *War in the Nursery* (London: Virago, 1983).

Ritchie, Charles, *The Siren Years: undiplomatic diaries, 1937–1945* (London: Macmillan, 1974).

Ritchie, Harry, *Success Stories* (London and Boston: Faber, 1988).

Rock, Paul and McIntosh, Mary (eds.), *Deviance and Social Control* (London: Tavistock, 1974).

Rodnitzky, Jerome L., *Minstrels of the Dawn* (Chicago: Nelson Hall, 1976).

Rolph, C. H., ed., *The Trial of Lady Chatterley* (Harmondsworth: Penguin, 1961).

Rosenberg, Bernard and White, David Manning, *Mass Culture* (New York: New York Free Press, 1957).

Rosenberg, Harold, *The Anxious Object* (London: Thames and Hudson, 1965). [*Anxious*]

——, *The Case of the Baffled Radical* (Chicago UP, 1985). [*Case*]

Ross, Andrew, 'Containing Culture in the Cold War', *Cultural Studies*, 1, part 3 (1987), pp. 328–48.

Rossi, Alice S., 'Barriers to the Career Choice of Engineering, Medicine, or Science among American Women', in *Women and the Scientific Professions, ed* Jacqueline A. Mattfield and Carol G. van Aken (Cambridge, Mass.: MIT Press, 1965).

Rowbotham, Sheila, *Woman's Consciousness, Man's World* (Harmondsworth: Penguin, 1973). [*Woman's*]

——, *Women, Resistance and Revolution* (Harmondsworth: Penguin, 1973).

Rowe, F. J. and Webb, W. T., *The Lady of Shalott* [*and other poems*] *by Alfred Tennyson* (London: Macmillan, 1938).

Russ, Joanna, *How to Suppress Women's Writing* (London: Women's Press, 1984).

Russell, Bertrand, *Bertrand Russell's America*, vol. 2; *1945–1970*, ed. Barry Feinberg and Ronald Kasrils (London: Allen and Unwin, 1984). [*America*]

——, *Has Man a Future?* (Harmondsworth: Penguin, 1961). [*Has Man*]

Russell, Charles, *Poets, Prophets and Revolutionaries* (New York and Oxford: Oxford UP, 1985).

Russell, John and Gablik, Suzi, *Pop Art Redefined* (London: Thames and Hudson, 1969).

Russell, Lord of Liverpool, *The Scourge of the Swastika* (London: Cassell, 1954).

Ryder, Judith and Silver, Harold, *Modern English Society*, 2nd edn. (London: Methuen, 1977).

Sack, Robert David, *Human Territoriality: its theory and history* (Cambridge UP, 1986).

Sage, Lorna, *Doris Lessing* (London and New York: Methuen, 1983).

Salinger, J. D., *Franny and Zooey* (1955, 1957; Harmondsworth: Penguin, 1964). [*Franny*]

——, *Raise High the Roof Beam, Carpenters and Seymour: an Introduction* (1955, 1959; London: Heinemann, 1963). [*Raise*]

Samuel, Raphael, 'The Lost World of British Communism', *New Left Review*, 154 (Nov.–Dec. 1985), pp. 3–53. ['Lost']

——, (ed.), *People's History and Socialist Theory* (London: Routledge, 1981). [*People's*]

——, 'Staying Power: the lost world of British communism, Part Two', *New Left Review*, 156 (March–April 1986), pp. 63–113. ['Staying']

Samuel, Raphael, MacColl, Ewan and Cosgrove, Stuart, *Theatres of the Left 1880–1935* (London: Routledge, 1985).

Sargant, William, *Battle for the Mind* (London: Heinemann, 1957).

Sartre, Jean-Paul, *Existentialism and Humanism*, tr. Philip Mairet (London: Methuen, 1948). [*Existentialism*]

——, *Literary and Philosophical Essays* (1946), tr. Annette Michelson, 1955 (London: Radius Book/Hutchinson, 1968). [*Literary*]

——, *La Nausée* (1938), tr. Robert Baldick (Harmondsworth: Penguin, 1965).

——, *What is Literature?* (1948), tr. Bernard Frechtman (London: Methuen, 1950). [*What Is*]

Schumpeter, Joseph A., *Capitalism, Socialism and Democracy*, 5th edn. (London: Allen and Unwin, 1976).

Scott, Paul, *The Alien Sky* (1953; London: Heinemann, 1967).

——, *Birds of Paradise* (London: Eyre and Spottiswoode, 1962).

Scott, Wilbur, *Five Approaches of Literary Criticism* (New York and London: Collier-Macmillan, 1962).

Selvon, Sam, *The Lonely Londoners* (1956; Trinidad and Jamaica: Longman Caribbean, 1972).

Sharp, Rachel, *Knowledge, Ideology and the Politics of Schooling* (London: Routledge, 1980).

Shaw, George Bernard, *Heartbreak House* (Harmondsworth: Penguin, 1964).

Shils, Edward, *The Intellectuals and the Powers and Other Essays* (Chicago UP, 1972).

Showalter, Elaine, *The New Feminist Criticism* (London: Virago, 1986).

Sigal, Clancy, *Weekend in Dinlock* (1960; Harmondsworth: Penguin, 1962).

Sillitoe, Alan, *Key to the Door* (1961; London: Star, 1978).

——, *The Loneliness of the Long-distance Runner* (1959; London: Pan, 1961).

——, 'Proletarian Novelists', *Books and Bookmen* (Aug. 1959), p. 13.

——, *Saturday Night and Sunday Morning* (1958; London: Pan, 1960).

Sinclair, Andrew, *My Friend Judas* (1959; Harmondsworth: Penguin, 1963).

Sinfield, Alan, 'Against Appropriation', *Essays in Criticism*, 31 (1981), pp. 181–95 ['Against']

——, *Alfred Tennyson* (Oxford: Blackwell, 1986). [*Alfred*]

——, 'Culture and Contest: *Oi for England* and the end of consensus politics', *Englisch Amerikanische Studien*, 8 (1986), pp. 418–26. ['Culture']

——, 'Power and Ideology: an outline theory and Sidney's *Arcadia*', *ELH* [*English Literary History*], 52 (1985), pp. 259–77. ['Power']

—— (ed.), *Society and Literature, 1945–1970* (London: Methuen, 1983). [*Society*]

——, 'Why the Arts Won't Save Us', *Gay Times*, 116 (May 1988), pp. 48–50. ['Why the Arts']

——, 'Who's for Rattigan?', *Gay Times*, 120 (Sept. 1988), pp. 44–6. ['Who's for Rattigan?']

Sissons, Michael and French, Philip (eds.), *Age of Austerity, 1945–51* (Harmondsworth: Penguin, 1964).

Sivanandan, A., *A Different Hunger* (London: Pluto, 1982).

Skeat, Walter W., *Shakespeare's Plutarch* (London: Macmillan, 1875).

Sked, Alan and Cook, Chris, *Post-war Britain* (Harmondsworth: Penguin, 1979).

Smith, Harold L. (ed.), *War and Social Change* (Manchester UP, 1986).

Snow, C. P., *The New Men* (1954; Harmondsworth: Penguin, 1959).

——, *Variety of Men* (London: Macmillan, 1967). [*Variety*]

Sparks, Colin, 'The Abuses of Literacy', in Centre for Contemporary Cultural Studies, *Working Papers in Cultural Studies*, no. 6 (Birmingham University, 1974).

Spender, Stephen, *The Creative Element* (London: Hamish Hamilton, 1953). [*Creative*]

——, *European Witness* (London: Hamish Hamilton, 1946). [*European*]

——, *The New Realism* (London: Hogarth, 1939).

——, *Poems* (London: Faber, 1933).

——, *The Struggle of the Modern* (London: Hamish Hamilton, 1963). [*Struggle*]

——, *The Thirties and After* (New York: Random House, 1978). [*Thirties*]

——, *World Within World* (London: Hamish Hamilton, 1951).

Stanworth, Philip and Giddens, Anthony, *Elites and Power in British Society* (Cambridge UP, 1974).

Steedman, Carolyn, *Landscape for a Good Woman* (London: Virago, 1986).

Steiner, Nancy Hunter, *A Closer Look at Ariel* (New York: Harper's Magazine Press, 1973).

Stimpson, Catharine R., 'Feminism and Feminist Criticism', *Massachusetts Review*, 24 (Summer 1983), pp. 272–88.

Storr, Anthony, *Human Aggression* (London: Allen Lane, 1968).

Sumner, Colin, *Reading Ideologies* (London, New York and San Francisco: Academic Press, 1979).

Sussex, Elizabeth, *Lindsay Anderson* (London: Studio Vista, 1969).

Sutherland, John, *Fiction and the Fiction Industry* (London: Athlone, 1978). [*Fiction*]

——, *Offensive Literature* (London: Junction Books, 1982).

Swingewood, Alan, *The Myth of Mass Culture* (London: Macmillan, 1977).

Taylor, Elizabeth, *A Wreath of Roses* (1949; Harmondsworth: Penguin, 1967).

Taylor, Helen, ' "Are We Talking About Literature?": a history of LTP', *LTP* [*Journal of Literature Teaching Politics*], 6 (1987), pp. 7–12.

Taylor, Jenny (ed.), *Notebooks/memoirs/archives* (London: Routledge, 1982).

Taylor, Jenny and Laing, Dave, 'Disco-pleasure-discourse: on "Rock and Sexuality" ', *Screen Education*, 31 (Summer 1979), pp. 43–8.

Taylor, John Russell, *Anger and After*, 2nd edn. (Harmondsworth: Penguin, 1963).

——, *John Osborne, 'Look Back in Anger': a casebook* (London: Macmillan, 1968). [*John*]

Taylor, Roger, *Art an Enemy of the People* (Brighton: Harvester, 1978).

Taylor-Gooby, Peter, *Public Opinion, Ideology and State Welfare* (London: Routledge, 1985).

Tennyson, Alfred, *The Poems of Tennyson*, ed. Christopher Ricks (London: Longman, 1969).

Thirkell, Angela, *Peace Breaks Out* (London: Hamish Hamilton, 1946). [*Peace*]

Thomas, Hugh (ed.), *The Establishment* (1959; London: New England Library, 1962).

Thompson, E. P., *The Making of the English Working Class* (1963), rev. edn. (Harmondsworth: Penguin, 1968). [*Making*]

——, (ed.), *Out of Apathy* (London: Stevens and Sons, 1960). [*Out*]

——, *The Poverty of Theory* (London: Merlin Press, 1978). [*Poverty*]

Tiger, Lionel, *Men in Groups* (London: Nelson, 1969).

Titmuss, Richard M., *Essays on 'The Welfare State'*, 2nd edn. (London: Allen and Unwin, 1963). [*Essays*]

——, *Problems of Social Policy* (London: HMSO and Longmans, 1950). [*Problems*]

Tomkins, Calvin, *Ahead of the Game* (Harmondsworth: Penguin, 1968).

Townsend, Peter, *The Family Life of Old People* (1957), abridged edn. (Harmondsworth: Penguin, 1968).

Trilling, Lionel, *Beyond Culture* (London: Secker, 1966).

Trotsky, Leon, *The Age of Permanent Revolution: a Trotsky anthology*, ed. Isaac Deutscher (New York: Dell, 1964).

Turnstile, Magnus, 'The PM and the Pirates', *New Statesman*, 10 Dec. 1965, p. 916.

Tynan, Kenneth, *A View of the English Stage* (St Albans: Paladin, 1976).

Upward, Edward, *The Rotten Elements* (1969): the second novel in the trilogy *The Spiral Ascent* (London: Heinemann, 1977).

Vanek, J. (ed.), *Self-management: economic liberation of man* (Harmondsworth: Penguin, 1975).

Veblen, Thorstein, *The Theory of the Leisure Class* (1899; New York: Mentor, 1953).

Volosinov, V. N., *Marxism and the Philosophy of Language*, tr. Ladislav Latejka and I. R. Titunik (New York and London: Seminar Press, 1973).

Wagner-Martin, Linda, *Sylvia Plath* (London: Chatto, 1988).

Wain, John, *Hurry on Down* (1953; Harmondsworth: Penguin, 1960).

——, (ed.), *Interpretations* (1955; London: Routledge, 1972).

——, 'Orwell in Perspective', *New World Writing 12* (New York: Mentor, 1957), pp. 84–96. ['Orwell']

——, *Sprightly Running* (London: Macmillan, 1962). [*Sprightly*]

——, *Strike the Father Dead* (London: Macmillan, 1962). [*Strike*]

Wandor, Michelene, *Look Back in Gender* (London and New York: Methuen, 1987).

Wardle, Irving, *The Theatres of George Devine* (London: Cape, 1978).

Warren, B., 'Capitalist Planning and the State', *New Left Review*, 72 (March–April 1972), pp. 3–29.

Watts, Cedric, ' "A Bloody Racist": about Achebe's view of Conrad', *Yearbook of English Studies*, 13 (1983), pp. 196–209.

Waugh, Evelyn, *Brideshead Revisited* (1945; Harmondsworth: Penguin, 1951).

——, *Put Out More Flags* (1942; Harmondsworth: Penguin, 1943). [*Put Out*]

——, *Unconditional Surrender* (1961; Harmondsworth: Penguin, 1964).

Webster, Paul and Powell, Nicholas, *Saint-Germain des-Près* (London: Constable, 1984).

Weeks, Jeffrey, *Coming Out* (London: Quartet, 1977).

Welch, Denton, *The Denton Welch Journals*, ed. Jocelyn Brooke (London: Hamish Hamilton, 1952).

—— , *Maiden Voyage* (London: Routledge, 1945).

Wells, H. G., *The Short Stories of H. G. Wells* (London: Benn, 1927).

Wesker, Arnold, *Chips with Everything* (1962), in *New English Dramatists* 7 (Harmondsworth: Penguin, 1963).

——, *The Wesker Trilogy* (*Chicken Soup with Barley*, 1958; *Roots*, 1959; *I'm Talking About Jerusalem*, 1960) (Harmondsworth: Penguin, 1964).

West, Rebecca, *The New Meaning of Treason*, rev. edn. (1964; Harmondsworth: Penguin, 1985).

Westergaard, John, 'Some Aspects of the Study of Modern British Society', in *Approaches to Sociology*, ed. John Rex (London: Routledge, 1974).

Whitley, John, *Golding: Lord of the Flies* (London: Arnold, 1970).

Widdowson, Peter (ed.), *Re-reading English* (London: Methuen, 1982).

Widgery, David, *Beating Time* (London: Chatto, 1986). [*Beating*]

——, *The Left in Britain, 1956–68* (Harmondsworth: Penguin, 1976). [*Left*]

Wiener, Martin, J., *English Culture and the Decline of the Industrial Spirit, 1850–1980* (Cambridge UP, 1981).

Wildeblood, Peter, *Against the Law* (London: Weidenfeld, 1955).

Williams, Francis, *Nothing So Strange* (London: Cassell, 1970).

Williams, Patrick, 'Colonial Literature and the Notion of Britishness', *LTP* [*Journal of Literature Teaching Politics*], 5 (1986), pp. 92–107.

Williams, Raymond, *Border Country* (1960; Harmondsworth: Penguin, 1964).

——, *Communications* (1962), rev. edn. (Harmondsworth: Penguin, 1968).

——, *The Country and the City* (St. Albans: Paladin, 1975).

——, *Culture* (Glasgow: Fontana, 1981). [*Culture*]

——, *Culture and Society, 1780–1950* (1958; Harmondsworth: Penguin, 1961). [*Culture and Society*]

——, *The Long Revolution* (1961; Harmondsworth: Penguin, 1965). [*Long*]

——, *Marxism and Literature* (Oxford UP, 1977). [*Marxism*]

——, (ed.), *May Day Manifesto 1968* (1967), expanded edn. (Harmondsworth: Penguin, 1968).

——, *Modern Tragedy* (London: New Left Books, 1979).

——, *Orwell* (London: Fontana, 1971).

——, *Politics and Letters* (London: New Left Books, 1979). [*Politics*]

——, *Problems in Materialism and Culture* (London: Verso, 1980). [*Problems*]

——, *Second Generation* (London: Chatto, 1964).

——, *Towards 2000* (1983; Harmondsworth: Penguin, 1985). [*Towards*]

Willis, Paul E., *Learning to Labour* (Farnborough: Saxon House, 1977). [*Learning*]

——, *Profane Culture* (London: Routledge, 1978). [*Profane*]

Wilmer, Valerie, *As Serious as Your Life* (London: Allison and Busby, 1977).

Wilson, Angus, *Hemlock and After* (1952; Harmondsworth: Penguin, 1956).

——, *Such Darling Dodos* (1950; St Albans: Panther, 1980). [*Such*]

Wilson, Colin, *The Outsider* (1956; London: Pan, 1978).

Wilson, Elizabeth, *Only Halfway to Paradise* (London and New York: Tavistock, 1980). [*Only*]

Wilson, Harold, *The New Britain: Labour's plan* (Harmondsworth: Penguin, 1964).

Winnicott, D. W., *The Child and the Family* (London: Tavistock, 1957).

Wolff, Janet, *The Social Production of Art* (London: Macmillan, 1981).

Woolf, Virginia, *Collected Essays, vol. 2* (London: Hogarth, 1966). [*Collected*]

——, *A Room of One's Own* (Harmondsworth: Penguin, 1945). [*Room*]

Worpole, Ken, 'Blowing Hot and Cold', *New Socialist* (Jan. 1985), pp. 36–8.

Worsley, T. C., *Flannelled Fool* (London: Alan Ross, 1967).

Wright, Erik Olin, *Class, Crisis and the State* (London: New Left Books, 1978).

Young, Michael, *The Rise of the Meritocracy* (1958; Harmondsworth: Penguin, 1961).

Young, Michael and Willmott, Peter, *Family and Kinship in East London* (1957), rev. edn. (Harmondsworth: Penguin, 1962).

Index

Index to 'The Politics and Cultures of Discord (1997)'